Indian Financial Reforms

Indian Financial Reforms

Priorities and Policy Thrust
Post Global Financial Crisis

Editor

Uma Kapila

ACADEMIC FOUNDATION
NEW DELHI

www.academicfoundation.com

First published in 2013
by

ACADEMIC FOUNDATION
4772-73 / 23 Bharat Ram Road, (23 Ansari Road),
Darya Ganj, New Delhi - 110 002 (India).
Phones : 23245001 / 02 / 03 / 04.
Fax : +91-11-23245005.
E-mail : books@academicfoundation.com
www.academicfoundation.com

Cataloging in Publication Data--DK
Courtesy: D.K. Agencies (P) Ltd. <docinfo@dkagencies.com>

Indian financial reforms : priorities and policy thrust, post global financial crisis / editor, Uma Kapila.

p. cm.

Contributed articles.
Includes index.
ISBN 9789332700079

1. Financial services industry--Government policy--India. 2. Monetary policy--India. 3. Financial crises--India. 4. India--Economic policy--1991- 5. Global Financial Crisis, 2008-2009. I. Kapila, Uma.

DDC 330.90511 23

Typeset by Italics India, New Delhi.

Printed and bound by The Book Mint, New Delhi.
www.thebookmint.in

CONTENTS

Acknowledgements

I am indeed grateful to Dr C. Rangarajan, Dr Ashok Lahiri, Prof Joseph E. Stiglitz, Dr Duvvuri Subbarao, Dr Y.V. Reddy, Dr N.A. Mujumdar, Dr Deepak Mohanty, Dr K.C. Chakrabarty, Dr Anand Sinha, Dr Harun R. Khan and Dr B. Mahapatra whose papers have been included in this book.

The papers by Duvvuri Subbarao, Joseph E. Stiglitz, Deepak Mohanty, K.C. Chakrabarty, Anand Sinha, Harun R. Khan and B. Mahapatra have been earlier published in the various issues of RBI Bulletin, Reserve Bank of India. I am thankful to Reserve Bank of India for making available such excellent research papers through the medium of RBI Bulletin.

—Uma Kapila

Editor/Contributors

Editor:

Uma Kapila

Reader (Retd.) Department of Economics, Miranda House, University of Delhi; Presently: Senior Editor, Academic Foundation, New Delhi.

Contributors:

Ashok Lahiri

Member, Board of Directors, Asian Development Bank, Constituency Office of Afghanistan, Bangladesh, Bhutan, India, Lao PDR, Tajakistan, Turkmenistan.

C. Rangarajan

Chairman, Prime Minister Economic Advisory Council, Government of India, New Delhi.

Y.V. Reddy

Chairman, Fourteenth Finance Commission, Government of India, New Delhi.

Joseph E. Stiglitz

Nobel Laureate (2001), University Professor, Columbia Business School; The Graduate School of Arts and Science (Department of Economics) and the School of International and Public Affairs.

Duvvuri Subbarao
Governor, Reserve Bank of India, Mumbai.

N.A. Mujumdar
Editor, Indian Journal of Agricultural Economics, Mumbai.

K.C. Chakrabarty
Deputy Governor, Reserve Bank of India, Mumbai

Deepak Mohanty
Executive Director, Reserve Bank of India, Mumbai.

Anand Sinha
Deputy Governor, Reserve Bank of India, Mumbai.

H.R. Khan
Deputy Governor, Reserve Bank of India, Mumbai.

B. Mahapatra
Executive Director, Reserve Bank of India, Mumbai.

UMA KAPILA

Introduction

The Indian financial sector has undergone wide ranging reforms during the last two decades. As part of the package of economic reforms launched after the 1991 crisis, financial sector reforms have progressed well in the initial years. The financial sector was one of the earliest to undergo significant changes. There was a clear recognition that for efficient mobilisation and allocation of resources, financial sector reforms had to keep pace with and in some cases, even precede policy reforms in the external and domestic industrial sectors. The main objective of financial sector reforms in India initiated in early 1990s was to create an efficient, competitive and stable financial sector that could contribute towards stimulating growth. Till the early 1990s, the Indian financial sector could be described as a classic example of financial repression. The financial system was characterised by extensive regulations such as administered interest rates, directed credit programmes, weak banking structure, lack of proper accounting and risk management system, lack of transparency in operation of major financial market participants (Mohan, 2004). Such a system hindered efficient allocation of resources. Financial sector reforms initiated in the early 1990s have attempted to overcome these weaknesses in order to enhance efficiency of resource allocation in the economy.

This edited volume comprising the writings of eminent economists, bankers and financial experts bring together at one place the story of financial sector reforms and its unfinished agenda. It also covers the next generation of financial sector reforms with a focus on lessons and responsibilities for central banks in wake of the global financial crisis—the new policy challenges arising from the new trilemma that is price stability, financial stability and sovereign debt sustainability; implications of Basel III and G-20; and the issues and challenges in financial inclusion.

The first three chapters are devoted to a discussion of financial sector reforms—the past, the present and the future agenda. Several committees set up from time to time have drawn up a long and important agenda for financial sector reforms. Reforms recommended by various committees—Chakrabarty Committee (April 1985) Narasimham I (November 1991), Rangarajan Committee (April 1993) in the first round, Tarapore I (1997) and Narasimham II (1998) in the second round (1997-2006), and Tarapore II (July 2006), P.M. Committee (February 2007) and Raghuram Rajan Committee (April 2008) have been discussed in chapter 1 in the book. According to Ashok Lahiri, reforms in the first phase 1991-1996 (see table 1.1, ch.1) were implemented more or less in a satisfactory manner. There are a large number of issues on which two recent committees have reiterated not only what Tarapore II said in 2006 but also what Narasimham II had emphasised in 1998. Ashok Lahiri has pointed out the untapped potential in the three reports of the most recent period. Some of the recommendations of these committees could not be implemented due to external developments in the form of a large commodity price shock in the world market and the ongoing global crisis. After providing a brief account of how the recent global crisis have affected financial sector reforms in India and how we may have sacrificed medium term reforms for short run considerations, Lahiri has focused on pending reform items.

The Second Generation Reforms

While India's financial sector remained resilient in the face of global shocks, there are a number of areas where the reforms would be needed to promote stability and generate growth impulses for the real economy. In the wake of turbulent global financial environments, banking and financial entities have to grapple with growing complexities and risks associated with their business. Against this backdrop, the policy initiatives such as adoption of tighter capital and liquidity standards, improved risk management practices and sound compensation practices are required to place the Indian banking system on a strong footing and enhance the banking sectors ability to absorb shocks arising from any financial and economic stress. (Chakrabarty, ch. 2). "Moreover, in India, while broader institutional reforms have taken place at the macro levels, the internal reforms among banks and financial institutions are yet to take place. Hence the need to go for second generation reforms particularly focusing on bringing down the cost of banking services, strengthening the credit delivery mechanism, improving customer service, reforming the human resource management systems and enhancing the financial out reach to hitherto unbanked areas," says Chakrabarty.

The Report of the Committees on Financial Sector Reforms (CFSR, 2008) headed by Raghuram Rajan advocated a national goal of ensuring that in 3 years 90 per cent of the households, if so desire, have access to a deposit account and to a payment system. This report indeed covers a wide range of issues: "the future role of the Reserve Bank of India, allowing entry of more private well governed small financial banks, modifying priority sector mandate and so on. More importantly, the committee believes in taking a hundred small steps in the same direction that will collectively take us vary far." Some such selective steps recommended by the committee have been discussed by N.A. Mujumdar in chapter 3. According to Mujumdar, in the contemporary financial scenario in India, there are three core issues: broad-based, decentralised growth in the real sector, the new architecture of the financial system to facilitate such growth, and the inequitable interest rate structure. Logically, the reinvention of the next generation financial sector reforms should have emerged from a holistic analysis of these three core issues.

Indian Banking System

The Indian banking system has emerged strong as a result of the reforms introduced since early 1990s says C. Rangarajan (ch. 4). "By dismantling the administered interest rate structure, by reducing the prescriptions in the form of CRR and SLR, by introducing prudential norms, by recapitalising public sector banks, by injecting a greater element of competition in the system through new banks as well as induction of private sector in the public sector banks and by revamping the system of regulation and supervision, we have succeeded in creating a banking system that is more safe and sound."

The current international financial crisis has important lessons for the management of the financial system in general and for the banking system in particular. According to Rangarajan what stands out glaringly in the current crisis is the regulatory failure in the developed world. "It is ironic that such a regulatory failure should have occurred at a time when intense discussions were being held in Basel and elsewhere to put in place a sound regulatory framework." "A competitive environment is essential to make the banking system cost-efficient. However, regulation is important to steer the banking system towards prudence and stability, but within this regulatory umbrella we must nurture a competitive banking system that will deliver efficient services at minimal cost."

According to K.C. Chakrabarty (ch. 5) banks have to look beyond the way banking is traditionally defined in a narrow fashion. They need to look towards the vulnerable and other excluded sections of the population as bankable.

Global Financial Crisis and Lessons for Central Banks

The crisis has triggered a wide-ranging debate on the role and responsibilities of central banks. What should be the right framework for monetary policy? Do we need to re-define the mandate of central banks independence? Although no definitive conclusions have emerged from the debate and hard thinking by central banking and academicians, the debate has continued and some broad lessons from the experience of handling the crisis can be derived. N.A. Mujumdar has discussed some of these like inflation targeting, bank regulation and supervision, role of central banks in preventing asset price bubbles, should financial stability be explicitly included in the mandate of central banks and the autonomy of central banks. (ch. 6)

There is another dimension of the impact of global financial crisis to which Y.V. Reddy has drawn our attention (ch. 7). The reference here is to erosion of trust in the financial sector as a whole, in particular in banking in the advanced economies. This decline of trust and confidence, according to Mujumdar, is partly the result of market failure and relate to incentives—in many cases, obscenely high level of remuneration of senior management and greed. Reddy advocates "inclusive finance"—a commitment to provide reasonable access to essential financial services to all segments of society. "Society expects central banks to restore this trust and confidence in money and finance and move the system towards inclusive finance. Society has put its trust in central banks. Central banks have to ensure that bank managements and the financial sector in general serve the masses, and not merely the elite or the financially active. In the ultimate analysis, central banks are trustees, agents to look after the interests of the masses," says Y.V. Reddy.

Global trends in financial sector regulation may see simultaneous re-regulation in some countries and deregulation in others. Innovations, by definition, are difficult to put into preconceived straight jackets and a disaggregated contextual approach would be appropriate. Above all, better regulation warrants effective regulation. Consideration of regulation, competition and ownership in an integrated manner, enhanced monitoring of financial market activities and the use of fiscal tools to supplement regulation could be helpful in this regard (Reddy, ch. 7).

According to Joseph E. Stiglitz (ch. 8) "most of the propositions that have been at the centre of monetary policy for the last quarter of a century need to be rethought. Monetary policy has not served our economies and societies well. It has arguably contributed to the growing inequality that has marked most countries around the world. But of this, there can be no doubt! It has not only failed to stabilise the economy in the way that was hoped, but the way that some central banks have conducted monetary policy and regulation has been at the centre of our greatest crisis in three quarters of a century. This should be the grounds for a revolution in monetary policy.

"Monetary policy (understood broadly, to include financial regulatory policy) is of such importance in part because the financial sector is so important: the financial sector has been likened to the brain of an economy, and if the financial sector does not work well, the economy does not work well. In many countries around the world-including the US and the EU—the financial sector has not done what it should have done and done what it should not have done; the costs of their failures in the US alone amount to trillions of dollars" (Stiglitz, ch. 8).

Financial Stability

Post crisis, there is emerging consensus that financial stability should be an objective of central banks. However, the key challenge is to evolve a consistent framework for implementation. According to Deepak Mohanty (ch. 9) financial stability has to be a shared responsibility wherein central banks have a predominant role. Also, there is a need for explicit recognition of financial stability objective particularly in the statute of the central bank to establish accountability framework. While it is not very apparent whether price stability can ensure financial stability, it is clear that price instability could jeopardise financial stability. "Financial stability, therefore can not and shall not override the price stability objective which continue to be the predominant objective of monetary policy," says Mohanty.

Price Stability, Financial Stability and Sovereign Debt Sustainability

"Even as central banks are grappling with balancing the demands of price stability and financial stability, there is now yet another powerful assault on central bank orthodoxy arising from the big elephant in the room—the Euro zone sovereign debt crisis. The European Central Bank (ECB) is being challenged and is being called upon to bend and stretch its mandate to bail out sovereigns who have forfeited the confidence of the market. The argument in its essence is that if a central bank is committed to financial stability, it can not ignore the feed back loop between financial stability and sovereign debt sustainability and by extension therefore, it has to be mindful of sovereign debt sustainability concerns," says D. Subbarao (ch.10). The new trilemma triggers several questions. How do the three objectives—price stability, financial stability and sovereign debt sustainability reinforce each other and in what ways do they conflict with each other? What is the nature and extent of the responsibility of central banks for each of three objective? Are central banks equipped to handle these additional responsibilities and what does this mean for the effectiveness and autonomy of central banks? Subbarao's paper throws light on these weighty questions centred around this new trilemma.

Crisis Management

Recent experiences have clearly demonstrated that resolving a financial crisis is complex and costly. This holds true regardless of what caused the crisis, and regardless of the solution. The best crisis management framework is one that prevents crises. No financial system can be completely immune from episodes of financial instability from time to time and therefore, there will be a need to manage crisis. As central bankers and regulators carrying the responsibility of fostering financial stability, the best service we can do to our objective, therefore, is to remain prepared to manage crisis says K.C. Chakrabarty (ch. 11). There are important lessons to be learnt from each crisis. Yet, we can count on each crisis to be sufficiently different from every other crisis. We can, but, be alert and flexible to evolving risks.

According to Anand Sinha for central banks, just as managing the crisis was difficult, managing the recovery is going to be equally, if not more, difficult. The policies that are most suited to crisis management are not necessarily the best for crisis resolution. An impressive range of regulatory reforms have been set in motion in the five years since the crisis first unfolded. But there are formidable implementation challenges ahead which will need to be carefully managed. In a concluding note Anand Sinha (ch. 12) remarks financial stability is a shared responsibility and therefore, Indian banks have a major role to play because while strong financial institutions need not necessarily make up a strong financial system, for a strong financial system, we would need strong banks. Indian banks are facing several challenges in the current scenario—implementation of Basel III and for some, implementation of advanced approaches of Basel II—in a situation where there is increasing pressure on asset quality.

Basel III

Papers by D. Subbarao and B. Mahapatra provide a comprehensive coverage of the implications of Basel III for capital liquidity and profitability of banks. According to B. Mahapatra (ch. 13) Basel III is the regulatory response to the causes and consequences of the global financial crisis. Learning the lessons from the crisis, the objectives of Basel III are to minimise the probability of recurrence of a crisis of such magnitude. Towards this end, the Basel III has set its objectives to improve the shock absorbing capacity of each and every individual bank as the first order of defence and in the worst case scenario, if it is inevitable that one or a few banks have to fail, Basel III has measures to ensure that the banking system as a whole does not crumble and its spill-over impact on the real economy is minimised. Therefore, Basel III will have some microprudential elements so that risk is contained in each individual institution; and a macro-prudential overlay that will "lean against the wind" to take care of issues relating to the systemic risk.

As banks and bankers have been at the heart of the crisis, enhancing the banking sector's safety and stability has been the thrust of the post-crisis policy reforms. While the work on this reform is still in progress, one segment of reforms that has taken a final shape is the Basel III framework for bank capital regulation. The final package was approved by the G-20 and the roll out has begun. We in India issued the Basel III guidelines on capital regulations in May 2012 after extensive consultations with all stakeholders. D. Subbarao in his paper (ch. 14) has discussed some of the conceptual and implementation issues underlying Basel III. He has raised 10 questions/charges that are often made against Basel III and has effectively answered them in this paper.

According to Subbarao effective implementation of Basel III is going to make Indian banks more strong, stable and sound so that they can deliver value to the real sectors of the economy (ch. 14).

G-20 and India

G-20 has been in the forefront for battling the financial crises—global financial crisis of 2008-09 and the Eurozone crisis since 2010. The G-20 according to D. Subbarao (ch. 15) is by all accounts a bold initiative in the sense that it is not formed by a charter, has no mandate for global governance and its decisions are not legally binding and enforceable. In short, it is based on the realisation that in a globalising world, our futures are all tied together and on the belief that the only way global governance can be pursued is through an honour code. "Received wisdom today is that financial deregulation shares the honours with global imbalances as being one of the twin villains of the crisis. Not surprisingly, therefore, reforms to the financial sector regulation have been on the top of the G-20 agenda", says Subbarao.

The broad contours of the international initiatives spearhead by the G-20 on financial sector reform rest on four broad pillars: regulation, supervision, resolution and assessment of the implementation of new standards. So far, according to Subbarao, one pillar that has received substantial public attention is regulatory reform where there have already been some notable achievements including agreements on the new Basel III capital and liquidity standards. All G-20 members have committed to the implementation of Basel III package.

Money Market and Monetary Operations

Over the last decade, there has been substantial development in the Indian money market in terms of depth, variety of instruments and efficiency which has enabled the RBI to change monetary operations from direct quantity based instruments to indirect interest rate based instruments to enhance the efficiency of monetary transmission consistent with international best practices. Against this background, Deepak Mohanty (ch. 16) has briefly captured the developments in the money market and discussed the experience with the recently modified operations procedures of monetary policy. Evidence so far suggests a significant improvement in monetary policy transmission under the new operating framework.

Forex Market

Economy and financial markets of India are in the midst of rapid transformation due to its increasing linkages with the rest of the world. Harun R. Khan's paper (ch. 17), discusses the role of FEDAI in the changing environment of Indian forex market—the future role and responsibilities including the challenge for internationalisation of the Indian rupee.

Financial Inclusion

Financial inclusion is a prerequisite for inclusive growth. While the last two chapters in the book by H.R. Khan and D. Subbarao are exclusively devoted to the subject of financial inclusion, the issue is of such great importance that it has been discussed in a large number of other papers by C. Rangarajan, D. Subbarao, Y.V. Reddy, K.C. Chakrabarty and N.A. Mujumdar as well.

One of the important effects of financial inclusion is that the entire national financial system benefits by greater inclusion, especially when promoted in the wider context of economic inclusion. The current policy objective of inclusive growth with financial stability can not be achieved without ensuring universal financial inclusion. Financial inclusion efforts do have multiplier effect on the economy as a whole through higher savings pooled from the vast segment of the bottom of the pyramid population by providing access to formal savings arrangement resulting in expansion in credit and investment by banks (H.R. Khan, ch. 18).

According to D. Subbarao (ch.19) what financial inclusion requires most of all is efficient and sympathetic customer service by banks. No amount of regulation, rules, policies and plans will deliver sustainable results unless banks serve their customers with efficiency, empathy and courtesy. Banks should look upon financial inclusion not as an obligation but as an opportunity to build 'fortune at the bottom of the pyramid'. So far the effort has been on the supply side—opening branches, appointing BCs and opening accounts that remain largely inoperative. We need to supplement the supply side effort by a demand side effort—by reaching out to people left behind, inspiring their trust and confidence in the banking system and supporting them in improving the quality of their lives. Such a change in mindset is very important if we are to achieve meaningful financial inclusion.

Conclusion

India has had remarkable success over the past two decades in its increase in GDP and now it seeks to ensure that the success continues and the benefits of growth are shared by all, for which we have to work towards creating an open democratic and inclusive society with a fair, efficient and stable financial system. The global financial crisis has shown how misguided were policies of financial market liberalisation and deregulation. "These are policies that served special interests well and the voices of those special interests are often heard more loudly than the voices of these that are hurt by these policies" (Stiglitz, 2013). There is a considerable agreement that better and more effective regulation is of vital importance in the financial sector. Financial sector regulation should be as much about protecting consumers as ensuring the availability of essential financial services to all sections of society keeping in view the expectations and needs of common person, says Reddy. It could be argued that a competitive financial system which is well regulated, keeping in view the needs for stability and consumer protection would automatically ensure inclusive finance (Reddy, ch. 7).

Society has put its trust in central banks. Central banks have to ensure that bank managements and the financial sector in general serve the masses, and not merely the elite. In the ultimate analysis, as Reddy emphatically remarks, "central banks are trustees, agents to look after the interests of the masses." Quoting Stiglitz again, "India is lucky in having a central bank that has earned recognition for its integrity—it is one of the few central banks that were not effectively captured by the financial crisis." It may be further noted that Reserve Bank is a multi-service central bank and has been discharging its responsibilities in a wide array of domains with a view to supporting long run growth and enhancing welfare of the common man. In addition to its pursuit of inflation control that helps the poor the most, the human face of Reserve Bank is reflected in its policies in the area of rural credit and regulation of banks and non-bank financial intermediaries, foreign exchange regulation, currency management, and payment and settlement system. Nothing represents the extent of human face of the banking than the progress it makes on the goal of financial inclusion. Financial inclusion has been adopted as a formal agenda for Indian banking following the Rangarajan Committee Report (2008) on financial inclusion. The task of financial inclusion is certainly a colossal one but it is in banks' medium to long term interest to do so. Financial inclusion may put short term pressure on banks' profitability but over the years would increase the size and scope of banking in India and thereby add to the banks' reserve stream making it commercially viable (RBI, 2012).

References

Mohan, Rakesh (2006). *Financial Sector Reforms and Monetary Policy: The Indian Experience* in (ed.) Uma Kapila (2011), "India's Economic Development Since 1947". *New Delhi: Academic Foundation*

Rangarajan, C. (2009). *India: Monetary Policy, Financial Stability and Other Essays*. New Delhi: Academic Foundation.

Reserve Bank of India (2012). *Reserve Bank of India Annual Report 2011-12.*

Joseph, E. Stiglitz (2013). "An Indian Social Democracy: Integrating Markets, Democracy and Social Justice", in (eds.) Sunil Khilnani and Manmohan Malhoutra, *A Social Democratic Agenda for a More Dynamic Indian Economy: Creating an Innovative and Learning Society*. Vol.II. New Delhi: Academic Foundation.

1

ASHOK K. LAHIRI

Indian Financial Reforms

National Priorities Amidst an International Crisis

Introduction

We are in the midst of an international financial crisis, and I think it is apt to focus on the national priorities of financial sector reform. Any crisis is also a window of opportunity. We reacted very boldly to the Gulf crisis in 1990. That initial burst of policy reform set off a remarkable period of accelerated growth with macroeconomic stability. In sharp contrast, our reaction to the East Asian Crisis was very different. It was marked by considerable conservatism. While we did respond swiftly and effectively in 1991 with far reaching economic reforms, conservatism was a hallmark of Indian policy making around 1997. With more than 1.1 billion people, and many below the poverty line, there are obvious limits to the risk that we can afford to take in policy making. Yet, too much risk aversion in policy making can impede growth, and slow down our efforts to alleviate poverty.

A majority of historic economic crises were preceded by financial liberalisation.[1] Consequently, there is a tendency to blame all crises on liberalisation, and for public and political opinion to turn against deregulation. It is a natural fall-out of an economic crisis anywhere in the world, for example in the contemporary US. We have seen it in the past after the East Asian Crisis of 1997. The report of the Committee on Capital Account Convertibility headed by S.S. Tarapore, submitted at the end of May, 1997, had a roadmap achieving some preconditions and moving towards capital account

1. See Kaminsky and Reinhart (1999).

convertibility by 1999-2000. The report of the first Tarapore Committee, which we shall call Tarapore I, could not have come at a more inopportune time. Starting with Thailand in June 1997, the countries of East Asia— Indonesia, Korea, Malaysia, Philippines, Singapore and Thailand—the then most rapidly growing economies in the world, were hit by a severe and sudden financial crisis. Tarapore I's recommendations were pretty much put in the cold storage. Safety first became the watchword of financial sector reform in India. Some argue that we learnt the wrong lessons, and safety was not only the first but also the last consideration.[2] There were some reforms, such as, the introduction of the Fiscal Responsibility and Budget Management Act, 2003 and pension reforms. Nevertheless, with the benefit of hindsight, perhaps more could have been done to profit the Indian economy.

We are going through yet another period of seriously adverse external economic developments. The onslaught of a steep commodity boom followed by a severe global financial crisis may have raised doubts about the validity of the reform strategy drawn up in more tranquil times. The doubts need to be dispelled or a new strategy drawn up. Inaction is not the answer. Delivering high growth and rapid removal of poverty is an imperative for the government. In the run up to the last election to the 14th Lok Sabha in 2004, the manifestos of the two major coalitions promised high growth. It is safe to assume that with rising popular aspirations in India and a constant benchmarking with China, political parties will have to promise high growth even in the run up to the next Lok Sabha elections. No matter who gets elected, there will be a host of reform issues that the new government will have to address.

There is a long and important pending agenda of financial sector reform already drawn up by very distinguished experts such as M. Narasimham, S.S. Tarapore, Percy Mistry and Raghuram Rajan. Is this long agenda going to be a victim of the current crisis? The answer to this question will determine the growth prospects of the Indian economy in the medium to long term. I want to share my thoughts on some of these pending reform issues. I shall start

2, See for example, conclusion by Mistry (2008) "...overall, 1997-2007 was a lost decade for Indian finance".

with a brief history of how three recent global crises have affected financial sector reforms in India and how we may have sacrificed medium-term reform for short-term considerations. Finally, I shall focus on five pending reform items: namely moving monetary policy to inflation targeting; modernising the delivery of financial services to the priority sectors and vulnerable and weaker sections; introducing capital account convertibility; moving to a streamlined financial regulatory architecture; and restructuring the banking industry.

I believe Sir Purushotamdas Thakurdas would have approved of the topic. To some of us who take an interest in monetary developments in India, Sir Purushotamdas Thakurdas, or Sir P.T. as he was more well-known as, is much more than just a name or a respected leader of the business community in pre-independence India. He was a stalwart in the evolution of monetary and credit policy and institutions in this country.

There is practically no debate on any issue of importance in the monetary field in India spanning across three decades from the mid-1910s to 1950 that Sir P.T. did not participate in. As early as August 1925, he was a member of the Hilton Young Commission.[3] And, almost a quarter century later, when the government of newly independent India appointed the Rural Banking Enquiry Committee in November 1949,[4] Sir P.T chaired the committee.[5] In the interim, as a member of the Legislative Assembly, and as a member of the Central Board of the Reserve Bank of India (RBI) right from its inception in 1935, he participated in every debate on monetary and credit issues.[6] Sir P.T. played a critical role in the Indianisation of the

3. Formally, Royal Commission on Indian Currency and Finance, under the Chairmanship of Lt. Commander Edward Hilton Young.

4. Reserve Bank of India (1970): 768.

5. Reserve Bank of India (1970): 532.

6. For example, back in 1927, speaking on the Gold Standard and Reserve Bank of India Bill in the Legislative Assembly, he along with Sir R.K. Shanmukham Chetty emphatically argued about how the Reserve Bank should be free from Government control and also from any influence of the legislature. See Reserve Bank of India (1970): 31. On the same grounds of protecting against political influence, Sir P.T. was opposed to the Governor General appointing the Governor and Deputy Governors of the Reserve Bank of India 'after considering the Central Board's (of the Reserve Bank of India) recommendations in this regard'. Of course, at that time, the Reserve Bank of India had not been nationalised. See Reserve Bank of India (1970): 91.

RBI on August 10, 1943, when Sir C.D. Deshmukh succeeded first an Australian and then an Englishman as Governor.[7]

Contrast between the Initial Thrust after the Gulf Crisis and the Troubled Second Round after the East Asian Crisis

Within less than a month of the first Tarapore Committee submitting its report, the East Asian Crisis was spreading from Thailand to other countries in the region. Tarapore I, more or less coinciding with the East Asian Crisis, started what we shall call the troubled second round of financial sector reform in India.

The troubled second round was dramatically different from the first round of financial sector reform of 1991-1996. It is important to remember that the 1991 reforms were launched in the midst of an international crisis. External shocks had deepened the problems of the economy in 1990. The Iraqi invasion of Kuwait in August 1990 resulted in a drying up of remittances, a massive airlift to repatriate the migrant Gulf labour, and a soaring import bill with a steep rise in the international petroleum prices. Inflation (on an end-of-period basis) was in double digits—12.1 per cent—in 1990-91. Foreign currency assets of the RBI came down to US$975 million on July 12, 1991, equivalent to less than a month of import cover. A part of the Government's gold had to be transported and pledged to borrow abroad, and foreign loans had to be raised on a continuous—often on an overnight—basis to avert a default on external debt. The government responded to the crisis resolutely with a major structural reform programme.

As part of the package of wide-ranging reforms launched after the 1991 crisis, financial sector reforms had progressed well in the initial years. The financial sector was one of the earliest to undergo significant changes. There was a clear recognition that for efficient mobilisation and allocation of resources, financial sector reforms had to keep pace with, and in some cases, even precede, policy reforms in the external and domestic industrial sectors. Reforms recommended by the various committees (Table 1.1) in the first phase between 1991 and 1996 were implemented more or less in a satisfactory manner.

---

7. Reserve Bank of India (1970): 273.

Table 1

Important Committees Set Up to Draw up the Financial Sector Reform Agenda

No.	Name of the Committee	Chairman	Year: Set Up	Year: Submission	Set Up By
Initial burst (1991-1996)					
1.	Committee to Review the Working of the Monetary System (Chakravarty Committee)	Sukhamoy Chakravarty	Dec-1982	10-Apr-1985	Reserve Bank of India
2.	High Powered Committee on Financial System (Narasimham I)	M. Narasimham	14-Aug-1991	Nov-1991	Government of India
3.	High Level Committee on Balance of Payments (Rangarajan Committee)	C. Rangarajan	19-Feb-1991	26-Apr-1993	Government of India
Troubled second round (1997-2006)					
4.	Committee on Capital Account Convertibility (Tarapore I)	S.S. Tarapore	28-Feb-1997	30-May-1997	Reserve Bank of India
5.	Committee on Banking Sector Reforms (Narasimham II)	M. Narasimham		Apr-1998	Government of India
Third round with untapped potential					
6.	Committee on Fuller Capital Account Convertibility (Tarapore II)	S.S. Tarapore	20-Mar-2006	31-Jul-2006	Reserve Bank of India
7.	High Powered Expert Committee on Making Mumbai an International Financial Centre (PM Committee)	Percy Mistry[8]	28-Nov-2005	10-Feb-2007	Government of India
8.	Committee on Financial Sector Reforms (Rajan Committee)	Raghuram Rajan	17-Sep-2007	07-Apr-2008	Planning Commission

8. Mistry resigned a few days before the submission of the report.

To better understand how the East Asian Crisis affected the pace of financial sector reforms, let us recall the three important reports that played a critical role in determining the financial sector reform agenda in India during the initial reform period: Chakravarty Committee, Narasimham Committee I, and Rangarajan Committee.[9] Following Chakravarty Committtee's recommendations, while the amount of RBI credit to Government for financing fiscal deficit may not have been curtailed with success during the initial years, the need for curbing such deficit for inflation control was well accepted. Government and RBI also implemented Chakravarty Committee's recommendation about adjustment of the administered rates of interest on Government borrowings.

Next came the recommendations of the High Powered Committee on Financial System headed by M. Narasimham, what we will call Narasimham I. In 1991, cash reserve ratio (CRR) was an all-time high of 15 per cent and statutory liquidity ratio (SLR) was also an all-time high of 38.5 per cent.[10] They were the main instruments of preempting banking sector funds. The fundamental recommendation of the Narasimham Committee was a change in the approach to banking development. It was a change from a supply-based, subsidy-linked and target-oriented one to a more demand-driven, self-sustaining, and market-friendly approach. This change in approach to banking development, Narasimham I argued, was essential for improving the financial sector's efficiency and effectiveness in responding to the emerging needs of the economy. The main recommendations were: (i) progressive deregulation of interest rates, (ii) reduction in SLR and CRR to reduce the preemption of bank funds, (iii) a phased achievement of capital-adequacy of 8 per cent for banks in line with Basel Committee[11] recommendations, and (iv) strengthening the balance sheets of

9. The RBI set up the Chakravarty Committee in 1982. On August 14, 1991, Government appointed the Committee on the Financial System, under the chairmanship of M. Narasimham. The High Level Committee on Balance of Payments under the Chairmanship of C. Rangarajan was set up by the Government on November 19, 1991. For a detailed discussion, see Lahiri (2006).

10. Both the ratios are as a proportion of net demand and time liabilities of banks.

11. In 1988, the Bank of International Settlements (BIS) based in Basel, the Central Bankers' bank, had set up a committee of several Governors of the Central Banks on Baking Regulations and Supervisory Practices. The broad framework of standards recommended by the Committee is known as Basel standards.

banks through proper asset classification, income recognition and provisioning norms. Most of these were implemented in what we call 'the initial burst' itself.

Prior to the initial burst, the rupee was considerably overvalued. There was a chronic shortage of foreign exchange at the 'official rate' and a scarcity premium reflected in the unofficial or black-market rate. Mirroring the permit-licence *raj* in industry, through its foreign exchange budget, the Government had an administrative mechanism for allocation of scarce foreign exchange. During the initial burst, when the Rangarajan Committee recommended a move to 'a realistic exchange rate' determined by market forces, the Government implemented the recommendations. This implementation was done in stages. The first was a move from an officially fixed overvalued exchange rate to the dual rate regime under Liberalised Exchange Rate Management System from March 1, 1992. Then, the dual exchange rates were unified on March 1, 1993. Finally, the rupee was made convertible under the current account from August, 1994. The issue that remained was of capital account convertibility. Capital account convertibility implies the residents' relatively unrestricted right to transact in financial assets with foreign countries.[12] Such convertibility can reduce the cost of capital in a capital-scarce developing country and thereby stimulate investment and growth. By allowing residents to invest abroad, it can reduce the susceptibility of their income streams and wealth to domestic real and financial shocks. Thus, it can also diffuse the risk of an asset-price bubble. Capital account restrictions tend to turn progressively ineffective, costly and even distortive. However, capital account convertibility also exposes a country to booms-and-bust cycles in international capital flows.

On February 28, 1997, the RBI appointed Tarapore I for outlining a roadmap for moving towards capital account convertibility. Tarapore I, in its report submitted on May 30, 1997, recommended a sequenced withdrawal of controls in moving towards capital account convertibility over a period of three years starting in 1997-

12. Although convertibility existed in respect of certain constituent elements of the capital account, such convertibility was, and is not complete, particularly with respect to residents borrowing abroad and acquiring large value foreign assets.

1998 and ending in 1999-2000. It outlined certain preconditions for sequencing the move towards such convertibility (Box 1.1).

Box 1.1

Tarapore I (1997): Preconditions for Full Capital Account Convertibility

(a) Fiscal consolidation—reducing the Centre's gross fiscal deficit (GFD) to 3.5 per cent of GDP, establishing a consolidated sinking fund for public debt and a 'public debt' office, and introducing a system of fiscal transparency.

(b) Mandated inflation rate—inflation to be maintained within 3.0-5.0 per cent in the medium term.

(c) Consolidation in the financial sector—full deregulation of interest rates, strengthening the financial system by bringing down gross non-performing assets (NPAs) of the banking sector to 5.0 per cent of total advances and the average effective CRR to 3.0 per cent.

(d) Exchange rate policy—monitoring the exchange rate within a band of +/- 5.0 per cent around the neutral real effective exchange rate (REER), non-intervention by RBI within the band, disclosing the neutral REER regularly along with its base period, ensuring that forward exchange markets reflect interest rate differentials.

(e) Balance of Payments—sustained increase in the current receipts/GDP ratio and reduction in debt service ratio to 20.0 per cent.

(f) Adequacy of reserves—reserves at no less than six months of imports and no less than three months of imports plus 50 per cent of debt service payments plus one month of exports and imports; short-term debt and portfolio stock at no more than 60 per cent of reserves and the net foreign assets/currency ratio at no less than 40 per cent.

(g) Strengthening of the financial system—uniform regulatory system for banks and financial institutions, reserve requirements on non-resident liabilities of banks on par with their domestic liabilities, RBI prescribed-prudential norms for rupee mismatches, banks adopting best practices of risk management and following international accounting and disclosure norms, and an effective regulatory regime for the financial sector capable of detecting warning signals.

A month after the Tarapore Committee submitted its report, crisis erupted in East Asia. The most rapidly growing economies in the world were hit by a severe and sudden financial crisis, which in R. Dornbusch's (2001) terminology, was a 'new style' crisis. Investors' concerns about the creditworthiness of the balance sheet of a significant part of the economy caused the crisis. It was very different from an 'old style' or 'slow motion' crisis.[13] As a reaction, India adopted a relatively cautious and calibrated approach to capital account convertibility. The deadline of 1999-2000 for Tarapore I came and went, and what we made were some modest moves such as replacement of the Foreign Exchange Regulation Act (FERA), 1974, by a more progressive Foreign Exchange Management Act (FEMA), in 1999, and permission to Indian mutual funds to invest in overseas securities.

There was a widespread perception that India was saved from the East Asian contagion because it had stringent capital controls. As Tarapore (2006b) has commented, "This is totally erroneous. India was saved from the East Asian contagion of 1997-98 not because of a restrictive capital account but because of a sound macroeconomic situation. It bears recalling that with extremely tight capital controls in 1990-91, India was inflicted by the worst balance of payments crisis in its history."

In this troubled second phase, shortly after Tarapore I, in 1998, M. Narasimham was asked again by the Government to head the Committee on Banking Sector Reforms. Narasimham II suggested some wide-ranging reforms for the banking sector (Box 1.2). It had better luck than Tarapore I, but not as good as those under the initial burst, including Narasimham I. Many of its recommendations were accepted and implemented. But, there were notable exceptions as well.

---

13. Countries in East Asia had witnessed enormous capital flows during the early-1990s. Except in Malaysia, the bulk of the capital flows to the rest of the countries were in the form of offshore borrowing by banks and the private corporations. Capital inflows had remained strong through 1996 and in most cases until mid-1997. But things changed in 1997.

Box 1.2

Narasimham II (1998): Main Recommendations

(i) Ensure orderly movements of the call money rate, by, if necessary daily, resetting Repo and Reverse Repo rates under RBI's liquidity adjustment facility (LAF);

(ii) An integrated system of regulation and supervision of banks, financial institutions and non-bank finance companies (NBFCs) under a Board for Financial Regulation and Supervision (BFRS);

(iii) A legal framework that clearly defines the rights and liabilities of parties to contracts and provides for speedy resolution of disputes, and suitable amendment of Transfer of Property Act 1882, Law on Mortgage, Indian Contract Act, and Banking Regulation Act;

(iv) Better balance sheet valuation, disclosure and stricter prudential standards;

(v) Reduce NPA of banks by setting up asset reconstruction companies (ARC);

(vi) Reform directed credit to priority sector, including by reducing its scope from 40 per cent;

(vii) Bank restructuring:

- allow mergers of banks and NBFC, and among banks;
- convert development financial institutions (DFI) into banks or NBFCs;
- remove restriction of 10 per cent voting rights;
- allow foreign banks to set up subsidiaries or joint ventures in India;
- progressively raise the statutory minimum net worth requirement for registration of NBFCs from ₹ 25 lakh to ₹ 2 crore, and withdrawing deposit insurance from NBFCs;
- move from a flat to a risk-based or variable rate premium for deposit insurance;

contd...

...contd...

- reduce the legally required public shareholding in public sector banks from 51 to 33 per cent;
- end the duality of control of urban cooperative banks by state governments and RBI, and bring them under the sole jurisdiction of the Board for Financial Supervision;

(viii) Market reforms:

- restrict access to inter-bank call and notice money markets strictly to banks and primary dealers, withdraw RBI from the primary market in 91 days treasury bills, and impose prudential limits on reliance of banks on the call money market;
- reduce minimum duration of certificates of deposits, commercial paper, treasury bills and money market mutual funds to 15 days to develop an active, deep and liquid secondary market;
- integrate the forward exchange market with the spot forex market by allowing all participants in spot to participate in the forward market up to their exposures.

The recovery of the East Asian countries after the 1997 crisis was fairly rapid and spectacular (Figure 1.1). Why were the recommendations of Tarapore I and Narasimham II not implemented after the East Asian crisis blew over? I do not know the answer, but perhaps three factors contributed. First, the misperception that India was saved from the contagion because it had stringent capital controls. Second, there was no crisis and hence no compelling reasons for reforms. The relation between reforms and crisis, and its obverse—namely, the absence of reforms without a crisis—is well-known. Third, there was a significant decrease in risk-aversion among international investors towards emerging economies, including India, resulting in buoyant capital flows.

Figure 1.1

Countries Bounce Back from East Asian Crisis

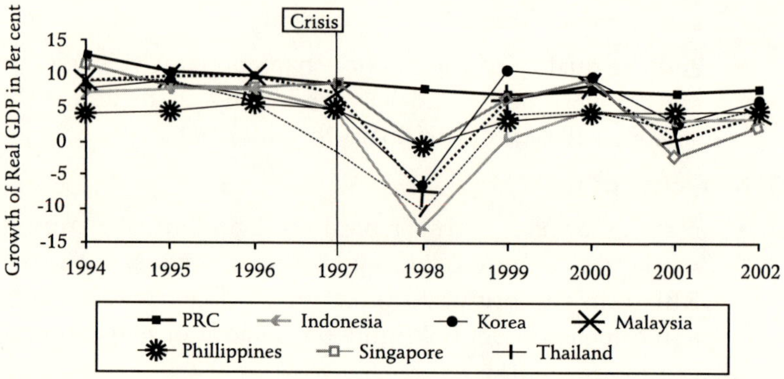

The Problem of Surfeit and the Impossible Trinity

By 2002, the East Asian crisis blew over, and the Indian economy also did well (Table 1.2). In fact, there were the problems of a surfeit on the foreign exchange front. After a gap of 24 years, the current account of the balance of payments recorded a surplus in 2001-02 (current account surplus was last recorded in 1977-78), and remained in surplus for the subsequent two years. It turned into a deficit subsequently, but albeit a small one. With buoyant capital flows, foreign exchange reserves were growing. The focus of monetary policy had to shift from protecting the economy from a precarious balance of payments situation to a problem of surfeit. Foreign exchange reserves almost doubled from US$76 billion at end-March 2003 to US$145 billion at end-March 2006.

As a matter of fact, by the end of 2003-04, the macroeconomic policy challenge had shifted dramatically from a problem of foreign exchange shortage to a problem of surfeit. It is well known that it is impossible to have the trinity of a fixed exchange rate, free capital movement and autonomous monetary policy. They are inconsistent with each other. We have to choose at most two of the three. Indeed, India did not and does not have a fixed exchange rate regime or capital account convertibility. But, there was a commitment to orderly exchange market conditions and *de facto* there was enough convertibility on the capital account. By the middle of this current decade, India was facing the impossible trinity.

Table 1.2

Growth Momentum with Macroeconomic Stability 2003-2007

	2002-03	*2003-04*	*2004-05*	*2005-06*	*2006-07*	*2007-08*
GDP growth	3.84	8.52	7.45	9.40	9.62	9.03
WPI Inflation (end of year)	6.49	4.64	5.70	3.98	5.94	7.75
Gross domestic savings as a per cent of GDP	26.4	29.8	31.8	34.3	34.8	...
Gross capital formation as a per cent of GDP	25.2	28.2	32.2	35.5	35.9	...
Current account deficit as a proportion of GDP	-1.25	-2.32	0.39	1.22	1.09	1.49
Fiscal deficit as a per cent of GDP	5.91	4.48	3.98	4.09	3.67	3.20
Foreign exchange reserves in billions of US dollars	76.1	113.0	141.5	151.6	199.2	309.7
BSE Sensex (end-March)	3048.72	5590.60	6492.82	11279.96	13072.10	15644.44

Reserve Bank of India (RBI) was intervening to maintain orderly conditions in the foreign exchange market and prevent the rupee from appreciating suddenly. The RBI by end of March 2002 was in a position to pay every holder of every rupee note anywhere an equivalent amount in foreign exchange and meet its obligation of "I promise to pay". It may be recalled that Tarapore I had recommended a statutory minimum net foreign asset to currency ratio of 40 per cent. The minimum had been achieved and well surpassed by 2001.

In the short-term firefight, initially, the strategy was that of sterilised intervention. First, the RBI bought the foreign currency by releasing rupees, and then sterilised it by selling bonds and mopping up the rupees released. The RBI could only sell government bonds that it had in its kitty, and with fiscal consolidation the government was borrowing a limited amount and there were not enough government bonds to sell. To solve this problem, in 2004-05, the government introduced the market stabilisation scheme (MSS) authorising the RBI to issue treasury bills and bonds beyond the government's own borrowing needs.[14] The cost of sterilisation accruing to the government, as a proportion of GDP, rose four-fold from 0.07 per cent (₹ 2,056.6 crore) in 2004-05 to 0.28 per cent (₹ 13,382.4 crore) in 2007-08 (RE).

Second, CRR had been on a downward trend almost continuously since 1991 until late 2003. CRR was doubled in stages from a low of 4.50 per cent of net time and demand liabilities of banks on June 14, 2003 to a high of 9.0 per cent on August 30, 2008 (Figure 1.2). CRR has long been recognised as a blunt instrument of monetary policy for two reasons. First, without market-related remuneration on such cash reserves, it is a tax on financial intermediation. With a non-interest bearing CRR of 10 per cent, a bank to break even, will have to charge at least 11 per cent on its loan when it raises deposits at 10 per cent. If CRR goes up to 20 per cent, the loan rate will have to rise to 12.5 per cent. CRR increases the spread between deposit and lending rates. Second, CRR is an across-the-board levy which does not take into account the relative liquidity position of different banks. Although originally CRR was considered appropriate more for safety reasons, now with good prudential norms, CRR has lost its popularity and has been dispensed with in many countries.[15] CRR continues to be popular in countries with shallow financial markets and hence weak mechanism for transmission of monetary policy. Tarapore I had recommended the reduction of CRR to 3 per cent and even as late as 2005, the RBI had announced that it "....continues to pursue its medium-term objective of reducing the CRR to the statutory minimum level of 3.0 per cent."[16] In the event, this medium-term objective became a victim of short-term exigencies.

---

14. The Government of India and RBI formally signed a Memorandum of Understanding (MoU) detailing the rationale and operational modalities of the market stabilisation scheme (MSS) on March 25, 2004. The scheme became effective from April 2004. The MSS is subject to a maximum limit specified by the Government.

15. Such countries include Australia, Canada, Mexico, New Zealand, Sweden and the UK.

16. See RBI (2005), Part II, Chapter 3, para III.9.

Figure 1.2

Cash Reserve Ratio

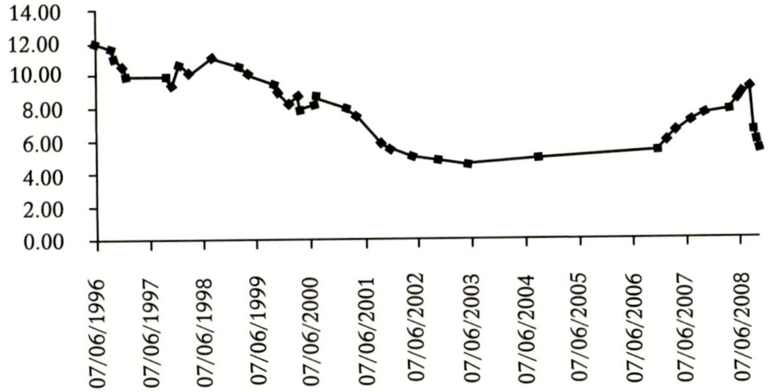

Third, following the recommendation of Narasimham II, to stabilise short-term interest rates through an informal corridor, a liquidity adjustment facility (LAF) was introduced on June 5, 2000. LAF is a daily exercise, in which only banks and primary dealers (PD) participate.[17] Acting as a banker of the last resort, RBI, under the LAF, injects liquidity by allowing participants to transfer securities to the RBI with a repurchase agreement at the repo rate, and absorb liquidity from them by getting into reverse repurchase agreement at the reverse repo rate. Like a bid-ask spread, the repo rate is always above the reverse repo rate.

The idea of Narsimham II behind LAF was to ensure orderly movements of the call money rate to "in a sense provide a reasonable corridor for market play," by resetting repo and reverse repo rates, if necessary daily. This was not achieved in any meaningful sense. With buoyant capital flows, RBI was worried about multiple considerations beyond orderly movements of the call rate within the LAF corridor. It fixed both the quantum of liquidity

17. RBI operates the LAF to inject/absorb liquidity through daily repos/reverse repos auctions in the forenoon between 9.30 a.m. and 10.30 a.m. For fine-tuning the management of bank reserves on the last day of the maintenance period, a Second LAF (SLAF) on reporting Fridays was introduced with effect from August 1, 2008.

to be absorbed or injected under LAF and the accompanying reverse repo and repo rates at the same time.[18]

You can either fix the price or fix the quantity. Fixing both denies the LAF corridor any chance of containing the call money rate. For example, in the 678 days of active trading between March 29, 2006 and December 22, 2008, the call money rate was above the repo rate on 253 days, and below the reverse repo rate on 108 days (Figure 1.3). In other words, on more than half the days, call money rate was outside the LAF corridor. Furthermore, the LAF corridor with the repo rate as the ceiling with the statutory bank rate remaining unchanged at 6 per cent since April 30, 2003 raises some questions about the significance of the bank rate in RBI policies.

Figure 1.3

Call Money and the LAF Corridor

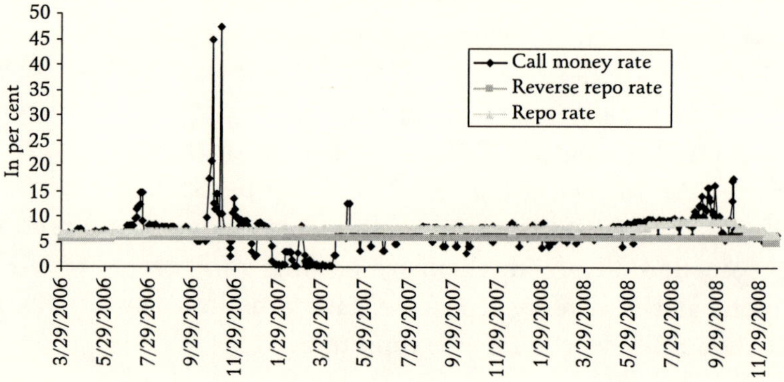

Overall, monetary policy had to shift gears with the remarkable turnaround of India's balance of payments situation between 2001-02 and 2005-06. The problem was no longer the traditional one of protecting the rupee from depreciating rapidly but one of preventing its rapid appreciation (Figure 1.4). With its multiple objectives of maintaining price stability, promoting growth by

18. RBI entrusted the Financial Markets Committee, consisting of the operational departmental heads, to meet every day in the morning to assess market conditions, and make decisions relating to the LAF. The Committee meets again at 12 noon to assess the bids received under LAF. The exact quantum of liquidity to be absorbed or injected and the accompanying reverse repo and repo rates are determined by the committee after taking into consideration, the liquidity conditions in the market, the interest rate situation and the stance of monetary policy.

meeting the legitimate credit needs of trade and industry and also maintaining orderly conditions in the foreign exchange market, RBI faced the impossible trinity.

Figure 1.4

Exchange Rate of the Rupee per US Dollar

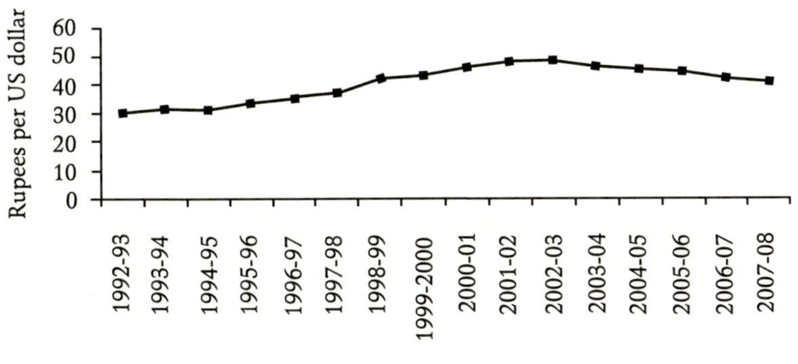

The Latest Round with Untapped Potential: 2006 Onwards

By end-March 2006, the Indian economy seemed to demonstrate a transition to a higher growth trajectory with more secure macroeconomic fundamentals. Growth in 2005-06 had exceeded 9 per cent, inflation was below 4 per cent, and the foreign exchange reserves already in excess of 11 months of imports were growing (Figure 1.5). This comfortable situation started off the third phase with untapped potential.

Figure 1.5

Growth in Foreign Currency Assets of the RBI

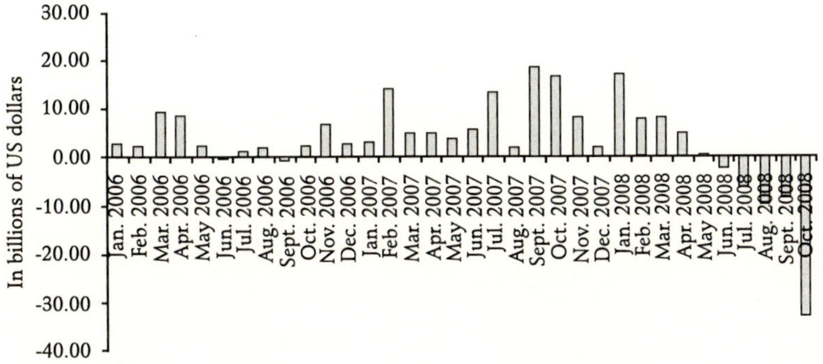

With most of the preconditions specified by Tarapore I (particularly in terms of inflation rate, consolidation and strengthening of the financial sector, exchange rate policy, external debt and reserve adequacy) having been achieved, there was a need to revisit the subject and consider a fresh roadmap for achieving full capital account convertibility. Accordingly, following the Prime Minister's directive to examine the issue afresh, the RBI, on March 20, 2006, appointed the second Tarapaore Committee (Tarapore II) to work out a framework for achieving the objective.

Tarapore II observed that there was progress towards capital account convertibility, but "….on an ad hoc basis and the liberalised framework continues to be a prisoner of the erstwhile strict control system."[19] The committee recommended various measures such as reduction of the gross borrowing requirement of the government, adopting the public sector borrowing requirement (PSBR) as a clear indicator of the public sector deficit, setting up of an Office of Public Debt outside the RBI, and a clear setting out of monetary policy objectives jointly by the government and RBI, for fuller capital account convertibility. The committee recommended a gradual approach towards fuller capital account convertibility consisting of Phase I (2006-07), Phase II (2007-08 and 2008-09) and Phase III (2009-10 and 2010-11). The substantive recommendations of Tarapore II are given in Box 1.3. Two other important committees appointed in the third phase by Government and the Planning Commission are the High Powered Expert Committee on Making Mumbai an International Financial Centre headed by Percy Mistry and the Committee on Financial Sector Reforms, headed by Raghuram Rajan, respectively. We shall call the two reports submitted in February 2007 and April 2008, respectively, the PM Report,[20] and the Rajan Report.[21]

---

19. Tarapore (2006a): 130.

20. Speaking at the Asian Corporate Finance Conference in Mumbai on March 18, 2006, Prime Minister Dr Manmohan Singh had said that making Mumbai a regional financial centre was under the Government's active consideration. The Committee was also chaired by Percy S. Mistry until February 7, 2007.

21. The Rajan Report submitted in April 2008 was a draft report. The final report came out as "A Hundred Small Steps" on September 12, 2008, and was due to be published in 2009.

Box 1.3

Recommendations of Tarapore II (2006) for Fuller Capital Account Convertibility

i. External commercial borrowings (ECB) (then subject to an annual ceiling of $18 billion):
   - Raising the ceiling gradually in Phases II and III;
   - Putting rupee denominated ECB outside the ceiling;
   - Removal of end-use restriction[22] on ECB in Phase I;
   - Removal of ECBs over 10-year maturity outside the overall ceiling in Phase I;
   - Removal of ECBs over 7-year maturity outside the overall ceiling in Phase II;
   - Raising the limit for automatic approval from $500 million to $750 million in Phase II and $1 billion in Phase III;

ii. Raising the limit of overseas investment by Indian companies from 200 per cent of net worth to 250 per cent in Phase I, 300 per cent in Phase II, and 400 per cent in Phase III;

iii. Prohibit foreign institutional investors (FII) from investing money through participatory notes (PNs);

iv. Raise the annual subceiling within overall ECB ceiling of FII investment in debt instruments:
   - For Government securities and treasury bills, from $2 billion to 6 per cent of total gross issuance by Centre and States in Phase I and further to 8 per cent of such issuance in Phase II and 10 per cent of such issuance in Phase III;
   - For corporate debt, from $1.5 billion to 15 per cent of fresh issuance Phase II and further to 25 per cent of fresh issuance in Phase III;

v. Allow non-resident corporates to invest in Indian stock markets through SEBI-registered entities;

contd...

22. End-use restrictions applied to working capital, repayment of rupee loans, investment in capital market, and investment in real estate.

...contd...

vi. Allow foreign institutions and corporates beyond multilateral institutions (such as International Finance Corporation and Asian Development Bank) to raise rupee bonds in India;

vii. Linking domestic banks' borrowings from overseas banks and correspondents to paid up capital and free reserves and not to unimpaired Tier I capital, and putting the limit at 50 per cent in Phase I, 75 per cent in Phase II, and 100 per cent in Phase III;

viii. Extending the permission for investment overseas by SEBI-registered Indian investors beyond mutual funds to all SEBI-registered portfolio management schemes and raising the annual aggregate ceiling on such investment from $2 billion to $3 billion in Phase I, $4 billion in Phase II and $5 billion in Phase III;

ix. Raise the annual limit on free remittance by resident individuals from $25,000 to $50,000 in Phase I, $100,000 in Phase II, and $200,000 in Phase III;

x. Allow non-residents (NRs) other than non-resident Indians (NRIs) also to open FCNR(B) deposit accounts without tax benefits in Phase I, and also NR(E)RA deposit accounts without tax benefits in Phase II; and

xi. Allow non-residents (NRs) other than NRIs to invest in companies in Indian stock exchanges through SEBI-registered mutual funds, and portfolio management schemes.

As an aside, the PM Committee report may not have attracted the right attention it deserves perhaps because of its name. The name may have given the mistaken impression to some that the report is all about making Mumbai an enclave for a few 'super-rich investment bankers and bonus-obsessed currency-and-options traders' supplying international financial service to the rest of the world. On the contrary, the PM Committee makes it very clear that making Mumbai an international financial centre is as much or more about the whole of India as it is about Mumbai. In its report submitted on February 10, 2007, it made five substantive points (Box 1.4).

Box 1.4

Recommendations of PM Committee (2007) on Making Mumbai an International Financial Centre

1. Make Mumbai an International Financial Centre not only to capture the domestic and foreign market for international financial services, but to get the real advantage coming from rooting it in a "large and efficient domestic financial market, ... that operates on global lines."[23]
2. Move aggressively on introducing full capital account convertibility.[24]
3. Have a monetary policy regime that targets inflation.
4. Shift financial regulatory regime from rules-based regulation to principles-based regulation by 2011.[25] Scrap subordinate law under a prescriptive approach.
5. Move from a fragmented to a unified financial sector regulatory architecture. In the interim, do a 'partial consolidation of extant regulators into a tightly knit quartet covering: (a) banking; (b) insurance; (c) pensions; and (d) capital, derivatives and commodities markets'. Transfer all regulation/supervision of any type of organised financial trading to SEBI.

Now, let us move to the Rajan Committee. Its very broad terms of reference included identification of the emerging challenges in meeting the financing needs of the Indian economy, examination of the performance of the various sectors of the financial sector, identification of changes needed in the regulatory and supervisory infrastructure. The Committee gave three reasons for financial sector reforms: for including more Indians in the growth process

23. See PM Committee (2007): 76.
24. See PM Committee (2007): 226: "..the HPEC is of the view that the capital account needs to be liberalised more rapidly and in a time bound fashion than is presently envisaged. CAC needs to be achieved within the next 18–24 months—i.e., by the end of calendar 2008 at the latest—preferably sooner."
25. The prime examples of such principles-based regulation were UK (pioneer), Ireland, and Australia. The Committee also cited appropriate moves in more recent times by Singapore and Commodity Futures Trading Commission in the US.

(or, more inclusive growth), more growth, and protecting the economy from external instability.[26] The Committee made 33 recommendations, of which the salient ones can be grouped into six categories (Box 1.5).

Box 1.5

Recommendations of Rajan Committee (2008) on Financial Sector Reforms

1. Inflation-targeting by RBI through the repo and reverse repo rates.
2. Reform of regulatory architecture with principles-based regulation.
3. Deregulation for more efficiency with opening up rupee bond markets to foreign investors, being more liberal in allowing takeovers and mergers, including by domestically incorporated subsidiaries of foreign banks, freeing banks to set up branches and ATMs anywhere, creation of a more innovation-friendly environment.
4. Deregulation for financial inclusion by allowing more entry of well capitalised deposit-taking small finance banks, liberalising banking correspondent regulation to allow local agents to extend financial services, allowing a system of exchangeable priority sector loan certificates (PSLC), and liberalising interest rate on loans subject to full disclosure, transparency and restrictions regarding eligibility under PSLC scheme.
5. Reforms for financial inclusion: to improve the collation of credit history, expedite the process of creating a unique national ID number with biometric identification, and open up credit bureau information to subscribers subject to verification of "need to know and authorisation to use" of the subscriber; and improve land registration and titling. Re-examine restrictions on tenancy so that tenancy can be formalised in contracts and extend the powers of Securitisation and Reconstruction of (SRFAESI) to all institutional lenders.

contd...

26. Rajan Committee (2008): 2.

...contd...

6. Restructure public sector banks (PSBs): by selling small underperforming PSBs to strategic investors and observing outcome; strengthening board of directors, and either creating bank holding companies or bringing down Government's share below 50 per cent.

The three recent reports provide valuable inputs for policy-making. What is striking is the commonality of recommendations. The two most recent committees, namely PM and Rajan, approach the issue of financial sector reform from two different angles—one for making Mumbai an international financial centre, and the other for accelerating growth and making it more inclusive. Yet, their recommendations are strikingly similar. This is not surprising since the PM Committee makes it very clear that development of Mumbai into an international financial centre has to be premised very differently from similar development of Singapore or Dubai. Mumbai is not just an entrepot, it has the vast Indian economy with immense potential behind its seagate. This advantage, which the PM committee calls 'the hinterland advantage', has to be fully utilised, and much of the advantage of developing Mumbai into an international financial centre will come from having a world-class financial sector that can serve the vast Indian economy. There are a large number of issues on which these two recent committees have reiterated not only much of what Tarapore II said in 2006, but also what Narasimham II had emphasised in 1998. There seems to be a lot of untapped potential in the three reports of the most recent period. I shall group the main pending recommendations under the following five headings:

1. moving to an inflation-targeted monetary policy regime;
2. modernising the delivery of financial services to the priority sectors and the vulnerable and weaker sections;
3. introducing capital account convertibility;
4. moving from a rules-based and fragmented regulatory architecture to a principles-based and unified architecture; and

5. reform of the banking system in general and public sector banks, in particular.

I believe that some of these measures would have been taken to implement some of these recommendations had it not been for adverse external developments in the form of a large commodity price shock in the world market and for the ongoing global crisis.

First too Hot to Handle and Then in the Midst of a Crisis

Before any action could be taken on the recommendations of the three committees of the latest sub-period, international petroleum prices started to rise steadily and food prices came under severe pressure. Relative to May 2007, the price of rice and wheat, for example, rose by 197 per cent and 137 per cent, respectively, by May 2008 and March 2008 (Figure 1.6). Simultaneously, with extremely buoyant capital inflows, foreign exchange reserves more than doubled again to $310 billion by end-March 2008.

Figure 1.6

International Rice and Wheat Price Flare Up

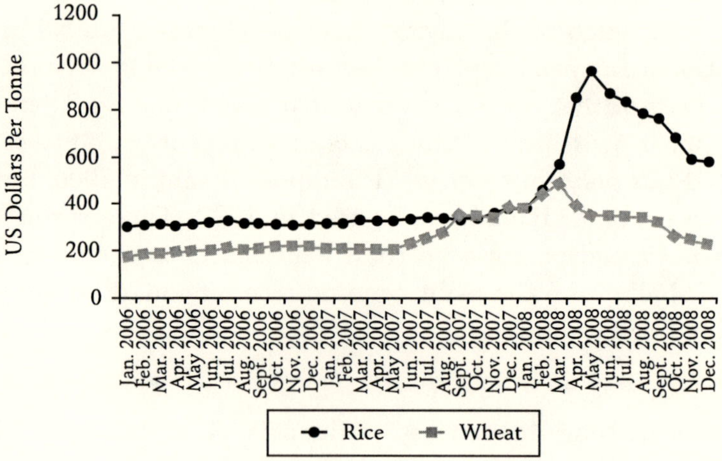

Rising world prices got transmitted to domestic prices of primary commodities. With primary commodity group prices rising, inflation continued to accelerate reaching a peak of 12.91

in the week ending August 2, 2008.[27] The inflation acceleration reflected not only a simultaneous flare up in the prices of both primary commodities and energy products but also a sharp rise in metal products, particularly those of iron and steel. Rising inflation became a matter of concern. India was described as "Too hot to handle" by some, as in *The Economist* dated November 25, 2006. Some alleged that India was 'too hot' or overheating, because it was growing beyond its growth potential thereby straining its labour force and capital stock and hence engendering inflationary instabilities.

In response to the inflationary surge, Government and RBI started to act on both the fiscal and monetary front. For example, the government allowed the subsidy bill for petroleum products to balloon by not raising the retail prices of motor spirit, high speed diesel, kerosene and LPG in spite of a large rise in their import cost, reduced import duties on a host of commodities and banned exports of some goods. In 2008, on the monetary front, the RBI increased the cash reserve ratio (CRR) from 7.5 per cent to 7.75 per cent from April 26, to 8 per cent from May 10, 8.25 per cent from May 24, 8.5 per cent from July 5, 8.75 per cent from July 19, and 9 per cent from August 30, 2008. Between May 7, 2008 and June 25, 2008, out of 34 trading days, on 31 days, the call money rate consistently was above the upper band of the LAF corridor. The RBI also increased the fixed repo rate under LAF from 8.00 to 8.50 per cent on June 25, 2008 and to 9 per cent on July 29, 2008. Yet, the call money rate continued to pierce the repo rate almost as a matter of bad habit. Liquidity was in high demand and prices were rising. Many of these measures were not consistent with the stated long-term policy stance of the government and the RBI. Governments and central banks all over the world have to take extreme measures to deal with extenuating circumstances of a temporary nature. With the benefit of hindsight, in the future, I believe economists will closely scrutinise the

27. With prices of primary commodities rising at an average annual rate of over 8 per cent between May 27, 2006 and June 23, 2007, the overall inflation rate, as measured by the year-on-year movement in the wholesale price index (WPI), crossed and remained above 5 per cent between the week ending August 9, 2006 and week ending June 2, 2007. Subsequently, after remaining subdued below 5 per cent until the week ending February 9, 2008, inflation reignited again to reach its peak on August 2, 2008.

necessity of all these short-term measures, their consistency with medium-term reform policy, and, if inconsistent, the speed with which they were rescinded to make them consistent again.

Let me come back to the main story. Relief on the inflation front came from the middle of the third quarter of 2008. Inflation after peaking at 12.91 per cent in the week ending August 2, started to decelerate (Figure 1.7). But as inflation started to decelerate, there was another major problem at hand. The global financial crisis was in full bloom. As preoccupation with curtailing inflation subsided, short-term concerns about risk-proofing the economy from the fall out of world recession became much more pronounced than financial sector reforms.

Figure 1.7

Success at Last: Inflation Declines

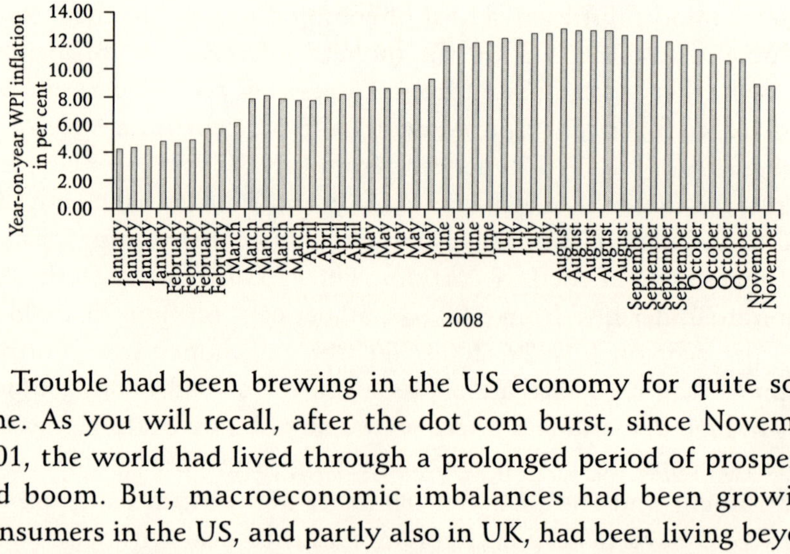

Trouble had been brewing in the US economy for quite some time. As you will recall, after the dot com burst, since November 2001, the world had lived through a prolonged period of prosperity and boom. But, macroeconomic imbalances had been growing. Consumers in the US, and partly also in UK, had been living beyond their means, borrowing money to buy houses and fund their other spending. Even the government in the US had been living beyond its means, and incurring large fiscal deficits. The excess of expenditure over savings in the US was getting reflected in large current account deficits, which reached a peak of US$811.5 billion, equivalent of 6.2 per cent of GDP in 2006. This current account deficit was financed by China and Japan, who invested their foreign exchange reserves in US paper. In other words, the US was paying for its excessive imports in dollars, which the Chinese and the Japanese in turn were investing in US securities. There were fears about a 'hard landing' of the US economy.[28]

To cut a long story short, home prices in the US, which had risen sharply since the second quarter of 2002, with excessively permissive mortgage financing, started to fall in the first quarter of 2007. In the second quarter of 2007, defaults increased sharply and some subprime mortgage lenders entered bankruptcy. Trust and confidence in mortgage-backed securities were lost and the credit market seized up. In mid-July 2007, the TED spread—the difference between the three-month London interbank-offer rate and the yield on a virtually risk-free treasury bill rate, which is a measure of credit conditions—spiked to 150-200 basis points. Banks faced problems in raising money in the money market. In August 2007, the credit crisis was on with US banks taking $500 billion in write-downs. Soon the crisis spread to the UK and Europe.[29]

With the benefit of hindsight, now we know that the US had entered a recession by December 2007.[30] The peak in December 2007 marked the end of the expansion that began in November 2001 and the beginning of a recession. But, at the end of 2007, without the

28. There were ominous predictions about brutal correction to the exchange value of the US dollar by Paul Volker. In 2005, he had said, "Altogether the circumstances seem to me as dangerous and intractable as any I can remember, and I can remember quite a lot....We are skating on thin ice." He had predicted presciently, "....it is more likely than not that it will be financial crises rather than policy foresight" that will correct the growing deficits of the US economy. See Volker (2005).

29. On August 9, 2007, the European Central Bank and the US Federal Reserve injected $90 billion into jittery financial markets. On August 16, 2007, Countrywide Financial drew down $11.5 billion from its credit lines. On August 11, 2007, Gordon Brown had said that Britain was in "as good a shape as it could be to weather the storm". Soon there was bad news from the UK. On September 14, 2007, British mortgage lender Northern Rock PLC ran into trouble and sought and received a liquidity support facility from the Bank of England. This led to loss of confidence among depositors and with customers queuing up outside branches to withdraw their savings, UK saw the first run on a British bank since the collapse of Overend and Gurney in 1866. On 22 February 2008, Northern Rock was taken into state custody.

30. On November 28, 2008, the Business Cycle Dating Committee of the National Bureau of Economic Research determined that a peak in economic activity occurred in the U.S. economy in December 2007.The Business Cycle Dating Committee of the NBER maintains a chronology of the beginning and ending dates (months and quarters) of U.S. recessions, defines a recession as "a significant decline in economic activity spread across the economy, lasting more than a few months, normally visible in production, employment, real income, and other indicators". The last expansion ending in November 2007 lasted 73 months, much shorter than the previous expansion of 120 months in the 1990s.

requisite data, the picture was far from clear. Even in mid-July 2008, there were even suggestions that the recession was only mental![31]

Meanwhile, the crisis continued. And around mid-September 2008, in the international financial markets, we lived through weeks when decades happened. In the US, regulators seized Fannie Mae and Freddie Mac on September 6, Lehman Brothers filed for bankruptcy on September 15. The crisis did not remain confined to the US. In no time almost, the Wall Street contagion swept across the Atlantic to Europe. And all hell broke loose in the western financial markets. House prices were down, stock markets faced a melt down and the credit markets seized up. The story is too well to merit recounting.

Indian reaction to the crisis was an easing of monetary policy. Governor Reddy relinquished office on September 5, 2008, and one of the first acts of the new Governor Subbarao was to reduce CRR from 9.0 per cent to 6.5 per cent on October 11, 2008. The global crisis was in full swing, and the RBI made the 2.5 percentage point reduction in CRR steeper than the 1.5 percentage points it had originally planned.[32] This was followed up by the introduction of a special fixed-rate term repo at 9.0 per cent per annum on October 14, with a view to enabling banks to meet the liquidity requirements of mutual funds and a reduction in the repo rate from 9.0 per cent to 8.0 per cent on October 21 (Figure 1.7).[33,34] Measures followed fast and thick. The repo rate and CRR were reduced again on November 3 and 8, respectively to 7.5 per cent and 5.5 per cent, respectively. The latest action of the RBI came on December 8, when it reduced the repo rate to 6.5 per cent, and for the first time since July 25, 2006, also reduced the reverse repo rate

31. In July 2008, Republican presidential candidate John McCain's top economic adviser Phil Gramm said "You've heard of mental depression; this is a mental recession,.... We may have a recession; we haven't had one yet." See *Washington Times*, July 9, 2008.

32. In a circular (Circular DBOD. No. Ret. BC.55 /12.01.001/ 2008-09) dated October 10, 2008, the RBI had notified a reduction of the CRR from 9.0 per cent to 7.5 per cent with effect from October 11, 2008. On October 15, 2008, RBI notified (DBOD.No.Ret.BC.61/12.01.001/2008-09) the reduction not to 7.5 per cent but 6.5 per cent.

33. Thus, there are three types of repos—standing facility, special LAF, second LAF.

34. With effect from October 29, 2004, the nomenclature of repo and reverse repo had been changed in keeping with international usage. From October 29, 2004, reverse repo indicates absorption of liquidity and repo signifies injection of liquidity.

to keep the LAF corridor in order. Furthermore, the government also announced some fiscal measures to stimulate the economy. Some of these measures, particularly the ones related to CRR, are more in line with the medium-term thrust of policies, yet overall they raise some fundamental questions about national priorities regarding financial sector reform policies amidst an international crisis.

With the decline in inflation, gone are the discussions of overheating of the Indian economy. Instead, the critical question has become: how do we avoid or minimise the backlash of the global crisis? Starting with the US, and the UK, a whole host of OECD countries have announced fiscal stimuli and monetary accommodation, including bail-out packages. If the Indian economy was overheated in 2006, does it need a fiscal stimulus today? Or, if it needs a fiscal stimulus today, was the overheating an exaggerated problem? Or, is it simply that the external economic environment has become so adverse that there has been a regime-switch from a supply-constrained overheated situation to a demand-constrained scenario? Such a switch is possible, but needs a careful scrutiny before coming to a definitive conclusion.

Beyond the Preoccupation with Short-term Concerns: Five Pending Reform Issues in the Financial Sector

Let me be very clear that a natural preoccupation with short-run firefighting has characterised policies all over the world, particularly in the US. In every country, however, there is the need for a satisfactory reconciliation of the dilemma of policies appropriate for the short run with those suitable for the long run. It is critical to distinguish between the immediate steps needed to manage the present crisis and long-run reforms needed to sustain growth and reduce the likelihood of future crises.[35] With the compelling need

35. Noble laureate Gary Becker (2008) has emphasised that "it is paramount to distinguish between the immediate steps needed to cope with the present crisis and the long-run reforms needed to reduce the likelihood of future crises." As an example, Becker cites the case of Bear Stearns. He says, "The moral-hazard consequence for banks receiving a bailout now is worrisome since they may expect to get rescued again by the government if their future investments turn sour. Yet while I find helping these banks highly distasteful, moral-hazard concerns should be temporarily relaxed when the whole short-term credit system is close to collapse. Still, the bank bill with its huge bailout does suggest that the $29 billion bailout of the bondholders of Bear Stearns in March was a mistake."

to grow and to ameliorate widespread poverty, the medium-term stakes of policies in developing countries such as India are very high, and policies need to have a longer-term vision. Allow me to focus on five of these medium-term issues.

Moving to an Inflation-targeted Monetary Policy

Perhaps it would be appropriate to describe RBI's approach to monetary policy as a combination of monetary targeting and 'just do it' discretionary approach, rather than inflation targeting. The objective of overall policy in India is accelerated inclusive growth with macroeconomic stability. Admittedly, the overall objective of monetary policy has to be the same as overall economic policy. The issue, however, is essentially one of Tinbergen's 'assignment rule': what objective do we assign to which policy? Both the PM Committee and Rajan Committee have strongly recommended the move to an inflation-targeted monetary policy. In contrast, Tarapaore II has recommended a real effective exchange rate (REER) rule. It reiterated the earlier recommendation of Tarapore I in 1997 about intervening in foreign exchange market to contain the REER in the band of ±5 per cent around the 'neutral' REER. All the three committees in the third and latest sub-period of reform have been much clearer about the objective that monetary policy should follow than the earlier committees. It may be recalled, for example, that Chakravarty Committee had recommended a flexible monetary targeting with feedback, that is, a system of targeting money stock with the target being revised "in the light of the information available on expected output performance." While conceding that multiple objectives tend to dilute the effectiveness of monetary policy and therefore disperse responsibility, on grounds of pragmatism, earlier committees had rejected the goal of monetary policy pursuing the single objective of an inflation mandate. As late as in 2000, for example, the Narasimham Advisory Group on Transparency of Monetary Policy and Other Financial Policies had suggested that there should be a primary objective (ostensibly an inflation target) and subsidiary objectives with a clear ordering of priorities. There are four concerns that normally are raised with regard to inflation-targeting. First is the issue of trade-off between growth and price-stability, or the so-called Philips curve. The temporary nature of this trade-off has been well established in the literature.[36] Furthermore, there is evidence that inflation beyond a single-digit threshold of around 6 per cent actually hurts growth. Second, is the fear of fixing too low an inflation target.[37] But, this objection is not sustained as it is possible to fix an inflation rate such as between 4 and 5 per cent, which is not too low. Third, is the sacrifice of the nominal exchange rate anchor with the pursuit of an inflation target. Fourth, is the sacrifice of a real exchange rate or REER rule. Let us turn to the last two objections one by one.

The advantages of maintaining a fixed exchange rate for the Indian rupee are well known. By eliminating exchange rate risk, it provides certainty to exporters and importers about their rupee income stream. Furthermore, it provides a nominal anchor to the economy. With a fixed nominal exchange rate, when inflation gets out of line with price rise in partner countries, the balance of payments adjusts to bring about equilibrium. If inflation is too high relative to partner countries, exports become uncompetitive and imports surge, money supply contracts through balance of payments deficits and inflation declines. The obverse happens when inflation is too low compared to partner countries. But, in reality, with exchange market intervention and the compulsions to avoid too much volatility in money supply for whatever reasons, including balance of payments, we know what happens is something else.

We know of many cases where a fixed exchange regime came to an end because the currency was overvalued. Central Bank intervened until it ran out of reserves, and then abandoned the fixed rate and devalued. There are enough examples of such unhappy ends to fixed exchange rate regimes in Latin America and

36. See Kannan and Joshi (1998).

37. Indeed, it may not be desirable to target too low an inflation for four reasons. First, some inflation of say around 3-4 per cent allows enough room for relative prices to adjust without any prices declining in absolute terms, and hence act as a lubricant for growth. Second, some inflation helps the government to mop up revenues in terms of inflation tax, or what is called seignorage. What the holders of cash lose in terms of erosion of real value, is gain to the government or its extended arm, the RBI, as cash is a public sector liability. Third, some inflation reduces the pressure on reducing the administered nominal interest rates on items such as small savings and PPF. Fourth, it allows the maintenance of the nominal exchange rate of the rupee without real appreciation even when some major currency such as the dollar is softening.

East Asia. But, what happens when the currency is undervalued? In such a case, the central bank or the government has to purchase foreign exchange to defend the rate and sterilise the injected liquidity to contain the monetary impact. Ultimately the cost of sterilisation becomes prohibitive, the peg has to be abandoned and the currency revalued. Though not as common as the breakdown of an overvalued peg, we know a few cases when an undervalued peg broke down in developed countries (Box 1.6).[38]

Box 1.6

Examples of Breakdown of Undervalued Currency under a Fixed Exchange Rate Regime

1. Even under the Bretton Woods Agreement about fixed exchange rate regime, Canada floated its currency from October 1950 under heavy upward pressures from rising commodity prices, improving trade balance, capital inflows and the speculation about a likely revaluation. The Canadian dollar floated through May 1962.[39]
2. With strong inflationary pressure coming from the US and an increasing concern about excess liquidity created through currency intervention to maintain the fixed exchange rate, Germany floated its currency in May 1971. After a short period of the Smithsonian fixed exchange rate system from December 1971 through February 1973, Germany again floated the German mark in February 1973. This was an internationally coordinated float with other major currencies including the Japanese yen, finally ending the era of the fixed exchange rate regime.

...contd...

38. I am grateful to Haruhiko Kuroda and Howard Brown for these examples. In Canada, the government and the central bank favoured float rather than revaluation because of the changing and unpredictable international factors like commodity prices and capital inflows. Initially, the float was seen as temporary but actually continued for 12 years. It is interesting that the IMF somehow found it not illegal despite clear violation of the charter oblibgation of all members to adhere to the fixed exchange rate under the Bretton Woods system.

39. Canada again floated its dollar from June 1970 before the demise of the Bretton Woods Agreement in February 1973. This again was caused by similar factors like rising commodity prices, increasing current account surplus, capital inflows attracted by high interest rates in Canada and increasing international reserves. Inflation was a real concern. But this time the problem was a global one, brought about by the Vietnam war and expanded welfare programme in the US. Eventually all major currencies were floated by 1971.

...contd...

3. Third, after the famous 'Nixon Shock' of August 15, 1971, while all European countries immediately floated their currencies, Japan floated its currency only after two weeks. Japan resisted revaluation or float for about two weeks by intensified currency market intervention and exchange control, but the overwhelming capital inflows (or, surging current account surplus through 'leads and lags') even under strict capital controls forced it to float the yen eventually.[40]

Now we come to the pros and cons of the REER rule recommended by the Tarapore II.[41] The REER rule in effect is an indexation of the nominal exchange rate to the price level. What are the problems with following an REER rule?

First, is the problem of choosing the target REER. How do we know what the correct REER is? If we do not hit the bull's eye and fix the REER at anything but the equilibrium level, either there will be persistent deficits or surpluses in the balance of payments leading to persistent declines or rises in money supply, downward or upward price-nominal exchange rate spirals and a total loss of monetary control. This is not just a theoretical possibility, but a real one that has been observed in some countries, for example, in the former Yugoslavia. In the former Yugoslavia, with the emergence of external financing difficulties in the late 1970s, the dinar was devalued by almost 30 per cent in 1980, and throughout the 1980s there were successive devaluations in line with inflation aimed at maintaining the REER at the new lower level. With a large degree of dollarisation through foreign currency deposits, Yugoslav inflation, which was in double-digit levels throughout the 1970s and 1980s,

---

40. Major reason for the government to float the currency appears to have been potentially large exchange loss from mushrooming foreign reserves rather than inflationary implications, though the Bank of Japan might have been more concerned about the loss of monetary control.

41. It is interesting to note that Tarapore I had recommended (p.62): ".. that there should be an early empowering of the RBI, on the inflation mandate. There should be a medium-term inflation mandate approved by Parliament and only Parliament should alter that mandate. Once the mandate is given, the RBI should be given freedom to use the instruments at its command to attain the medium-term inflation target."

unfolded as a classic wage-price exchange rate spiral and exploded into hyperinflation in the last quarter of 1989.[42]

Second, quite apart from getting the REER level wrong, an REER rule can exacerbate instabilities in output levels. In the late 1970s and early 1980s, for small open economies, such an indexation was quite popular to isolate the foreign trade sector from the vagaries of the macroeconomy. But, it can be demonstrated that such an indexation of the exchange rate not only creates potential instabilities in the price level, but also results, under realistic assumptions, from the supply-side interactions, in increased instabilities in output as well.[43]

On the institutional arrangements, the PM Committee recommends "an explicit and legally mandated *de jure* inflation-target regime" over "a *de facto* pegged exchange rate regime ....or a *de facto* inflation targeting regime (as is the case in the US)."[44] What is needed is a debate as to whether we need to move immediately to an explicit and legally mandated inflation-target regime, or pending such legislation, to a *de facto* inflation-target regime with adequate understanding between the government and the RBI.

There are three very compelling reasons to shift to an inflation-targeting regime amidst the current international financial crisis. First, inflation, worldwide, is on a downward phase. Targeting moderate inflation when world prices are soft is easier to achieve than when the world commodity markets are flaring up. Reputation for delivering a modest inflation target is easier to build now than it was a year ago when world petroleum prices were around $150 per barrel. Second, targeting a moderate inflation rate will effectively also provide a floor to the extent the RBI will allow deflationary forces to operate. A modest inflation target, in case the world crisis proves to be more severe than what is expected now, will act as a guarantee for reflation. Third, with aversion to risk growing among the international financial investors, capital flows have reversed direction. The rupee is no longer under upward pressure. Thus,

42. See Lahiri (1991).

43. See Dornbusch (1982).

44. See PM Committee, p.95.

choosing an inflation target need not necessarily mean an inevitable appreciation of the rupee in real terms.

Modernising the Delivery of Financial Services to the 'Priority Sectors', and Vulnerable and Weaker Sections

Provision of adequate and timely institutional credit at competitive rates to the rural areas in general and agriculture, export and small-scale sector and weaker and vulnerable sections in particular has remained a major challenge for Indian banking for decades. As far back as 1933, when the Reserve Bank of India Bill was referred to the Joint Select Committee, two issues that have been a matter of some serious discussion have been: (i) how to provide adequate finance in the rural areas, particularly for agriculture, and (ii) the inclusion of indigenous bankers and other parties doing banking business in the country within the RBI's scope.[45] The legislature was very keen that the services of the indigenous bankers and moneylenders should be utilised in the scheme of provision of credit to the rural economy. By statute, the RBI, in its Central Office, has always had an Agricultural Credit Department.[46]

As a matter of record, however, it is important to note that starting from the Darling Report of June 1935, the emphasis has been on affording credit and other assistance through cooperative banks (including land mortgage banks). Other channels of assistance have been dealt with rather sketchily.[47] Indeed, there was reluctance on the part of indigenous bankers and moneylenders to collaborate with the RBI as well. The RBI had suggested the possibility of registering indigenous bankers and moneylenders 'carrying business on proper lines' and accepting the names of such parties 'as one of the names on two-name paper coming through scheduled banks' for rediscounting.[48] RBI was even willing to deal directly with the indigenous bankers provided they confined their business to

45. See RBI (1970): 111-114.
46. Section 54, RBI Act.
47. See RBI (1970): 201.
48. RBI (1970): 204.

banking proper and had a specified minimum capital. This proposal to use indigenous bankers either as agents for collection of cheques and bills or after some restructuring was, however, rejected by the indigenous bankers.[49]

The post-independence period with its emphasis on cooperative banking has not produced enough success in extending adequate and timely credit to the agricultural sector. It is in this context that the Rajan Committee recommendation of liberalising banking correspondent regulation to allow local agents to extend financial services[50] becomes important. This needs to be implemented.

After the two drought years and associated shortfall in food production in 1965-66 and 1966-67, under the concept of social control over banking introduced in December 1967 came the directed credit programme involving loans on preferential terms and conditions to priority sectors.[51] Priority sector was initially defined as agriculture, exports and small-scale industry.[52] Fourteen (14) banks were nationalised and one of the objectives of nationalisation was to ensure that no productive endeavour in agriculture and small scale industries fell short of credit support.

As a matter of record, directed credit is an instrument that has been followed by many developing countries. Japan used direct government allocation of funds to industry during the reconstruction period of 1945-55, and in a less direct fashion, but with a rigidly segmented financial system under wide-ranging controls, between 1955 and 1970.[53] Korea used directed credit through government-owned banks for promoting exports and industrial investment in the 1950s and 1960s, and heavy and chemical industries during the 1970s. Unlike Japan, Korean directed credit involved heavy subsidisation. With political democratisation, in the 1980s credit was directed towards social programmes

49. See Bombay Shroffs Association's reaction and letter of Seth Fatichand Gokaldas of Madura dated September 27, 1937, RBI (1970): 215-16.

50. Rajan Committee (2008): 8.

51. See RBI (2008): 100.

52. The definition of priority sector as well as that of small firms have undergone various changes over time.

53. See Vittas and Cho (1995)

and income redistribution. The conclusion about directed credit programmes appears to be that they should be small, narrowly focused, and of limited duration with clear sunset provisions. Experience in most countries shows that they stimulated capital-intensive projects, that preferential funds were often diverted for non-priority purposes, and were associated with low repayment rates. Subsidies should be low to minimise distortion of incentives as well as the tax on financial intermediation that a directed credit programme entails.

As far back as 1991, Narasimham I had recommended a re-examination of the continued relevance of directed credit programme and its phasing out. It also recommended that the priority sector be redefined to comprise small and marginal farmers, tiny sector of industry, small business and transport operators, village and cottage industries, rural artisans and other weaker sections and the credit target for this redefined priority sector should be reduced from 40 per cent of aggregate credit. The RBI rejected the proposal ".... to ensure that any changes in the policy on priority sector credit did not result in a disruption in the flow of credit for productive purposes."[54]

After Narasimham I, at least two committees have reiterated the recommendation about phasing out the system of directed credit. More than a decade ago, Narasimham II again recommended reduction of the scope of directed credit to priority sector from 40 per cent.[55] The effect of financial repression through micro-level controls on financial deepening and hence growth is also well-known.[56] Last year, Rajan Committee concluded that "India's experience with directed credit has been abysmal, with flows historically going into sectors with low productivity that happen to be favoured."[57] The fact that important segments of the Indian economy are credit-constrained is well-accepted by most economists.

54. RBI (2008): 118.

55. It also recommended inclusion of employment-oriented, important sectors like food processing and related service activities in agriculture, fisheries, poultry and dairying, under such lending; and consideration of the debt securitisation concept within the priority sector for improving efficiency and imparting a measure of flexibility.

56. See for example, Demetriades and Luintel (1996).

57. Rajan Committee (2008): 101 (new)

Many farmers, and small and medium firms in developing countries such as India take loans at 60 per cent interest rates or more and defaults are rare showing that rates of return or marginal products of capital in related activities are sufficiently large.[58] Yet, some of these farmers or firms are credit-constrained. The productivity loss as a result of misallocation of capital due to credit constraints can be fairly large. The problem with a directed credit programme is essentially two-fold. First, how to price such directed credit at its 'true' market level? Second, how to avoid such directed credit going to farmers or firms or people who are not credit-constrained? The second problem becomes serious when directed credit is required to be cheap as well. That creates an incentive for even non-credit-constrained agents to avail such directed credit.

How do we solve the problem of credit inadequacy in the priority sectors and among the weaker sections? Can we have the desired results of financial inclusion through a more market-friendly hybrid approach with directed credit? Narasimham II clearly stated that "The Committee believes that it is the timely and adequate availability of credit rather than its cost which is material for the intended beneficiaries."

Directed credit with far below-market interest rate harms the priority sectors and the weaker sections by denying them adequate and timely institutional credit and compelling them to borrow from non-institutional sources at usurious rates. Too low a rate of interest denies the banks any incentive to lend. Perhaps, a good way of starting the reform for financial inclusion is retaining the directed credit programme to ensure that productive small farmers and small and medium firms are not credit-constrained, while deregulating and increasing the interest rate that can be charged on such directed credit.[59] Allowing higher interest rates to be charged for such directed credit will create an incentive for banks to lend more to the priority sectors and also discourage non-credit-constrained farmers and firms from preempting such directed credit.

---

58. See Banerjee and Duflo (2004)

59. Even the cost of administering credit is higher for priority sector loans. Labour and administrative cost of lending by banks to the priority sector has been estimated to cost them ₹ 1.50 more per ₹ 100 than lending to the unreserved sector, see Banerjee and Duflo (2000).

Box 1.7

Some Detailed Recommendations of Rajan Committee (2008) for Improving Financial Sector Inclusion

- Deregulate and allow more entry of well-capitalised deposit-taking small finance banks subject to higher prudential norms;
- Liberalise banking correspondent regulation to allow local agents to extend financial services;
- Allow a system of priority sector loan certificates (PSLC) and make it exchangeable;
- Liberalise interest rate on loans subject to full disclosure, transparency and restrictions regarding eligibility under PSLC scheme;
- To improve the collation of credit history, expedite the process of creating a unique national ID number with biometric identification;
- Open up the information of the credit bureau to subscribers subject to verification of "need to know and authorisation to use" of the subscriber by the credit bureau;
- Expedite ongoing efforts to improve land registration and titling—including full cadastral mapping of land, reconciling various registries, forcing compulsory registration of all land transactions, computerising land records, and providing easy remote access to land records, with the Centre playing a role in facilitating pilots and sharing experience of best practices. Explore the possibility of setting up special law courts to clear the backlog of land disputes;
- Re-examine restrictions on tenancy so that tenancy can be formalised in contracts, which can then serve as the basis for borrowing;
- Extend the powers of SRFAESI that are currently conferred only on banks, public financial institutions, and housing finance companies to all institutional lenders;

contd...

...contd...

- Bring supervision of all deposit-taking institutions under the RBI and ending the system of shared responsibility, such as with the State Registrar of Cooperative Societies; and
- Convert trade receivable claims of small and medium enterprises on large firms to electronic format, accepted by the large firms, and sold as commercial paper.

Furthermore, many of the recommendations of the Rajan Committee (Box 1.7), which is appropriately called "A Hundred Small Steps", can be implemented to improve financial inclusion.

Introducing Capital Account Convertibility

Tarapore I, Tarapore II, PM Committee and Rajan Committee have unanimously recommended a move towards fuller capital account convertibility. As already mentioned, capital account convertibility, by reducing the cost of capital, can stimulate investment and growth. By allowing residents to diversify their portfolio into foreign assets, such convertibility can reduce the variability of their income and wealth from domestic shocks and also diffuse the risk of an asset-price bubble. Capital account restrictions tend to turn progressively ineffective, costly and even distortive. The PM Committee has observed that India has a *de facto* open capital account for the real economy, but not for financial services.[60] Lack of capital account convertibility has reduced competition in the Indian financial sector and denied the country competition-induced efficiency gains. According to some experts, the benefits from capital account convertibility for the financial sector in India will be analogous to the benefits that accrued to the real sector from the policy of opening-up in the early 1990s.

Many of the milestones recommended by Tarapore I have already been achieved. What about the others? While considerable progress has been made on the fiscal front both by the Centre

60. PM Committee (2007): 99.

and the states after the implementation of the FRBM Acts, some susceptibilities remain on account of off-budget liabilities such as oil bonds. It is also well-known that "Running a large fiscal deficit constrains a country's ability to open its capital account without running undue risks. Countries that have opened capital accounts and stabilised or pegged their exchange rates—while running large fiscal deficits financed in foreign currencies—have triggered an economic crisis."[61] Now, with the current global crisis, we need not look any further than the US for vulnerabilities on the external front from large fiscal deficits.

Is fiscal consolidation the right policy when most countries in the world are talking about fiscal stimuli? There seems to be a consensus among mainstream economists that there is no case for "one-size-fits-all fiscal expansions but for fiscal actions tailored to the circumstances of individual country and taken with a view toward the impact on the rest of the world."[62] India does not have a trade or current account surplus and the case for a fiscal expansion in a country with a large trade deficit needs a careful examination.[63] A large part of any fiscal stimulus will spill over as benefits to the rest of the world. Furthermore, it is important to remember the long and variable lags with which policies affect the economy. We need a clear deadline for solving the problem of attaining the necessary milestones, including removal of fiscal susceptibility, and introducing capital account convertibility. Here, it is also critical to remember the interdependence between institutions and capital account convertibility. It is possible that capital account convertibility, with its magnified penalty scheme for policy lapses, may become the cause for preferred institutional outcomes even with regard to fiscal prudence.

The current crisis may provide an opportunity for introducing capital account convertibility. The dominant worry about introducing convertibility has been an upsurge of capital flows with large upward pressure on the exchange rate of the rupee followed

61. PM Committee (2007): 88.
62. See Eichengreen and Baldwin (2008).
63. See Dani Rodrik in Eichengreen and Baldwin (2008).

by a sudden sucking out of such capital, precipitating a crisis. Risk aversion on the part of international investors is an all-time high now, and the risk of large inflows is limited. The residual risks, as the PM Committee has observed, can be managed given: (a) the proven skills and capabilities of the RBI in managing India's external accounts with extraordinary competence; (b) the trends that are now manifest in accelerating two-way financial flows at a very rapid rate—i.e., at two or three times the output growth rate; and (c) the problems that will increase as the partially closed regime is maintained. Furthermore, according to the Committee "Opening the capital account decisively is not a matter of tweaking technical ratios and tinkering with the present limits of what is allowable and what is not. That process adds little of value."[64]

As immediate steps, what can be done are: (i) removing end-use restriction on external commercial borrowing or ECBs; (ii) removing ECBs over 10-year maturity and rupee-denominated ECBs outside the overall annual ECB ceiling; (iii) allowing non-resident corporates to invest in Indian stock markets through SEBI-registered entities; (iv) allowing foreign institutions and corporates beyond multilateral institutions (such as International Finance Corporation and Asian Development Bank) to raise rupee bonds in India; and (v) linking domestic banks' borrowings from overseas banks and correspondents to paid up capital and free reserves and not to unimpaired Tier I capital, and putting the limit at 50 per cent. Tarapore I recommended them for immediate implementation more than 10 years ago.

Moving to a Streamlined and Principle-based Financial Regulatory Architecture

The ongoing global financial crisis has raised important questions about the optimal regulatory architecture. This is best exemplified by the case of derivatives, which is a generic name for products such as futures, mortgage-backed securities or options and which 'derive' their value from underlying assets such as stocks, bonds or commodities. Derivatives market grew exponentially during the 1990s and quintupled between 2002 and 2008 to over

64. PM Committee (2007): 99.

$500 trillion under the regime of Alan Greenspan, the former Chairman of the US Federal Reserve. Greenspan saw derivatives as "an extraordinarily useful vehicle to transfer risk from those who shouldn't be taking it to those who are willing to and are capable of doing so." Warren Buffett, the legendary US investor, however, had presciently observed in 2003 that derivatives were "financial weapons of mass destruction, carrying dangers that, while now latent, are potentially lethal."[65] There were demands for stricter regulation of derivatives, but Greenspan favoured self-regulation on Wall Street. In 1997, when Brooksley Born, the former Chairperson of the Commodity Futures Trading Commission, a US government agency that regulates options and futures trading, began exploring derivatives regulation, Greenspan argued against it, and US Treasury came to the conclusion that even discussing new rules could threaten the booming derivatives market.

We know now the absence of rules requiring institutions to disclose their positions, to be adequately capitalised, to limit leveraging, and to set aside funds as a reserve against bad bets, and protection against counterparty risk in settlement, and stripping the Commodity Futures Trading Commission of regulatory authority over derivatives may not have been good ideas. At the same time, there is a lot of force in Greenspan's argument that "You can have huge amounts of regulation, and I will guarantee nothing will go wrong, but nothing will go right either." The regulatory reform agenda is a complex one and there should be no hasty conclusions. Too much regulation can be as harmful as too little regulation. Nobel laureate Michael Spence has observed that "The longer term regulatory issues should await a careful analysis of the causes of the crisis."[66]

Currently, in India, what we have is a regulation by silos with banks regulated by the RBI, stock markets by SEBI, pensions by Pension Funds Development and Regulatory Authority, insurance by Insurance Regulation and Development Authority, and commodity futures by Futures Market Commission. Regulation by independent authorities is not unique to India alone. India is not alone in having

65 See Goodman (2008).

66. See Spence in Eichengreen and Baldwin (2008).

such a fragmented regulatory structure. In the US, for example, four regulators—Federal Reserve, Federal Deposit Insurance Corporation (FDIC), Office of the Controller of the Currency (OCC), and State Regulators—regulate banks, two regulators—Securities and Exchange Commission (SEC) and Commodities Futures Trading Commission (CFTC)—control securities business, Federal Reserve and SEC regulate investment banks, and insurance is regulated by different State Regulators.

Yet, the increasing dynamism and complexity of financial products have blurred the borders between financial products, and compartmentalising them, for example, into pure banking, or pure security or pure insurance products has become increasingly difficult. The easiest example of such a hybrid product is a unit-linked insurance policy. Even in India, banks, insurance companies and securities firms are now competing in the same market for the same customers. They have similar and often even identical products, and compete via the same distribution channels. Individual financial institutions increasingly have comparable organisation and management structures. Consequently, the balance of the argument has moved away from retaining or creating multiple financial services regulators differentiated by the types of firm they regulate, the activities they regulate, or the objectives of regulation. Many countries have moved to unified regulation (Table 1.3).

While awaiting a careful analysis of the causes of the current global crisis from the regulatory angle, most experts seem to agree that the fragmented regulatory architecture in the US may have contributed to the problem. In the US, no regulator had the clear remit to regulate derivatives. It is in this context that it is important to note that the PM Committee has recommended a move towards unified regulation. Although the Rajan Committee has not stated such a move towards unification in explicit terms, the spirit of its recommendation appears to be in favour of unification. This is so when it recommends a statutory Financial Sector Oversight Agency (FSOA) to supervise and monitor the functioning of large, systemically important, financial conglomerates; anticipate potential risks, initiate balanced supervisory action by the

Table 1.3

Countries with a Single Supervisor, Semi-integrated Supervisory Agencies and Multiple Supervisors in 2002[a]

Single Supervisor for the Financial System		*Agency Supervises Two Types of Financial Intermediaries*			*Multiple Supervisors*	
		Banks & Securities Firms	*Banks & Insurers*	*Securities Firms and Insurers*	*(At Least 1 Each for Banks, Insurers, and Securities Firms)*	
1. Austria	12. Japan	24. Dominican Republic	30. Australia	41. Bolivia	48. Argentina	65. Jordan
2. Bahrain	13. Latvia	25. Finland	31. Belgium	42. Chile	49. Bahamas	66. Lithuania
3. Bermuda	14. Maldives	26. Luxembourg	32. Canada	43. Egypt	50. Barbados	67. Netherlands
4. Cayman Islands	15. Malta	27. Mexico[b]	33. Colombia	44. Mauritius[b]	51. Botswana	68. New Zealand
5. Denmark	16. Nicaragua	28. Switzerland	34. Ecuador	45. Slovakia[b]	52. Brazil	69. Panama
6. Estonia	17. Norway	29. Uruguay	35. El Salvador	46. South Africa[b]	53. Bulgaria[b]	70. Philippines[b]
7. Germany	18. Singapore		36. Guatemala	47. Ukraine	54. Cambodia	71. Poland
8. Gibraltar	19. Republic of Korea		37. Kazakhstan[b]		55. China	72. Portugal
9. Hungary	20. Sweden		38. Malaysia		56. Cyprus	73. Russia[b]
10. Iceland	21. Taipei[c]		39. Peru		57. Egypt	74. Slovenia
11. Ireland	22. UAE		40. Venezuela		58. France	75. Sri Lanka
	23. UK				59. Greece	76. Spain
					60. Hong Kong	77. Thailand
					61. India	78. Turkey
					62. Indonesia[b]	79. USA
					63. Israel	80. Vietnam
					64. Italy	

Notes: a Sample includes only countries that supervise all the three types of intermediaries (Banks, Securities Firms and Insurers).
b Countries reported to be considering adopting partial or full integrated supervision as well.
c Established in 2004.

Source: Milo (2007).

concerned regulators to address those risks; it will address and defuse interregulatory conflicts, and look out for the build-up of systemic risks (Proposal 25[67]).[68]

One of the major reasons behind unified regulation is the economies of scope and scale available from operating in all sub-segments of financial product/services markets. A fragmented regulatory architecture leads to contrived corporate structures (for example, through holding companies) to create virtual unified financial firms. Unified regulation will redress the segmentation of the financial market into banking, insurance, capital markets, asset management activities and derivatives market.[69]

In the interim, until we move to unified regulation, PM Committee has recommended a "Partial consolidation of extant regulators into a tightly-knit quartet covering: (a) banking; (b) insurance; (c) pensions; and (d) capital, derivatives and commodities markets."[70] Thus, it urged the transfer of all regulation/supervision of any type of organised financial trading to SEBI. The Rajan Committee has also endorsed the recommendation that all regulation of trading should be brought under the Securities and Exchange Board of India (SEBI) (Proposal 13[71]).[72] The case for implementing these recommendations appears very strong.

---

67. Rajan Committee (2008): 17-18.

68. Rajan Committee also recommends a Financial Development Council (FDC) with the Finance Minister as the Chairman to focus on macro-risk assessment and developmental issues, with the FSOA as its secretariat (Proposal 26: 18). A Financial Sector Appellate Tribunal should be set up along the lines of, and to subsume, the Securities Appellate Tribunal, and make regulatory actions subject to appeal to the Tribunal (Proposal 22: 16). An Office of the Financial Ombudsman (OFO), incorporating all such offices in existing regulators, should be set up to serve as an interface between the household and industry. (Proposal 27: 18-19).

69. See PM Committee, pp.147-148, and 196-197.

70. Rajan Committee has recommended that Parliament should set a specific remit for each regulator, consistent with the principles enshrined in the relevant law, every five years. Every year, each regulator should report to a standing Committee (possibly the Standing Committee on Finance), explaining in its annual report the progress it has made on meeting the remit. The interactions should be made public (Proposal 21: 12).

71. Rajan Committee (2008): 13.

72. It recommended the introduction of markets that are currently missing such as exchange traded interest rate and exchange rate derivatives should be encouraged (Proposal 14) (p. 13). It also recommended creating the concept of one consolidated membership of an exchange for qualified investors (instead of the current need to obtain memberships for each product traded). Consolidated membership should confer the right to trade all the exchange's products on a unified trading screen with consolidated margining (Proposal 16: 13).

Furthermore, both the PM Committee and Rajan Committee (Proposal 20)[73] have recommended a move from rules-based regulation to principles-based regulation, by redrafting securities and banking laws as well as re-skilling of all regulatory staff. PM Committee recommends scrapping the large repository of subordinate laws under a prescriptive approach. It argues against writing down every minute detail either into the basic legislation or into detailed subordinated rules and regulations. "Under such a system if something is not specified, it is proscribed; or conversely, if something is proscribed then non-proscribed activities remain contentious as to whether they are permissible or not."[74] The spirit of the recommended move towards principles-based regulation is to promote financial innovation and avoid the mistake of over-regulation.[75] Rajan Committee's specific recommendations included creating a more innovation-friendly environment, speeding up the process by which products are approved by focusing primarily on concerns of systemic risk, fraud, contract enforcement, transparency and inappropriate sales practices (Proposal 18[76]). What we need to debate is the extent of innovation that we shall allow. But, it appears that we may have been rather conservative in allowing innovation. Let the excesses of derivatives in the US not detract us from the fact that it was mortgage-backed securities issued by Fannie Mae and Freddie Mac—two much maligned institutions in the US today—that promoted widespread home-ownership in the US.

The transition from rules-based to principles-based regulation may require a graduated move. Principles-based regulation can succeed with only a very skilled set of staff in the regulatory bodies. Given the problems associated with salaries that can be paid to such staff in the regulatory bodies because of their public sector nature,

73. See Rajan Committee (2008: 16). Furthermore, Rajan Committee has recommended allowing greater participation of foreign investors in domestic markets and reducing the extent to which regulators restrict a domestic institutional investor's choice of investments by moving gradually instead to a "prudent man" principle (Proposal 19). See Rajan Committee (2008): 13.

74. See PM Committee: 132.

75. PM Committee's recommended regulatory impact assessment for evaluating the cost-benefit of various aspects of the regulatory architecture and implementation is to guard against this error of over-regulation.

76. Rajan Committee (2008): 13.

attracting the appropriate skill set may prove to be a challenge. That challenge needs to be faced before the transition to a principles-based regulatory architecture. Nevertheless, while a full-fledged move to principles-based regulation may not be possible, the move should be towards such a regulatory architecture.

Finally, I must sound a word of caution about too hasty a move to principles-based regulation. The current crisis in North America and Europe has exposed some serious deficiencies in their regulatory architecture. The dust around the current crisis needs to settle a bit, before the verdict on contemporary international best practice in regulation emerges. While this should not become an excuse for inaction on the regulatory reform front, it may be good to avoid any undue haste. In the interim, what we should focus on is to move towards unified regulation to prevent any financial institutions to slip past the regulatory net, insist on these institutions to be adequately capitalised, for them to limit leveraging, and for them to set aside funds as a reserve against bad bets, and have protection against counterparty risk in settlement.

Restructuring the Banking Industry

Many unexpected things have happened in the last six months in free market economies. For example, in the US, Fannie Mae and Freddie Mac have been taken over by the government. Starting with Northern Rock, and continuing with Bradford and Bingley, the British retail banking system has been partly nationalised. Iceland has nationalised three of its largest banks. Although such nationalisation has often been described as conservatorship, the current crisis has posed a considerable threat to the free functioning of the market economy. The current crisis has even been seen as the death of capitalism. This is nothing new. As Gary Becker (2008), the Noble laureate, has noted, death of capitalism has been prophesied after every major recession and financial crisis since the mid-19th century. While the current global crisis is a reminder of the potential danger from market failure, given our knowledge of extensive cases of government failure, the merits of bringing dynamism to the functioning of the economy through enhanced competition and an appropriate incentive structure remain more or less unquestioned.

It is in this context that the pending recommendations of Narasimham II regarding restructuring the banking sector deserve attention. Out of these, the three major ones are: removing the restriction of 10 per cent voting rights; reducing the legally required public shareholding in public sector banks from 51 to 33 per cent, and allowing foreign banks to set up subsidiaries or joint ventures in India.[77]

Narasimham II argued that given that no promoter group's holding can exceed 40 per cent of a bank's equity, the voting right restriction of 10 per cent prescribed in section 12 (2) of the Banking Companies Act, 1949 does not have much justification. It may be recalled that the last amendment to voting rights came into effect in 1994, when the ceiling was raised from 1 per cent to 10 per cent paving the way for entry of the new private banks that have grown rapidly in the last decade and a half. The Banking Regulation (Amendment) Bill, 2005 introduced in the Lok Sabha on May 13, 2005, seeks to remove the restriction on voting rights and introduce the requirement of prior approval of the RBI for acquisition of shares or voting rights above the specified limit. It empowers the RBI to satisfy itself that the applicant is a 'fit and proper person' to acquire shares or voting rights, and to impose such further conditions that the RBI may deem fit to impose. The passing of this amendment will pave the way for implementing an important pending recommendation of Narasimham II. It is interesting to note that voting rights of shareholders of nationalised banks are capped at not 10 but 1 per cent of the total voting rights (under section 3(2E) of the Banking Companies (Acquisition and Transfer of Undertakings) Acts, 1970 and 1980). There are two different laws governing public sector banks and private banks. Treating shareholders of public sector banks differently from those of private banks is difficult to justify. There have been suggestions of corporatising the public sector banks and leveling the playing field for all. Corporatisation of public sector banks by bringing these banks under the purview of the Companies Act will not only help the process of consolidation—a cherished goal of public policy—

---

77. In case of the State Bank of India (SBI), the Committee recommended bringing down the legal requirement of RBI shareholding from 55 per cent to 33 per cent.

but also be in line with the Rajan Committee's recommended major restructuring of public sector banks. The Committee also recommends strengthening the board of directors of PSBs by devolving more powers to outside shareholders and granting boards the power to appoint top executives, and delinking banks from oversight of Central Vigilance Commission (VC) and Parliament.

Public sector banks dominate the Indian banking scene, and getting the best out of them is of paramount importance. The legal minimum public shareholding in nationalised banks and State Bank of India are 51 per cent and 55 per cent, respectively. Majority shareholding by the government has created quite a few complications for public sector banks including revision of salary in line with market trends, oversight of Central Vigilance Commission and Parliament, and employees using Right to Information Act to harass management. Narsimham II has recommended bringing down this legal requirement to 33 per cent. Tarapore II has not only endorsed this recommendation but also added that majority public ownership should be given up in both public sector banks and the State Bank of India. Bringing down its shareholding to 33 per cent will allow the government to raise enough capital from the market for the public sector banks and also increase the efficiency of these banks through private-public partnership. All this will be achieved while, as a very large shareholder with the power to block special resolutions, retaining enough leverage to guide the affairs of these banks in a gentle and indirect way. Rajan Committee has endorsed this recommendation and suggested that the Government should either create bank holding companies or bring down its share in these banks below 50 per cent. Rajan Committee has also suggested selling small underperforming public sector banks to strategic investors and observing outcome.

In 1998, Narasimham II had recommended allowing foreign banks to set up subsidiaries or joint ventures in India. After a year of announcing it in the 2003-04 Budget, Government of India increased the foreign direct investment limit in private banking, which is under the automatic route, from 49 per cent to 74 per cent including investments by foreign institutional investors (FII), non-resident Indians (NRI) and overseas corporate bodies.[78] Press Note 2 (2004 Series), on March 5, 2004, also announced that foreign banks will be permitted to set up either subsidiaries or joint ventures but not both. Again after almost a year of the Press Note, on February 28, 2005, RBI announced a roadmap for a two-phased implementation of the Government decision.[79] The first phase, running from March 2005 to March 2009, allowed a one-mode presence of either though a wholly-owned subsidiary or branches, promised a more liberal approach than the WTO-commitment of 12 branches per year for existing and new foreign banks, and restricted acquisition by foreign banks of only in private sector banks identified by RBI for restructuring. The second phase is to start from April 2009, which is just three months away. It is supposed to accord full national treatment to wholly-owned subsidiaries of foreign banks "after reviewing the experience with Phase I and after due consultations with all stakeholders in the banking sector."

In China, by the end of 2007, 72 foreign banks, representing 23 different countries, had opened 126 branches and sub-branches; 193 foreign banks, from 47 countries, had opened up 242 representative offices; and a total of 24 foreign banks, with 295 branches and sub-branches, had incorporated locally.[80] But, the Chinese permission to foreign banks was a part of its five-year commitment for entry into the WTO to be fulfilled by December 2006. The critical question is whether such an opening up is good for China and whether China should have done it anyway even without the WTO commitment. It is interesting to note that Narasimham II, PM Committee and Rajan Committee appear to believe that opening up to foreign competition will be good for the efficiency of the domestic banking industry. In 1991, faced with a severe balance of payments crisis, India opened up to external competition in the goods

78. Under Portfolio Investment Scheme through stock exchanges, the individual holding of FIIs was limited to 10 per cent with an aggregate limit for all FIIs of 24 per cent. This limit could be raised to 49 per cent by the Bank through resolutions of its Board of Directors and General Body. The FIIs investment limit continued to be within 49 per cent. In case of NRIs, the individual holding was restricted to 5 per cent with an aggregate limit to 10 per cent. This again could be raised to 24 per cent by the Bank through special resolution of General Body.

79. *http://www.rbi.org.in/upload/content/pdfs/RoadMap.pdf.*

80. See *China, Country Finance 2008*, Economist Intelligence Unit.

market. Proving the doomsday predictors wrong, it was Indian manufacturing that rose to the challenge of global competition, and improved its efficiency and performance. If this unanimous recommendation of all the three committees about opening up the banking sector is not to be implemented, we need to make a strong case to prove that the maturity of Indian banking in 2009, in terms of coping with competition and globalisation, is less than what Indian manufacturing had in 1991.

Conclusion

I have come to the end of my long discourse. I want to end with two observations. First, according to Kishore Mahbubani, the Chinese translate the western word crisis by combining two Chinese characters, "danger" and "opportunity".[81] When looking at financial sector reform, let us look as much at the "opportunity" part of the current global crisis as to its "danger" part. Let us not forget that reform is all about destabilising the status quo. A crisis often provides an excellent opportunity to destabilise the status quo.

Second, Finance Minister Chidambaram after promising in his budget speech for 2008-09, measures to develop the bond, currency and derivatives markets, launched the NSE exchange traded currency futures on August 29, 2008. Let us hope that more measures will be forthcoming in the coming months and years to develop the missing bond, currency and derivatives markets with the right level of transparency and appropriate safeguards. This will be important to move to an inflation-targetted monetary policy. Furthermore, let us hope that the roadmap for financial sector reform suggested by the expert committees will be implemented in good earnest to ensure that a vibrant and robust financial sector aids accelerated growth and rapid amelioration of poverty rather than becoming a hindrance in the process. In particular, let us hope that we will consider moving to an inflation-targeted monetary policy regime; modernising the delivery of financial services to the priority sectors and the vulnerable and weaker sections; introducing

81. See Mahbubani (2008): 9.

capital account convertibility; moving from a rules-based and fragmented regulatory architecture to a principles-based and unified architecture; and reforming the banking system in general and public sector banks, in particular. The current global crisis provides an opportunity to think hard about financial sector reform. All and any change is not necessarily good, but neither is the status quo. We need to reform, and reform in the right way. Inaction is not the way forward.

References

Banerjee, Abhijit and Esther Duflo (2004). "Do Firms Want to Borrow More: Testing Credit Constraints Using a Directed Lending Program", *http://econ-www.mit.edu/files/791.*

——. (2000). "Efficiency of Lending Operations and the Impact of Priority Sector Operations", *Mimeo*. MIT.

Becker, Gary (2008). "We're Not Headed for a Depression — No, this isn't the crisis that kills global capitalism", *Wall Street Journal*, October 7.

Chakravarty Committee (1985). *Report of the Committee to Review the Working of the Monetary System* (Chairman: Prof. Sukhamoy Chakravarty). Mumbai: Reserve Bank of India, April 10.

Demetriades, Panicos O. and Kul B. Luintel (1996). "Financial Development, Economic Growth and Banking Sector Controls: Evidence from India", *Economic Journal* 106: 359-74, March.

Dornbusch, Rudiger (1982). "PPP Exchange Rate Rules and Macroeconomic Stability", *Journal of Political Economy* 90; 1: 158-65.

——. (2001). "A Primer on Emerging Market Crises", *NBER Working Paper* No. 8326. Cambridge, Massachusetts: National Bureau of Economic Research.

Economist (2006). "Too hot to handle", November 25.

Eichengreen, Barry and Richard Baldwin (2008). "What G-20 leaders must do to stabilise our economy and fix the financial system". London: Centre for Economic Policy Research (CEPR), *http://www.voxeu.org/reports/G20_Summit.pdf*

Goodman, Peter S. (2008). "Taking Hard New Look at Greenspan Legacy", *The New York Times*, October 8.

Government of India (2004). "Press Note 2 (2004 Series)—Revision of Existing Sectoral Guidelines and Equity Cap on Foreign Direct Investment (FDI), including Investment by Non-Resident Indians (NRIs) and Overseas Corporate Bodies (OCBs)/Foreign Institutional Investors (FIIs) in the Banking Sector", No.5/6/2000-FC Dated 5th March. New Delhi: Ministry Commerce & Industry, Department of Industrial Policy and Promotion, Government of India.

Kaminsky, Graciela and Carmen M. Reinhart (1999). "The Twin Crises: The Causes of Banking and balance of Payments Problems", *American Economic Review* 89: 473-500.

Kannan, R. and Himangshu Joshi (1998). "Growth-Inflation Trade-Off: Empirical Estimation of Threshold Rate of Inflation for India", *Economic and Political Weekly*: 27-28, October 17-24.

Lahiri, Ashok K. (1991). "Money and Inflation in Yugoslavia", International Monetary Fund, *Staff Papers* 38(4): 751-88, December.

——. (2006). "Macroeconomic Policy" in S. Narayan (ed), *Documenting Reforms—Case Studies from India*. Mcmillan India Ltd.: Observer Research Foundation.

Mahbubani, Kishore (2008). "The New Asian Hemisphere: The Irresistible Shift of Global Power to the East", *Public Affairs*. New York, USA.

Milo, Melanie S. (2007). "Integrated Financial Supervision: An Institutional Perspective for the Philippines", *ADB Institute Discussion paper* No. 81, Asian Development Bank Institute, Tokyo, Japan, October.

Mistry, Percy S. (2008). "Let us not repeat post-1997", *Business Standard*, New Delhi, February 28.

Narasimham, M. (1991). *Committee on Financial System*. Mumbai: Reserve Bank of India.

——. (1998). *Committee on Banking Sector Reforms*, Mumbai: Reserve Bank of India.

PM Committee (2007). *Mumbai: An International Financial Centre*. Ministry of Finance, Government of India. India: Sage Publications.

Rajan, Raghuram (2008). *A Hundred Small Steps: Report of the Committee on Financial Sector Reforms*. New Delhi: Planning Commission, Government of India, April.

Rangarajan, C. (1993). *Report of the High level Committee on Balance of Payments*, April. Reprinted in C. Rangarajan (2004). *Select Essays on Indian Economy* 2: 241- 334. New Delhi: Academic Foundation.

Reserve Bank of India (1970). *History of the Reserve Bank of India: 1935-51*. Bombay: Reserve Bank of India.

——. (2005). *Reserve Bank of India Annual Report 2004-05*. Mumbai: Reserve Bank of India.

——. (2008). *Report on Currency and Finance, 2006-08*. Mumbai: Reserve Bank of India.

Tarapore, S.S. (1997). *Report on Capital Account Convertibility*. Mumbai: Reserve Bank of India, May.

——. (2006a). *Report of the Committee on Fuller Capital Account Convertibility*. Mumbai: Reserve Bank of India. July 31.

——. (2006b). "Fuller Capital Account Convertibility: Interaction of Concomitants and Measures", Keynote address at the Federation of Indian Chambers of Commerce and Industry (FICCI), November 15, New Delhi.

Vittas, Dimitri and Yoon Je Cho (1995). "Credit Policies: Lessons from East Asia", *World Bank Policy Research Working Paper* No. 1458. Washington DC: World Bank, May.

Volker, Paul (2005). "An Economy on Thin Ice", Washington Post, April 10. Adapted from a speech in February, 2005 at an Economic Summit sponsored by the Stanford Institute for Economic Policy Research.

Washington Times (2008). "McCain Advisor talks of 'Mental Recession", July 9.

Sir Purushotamdas Thakurdas Memorial Lecture organised by IIBF, Manila, January 16, 2009, Mumbai.

2

K.C. CHAKRABARTY

Indian Economy

Imperatives for Second Generation Reforms

The Indian financial sector has seen wide ranging reforms during the last two decades. However, these reforms were broader and focussed at the macro level with internal reforms at the institutional level yet to take place. Thus, the need of the hour is to go for second generation reforms. Nonetheless, the reforms in the financial sector alone will not bring perpetual prosperity. It is the real sector which needs reforms. The financial sector has to grow and keep pace with the developments in the real sector.

Why Financial Sector Regulation?

On an intuitive basis, the business of finance and banking is different from other businesses. This is on account of the fact that while other businesses operate with their own funds, banks are highly leveraged institutions that operate with public money and hence, require to be closely regulated and supervised. Besides, unlike other businesses where, due to absence of entry barriers, free market competition can be expected to ensure efficiency and fair treatment of customers, in the banking business, high entry barriers imply that banking operations cannot be carried out without a licence. This restricts the free play of competitive forces and hence, makes it all the more imperative to have a sound regulatory framework, particularly for protection of customers. In the business of banking and finance, there is an inherent inequity between the provider of

---

The assistance provided by Smt Rekha Mishra and Shri S.M. Lokare in preparation of this address is gratefully acknowledged.

the service and the consumer and this, again, presents the need for a framework of rules and procedures, which we call as regulation.

The health of the financial sector is a matter of public policy concern in view of its critical contribution to economic performance. Financial regulation and supervision assumes importance in ensuring that the financial system operates along sound lines. The primary justification for financial regulation by authorities is to prevent systemic risk, avoid financial crises, protect depositors' interest and reduce asymmetry of information between depositors and banks. As the costs of financial crises are perceived to be very high, the authorities realised that they should be avoided at all costs. As a result, banks came to be regulated everywhere. Besides, financial regulation attempts to enhance the efficiency of the financial system and to achieve a broad range of social objectives. Going by the experience in several countries, effective regulation is in the interests of all concerned, though it cannot be based on a 'one-size-fits-all' approach. However, it is important to bear in mind that while financial institutions do benefit from an appropriate regulatory regime, there is not much evidence that the existence of a regulatory jurisdiction makes institutions stronger and less prone to shocks. There is neither a unique theoretical model, nor just one practical approach to the regulation and supervision of a financial system. The existence of different types of regulatory models of the financial system makes the ideal choice a difficult exercise.

The regulation and supervision of the financial system in India is carried out by different regulatory authorities. The Reserve Bank regulates and supervises the major part of the financial system. In the past five decades, the Indian banking system has traversed through a difficult path endeavouring to balance several competing and conflicting demands on it from large, medium, small and tiny borrowers in both the organised and unorganised sectors. The banking system's activities were initially tightly regulated and their freedom was restricted. It also confronted several domestic stresses and external shocks. However, the regulations have changed over time to ensure that the banking system steps out of the restrictive operational environment and functions in an atmosphere that provides the freedom to innovate.

In recent years, innovations in instruments and processes, advances in technology and the increasing volumes of capital intermediated by the financial system have necessitated a proactive strengthening of the regulatory and supervisory framework. Emergence of several players with diversified and significant presence in the financial sector makes it imperative for supervision and regulation to be spread across various segments of the financial system. In recent years, there has been a shift in emphasis from microregulation to macromanagement, supported by a tightening of prudential norms and improvements in the functioning of the financial system.

Since the global crisis, there has been a decisive shift in trend towards assigning increased responsibility to the central banks for both 'systemic oversight' and 'macroprudential regulation'. This greater responsibility is driven by the capability of the central banks among regulators and public institutions to perform the intended task. Central banks have robust frameworks for macroeconomic analysis, and in India, the Reserve Bank has the responsibility for microprudential supervision of banks and non-banking financial companies (NBFCs). As a result, while macroeconomic analysis has helped in strengthening the microprudential supervision, supervisory information aggregated for the financial system as a whole has also helped in conducting more appropriate macroeconomic policies.

The Reserve Bank has been deeply involved in the development of markets, and it monitors and analyses the impact of market trends on the economy and financial institutions. Another important reason why central banks have to be the systemic risk regulator is because of their mandate of Lender of Last Resort (LOLR). Going forward, given the complex nature of the challenge, significant strengthening of the capacity for systemic risk assessment and macroprudential regulation would be critical for the Reserve Bank.

Macroeconomic and Financial Sector Reforms

In response to the macroeconomic crisis, a programme of stabilisation and structural adjustment was initiated in July

1991, with wide ranging reform measures encompassing the areas of trade, exchange rate management, industry, public finance and the financial sector. Fiscal correction, exchange rate adjustment, monetary targets and inflation controls constituted the immediate measures for macroeconomic stability. These measures were supported by structural reforms in the form of industrial deregulation, liberalisation of foreign direct investment (FDI), trade liberalisation, overhauling of public enterprises and financial sector reforms. Apart from aiming at restoring the economic stability on both domestic and external fronts, the economic reform programme strived towards achieving a higher growth trajectory through increased levels of investment and improvements in productivity, efficiency and competitiveness. Structural reforms aimed at reorientation of the economy from a centrally directed command and control economy to a market oriented one, to foster greater efficiency and growth. This was done by introducing greater competition in the economy through progressive internal deregulation accompanied by external competition promoted by FDI and trade liberalisation.

The reform measures had sectoral dimensions as well. Beginning with the industrial policy of 1991, reforms in the industrial sector were undertaken with a view to remove distortions in the resource allocation and improve competitiveness of Indian industry. The reform measures included removal of industrial licensing, reduction in the number of industries reserved for the public sector, abolition of restrictions on investment and expansion under the Monopolies and Restrictive Trade Practices (MRTP) Act, 1969, automatic approval of foreign investment, elimination of quantitative import restrictions on intermediate and capital goods and steady reduction in protective customs tariffs. These measures created a favourable environment for industry to upgrade its technology and build-up capacity in order to cater to growing domestic and external demand. A series of policy initiatives were undertaken in agricultural sector as well. These included, *inter alia*, replacement of quantitative controls by tariffs, partial decontrol of fertiliser prices, removal of bottlenecks in agricultural marketing, relaxation of restrictions of the Essential Commodities Act, 1955, replacement of the Revamped Public Distribution System (RPDS) with Targetted Public Distribution System (TPDS), and establishment of Rural Infrastructure Development Fund (RIDF). Moreover, price reforms improved terms of trade for agriculture. Also, exchange rate and international trade reforms improved the incentive structure facing agriculture.

Several initiatives were undertaken for the development and reform of financial markets, particularly since the 1990s. The reforms in various segments of financial markets such as money, government securities and foreign exchange markets were introduced in a calibrated, sequenced and careful manner, in step with those in other markets in the real economy. The sequencing has also been influenced by the need to develop market infrastructure, technology and capabilities of market participants and financial institutions in a consistent manner. In India, the initiation of the structural reforms in the early 1990s encompassed a process of phased and coordinated deregulation and liberalisation of financial markets. Financial markets in India, in the period before the early 1990s, were marked by administered interest rates, quantitative ceilings, statutory pre-emptions, captive market for government securities, excessive reliance on central bank financing, pegged exchange rate, and current and capital account restrictions. As a result of various reforms, the financial markets have transited to a regime characterised by market-determined interest and exchange rates, price-based instruments of monetary policy, current account convertibility, phased capital account liberalisation and an auction-based system in the government securities market. Enhancing efficiency, while at the same time avoiding instability in the system, has been the challenge for the regulators in India. This approach to development and regulation of financial markets has imparted it greater resilience. India's reform programme has had a definite positive and significant impact on the economy as compared with the past.

Who are the Stakeholders?

In the whole process of reforms, the key stakeholders are the customers themselves. The regulators have a critical role in ensuring fair treatment to customers and it cannot be left to the market forces alone. The key to a prompt, effective and courteous customer service emanates from having the right attitude. A radical transformation of attitude right from top management to ground level employees is the first step towards improving customer service. Communication is at the root of effective customer care in a service industry, especially like banking, where the documents, terms and conditions, practices and precedents are all heavily loaded against the customer. In many fields and in different countries, regulators determine the price. But, the financial sector regulator in India does not do so. Therefore, whatever charges are levied, it is expected that they are reasonable and that the pricing is fair, transparent and non-discriminatory. Globally, regulators are expected to usher in much stricter regulations in the area of fair treatment to customers. Banks need to price their products and services fairly and competitively and ensure higher transparency in their products and pricing. Lack of transparency in designing and pricing of products and services and selling them to inappropriate customers could expose banks to litigation and reputational risks, besides making them liable for supervisory action. There should be no unreasonable post sale barriers if the customers wish to change product or bank. Customer education is also critical in providing appropriate and need based products and services and the Indian Banks' Association (IBA) may have a critical role to play in this regard. The banking business would, thus, have to turn customer centric in all its true dimensions.

Financial Sector Reforms: What Next?

The Indian approach to financial sector reforms, so far, has been driven by the predominant objective of enhancing the role of finance in promoting growth and economic development, while preserving financial stability, which is equally critical for sustained economic progress. While balancing the goals of efficiency and stability in introducing reforms, the Reserve Bank has moved towards deregulation of interest rates, promoted development of markets, and strengthened the legal infrastructure to facilitate better enforcement of financial contracts. Going forward, three areas will continue to be important in policy debates, i.e., development of long-term corporate bond markets, derivative markets to facilitate better price discovery and risk transfers, and more competition by allowing greater foreign participation.

The regulatory and supervisory framework of the financial system across the world is undergoing a paradigm shift following the problems experienced during the global financial crisis. In this regard, multilateral and standard setting bodies like the G-20, IMF, BIS and FSB have been in the forefront to design an advanced regulatory framework to prevent the recurrence of such crisis. Addressing the regulatory gaps based on the lessons from the global financial crisis in advanced economies will be a major challenge for regulators all around the world. Much of the challenges in the domain of financial stability regulation would arise from complexities surrounding the assessment of systemic risk, interconnectedness, common exposures, risk concentrations in complex innovative products and use of models to manage and price risks which, at times, mask information.

While India's financial sector remained resilient in the face of global shocks, there are a number of areas where the reforms would be needed to promote stability and generate growth impulses for the real economy. In the wake of turbulent global financial environment, banks and financial entities have to grapple with growing complexities and risks associated with their businesses. Against this backdrop, the policy initiatives such as adoption of tighter capital and liquidity standards, improved risk management practices and sound compensation practices are required to place the Indian banking system on a strong footing and enhance the banking sector's ability to absorb shocks arising from any financial and economic stress and encourage prudent risk taking.

Moreover, in India, while broader institutional reforms have taken place at the macro level, the internal reforms among banks and financial institutions are yet to take place. Thus, there is a need to go for second generation reforms, particularly focusing on bringing down the cost of banking services, strengthening the credit delivery mechanism, improving customer service, reforming the human resources management systems and enhancing the financial outreach to hitherto unbanked areas.

Second Generation Reforms

Let me talk about some of the elements of these second generation reforms.

Adopting Improved Risk Management Practices

One fundamental principal of finance that I would like to emphasise is the direct relationship between risk and return. Any investment that offers greater returns, invariably involves more risk. Similarly, if you avoid taking risk, then the returns could even be negative. Banks, for instance, are in the business of taking risks and hence, cannot be expected to shun risk in its entirety. Four basic requirements that banks and professionals in the field need to develop is to:

- Understand Risk.
- Define Risk.
- Measure Risk.
- Manage Risk.

One should never take a risk where you cannot meet the above four requirements.

Globally, there is an increasing move towards more advanced approaches to risk management. Banks in India have made progress in moving towards the advanced risk management approaches. Banks, however, need to traverse a long distance in this regard. As capital always comes at a cost, banks need to have in place a fair and differentiated risk pricing of products and services. This involves costing, quantitative assessment of revenue streams from each product and service, and an efficient transfer pricing mechanism, which would determine capital allocation. Each business unit in the enterprise would have to aim at being a profit centre within the overall risk–return framework. In essence, it would mean accountability for profit, tempered by the discipline of risk–return within a deeply embedded culture of good governance. Our past experience has been of poor savers subsidising the rich borrowers. Also, there are incidences of rampant mispricing of risks. From a business perspective, pricing of assets should be non-discriminatory and in line with risk rating of the customer. A lower rated customer should not get a better price than a higher rated customer. Once these basic issues are addressed, other issues such as migration to advanced approaches, etc., would gain importance.

While all Indian banks have adopted the standardised approaches under the Basel II framework in 2009, the pace of migration to the advanced approaches has, naturally, been very slow. Though the Reserve Bank has set an indicative time schedule for implementation of the advanced approaches, banks' response has been less than encouraging so far. Migration to the advanced approaches is important for larger banks as it involves adoption of more sophisticated risk management systems. Moreover, there are reputational issues also in large banks continuing with standardised approaches. Apart from these fundamental issues, much of this sluggishness could be attributed to issues relating to development of human resource skills, technology upgradation, branch interconnectivity, availability and management of historical data, robustness of risk management systems, etc., within the banks. Even within the Reserve Bank, the supervisors would have to make rapid strides to be able to appreciate the nuances associated with the quantitative techniques and models.

The objective of the Basle III reform package is to improve the banking sector's ability to absorb shocks arising from financial and economic stress, whatever the source, thus reducing the risk of spillover from the financial sector to the real economy. An assessment of Indian banks' capital requirements under Basel III has revealed that, notwithstanding some issues with a few individual banks, the system as a whole, is very well capitalised and the transition to the revised capital norms of overall capital adequacy, Tier I component or equity component would be smooth. The implementation period of Basel III capital requirements, including capital conservation buffer and regulatory deductions, will begin from January 1, 2013 and will be fully implemented by March 31,

2018, before the timeline (January 1, 2019) indicated in Basel III rules.

Reforming Human Resources (HR) Management

There is an imperative need to improve the productivity and efficiency of human resources. An organisation can only be as good as its people. They are the force behind innovation, business process re-engineering and making the difference between success and failure. A committed and highly motivated workforce can make the difference in winning and retaining customers as banking is a people oriented business. Banks have to be knowledge organisations, able to attract and retain talent. HR policies should look at right size, right fit and career growth with market related compensation. Increasingly, there is going to be intense competition for the right kind of talent as they are likely to be in short supply. The demand for efficient manpower will not only stem from domestic institutions but also from foreign institutions/countries; and not just from the banking industry but from other financial/non-financial sectors. The challenge before Indian banks is, therefore, to revitalise themselves by hiring the right talent, investing in training and bringing about a vibrant transformation in their DNA.

Technology to be More Customer Focussed

Most banks are already on 'Core Banking Systems' (CBS) which covers banking operations pertaining to deposits, withdrawals, credit delivery, back-office operations, etc. Banks need to look beyond core banking to harness the benefits of technology. CBS could provide inputs for developing customised products based on customer database. It would help in planning product delivery and service at selected/multiple delivery points, better customer relationship management and building lasting customer relationships which will translate into higher revenues. Technology needs to be more customer focused than employee or vendor focused. In case of glitches, the rectification must be swift to instill faith and confidence in the system. It is only the more agile and innovative players who will stay ahead in the game. Along with IT solutions arise allied issues such as IT security, governance and audits. Gaps in IT security could make banks vulnerable to data piracy, fraud and operational risk leading to reputation risk and erosion of customer confidence.

Focusing on MIS and Information Literacy

MIS is an inseparable part of bank's decision-making process. The integrity and timeliness of data is critical in formulating the bank's capital planning, business strategies, reviewing achievements *vis-à-vis* targets, formulating course correction exercises where required, feeding data into stress tests and importantly, taking action on the outcomes. This brings us to technology support for decision-making. Banks have made huge investments in technology, which should be translated into better MIS through decision support systems and yield returns on investment by providing economical, affordable and customised customer centric banking solutions. The use of technology should not be seen as an end in itself but as a means to an end.

Business Strategy and Vision

The role of banks' Boards would become increasingly crucial in the next decade in view of the looming competition. The board would need to have a clear vision for the bank, a strategy to achieve its objectives, both medium and long-term, and a well laid out long-term plan. Banks would need to look beyond their existing customer base and large corporates and reach out to rope in the vast number of small, retail and SME clients which are presently deprived of bank credit. Alongside extending the reach of their banking services, there would be a need to improve the products offered to customers and the quality of services. They need to have proper business model and delivery model.

Reaching to the Unbanked/under-banked Areas

In India, growth with equity has been the central objective right from the inception of the planning process. The objective of financial inclusion is to provide financial services at affordable cost to those who are excluded from the formal financial system. This is vital for sustaining long term equitable development, since a large proportion of the households/areas do not have access to basic banking facilities, notwithstanding the existence of vast institutional framework in the country. An important challenge is to channelise more savings to the financial system, particularly in rural areas and from the urban informal sector. This would need further penetration of the banking system. The Reserve Bank's emphasis on financial inclusion is important in attaining this objective over time. There is also enormous potential for extending finance in semi-urban and rural areas for productive activities, which may require strengthening the banking correspondent (BC) relationship, simultaneously enhancing the risk assessment and risk management capacities in order to maintain credit quality and sustain the credit growth in these sectors. Besides benefiting the unbanked masses, this will also ensure viability and scalability of banks' financial inclusion initiatives.

Bringing Down the Cost of Banking Services

Further reduction in the cost of banking services may require greater competition among product lines, improved delivery mechanisms and increasing use of information technology. The costs of banking transactions need to be dramatically reduced as has happened in many other fields such as telecom, after the advent of technology. However, it is observed that, in banking, the transaction costs continue to be high, particularly in agriculture sector, which include costs incurred in appraisal of borrowers, processing, documentation and disbursement charges, loan monitoring/supervision and collection. It is essential to bring down such transaction costs to make available credit at affordable price to the farmers.

Balancing the Real and Financial Sector Reforms

Financial sector reforms alone will not bring continued prosperity. In the recent years, we see, growing evidence on growth deceleration in the Indian economy. For sustaining the high growth path, improving the investment climate and enhancing the absorptive capacity by bringing in the real sector reforms would be critical. The fact that a well-developed financial sector is necessary to act as the intermediary between entrepreneurs/investors and savers can hardly be overstated. An efficient financial sector reduces the cost and risk of producing and trading goods and services and, thus, makes an important contribution to raising standards of living. The recent crisis, however, showed that the financial sector had apparently taken a quasi-autonomous existence without close connection with the financing requirements of the real economy. The financial industry, indeed, grew oversized in the preceding years, reflected in rapid credit creation, asset price bubbles and high levels of indebtedness, particularly in advanced financial systems. The disproportionate growth in the global financial sector was largely due to the aggressive search for yield, engendered by the easy liquidity in the global system that triggered a wave of financial innovation. Complex financial products were created by structuring and hedging, originating and distributing, all under the belief that real value could be created by sheer financial engineering. There were hardly any signs of growing capital formation due to the growing and increasingly complex financial sector.

The financial sector grew more rapidly than other goods and services. In a way, that made growth of finance an end in itself and not a means to meet human needs such as food, fuel, health and education. Given that the busting of the oversized financial sector has a devastating impact on the real sector, it becomes important to: (i) examine the optimal size of the financial sector relative to growth and development needs, and (ii) make financial sector innovations more meaningful to cater to the needs of the real sector.

For sustaining the high growth path, it is imperative that we bring in reforms in the agriculture, industry, infrastructure and services sectors. I would like touch upon some of the elements of these reforms.

Improving Agricultural Governance and Productivity

In order to step up agriculture growth, a judicious use of technology is required along with institutional reforms, including those relating to land, incentives for supply response and better input use. Given the dependence of a vast majority of workforce on agriculture, enhancing the agricultural output, driven by higher yield and diversification of crops, assumes importance. Higher investment, backed by sustained research and extension activities, could be critical for augmenting yield. The policy focus, so far, has been on using higher MSP to generate supply response and public investment on expanding the irrigation potential. However, there is a need for improving the market structure for agricultural commodities, ensuring competitive pricing, enhancing warehouse facilities and improving rural roads for enhancing better connectivity with urban markets. Better water management, with an emphasis on water harvesting, would be important for enhancing the farm productivity and output.

Improving the Performance of Manufacturing Sector

The manufacturing sector's performance in a competitive environment and in the face of risks of rising protectionism could encounter several challenges. Despite the advantages of a large domestic market, abundant availability of skilled labour force, and the proximity to the fast growing Asian markets, productivity growth needs to catch up with the Asian economies, including China. This requires greater emphasis on quality, better adoption of technology, more flexible labour laws, significantly improved infrastructure and a policy environment supportive of the SMEs sector. The industry-education linkages must be strengthened vigorously. Persistent problems like frequent disruptions in the availability of power and lack of stable demand also affect the performance of the manufacturing sector.

Harnessing the Potential of Services Sector

Notwithstanding the high growth and resilience of the services sector in the recent past, the sector faces multiple challenges for sustained growth over the years. A number of services, where India enjoys comparative advantage, experience lack of clear policy thrust. For instance, despite the high quality of health care services, it attracts a number of regulations. Similarly, in education, multiple regulation points and lack of credible accreditation systems hamper the growth potential. Given the medium to long-term contribution of investments on education and health to growth and productivity, availability of these services at affordable cost, while enhancing their global competitiveness, must form part of the priority in India's development process. A number of services in India are either predominantly associated with the government or not liberalised enough to ensure growth through organised private initiatives. Services like professional, legal, postal, accountancy and insurance need further liberalisation to harness their potential.

Facilitating Infrastructure Finance

As per the assessment of the Planning Commission, during the Twelfth Plan (2012-2017) India may need infrastructure investments of over US$ 1trillion. This poses a mammoth financing task. The infrastructure gap in India, both in relation to other major countries and its own growing demand, has been a key factor affecting the overall productivity of investments. The requirement of high initial capital outlay, that too over longer terms, necessitates measures to address the financing constraint to capacity expansion in infrastructure. The financing issue relates not only to possible resource gap, but also to ensure commercially viable funding that remains so over business cycles. Infrastructure investment during the Twelfth Plan will need to be funded by both, public and private sectors. Despite increasing participation of the private sector in bridging the infrastructure gap, public investment still has to play a significant role. Fiscal consolidation and reorientation of expenditure towards capital expenditure is required to meet the target. The banking system, despite the risk of asset-liability mismatch (ALM) while lending for long-term infrastructure projects, has seen high growth in credit to this sector in recent years.

To Sum Up

The first round of financial sector reforms resulted in strengthening of the financial system and making it more vibrant and resilient. However, over time, the pace of reforms and growth has slowed down and the need for second generation of reforms is strongly felt. These reforms would have to focus on individuals and corporates and work towards improvement in productivity and efficiency of the economy as a whole.

Financial sector reforms, in isolation, will not have a significant impact unless there is improvement in the absorption capacity of the economy. Real sector reforms should precede financial sector reforms for bringing in inclusive and sustainable development of the country. Even in the financial sector, there is an imperative need for internal institutional reforms, particularly focusing on improving the risk management practices, reducing the cost of transactions, both borrowing and lending, and improving the overall customer service. I hope all concerned stakeholders work towards implementation of these second generation reforms, which is essential for moving the economy back to the high growth trajectory.

Address at the Inaugural Session of the State level seminar organised by the Department of Economics of the Viveananda Education Society's College of Arts, Science and Commerce, Mumbai, September 14, 2012. RBI Bulletin October 2012.

3

N.A. MUJUMDAR

Next Generation Financial Sector Reforms and Inclusive Growth

The Eleventh Five Year Plan (2007-2012) is based on the strategy of inclusive growth that is, broad-based, decentralised growth. If the growth in the real sector has to be not only higher but also more inclusive, what is the kind of financial engineering required—in terms of institutional framework, financial instruments and lending procedures and practices—to facilitate such more inclusive growth? The Planning Commission, in August 2007, appointed a High Level Committee on Financial Sector Reforms (CFSR) with, among others, the following terms of reference:

> To identify the emerging challenges in meeting the financing needs of the Indian economy in the coming decade and to identify real sector reforms that would allow those needs to be more easily met by the financial sector (Government of India, 2008).

The terms of reference, provided an outline of "the next generation of financial sector reforms" (p.1).

While there are so many reports on different segments of financial sector—for instance, Dr Vaidyanathan's Report on the Cooperative Credit institutions and Dr Rangarajan's Report on Financial Inclusion—this Report was expected to paint a broader canvass of the entire financial sector. The Report claims to attempt to "see links that others have not" and to create mutually reinforcing influences in the financial sector. The Committee puts forward its proposals for financial reform with a three fold objective: "to foster growth itself; to include more Indians in the growth process; and to improve financial stability" (p.2). The third objective has become important in the contemporary situation when the sub-prime crisis has engulfed many developed countries and has threatened to spill over to some emerging economies. The committee does not make a secret of its high profile nature in the sense that it does not suffer from the traditional virtue of scholarly work, namely "modesty". Take the following statement: "...practical pieces of legislation that seem to be exempt from any intellectual influence, are usually drawn from some long forgotten report. Despite the current political climate this is indeed the reason we have no doubt this report will not be a wasted report" (p.5).

This Report indeed covers a wide range of issues: the future role of Reserve Bank of India (RBI), a national goal of ensuring in three years that 90 per cent of households have access to a deposit account, allowing entry of more private well-governed small finance banks, modifying priority sector mandate, discontinuing government ownership of banks, by selling small under performing public sector banks, promote exchange rate derivatives, establishment of financial ombudsman, and so on. More importantly the committee believes in taking a hundred small steps towards reforms. "Instead of focusing primarily on a few large and usually politically controversial steps, we need to take a hundred small steps in the same direction that will collectively take us very far" (p.3). We will have occasion to discuss later some such selective small steps recommended by the committee.

This Report needs to be analysed in depth because of the following two reasons. First, in view of its high profile nature there is the danger that government may accept its major recommendations, some of which have far reaching implications for the economy. Unfortunately, most of these recommendations are based on an amateurish understanding of the Indian economy and hence, if implemented, they may prove counter-productive. Secondly, the committee has failed to address the basic issue we raised at the beginning: how to reshape the financial system with a view to promote more inclusive growth?

This Report belongs to the genre of IMF/World Bank Reports, characterised by excellent presentation, obsessed with market theology and marked by a sense of superciliousness. The report embodies doctrinaire policy prescriptions inspired by pure market theology, and not rooted in the Indian specific socioeconomic milieu. To borrow a phrase from the committee's report, market theology overtakes reasoned debate. The authors of the report lack a sense of Indian economic history and have presented their recommendations in the form of a series of *obiter dicta* rather than as recommendations emerging from analyses of empirical data or experience, as we will seek to illustrate. The authors of the report seem to have been carried away, as it were, by the rhetorics of international best practices. The bulk of the recommendations lack intellectual support. The committee's commitment to market theology has eclipsed all other commitments like commitment to enlarge employment opportunities or reduce poverty. Finally, the random assortment of proposals for financial sector reforms lack the vision to portray the kind of financial structure we need to aim to build. Some core issues, as we will discuss later, involved in the transfiguration of the financial sector, with a view to enabling it to facilitate inclusive growth in the real sector, have been conveniently bypassed.

Privatisation, liberalisation, independent central banks focusing exclusively on inflation control, non-intervention by government in the agricultural sector—these are some of the essential ingredients of neo-liberalism; neo-classical market fundamentalism that underlay the so-called "Washington Consensus". And this market fundamentalism is, writ large on the committee's report. The committee should have realised that countries which followed this ideology have been disillusioned by empirical experience. Pragramatic economists and multilateral financial institutions are already discarding this thesis.

In fact this question forms part of the larger issue of the changing face of development economics itself. As Prof John Humphery (2007) puts it:

> Historically, much development thinking assumes the superiority of, or at least the dominance of the West. The rise of Asia shows that new economies are the global success stories and their expansion is shaping growth and development...

> New multiple Southern policy agendas—backed up by financial muscle, the credibility that goes with rapid growth, an intellectual and policy making capacity—are forcing a reinvention of development studies.

One would have thought that the High Level Committee would at least seek to reinvent, in the sense mentioned by Prof Humphery, the financial system which would be best able to promote inclusive growth in the real sector. Instead, the committee is content with merely recommending the mimicking of the systems or institutions of the West. Elsewhere I have made an exploratory attempt to draw a blue-print of the kind of financial system we need to build, if the objective of inclusive growth in the real sector is to achieved: the need to integrate banks, microfinance institutions (MFIs), self-help groups (SHGs) and non-government organisations (NGOs) (Mujumdar, 2007).

Congenital Dislike of Public Sector

Congenital dislike of public sector is an integral part of the IMF/World Bank philosophy. This Report reflects faithfully this theology:

> The majority of this Committee does not see a compelling reason for continuing government ownership. There are other activities where government attention and resources are more important. However, the Committee does recognise that public opinion in this country is divided on the issue of privatisation. A parallel approach is to undertake reforms that would remove constraints on the public sector banks, even while retaining government ownership. Intermediate steps such as reducing the government ownership below 50 per cent while retaining its control (as suggested by the Narasimham Committee) are possible (p.10).
>
> The Committee has therefore recommended, to begin with, "sell small under performing public sector banks, possibly to another bank or to a strategic investor to gain experience with the process and gauge outcomes" (p.11).

This doctrinaire prescription shows that the committee is innocent of the recent financial history of India. The branch expansion programme in the post-nationalisation period (post-1968) was unprecedented in the history of world banking. In retrospect one could see the widening and deepening of the Indian banking system as a process of modernisation of the Indian economy (Mujumdar, 2002). Only the public banking system and directed credit policy could have achieved these goals. No private sector banks would even think in terms of such goals. The history of banking in former British colonies like say, Zambia or South Africa provides enough evidence of this statement. And all this was achieved in India well before the concept of "financial inclusion" became fashionable.

Ironically, the High Level Committee also advocates "a national goal of ensuring in 3 years that 90 per cent of the households, if they so desire, have access to a deposit account and to a payment system" (p.7). It would be naive to expect private sector banks, either domestic or foreign, to address this issue.

After the implementation of banking sector reforms in 1990, including the Basle norms, the Indian banking system has become "strong and sound", as D.T. Pai (2007), a professional banker has demonstrated, with all the relevant data.

> The banks have been able to show strong balance sheet growth in the post-reforms period in an environment of operational flexibility. Improvement in the financial health of banks is reflected in the improvement in capital adequacy and asset quality. This progress has been achieved despite the adoption of international best practices and prudential norms and renewing out goals of social banking *viz.*, maintaining wide reach of banking system and directing credit towards important disadvantaged sections of the society.

Thus, it is to the credit of the Indian banking policy makers that they have been able to successfully blend the objectives of social banking with the market theology of maximising profitability of banks. Where is, then, the case for privatisation?

While on this subject, we may also consider the committee's other recommendation that small private sector banks should be allowed to be set up and the minimum capital requirement could be reduced significantly from the present minimum of ₹ 300 crore (p.8).

This proposal also shows that the committee is innocent of history of Indian banking. Visceral memories of the pre-1960 mushrooming of small banks of indifferent quality should sound a note of warning. During the post-war period 1946 to 1950, 207 banks with paid up capital of ₹ 5.33 crore had failed. It was really the failure of Laxmi Bank and Palai Bank in 1960 which triggered Reserve Bank of India's action to weed out a large number of unviable commercial banks. Through a process of moratorium and merger the number of scheduled commercial banks (SCBs) was reduced to about 100.

More recently, some not-so-viable, small, private sector banks had to seek shelter under public sector banks: Lord Krishna Bank merged with the Punjab National Bank, Global Trust with Oriental Bank of Commerce, and United Western with the IDBI bank. The committee should have realised that banking efficiency is ownership neutral. Reform of the public sector banks? Yes. Their total elimination? No.

Reserve Bank of India (RBI)

Let us now turn to another major recommendation of the Committee relating to the future role of RBI. First, the committee seems to have set out to cut the RBI to size, for no rhyme or reason. "The RBI should formally have a single objective, to stay close to a low inflation number, or within a range, in the medium term and more steadily to a single instrument, the short-term interest rate (repo and reverse repo) to achieve it" (p.5). This recommendation would have made sense if the committee had demonstrated with the necessary data and empirical evidence that RBI had failed to contain inflation because it has pursued multiple objectives. It has not even attempted this exercise. On the contrary, RBI's track record in this area is excellent. Taking more recent years, inflation decelerated from an average of 10.3 per cent between 1991-1994 to 8.9 per cent between 1995-1999 and to 4.3 per cent during the current decade. Equally important is the fact that the regime of inflation control has, in turn, stabilised inflation expectations. In fact RBI has further lowered the 'policy tolerance threshold' from 4 to 4.5 per cent to around 3 per cent, as a medium term objective.

Parenthetically, one must add that the alarm regarding inflation reaching 11 per cent during the financial year 2008-09 was an aberration brought out primarily by external factors like the international oil prices soaring to unprecedented levels. It has not much to do with RBI's capability of controlling inflation.

In terms of instruments also, if RBI has been able to use a mix of instruments to successfully rein in inflation, why should it restrict its operations to a single instrument? The committee's recommendation lacks intellectual support.

Basically, central banks in developing countries or even in emerging economies, have to play a development role. That is why the founding fathers of RBI built into its statute, the responsibility of developing the infrastructure for rural credit. As we have spelt out earlier, historically, RBI has played an active role in widening and deepening of the banking system.

Even at the current juncture, financial inclusion has become a pre-condition for promoting inclusive growth in the real sector. Ironically, the committee itself has, as we have mentioned earlier, set a target for wider banking coverage of the population. Given these objectives, to restrict RBI's function to "one objective one instrument" regime hardly make any sense.

The Committee makes another textbookish recommendation: RBI should cease to manage the exchange rate of the rupee and should be "intervening in currency markets only to limit excessive volatility" (p.5). The committee believes that, given capital flows, "the real exchange rate, which is the key factor determining India's competitiveness, is influenced by factors such as productivity growth and demand supply imbalances that are not changed by central bank intervention against the dollar" (p.5). In the real world, we all know, managed currency is the rule rather than an exception. The contemporary example is China whose monetary authorities refuse to up-value its currency *vis-à-vis* dollar, despite pressures from the US. Historically, Japan also followed a similar policy. Leaving the exchange rate to be solely determined by market forces is a sure recipe for disaster. Speculative capital flows can play havoc with exchange rates.

Warehouse Receipts and Bill Market Schemes

Among the random assortment of recommendations of the committee two rather minor recommendations may be briefly discussed. First, "trading of warehouse receipts". To quote:

> With the promulgation expected soon of the Warehousing (Development and Regulation) Act, 2008, warehouse receipts will become a negotiable instrument: They will become a new reliable form of collateral in the agricultural sector, where till now there was no other security except land, which has its own infirmities. ...Warehouse receipts can be in physical or electronical form and must be issued by registered warehouses which will be accredited by the Warehousing Development and Regulating Authority" (p.3).

Further, the committee proclaims grandiloquently: "Assuming that at any time, about 11-20 per cent of the annual agricultural produce is stored in warehouses, the Act has the potential to inject over US $30 billion of agricultural credit" (p.3). The unwary reader may be led to believe that this instrument is the 'discovery' of the committee. But those who are familiar with the recent economic history of India however, would point out that the warehouse receipts issue dates back to the recommendations of the famous All-India Rural Credit Survey 1956. If the committee were serious, they should have investigated why warehouse receipts, as a financial instrument, have failed to gain wider acceptance during these 50 years and what should be done to remove the impediments which come in the way of popularising the instrument. The committee did not condescend to undertake such an exercise.

A similar homily is reflected in their recommendations relating to small and medium industries. "As another example, credit to small and medium enterprises could be boosted enormously if the trade receivable claims they have on large firms could be converted to electronic format accepted by large firms and sold as commercial paper" (p.3). If the committee had cared to study the efforts made by RBI in the past in this area, it would have been in a position to go beyond this textbook recommendation. RBI had even tried to make it mandatory for large firms to clear their dues to small industries as part of the conditionality of access to bank credit. There were also several aborted efforts of RBI to promote the Bill market schemes. But the committee did not condescend to examine why these schemes failed to take off.

Absence of Intellectual Macro Framework

The trouble with the Committee is that there is no intellectual macro framework against which its main recommendations have been formulated. This has led to several internal inconsistencies, disjointed recommendations, and failure to identify the basic issues. Let us take three examples. First, focus on rural areas. "In addition, this Committee would suggest moving away from a sole focus on rural areas, where undoubtedly many of our poor live, to also include the urban areas, where, more of them are migrating" (p.7). In contrast, the committee asserts elsewhere "... Indeed the road to making Mumbai an international financial centre runs through every village and slum in India" (p.21).

Second, the committee is against concessional interest rates to the poor. "Liberalising interest rates would allow the formal sector to lend to the poor and keep them from the moneylender, though liberalisation would require the political will to accept the widespread evidence that low interest rate ceilings simply do not help the poor" (p.9). This reflects an amateurish understanding of the rural realities. Even the World Bank, the fountain head of market theology, has now accepted the thesis that concessional lending is essential at least initially, to facilitate the poor escape from the poverty trap. The committee did not bother to examine why the present interest rate structure in India is inequitable, biased against the low-income borrowers. More of it later.

The third point pertains to the very rationale of why inclusive growth in the real sector has become necessary. Here the committee exposes its innocence: "Ultimately, though it is opportunities in the real sector, created by broader growth, which will give the poor the ability to use credit effectively. Instead of forcing credit to household that could thereby become heavily indebted, the focus should be on making them credit-worthy so that when opportunities arise, they have access" (p.7).

Basically, as I have spelt out elsewhere, inclusive growth in the real sector has now become a growth and development imperative: growth because a high GDP growth like the 8 or 9 per cent targetted in the Eleventh Plan (2007-2012) can be sustained only if other sectors or segments of the economy, which have been sluggish because of a number of reasons, including policy neglect, can be activated. Development, because this is perhaps the best route by which the bulk of the poor can be provided with livelihood and food security (Mujumdar, 2007). In other words, we can no longer depend on 'autonomous' forces for growth of the real sector; this growth has to be policy-induced with a view to enabling sections of the population, whom the growth process has bypassed, to fully engage themselves with the development process. An interventionist and proactive policy is therefore warranted. This should be the starting point for designing what the committee calls "the next generation financial sector reforms." In this context, the contemporary experience of China is illuminating. China's Township and Village Enterprises (TVEs) provided increasing job opportunities outside agriculture and this phenomenal expansion of non-farm sector played a critical role in reducing poverty.

Three Core Issues

In the contemporary financial scenario in India, there are three core issues: broad-based, decentralised growth in the real sector; the new architecture of the financial system to facilitate such growth; and the inequitable interest rate structure. Logically, the reinvention of the next generation financial sector reforms should have emerged from a holistic analysis of these three core issues. Judged by these criteria, the committee has frittered away its energies on a random assortment of recommendations: some relevant, some not so relevant, many aimed at mimicking the 'best practices' of banking in the developed world. Thus, the report has acquired the characteristics of a PhD Thesis: prolixity and discursiveness. The committee has not done its homework on the economic realities at the ground level, as the ensuing discussion would demonstrate.

First, the unorganised sector holds the key to broad-based decentralised growth. The recent Report on the sector spells out that micro enterprises—an investment of below ₹ 0.5 million—constitute 94 per cent of small enterprises in the country and provide employment to 70 million people and contribute 30 per cent of industrial production. Despite occupying this central position these enterprises receive only 2 per cent of net bank credit (Government of India, 2007). If additional credit is injected into this sector it may lead not only to higher production, but it may also promote upgradation of technology, improvement in marketing efficiency, and so on.

With the growing importance of small and medium-sized enterprises (SMEs), the credit delivery system needs to be streamlined. For instance, since there is no or little information about such SMEs credit history, banks are prone to insist on collateral for their advances to this segment. The goal of collateral-free lending both for microenterprises and SMEs seems to be far away.

Second, the institutional infrastructure. Microfinance is expected to play an important role in promoting financial inclusion and inclusive growth. It is a sort of supplementary credit delivery system that is cost effective and user friendly for both banks and the poor borrowers. RBI's initiatives in promoting this channel of credit delivery have centred around two models, namely SHG-Bank Linkage programme and Microfinance Institutions (MFI) Model (Mujumdar, 2008). At the same time, the cooperative credit structure is being reorganised, on the lines recommended by the Vaidyanathan Committee. Similarly, the more recent developments reveal that regional rural banks (RRBs) could become the main institutional mechanism for providing credit to the poor. As Dr Thingalaya (2007), a professional banker puts it:

> The process of their merger at the state level, reducing the number from 196 to 96 has expanded their operational base considerably. The best among them like the Karnataka Vikas Grameen Bank or Pragathi Grameen Bank are comparable to the best grameen bank, anywhere in the world, including the much publicised banks of Bangladesh..... Out of the 1.29 crore of borrowing accounts handled by them, 1.07 crore or 83 per cent are in the advances group of less than ₹ 25,000.

The blue print for the future institutional structure should clearly indicate how the pyramid comprising banks, RRBs, co-operatives, MFIs and SHGs needs to be built.

Finally, the inequitable interest rate structure. The committee's pontification on why the concessional lending rates do not help the poor further exposes its innocence of the realities of the present interest rate structure. Financial sector and banking sector reforms implemented in the 1990s have resulted in the emergence of an inequitable interest rate structure, a structure designed to pamper the private corporate sector, and which is biased against agriculture and the small borrower generally. For instance, a small farmer was made to pay an interest rate of 12 per cent at a time when a highly rated corporate entity could raise money from banks at 6 per cent.[1] This paradoxical situation was the result of mindless implementation of Basel norms and adoption without adaptation concept like 'risks' as understood in the developed world. RBI *Report on Currency and Finance, 2005-06* provides valuable insights into the structure of interest rates. The bulk of bank lending has been taking place at sub-BPLR (Benchmark Prime Lending Rate). For instance, the share of sub-BPLR lending increased to 82 per cent by March 2007. While higher credit rated corporates are getting credit at sub-BPLR rates, agriculture and small industry and other small borrowers are generally charged BPLR, or in some cases, above BPLR rates. To quote the RBI Report: "to compensate for such sub-BPLR lending, other segments are charged higher rates of interest, thus leading to cross subsidisation of the economically well-off borrowers by the economically poor borrowers" (RBI; 2006: 159).

1. For an in-depth discussion see: Mujumdar (2002). .

This is indeed disturbing especially when the objective of both the inclusive growth in the real sector as envisaged in the Eleventh Plan and financial inclusion is to promote growth with equity. The next generation financial reforms must address this question.

In this context, it is important to highlight that the World Bank—the citadel of market theology—has itself changed its attitude to concessional lending and support systems to poor farmers or poor borrowers generally. As Jeffrey Sachs has pointed out recently, during the debt crisis of the 1980s and 1990s, both the IMF and World Bank forced dozens of poor food-importing countries to dismantle their state support systems, including concessional lending to the poor farmers. Poor farmers were told to fend for themselves, to let market forces provide for farm inputs. Empirical experience showed that this proved counter-productive. Under its new president, Robert Zoellick, the World Bank has now stepped forward to provide grants to state governments to establish the support systems, including concessional lending, for poor farmers to enable them to gain access to inputs like seeds fertiliser and irrigation (Sachs, 2008). One would wish that the committee should have updated itself with these new developments in market theology, before offering their advice on interest rates.

Overall, any blue print for the next generation financial sector reforms can be meaningful only if it addresses these three core issues.

References

Government of India (2008). Draft Report of the Committee on Financial Sector Reforms (CFSR), Planning Commission, April.

———. (2007). *Report on Conditions of Work and Promotion of Livelihoods in the Unorganised Sector.* p.221.

Humphrey, John (2007). "Asian Drivers: China, India and Development", in *Moving Towards 360 Degree Research: IDS Annual Report, 2006-07*, Brighton: University of Sussex.

Mujumdar, N.A. (2008). "Rural Lending, Inclusive Growth and Financial Inclusion", *The Journal of the Indian Institute of Banking and Finance*, January-March.

———. (2007). *Inclusive Growth: Development Perspectives in Indian Economy.* New Delhi: Academic Foundation.

———. (2002). *Financial Sector Reforms and India's Economic Development.* New Delhi: Academic Foundation.

———. *Financial Sector Reforms and India's Economic Development* (2 Volumes). New Delhi: Academic Foundation.

Pai, D.T. (2007). *Overview of Banking Development, 1947-2007*. Manipal. p.111.

Reserve Bank of India (2006). *Report on Currency and Finance, 2005-06*. Mumbai. p.159.

Sachs, D. Jeffrey. (2008). "A New Deal for Poor Farmers", *Economic Times*, May 23.

Thingalaya, N.K. (2007). "Annals of a Central Bank", *Indian Economic Journal*, April-June.

4

C. RANGARAJAN

The Indian Banking System

Some Issues

The year 1991 is an important landmark in the post-Independent Indian economic history of our country. It is an equally important landmark in evolution of the Indian banking system. Financial sector reforms were introduced as part of the liberalisation process. These reforms were aimed at enhancing the viability and efficiency of our banking system. While the rapid growth of the Indian banking system in terms of geographical diversification was well recognised, the banking system in 1991 was weak in terms of net worth and profitability. It needed rejuvenation. This was provided by the banking sector reforms. By dismantling the administered interest rate structure, by reducing the prescriptions in the form of CRR and SLR, by introducing prudential norms, by recapitalising public sector banks, by injecting a greater element of competition in the system through new banks as well as induction of private sector in the public sector banks and by revamping the system of regulation and supervision we have succeeded in creating a banking system that is more safe and sound.

There is no doubt that the financial sector plays a critical role in any economy. Financial institutions, instruments and markets which constitute the financial sector act as a conduit for the transfer of financial resources from net savers to net borrowers. Institutionalisation of savings and investment leads to augmentation of savings and better allocation of resources. The gain to the real economy therefore depends on how efficiently the financial sector performs the basic function of intermediation. Financial sector development and economic development have a mutually interacting beneficial effect. The one helps the other. With respect to financial sector development and more particularly banking development, there are two possible scenarios. One is supply leading and the other is demand following. In the first case, banking institutions come first into existence and then create the demand for their services. In the second scenario, banking institutions are set up to meet an emerging and existing demand. In the banking development of our country, we have seen both types of phenomena operating.

The Indian financial system comprises an impressive network of banks and financial institutions and a wide range of financial instruments. There is no doubt that there has been a considerable widening and deepening of the Indian financial system, particularly in the last two decades. The extension of banking and other financial facilities to a larger cross-section of people stands out as a significant achievement. As a ratio of GDP at current prices, bank deposits increased from 18 per cent in 1969–70 to 45.3 per cent by end-March 1995, and now stand at 73 per cent. All indicators of financial development, such as the 'finance ratio', 'financial interrelations ratio' and 'intermediation ratio', have significantly increased, highlighting the growing importance of financial institutions in the economy and the growth of financial flows in relation to economic activity.

Challenges Ahead

The Indian banking system has emerged strong as a result of the reforms introduced since early 1990s. However, as we go ahead, there a few challenges to which I would like draw your attention.

Capital Adequacy

Maintaining adequate capital has become imperative. In a globalised financial system, every country has to conform to international standards. The Basel III guidelines drafted after taking into account the lessons learnt from the recent crisis have emphasised on both the quality as well as quantity of capital maintained by banks to strengthen the resilience of banking sector. The redesigned regulatory framework calls for higher quantum as well as better quality of capital. The minimum equity capital requirements have in fact been increased to 7 per cent (inclusive of 2.5 per cent of capital conservation buffer) of risk weighted assets as against the requirement of just 2 per cent under Basel II. The new requirements have triggered a serious debate over the impact they may likely to have on economic growth as well as the profitability of banks. Different studies show different conclusions based on differing assumptions.

The Indian banking system remains well capitalised. The capital adequacy ratio (CAR) for all scheduled commercial banks (SCBs) is now estimated at 14.17 per cent, well above the required 9 per cent. This high ratio means that the implementation of even Basel III standards will not pose much difficulty at least initially. However, it needs to be noted that the capital requirements consequent upon the introduction of Basel III norms as well as the growth in credit consistent with a rapid economic growth of 8 to 9 per cent will require fairly large amount of capital to be injected. According to the recent Annual Report of RBI, in order to achieve the full Basel III implementation by March 31, 2018 the public sector banks (PSBs) would require common equity to the tune of ₹ 1.4 to 1.5 trillion on top of internal accruals and in addition to ₹ 2.65 to 2.75 trillion in the form of non-equity capital. Similarly, major private sector banks would require common equity to the tune of ₹ 200 to 250 billion on top of internal accruals and in addition to ₹ 500 to ₹ 600 billion in the form of non-equity capital. The estimates for common equity capital may turn out to be an underestimate. While the private sector banks will have to meet these requirements by accessing capital markets, PSBs will require additional budgetary support. Under the present dispensation, about 50 per cent of the additional capital requirements in the case of PSBs will have to come from the government. While several innovative suggestions have been made for raising the capital, it is quite evident that the capital infusion by the government will remain large and has to be a continuous process and as such a long term programme will have to be drawn up. Otherwise, the market share of the PSBs will come down. In addition, banks will have to perform in such a way that they will be in a position to attract the required capital from the market. Investors' confidence in the banks' performance must be built up.

Quality of Assets

Besides the CAR, the other important indicator of the soundness of the banking system is the level of non-performing assets (NPAs). The asset quality of the Indian banks has improved over time with the gross and net NPA ratios showing a continuous decline. The gross NPA of all SCBs came down from 14.6 per cent in March 1999 to 2.25 per cent in March 2008. However, there is some concern about the deterioration in asset quality in the last two years. Gross NPAs of the PSBs increased from 2.3 per cent at the end of 2010-11 to 3.2 per cent at the end of 2011-12. This is indeed a significant increase. In net terms, the ratio went up from 1 per cent to 1.5 per cent. This is in part a reflection of the slower growth of the Indian economy. In any economic downturn, asset quality deteriorates. In the wake of the international financial crisis in 2008, banks were allowed to restructure the debt of firms. The restructured loans at the end of 2011-12 stand at 5 per cent of the loans outstanding. Because of the slow growth, some of the restructured debts are in difficulties in restructuring. The Indian banking system is also exposed in a big way to certain sectors such as power and aviation which are not doing well. Further, banks need to watch out for liquidity risks which will increase because of maturity mismatches. Increased exposure to real estate and infrastructure will lengthen the maturity of bank assets. The challenge for banks lies in efficiently managing risks both in the upswing and downswing.

Entry of New Banks

If the Indian banking system is to remain competitive over time, there should be periodic entry of new banks; a closed system can only become oligopolistic. The 'threat' of entry should not therefore be eliminated, and the central bank should lay down entry norms as also decide on who satisfies the criterion of 'fit and proper'. It must be noted that new banks take about two decades to achieve a sizeable level. Our decision on how many new banks to be licenced must be based on what the economy will need not today but over the next several decades.

Financial Inclusion

Financial Inclusion, a term which has received much attention lately has many dimensions. First, it relates to bringing the economic and socially vulnerable sections into the ambit of the organised financial system. Second, it denotes inclusion of all sectors of the economy; agriculture, industry and services. Third, it implies the extension of the organised financial system to all geographical regions. Thus, it has social, sectoral and regional dimensions. However, the term financial inclusion has largely been used in the context of providing finance to the bottom deciles of population.

NSSO data reveal that 45.9 million farmer households in the country (51.4%), out of a total of 89.3 million households do not access credit, either from institutional or non-institutional sources. Further, despite the vast network of bank branches, only 27 per cent of total farm households are indebted to formal sources (of which one-third also borrow from informal sources). Farm households not accessing credit from formal sources as a proportion to total farm households is especially high at 95.91 per cent, 81.26 per cent and 77.59 per cent in the North Eastern, Eastern and Central regions respectively. Thus, apart from the fact that exclusion in general is large, it also varies widely across regions, social groups and asset holdings. The poorer the group, the greater is the exclusion. What is true of the banking system must be true in relation to the provision of other financial services.

Financial exclusion is also caused by demand side issues. Unless steps are taken on the demand side, that is in the 'real sectors', mere supply side solutions from the financial sector will not work. Credit is necessary for this, but not sufficient. Credit has to be an integral part of an overall programme aimed at improving the productivity and income of small farmers and other poor households. Putting in place an appropriate credit delivery system to meet the needs of marginal and sub-marginal farmers must go hand in hand with efforts to improve the productivity of such farm households.

As far as banks are concerned, financial inclusion has two dimensions: (a) providing deposit and payment facilities to the disadvantaged and underprivileged, and (b) providing credit facilities to such people. In some ways, it is easier to tackle the former than the latter. Technology has facilitated improved facilities for depositing and withdrawing cash. The business correspondent (BC) model, combined with new technology, should be able to extend banking facilities to the interiors of the country and to the existing unbanked. The provision of credit facilities to low income peoples, however, is a much harder task. Once credit is granted, BCs can take over, but the grant of credit itself requires some fundamental changes in the way the rural bank branches function.

In order to increase the outreach of the banking sector, the Reserve Bank has permitted banks to use the services of specified institutions and individuals as intermediaries for providing banking services. However, this scheme is yet to gather full momentum. In fact, the appointment of well-chosen individuals holds out the best promise in this regard. The emergence of corporate entities as BCs has both positive and negative features. While corporates with large retail network can bring in larger resources and higher organisational strength, the local touch which is very much required for the success of the scheme may be absent. While large corporates or technology service providers may try to employ local people, it is not clear at this point how successful they will be. The appointment of one BC to transact on behalf of several banks can also create conflict of interests and lack of commitment. However, one critical issue in the effective use of this model revolves around as to who should bear the additional transaction costs resulting from the employment of facilitators and correspondents. This, of course, depends upon the level of use. When large transactions such as those involved in NREGA are entrusted to the banks with compensation, the scheme can take off easily. There has to be some flexibility with respect to the charging of transaction costs. In the interests of overall expansion of financial inclusion, while all efforts must be made to minimise the costs, we cannot overlook the fact that there are legitimate transactions costs which the system must be willing to bear. Beating them down even through competitive bidding may turn out to be counter-productive. If necessary, government must become part of the burden sharing arrangement.

Regulation and Innovation

The current international financial crisis has important lessons for the management of the financial system in general and for the banking system in particular. Regulation has emerged as a major factor in maintaining the solvency of individual financial institutions and preventing systemic risk. What stands out glaringly in the current crisis is the regulatory failure in the developed world. The failure was two-fold. First, some parts of the financial system were either regulated loosely or not at all, leading to 'regulatory arbitrage' with funds moving more towards the unregulated segments. Examples of 'soft-touch' regulation are investment banks, hedge funds and rating agencies. Second, there was an imperfect understanding of the implications of various derivative products. In addition, regulators failed to recognise the limits of financial markets.

It is ironic that such a regulatory failure should have occurred at a time when intense discussions were being held in Basel and elsewhere to put in place a sound regulatory framework. There is a degree of consensus on how the regulatory framework should be reshaped.

Apart from protecting individual financial institutions, there is a greater focus on limiting systemic risk, which is defined as widespread disruption to the provision of financial services. In view of this, efforts are on to identify macroprudential indicators—which include aggregate indicators of imbalances, indicators of market conditions, and matrix of concentration of risks in the system—and the appropriate tools aimed at containing systemic risk. The macroprudential instruments that are used commonly fall into three categories: (a) tools to address threats from excessive credit expansion in the system, (b) tools to address key amplification mechanisms of systemic risk, and (c) tools to mitigate structural vulnerabilities and limit spillovers from stress.

As I mentioned earlier, the development of the financial system is considered crucial to sustaining high economic growth. However, in the wake of the current international financial crisis some questions have been raised whether the unfettered development of the financial markets and products is good for the economy. It has been argued that not all financial innovations are welfare maximising. Thus, the recent financial crisis has forced us to reevaluate the size, role and rate of growth of the financial sector.

Banking development has taken big strides in the last two decades. The basic motivation for inducting new financial products is to improve customer satisfaction. A question that is being asked increasingly is whether the financial sector today is inherently more volatile and vulnerable than before. The very factors that have contributed to the growth of the financial sector may well have contributed to increase fragility. Close interdependence among markets and market participants have increased the potential for adverse events to spread quickly. They have increased significantly the scope for and speed of contagion. Some question whether the new financial products serve any socially useful purpose. The Stiglitz Commission said, "Much of the recent innovation in the financial system has sought to increase the short-run profitability of the financial sector rather than to increase the ability of financial markets to better perform their essential functions of managing risks and allocating capital. In addition, innovation has engendered financial instability. Indeed from the point of view of the economy as a whole, some innovations had a clearly negative impact." It would be inappropriate to classify all or even most of the financial innovations introduced in the last few decades as socially unproductive. Many of the financial products satisfy a felt need. We are living in a world of uncertainty. Customers need to protect themselves from the volatility in exchange rates and interest rates. Appropriate hedging mechanisms are therefore needed. It is the function of an efficiently organised financial system to provide these instruments. It is wrong to argue that the economic growth seen by the industrially advanced countries in the recent period particularly in the last decade and a half has not been helped by the improvements in the financial markets. But excesses in any field have their own dangers. There is no argument that the regulatory regime needs to be restructured to make the banking system more sound. Excessive risk taking and leveraging by banks need to be discouraged by appropriate regulatory measures or controls. Of course, there is the larger question whether the financial sector is growing at a rate highly disproportionate to the growth of the real sector. On this again, there is no consensus. Financial assets as a proportion of GDP vary widely across countries. Some argue that an important determinant of demand for financial services is the nature of the firms engaged in real economic activities. In particular, when firms with low levels of cash have high investment opportunities, they are unable to use current earnings to finance their new ideas. This naturally leads to growth in the financial sector, to enable the transformation of these idea-rich, cash-poor firms into engines of economic growth. Conversely, when firms with high levels of cash are the main source of investment opportunities, we should expect low growth in the financial sector, since ideas and cash reside in the same entities. In developing economies like India the structure of the economy is undergoing rapid change. The financial system must be able to meet the diversified needs of a growing economy. In this context, we must actually encourage financial innovations. For example, in the Indian context, I would like to cite two instances. First, there is the need to encourage the emergence of a vibrant corporate debt market. Efficient debt market will help not only large industries but also small and medium enterprises. A number of suggestions have been made to create an efficient debt market in our country. Apart from other things, we will also need institutions which will serve as market makers offering two way quotes. This will provide the required liquidity to the market and make it attractive to the investors. Second, there is the need to explore innovative ways of financing infrastructure. Banks at present have certain limitations. They have to take care of the mismatch in liability and asset management. Of course, a vibrant debt market will also help investors' need for long term funding. 'Take out financing' has been suggested as one way by which the tenure of loan can be increased. Thus, the scope for financial innovation continues to remain wide in India. We need to draw appropriate lessons from the current international financial crisis. Too little regulation may encourage financial instability but too much of it can impede financial innovations which are badly needed.

Regulatory oversight of innovations is necessary. But the regulatory perspective on innovation must not become too restrictive. In short, the policy makers must strike an appropriate balance between the need for financial innovations to sustain growth and the need for regulation to ensure stability. Financial innovations and regulations must go hand-in-hand in order to ensure growth with stability in real and financial sectors.

Conclusion

In many ways, the coming decade will be crucial for India. If India grows at 8-9 per cent per annum, it is estimated that her per capita GDP will increase from the current level of US$ 1,600 to US$ 8,000–10,000 by 2025. Then, India will transit from being a low income to a middle income country. For this to happen, the Indian banking sector must develop so as to meet the needs of this diversifying economy, and assist the transition. A competitive environment is essential to make the banking system cost-efficient. Adequate availability of services to customers, both as depositors and borrowers, must remain the driving force. Obviously, regulation is important to steer the banking system towards prudence and stability, but within this regulatory umbrella we must nurture a competitive banking system that will deliver efficient services at minimal cost.

Valedictory address delivered at FICCI-IBA Conclave (FIBAC 2012) at Mumbai, 6th September 2012.

5

K.C. CHAKRABARTY

Banking and Beyond

New Challenges before Indian Financial System

Winston Churchill once said that, "in finance, everything that is agreeable is unsound and everything that is sound is disagreeable." I suspect many of my views may spark a strong feeling of disagreement but will hopefully stimulate passionate public debate. I am more convinced than ever that financial markets require a healthy dose of regulation to function efficiently. I am more convinced than ever that too-big-to-fail, or too-big-to-save banks represent veritable systemic risk concerns, which are sure to bring in more unpredictability in the system, need to be credibly and effectively tackled. And I am more convinced than ever that central banks operate most effectively and optimally when insulated from any external interference.

Even though it is a bit customary nowadays to have a discussion on any topic with the tag 'next' or 'beyond', this particular issue holds enormous importance for all of us in India. However, in today's integrated world, what I shall be talking would be very much relevant for other emerging markets also. Hence, I would dwell upon the issues that stare the global economic recovery in the face and the key elements that will shape the emerging new financial architecture. These issues are pretty much similar to what banks in India are/will be struggling with.

Although, the recent global financial crisis and the resultant recession had its origin in the developed western world; but its contagion did not spare the emerging economies like India. Once in a life-time crisis warranted a commensurate response in terms of a major overhaul of the financial system involving almost everything from regulation to risk management to mergers/acquisition to capitalisation to executive compensation to financial engineering to governance.

In this connection, interface between banks and financial markets has undergone a fundamental shift in the recent times—banks have become intricately linked to financial markets and hence more vulnerable to financial markets stress. At the same time, functioning of markets has become intricately linked to banks which then emerge as the carrier for most of risks within the financial markets. We have seen these correlations at their most devastating during the sharp deepening of recession triggered off by the collapse of the apparently infallible Lehman Brothers which encompassed the whole world in its whirlwind spiral. However, I would restrict myself to sharing my thoughts in terms of 'next' issues and, that too, to the banking system, which are somewhat already visible in the global financial firmament.

Financial Inclusion

Before I address other individual issues, I shall highlight a very basic and core issue of the Indian banking system and that is the challenge of achieving financial inclusion. Without being inclusive, financial and economic stability cannot be sustainable. Financial inclusion is about credible access to appropriate financial products and services needed by vulnerable groups such as weaker sections and low income groups at an affordable cost in a fair and transparent manner from mainstream institutional players. More recently, there has been a strategic shift in sustainable financial inclusion to the adoption of market oriented approach viewing financial inclusion as a viable business proposition. It has been made possible by the availability of information and communication technology (ICT) required by the formal financial sector for penetrating widespread unbanked areas in a cost-effective way and the realisation that the 'poor is eminently bankable'. Financial inclusion is related to financial stability also through the key of financial education and literacy. In my opinion, financial literacy is an integral part of financial inclusion of the public or users of financial products/services. Financial literacy is instrumental in expanding financial inclusion and financial inclusion is itself helpful in further expanding financial literacy, thus mutually reinforcing each other in a positive manner. The knowledge about the risk and return framework holds the key to prudent participation in the market and welfare maximisation within the given constraints for each market player. As financial literacy involves imparting the required knowledge of risks and returns of financial products to the users and suppliers of these products, it would help in controlling risks in the financial system thus helping in maintaining systemic stability. It would be inappropriate to assume that financial literacy and inclusion are not global challenges. At the present juncture as the global financial system is dealing with the after-effects of financial crisis, it is not so much a question of access but advanced countries are more in need of financial literacy/education than ever before. In India, it is a question both of access to financial products and services and financial literacy. It implies not just providing access but also to educate all stakeholders about the fairness and other characteristics of the financial products/services, such as their risks and returns.

Capital

Let me now turn to some other specific issues. First issue staring in the face of banking industry is capital. Even though reasonably well capitalised today, banks will be facing the challenge of growing their business due to capital constraints. India's financial system is better at capital allocation than most of the emerging market players. It has some high performing banks, very low stock of gross non-performing loans of about 2.5 per cent and deep and liquid equity markets that efficiently discover price in stocks of globally competitive companies in BPO, IT, R&D, pharmaceuticals, automobiles, telecom and hospitality space. Still one of the challenges will be capital raising by corporate sectors but not at the expense of agriculture, small industries and business. Debate over channelling larger portion of available credit to the most potentially productive sector or to the sectors where the investment efficiency is lower is yet to be fully resolved. In any case, to make banks allocate increased credit to the productive sectors of the economy is strongly predicated on the bank capital strength. To do so, more capital would be required to be infused into banks. With requirements of Basel III looming large, banks would be facing challenges in raising additional capital for meeting the funding needs of Indian economy potentially growing at 9 per cent plus.

Post-crisis, regulators worldwide are discussing a macroprudential framework that would involve a regulatory policy focussed on the system as a whole, rather than individual players. Capital buffers are an extremely important component of the new macroprudential regulatory framework. The new framework aims at improving both quality and quantity of capital. Let us understand that capital is a competitive charge on the resources available for lending with a bank and hence, stepping up countercyclical capital requirements and providing capital buffers comes with a cost for the banking system. Capital enhancement, however, is a prudential requirement, as financial products and transactions are becoming increasingly complex and prudent risk management has assumed considerable importance. With higher and modified nature of capital requirements proposed through the new Basel III accord in the aftermath of the financial turmoil, keeping banks well capitalised would be an added challenge.

Banks are already suffering from inadequacy of capital as the return on such capital does not encourage new investors. Era of cheap capital is over and investors are also wary of the volatility of returns. Newer instruments and techniques would be required to attract investors. While creation of enabling conditions for capital flow to the sector would continue to remain on the top of the reform agenda, banks would need to grow their balance sheets by raising capital from the markets rather than count on government. Considering the back-to-basics common equity focus of Basel II, growing bank balance sheets will increasingly pose the challenge of balancing interests of shareholder and depositors/financial stability.

Liquidity Management

Traditionally, capital adequacy requirements have been imposed to ensure solvency. However, that is not the only issue. The next issue that will continue to engage substantial management attention is the management of liquidity. Is liquidity an offshoot of economic crisis or management crisis? I think a bit of both. In short, banks and financial institutions (FIs) are destined to be facing the unpredictability they like to believe as non-existent. Liquidity crises, although recurrent, are yet to be effectively managed. Responses are varied and such crises leave a trail of devastation clearly visible in the post-crisis stage. Issue of liquidity management requires much defter response than what is so far seen. How the banks will graduate from 'lazy banking' (as response to credit market growing more unsecure) to 'crazy banking' (when it became more fashionable to jump onto retail lending bandwagon with some of the banks burning their fingers) to 'edgy banking' is an issue which is yet to find a resolution. The truth is that the liquidity management requires more sophisticated, comprehensive, nuanced and razor-sharp approach in order to prevent it from being the carrier of contagion.

Implementation of International Financial Reporting Standards (IFRS)

The third issue that is going to cast a spell over the financial sector players is the compliance with IFRS. Globalisation of financial markets has meant an increased focus on international standards in accounting and has intensified efforts towards a single set of high quality, globally acceptable set of accounting standards. Financial statements prepared in different countries according to different set of rules, mean numerous national sets of standards, each with its own set of interpretation about a similar transaction, making it difficult to compare, analyse and interpret financial statements across nations.

In respect of banks and non-banking financial companies (NBFCs), in view of the special issues involved (finalisation of IFRS 9 expected in the middle of 2011), a separate roadmap was prepared in March 2010 for convergence with IFRS for the banking industry and NBFCs. The convergence process would be from period beginning April 1, 2013, with a phased approach for urban banks and NBFCs. This gives the banking system some time to adapt to the standards in a smooth and non-disruptive manner. It has to be noted, however, that banks will be significantly affected by the IAS 39 replacement project and a number of other accounting developments including those relating to financial instruments, fair value measurement, financial statement presentation and consolidation. Some of the major changes pertain to certain critical areas such as classification and valuation of financial assets, classification and valuation of liabilities, impairment provisions and fair value measurement. One area of concern has been the drawback of the incurred loss model of IAS 39 and the need to introduce more forward looking provisioning. We have seen how the concept of 'marked to market' turned to be useless at the time of real crisis through the potential futility of the idea of 'marked to model' as being divorced from real market and virtually ended up with a situation that can best be described as 'marked to madness'. The IFRS convergence process will involve significant challenges for the banking system in general. Banks would need to upgrade their infrastructure, including IT and human resources, to face the complexities and challenges of IFRS. Some major technical issues arising for Indian banks during the convergence process would be differences between the IFRS and current regulatory guidelines on classification and measurement of financial assets, focus on the standard of the business model followed by banks and the challenges for management in this area, application of fair values for transactions where not much guidance is available in India in terms of market practices or benchmarks, and expected changes in impairment rules.

Beyond Core Banking Solutions (CBS)

Today we cannot think of banking services without technology. IT has become the central cog in whatever banks are doing or strategising to do in future. All of us would agree that technology has no longer remained just a means for automating processes. It has revolutionised every industry in the world by rendering faster and cost-effective delivery of products and services to customers, who in the normal course could not have afforded the same.

Technology is the surest and most appropriate way of bringing inclusion in respect of any product and/or service. Is technology in banks being leveraged adequately?

Technological advancement enables a broader and inclusive banking sector and in the process, is a key driver for the sustained and inclusive growth of the economy. Technology by itself is not a panacea. But technology has evolved to such an extent that it can hold the key to achieving goals—if banks are willing to accept the changes that they will need to make to get there. Banks have implemented CBS which marked a paradigm shift in more senses than one and branch customers are now bank customers as they can access their accounts from any branch for defined purposes. It was envisaged that the CBS would offer new opportunities for information management, better customer service and improved risk management. However, banks have not been able to reap the benefits of this technology in terms of reduction in costs of small value transactions, speed with which the transactions are done if both successful and unsuccessful transactions are considered, improved customer services and effective flow of information within the banks as also to the regulator. Banks have not gained in terms of efficiency partly because the much needed business process re-engineering was not done. Further, banks have deployed technology for transaction processing and the same has not been explored extensively for analytical processing like customer relationship management and decision-making. Thus, there is a need to take care of what we could not achieve in the first round of technology implementation and think beyond CBS. Supported by the latest technology, banks would need to identify new business niches, to develop customised services, to implement innovative strategies and to capture new market opportunities.

Optimum leveraging of technology would critically hinge upon the following:

a. skilled resources,

b. supportive HR policy,

c. appropriate IT governance structure,

d. effective business continuity plan.

Banks and FIs would require review of the issues relating to recruiting appropriate skill, retain them over a longer time horizon by offering them a clear career growth opportunities and supporting enabling process. However, it is equally important to embed inside the management structure a proper IT governance structure which will also enable the technology strength of the banks to play a supporting role with a degree of assurance and sustainability.

Risk Management

Issue of risk management in banks and FIs would, however, continue to be at the centre of an ongoing search for the right policy prescription. While newer skill set for managing newer areas and unfamiliar elements of risks would continue to pose questions even to the most savvy of banks. Banks will have to adopt a converged approach to risk where they will re-evaluate their risk management acumen in a manner that calls for higher levels of transparency, structural integrity and operational control. To combat internal fraud and protect clients and accounts, behaviour and rules-based tools will have to be brought in. Better risk management and surveillance applications that address systemic and customer-oriented risks, potential conflicts of interest, financial valuation, volatility of market movements and regulations will have to be embedded into the operational structure. Future pricing will be dependent on risk minimisation even while relationship-based pricing will continue to hold sway. Today banks and FIs are facing with the risks of mispricing, adverse selection and mis-selling. On the one hand, banks are operating in the market where only about one-third of the adult population are within the banking fold leaving out the market potential to grow twice the current size and, on the other, banks' propensity to take banking services to the silent majority is very slow. While expanding market is a matter of survival, further challenge for the banks would be to ring-fence its operations by establishing a sound risk management system that is not only protective but also inclusive and acts as a business enabler. But for this to happen, analytics have to be developed and data integrity has to be improved.

Going forward, more focussed approach would have to be given to strict adherence of anti-money laundering (AML)/know your customer (KYC) norms so as to prevent the elements of fragility to come into the system. Strong tracking system for verifying the movement of funds, especially cross-border transaction and skillful analytical capabilities will be the prescription of the future. Along with that, the most important issue will be customer protection. When I talk of the customer protection, I mean making banking services or banks economically feasible for the customers and protect them from the bad banking practices. Can we devise a system by which poor subsidising the rich can be reversed? When banks make huge profit, it is because the customers are paying through their nose. When the banks incur loss, again it is the customers who are made to take less for their deposits or pay more for the loans. When the banks go out of business, it is the millions of tax payers' hard-earned money that goes down the drain. Customer protection also needs to be seen from protecting customer information and transaction security. The writing on the wall is clear: "keep your customers happy and survive."

Risks and Rewards

Next important issue that warrants a really careful consideration is the issue of executive compensation. How much compensation is too much? Can the industry have a different kind of compensation structure for the same job? Can there be uniform board level accountability? Flawed incentive compensation practices in the financial sector were one of the important factors contributing to the recent global financial crisis. I am aware that booms are propelled by greed and busts are born out of fear. This quirk of human nature will always ignite the euphoria that fuels the ups and exacerbates the downs. Employees were too often rewarded for increasing the short-term profit without adequate recognition of the risks the employees' activities posed to the organisations.

These perverse incentives amplified the excessive risk-taking that severely threatened the global financial system. The compensation issue has, therefore, been at the centre stage of the regulatory reforms. Issue of appropriate compensation commensurate with risk or built-in checks to avoid excessive risk-taking would have to be managed through a sound corporate governance framework based on strong corporate ethics principles and with reference the principles laid down by Financial Stability Board (FSB). The principles are intended to reduce incentives towards excessive risk-taking that may arise from the structure of compensation schemes. The principles call for effective governance of compensation and its alignment with prudent risk-taking and effective supervisory oversight and stakeholder engagement. The principles have been endorsed by the G-20 countries and the Basel Committee on Banking Supervision (BCBS), and are under implementation across jurisdictions. However, banks and other financial system players need to appreciate that good governance is more a matter of practice rather than a matter of compliance.

Now the question is: With so much of constraints and problems, whether the system will survive? The answer is an emphatic yes, because banking is a highly regulated business. But having flagged some of the challenges before the banks, it is incumbent upon me that I flag certain challenges for regulators. We all know that:

- The financial system is growing to be highly complex and opaque—sometimes making it difficult to assess the extent of exposures and potential spillovers. This opacity magnified the shock to confidence as the recent crisis unfolded.
- The financial system has a propensity to become over-leveraged and heavily interconnected, leading to massive deleveraging and easily available propagation channels, both domestically and globally.
- Liquidity risks, both the funding risks incurred by institutions and the associated market liquidity risks of assets, are often much higher than recognised.
- Financial intermediation has increasingly shifted to the non- or less-regulated 'shadow' banking sector, in large part to avoid the more stringent requirements imposed on banks.
- There is a critical absence of effective mechanisms to deal with institutions that were deemed 'too big to fail.'

How do Regulators meet the above Challenges?

Central banks must take a long-term view of the economy and craft appropriate policy responses. We must have the latitude to raise interest rates when others want cheap credit and rein in risky financial practices when others want easy profits. There has to be greater societal consensus on taking tough corrective actions.

While progress on macro and microprudential regulations will be the key for moving forward, some work is still needed from the regulators in providing guidance to the market in instituting a mechanism in the area of managing not only several 'known unknowns' but also a number of 'unknown unknowns.'

With the benefit of hindsight, low nominal interest rates, abundant liquidity and a favourable macroeconomic environment encouraged the private sector to take on ever-increasing risks. Financial institutions provided loans with inadequate checks on borrowers' ability to pay and developed new and highly complex financial products in an attempt to extract ever higher returns. Meanwhile, many financial regulators and supervisors were lulled into complacency and did not respond to the building up of vulnerabilities. We have to develop more sensitivity in our policy tools to capture and quickly correct our policy stance to control such covert signs of overheating.

Conclusion

In summing up, I would like to reiterate that though each one of the key challenges facing the Indian financial system begins with the banking system, it does not and should not stop at the banking system. Banks have to look beyond the way banking is traditionally defined in a narrow fashion; they need to look towards the vulnerable and other excluded sections of the population as bankable. Stakeholders other than banking too need to involve themselves in the process of expanding the outreach of the financial services, and thus partner with banks in the process of inclusive economic growth. That is the key challenge.

Address at the Mint's *Clarity through Debate*, Mumbai, 15th March 2011. RBI Bulletin April 2011.

6

N.A. MUJUMDAR

Global Financial Crisis

Some Lessons for Central Banks

Introduction

The global financial crisis of 2008 has changed the policy making landscape for central banks. Three aspects of these changes can be briefly discussed. First, some broad lessons for central banks from the experience of handling the crisis can be derived. These are summed up in section II. Second, the crisis has resulted, in the advanced countries, in the erosion of trust and confidence of the society in the financial sector. These issues are taken up for discussion in section III. The erosion is partly the result of a comprehensive regulatory capture. As Reddy (2012) puts it: "There is, perhaps, what may be described as unionisation of global capital against attempts by public policies to regulate the financial sector effectively." There is public resentment at several irregularities in the functioning of financial institutions and at obscenely high level of remuneration paid to senior management in some cases. How can this confidence be restored? Is inclusive finance the answer? Third, looking back at history, India offers a refreshing contrast. This is an occasion when we should pay tributes to the vision of the founding fathers of Reserve Bank of India (RBI) and the policy makers of the 1970s. Much before financial inclusion became internationally fashionable, the Indian policy makers laid the foundation for financial inclusion. These issues are discussed in section IV.

Lessons for Central Banks

It is now five years since the outbreak of global financial crisis in 2008. These years have been defining moments in the history of central banking. The developments during the period have challenged the intellectual framework and conventionally held beliefs about the functioning of the financial system and theory and practice of central banking. Financial stability has come to occupy the centre stage of policy making (Sinha, 2012).

The crisis has triggered a wide-ranging debate on the role and responsibilities of central banks. What should be the right framework for monetary policy? Do we need to re-define the mandate of central banks independence? Although no definitive conclusions have emerged from the debate and hard thinking by central banks and academicians, the debate has continued and some broad lessons from the experience of handling the crisis can be derived. Let us enumerate some of them.

First, inflation targeting. Before the crisis, there was a broad intellectual consensus in favour of inflation targetting, that is, basing monetary policy on achieving a target inflation rate, usually as expressed in consumer prices. There are formal inflation targetting central banks like those in Canada, New Zealand, and Thailand. This solely inflation targetting appeared to have worked well for some extended period, when price stability was accompanied by stable growth and low unemployment. Thus, inflation targetting became 'fashionable' and even some experts in India began to advocate its adoption. The mainstream view before the crisis was that price stability and financial stability reinforce each other. The crisis has demonstrated that this is wrong. Price stability does not necessarily ensure financial stability. The crisis has proved that price inflation targetting alone is inadvisable and that the mandate of central banks should extend beyond price stability to include bank regulation and supervision, financial stability and preventing asset price bubbles. Reserve Bank of India's multiple objectives approach with low inflation not necessarily a dominant, far less the sole objective, stands vindicated. Growth, employment and equity are among the other objectives.

Second, bank regulation and supervision. There is a variety of regulatory models. In some countries, central bank is a purely monetary authority, with bank regulation and supervision entrusted to another agency. The global crisis was caused, in large part, by a lack of coordination and communication between central banks and supervisors. The consensus that seems to be emerging after the crisis is that in the interest of financial stability, it is optimal to entrust regulation and supervision of banks to central banks.

The third point relates to the role of central banks in preventing asset price bubbles. We have seen how price bubbles in housing can have destructive effects on the financial system or the economy as a whole. It has now been conceded that preventing an asset price bubble should form part of the responsibility of a central bank. Whether this objective should be sought to be achieved through proper monetary action or regulatory action, should better be left to the concerned central bank to decide.

Fourth, should financial stability be explicitly included in the mandate of central banks? There is an ongoing debate on the issue. Of course, one could argue that financial stability is a necessary but not a sufficient condition for achieving the conventional objectives of central banks like growth, employment and equity, to which we have referred earlier. Basically, defining stability in a precise, comprehensive and measurable manner is difficult. In any case, the involvement of central banks in the stability exercise is now accepted. It may be recalled that during the global crisis, Central banks injected large doses of liquidity, as part of their lender-of-last-resort function to unfreeze the system. The need for fundamental changes in the way banks and financial institutions are regulated is recognised. At the international level, important steps have been taken under the auspices of G-20, Financial Stability Board (FSB) and Basel Committee on Banking Supervision (BCBS). The emerging framework includes ring-fencing of banking institutions with more and better quality capital under Basel III, appropriate framework for systemically important financial institutions (SIFIs), aligning compensation practices to prudent risk-taking. The Reserve Bank of India has now begun to conduct macroprudential surveillance of the financial system, on an ongoing basis. The assessment of financial stability and their findings are shared with financial institutions, market players and the general public in the form of financial stability reports (FSRs). The first Report was published in March 2010 and the fifth in 2012.

Finally, autonomy of central banks. Central bank independence is under assault following the global financial crisis of 2008. During the crisis, government and central banks coordinated their efforts to launch unprecedented expansionary fiscal and monetary policies. As countries now contemplate exiting these extraordinary expansion policies, the familiar conflicts between monetary and fiscal policies are resurfacing. A possible return of fiscal dominance may undermine the autonomy of central banks. In the US, for example, the Congress was threatening to put the Federal Reserve under greater surveillance. Admittedly, the responsibility for financial stability must be shared by both the Government and the Central Bank. RBI Governor, D. Subbarao, points out two concerns in this context. First, the rescue of financial institutions is an inherently political act and involvement in such decisions may compromise central bank's technocratic credentials. Second, there is the risk that coordination with the government for the purpose of financial stability may spill over into other areas within the central bank's purview thereby undermining its independence. "Central bank independence is perhaps not an unalloyed virtue", and Subbarao recommends: "Central Banks must advocate for independence not with weighty arguments but through more vigorous and voluntary efforts to be transparent, responsive, and accountable."

As Y.V. Reddy (2012) points out: "First, large sections of the population have[1] been affected by the financial crisis and they consider themselves innocent victims of the crisis in the financial sector. In particular, they feel that those involved in the finance sector have enjoyed disproportionate gains and shifted the pains of adjustment to the rest of the population." Reddy feels that to correct this perception by the majority it is not enough to provide consumer protection and ensure, systemic stability.

1. Redefining Central Banking Dr. Duvuuri Subbarao

Imperatives of Inclusive Finance

There is another dimension of the impact of global financial crisis, to which Reddy (2012) has drawn our attention in his recent Par Jacobson Foundation lecture. The reference here is to erosion of trust in the financial sector as a whole, in particular in banking in the advanced economies. This decline of trust and confidence is partly the result of market failure and relates to incentives—in many cases obscenely high level of remuneration of senior management—and greed. Partly, it is also due to misplaced faith in the self-correcting powers of the market. Whatever may have been the reasons, the resultant effect—is clear. "It is evident that public authorities in major financial centres genuinely believed that the financial system, even in its complex evolution, was contributing to the public good. But this faith *ex post* proved to be misplaced." Reddy therefore advocates 'inclusive finance'—a commitment to access of essential financial services to all segments of the society. He outlines the course of future action towards achieving this objective.

> Society expects central banks to restore this trust and confidence in money and finance and move the system towards inclusive finance.
>
> Society expects central banks to restore this trust and confidence in money and finance and move the system towards inclusive finance.
>
> Society has put its trust in central banks. Central banks have to ensure that bank managements and finance sector in general serve the masses, and not merely the elite or the financially active. In the ultimate analysis, central banks are trustees, agents to look after the interest of the masses.

The Indian Experiment

Viewed in this broader context, Indian empirical experience is interesting. The evolution of the Indian financial system is unique in a number of ways. The founding fathers of RBI built into the statute of the RBI the responsibility of promoting agricultural credit. This was rather unusual for a country which was still a British colony. Nationalisation of major commercial banks in 1969, the phenomenal branch expansion programme, unprecedented in the history of world banking and fixing credit targets with a view to ensuring wider disbursal of credit—these were indeed bold steps at that point of time in financial history. Reaching the small borrowers and the poor thus became the objective of the whole financial system. The Indian financial system is thus a product of state and central banks' direction and guidance. This approach brought about a structural transformation in the deployment of bank credit. The share of large and medium industries in the total credit which was around 61 per cent in March 1968 declined significantly to 38 per cent in June 1982. Simultaneously, the share of priority sectors which include agriculture and small industries rose from 11 per cent to 36 per cent during the period. Those who came to scoft at the Indian experiment have remained to pray.

As a postscript it may be added that more recently top regulators in the US have begun to articulate what needs to be done for banking. Banks have become too complex to manage as opposed to just too big to manage. The biggest banks must become simpler. More broadly, we have lost sight of what banking is supposed to do. Their role is not to assume a huge amount of risk with downside losses covered by society. Wilber Ross the legendary investor states: "I think that the real purpose and the real need that we have in this country for banks is to make loans particularly to small business and to individuals. I think that's the hard part to fill" (Johnson, 2012). Back to the basics!

References

Johnson, Simon (2012). "Big Banks: Too Big to Handle", *Economic Times*, October 26.

Prasad, Easwar (2010). *After the Fall, Finance and Development*. Washington, D.C.: IMF. June.

Reddy, Y.V. (2012). "Society, Economic Policies and the Financial Sector", *Economic and Political Weekly*, August 18.

Sinha, Anand (2012). "Financial Stability: 2007 to 2012 Five Years On", *RBI Monthly Bulletin*, October.

7

Y.V. REDDY

Society, Economic Policies and the Financial Sector

The future of finance, and in particular saving it from a popular backlash against the global financial crisis and related crisis-management policies, has rightly become a matter of great concern. There is broad agreement that finance has, as in the past, the potential to do good, which should be harnessed by all. However, it is essential to minimise its potential to do harm. In the commendable search for good finance, central bankers do not have just a stake but also a legitimate role to play. From a central banker's point of view, there are several issues in this search for good finance for the future, but there are three interrelated issues that I want to comment on: (a) how to ensure that the financial sector serves society better; (b) how to integrate financial sector policies better with national economic policies; and (c) how to ensure that the financial industry functions as a means and not as an end in itself.

The discussion here considers many issues raised on the future of finance (e.g., Ferguson, 2009; Sheng, 2009; Chittenden, 2010; Roubini and Mihm, 2010; Turner and others 2010; Pringle and Jones, 2011; CAFRAL-BIS, 2011; Blanchard *et al.*, 2012; Shiller 2012). My reflections are moulded by not only a decade in central banking but also many years in macroeconomic management in the central government and the Bretton Woods Twins, in addition to a much longer period at state and local levels of government dealing directly with the public. I will explore select themes of operational significance to central banks at the present juncture.

Society and Finance

An assessment of the impact of the recent global financial crisis on the trust and confidence of society in the financial sector is a useful starting point when considering ways of restoring the trust. A major reason for the erosion of trust may be a sense that there has been a comprehensive capture of regulation of the financial sector by the finance industry, particularly in the leading advanced economies. A demonstrable commitment to provide reasonable access to essential financial services to all segments of society would reinforce the assertion that finance serves the larger community. This approach, which may broadly be described as inclusive finance, goes beyond the current concerns with providing consumer protection and ensuring systemic stability.

Restoring Trust

It is true that the Occupy Wall Street movement directed at the financial sector has petered out. This may signify a lack of popular support for the movement, or equally it may signify a lack of hope that things will change or that better alternatives are on the horizon. A society's trust and confidence in finance, like in any other sector, is derived partly from formal laws, regulations and procedures, and is based partly on the manner in which they are implemented, through both formal and informal channels. Trust is, therefore, difficult to measure, but on the basis of surveys conducted and anecdotes reported in the media, there appears to be an erosion of trust in the financial sector as a whole, in particular in banking, in advanced economies. The perceptions of such an erosion of trust, however, differ.

What are the plausible reasons for the erosion of trust in some jurisdictions? We can only speculate.

First, large sections of the population have been affected by the financial crisis and they consider themselves innocent victims of the crisis in financial sector. In particular, they feel that those involved in the financial sector have enjoyed disproportionate gains and shifted the pains of adjustment to the rest of the population.

Second, in the discharge of semifiduciary functions that are critical to the integrity of financial markets, such as fixation of LIBOR and credit rating, the major global players in financial markets discredited themselves by resorting to questionable practices.

Third, when several irregularities in the functioning of large financial intermediaries were found, the regulators reacted to the wrongdoing by imposing penalties. The public at large was often left in the dark about the details of the malfeasance and the losses they had suffered.

Fourth, the shareholders in a few large financial conglomerates are actively questioning the remuneration of senior management in some cases. This is unprecedented, reflecting the loss of trust by shareholders in the management of financial firms.

Fifth, although public policies provided liquidity, extended bailouts in some cases, and in a few cases tax breaks, the much-needed credit from the financial sector to the economies is not forthcoming, even after accounting for the muted demand for credit.

Finally, there is resistance from finance industry leaders to suggestions for strengthening regulations. In advanced economies, operational details of important reforms in the banking sector, shadow banking activities and innovations in financial markets are yet to take a final shape. There is, perhaps, what may be described as unionisation of global capital against attempts by public policies to regulate the financial sector effectively.

It is also possible to argue that erosion of trust, if any, may be temporary, as seen in the past when the financial sector faced crises. It is also possible that central bankers have no tools for managing society's trust except by delivering their mandate through price stability and financial stability consistent with maintaining employment and growth. But it is undeniable that maintaining trust and confidence in finance is essential for the good of society at large.

The mandate for maintaining financial stability, which often rests primarily on central banks, has two related dimensions, namely, the avoidance of disruptions in the functioning of the financial system and (more positively) the promotion of trust and confidence in the system. If there is any wing of public policy authority that has a stake in building such trust, it is the central bank. Hence, the central bank should be watchful of developments related to trust in their jurisdictions and take a conscious decision whether to monitor and act, as necessary, to ensure continued trust and confidence in the financial sector.

Comprehensive Regulatory Capture

As noted earlier, the decline of trust and confidence is partly the result of the perception that there has been a comprehensive regulatory capture. While the popular explanations for market failure relate to incentives, and possibly greed, the regulators' failures are generally attributed to misplaced faith in the selfcorrecting powers of markets, a lack of skills in regulatory agencies and capture by vested interests. Such a capture can be described as comprehensive, particularly in the countries that were most affected during the crisis, in the sense that it was not restricted to the economic concept of regulatory capture, but extended to the overall public policy relating to financial sector.

What could be the reasons for this? First, the political leadership has a short-term horizon, and financial markets also have a short-term horizon. This creates a natural tendency for their priorities to converge. Available evidence shows that financial contributions to political activity from the financial sector in many affected countries increased significantly in recent years. Moreover, large global financial conglomerates seem to be in a position to influence not only political governance but also corporate governance, to suit their own interests.

Second, regulators, as part of their public consultation process, often depend on the regulated for consultation, which is a feature common in most industries. But the dominant market shares of the few giants in the finance industry, combined with the characteristic externalities of finance, make a difference to the process and outcomes. In the past, the excessive deregulation of the financial sector was often designed to a significant extent based on the advice of the interested market participants themselves.

Third, in cases where academics are advising on the design of reforms, they are often finance experts, sometimes engaged with market participants in remunerated advisory or consulting capacities. A large part of economic research on regulation is funded by the financial sector. In fact, most of the analysis of macroeconomic trends available in the public domain is from economists employed by large financial conglomerates. There may be, as a result of several of these factors, a tilt in favour of the financial sector in media coverage too.

Fourth, in many countries, the finance industry offers prospects of highly paid jobs for those employed in the regulatory agencies and treasuries or ministries of finance.

Finally, finance and its regulatory framework are somewhat intangible and difficult for a common person to fully understand. Hence, interested groups can tilt the intended policy changes in their favour by presenting their initiatives to shift equilibria between competing considerations as mere technical issues.

It is possible to argue that capture of regulators is inevitable, and that a case can therefore be made in favour of reducing formal regulation, and encouraging selfregulation and promoting principles-based regulation. On the contrary, there is a widespread feeling that those were the very prescriptions that brought about the global financial crisis. The biggest challenge for the future of finance lies, therefore, in designing governance practices that avoid the dangers of comprehensive regulatory capture.

I would, however, hasten to add that public policy failures cannot at the same time be wished away by placing undue blame on regulatory capture. It is evident that public authorities in major financial centres genuinely believed that the financial system, even in its complex evolution, was contributing to the public good. But this faith *ex post* proved to be misplaced. Levine (2012) observes that the absence of an informed, expertly staffed and independent institution that evaluates financial regulation from the public perspective is a critical defect in the governance of financial regulation. He suggests establishing a body that would submit a periodic report to the legislative and executive branches of government assessing the impact of financial regulation on the public. The body would be politically independent, independent of financial markets and staffed with experts, while having no official power over the central bank or other regulatory bodies. This may sound utopian, but is worth trying in the present day turbulent market environment.

Consideration may also be given to the formulation of a "fair practice code" for finance professionals, regulators and academia, extending the idea mooted by the American Economic Association on a Code of Ethics. A similar approach has been suggested by Shiller (2012: xi) in the context of financial innovation supporting the stewardship of society's assets. He observes that "the best way to do this is to build good moral behaviour into the culture of Wall Street through the creation and observance of best practices in its various professions—CEOs, traders, accountants, investment bankers, lawyers, philanthropists." However, experience suggests that there are limits to the effectiveness of such codes. In fact, ethical behaviour can be felt and understood, but it is difficult to formulate it fully in a code intended for day-to-day organisational purposes. Moral behaviour, in the final analysis, is a matter of individual choice. But what best practices can do is to exemplify the inherent morality in the individual.

I would argue that serious consideration should be given to evolving trustworthy institutional structures and adoption of best practices to reassure the public that the scope for comprehensive regulatory capture is being minimised. These assurances could be further reinforced through improving the public image of central banks and, in particular, of the governors.

Inclusive Finance

Inclusive finance implies that the objective of financial sector regulation should be as much about protecting consumers as ensuring the availability of essential financial services to all sections of society, keeping in mind the expectations and needs of the common person. Emphasis on financial literacy by central banks has been advocated to enable consumers to take advantage of competitive efficiency. However, the issue is not one of financial literacy but of the behavioural patterns of common people dealing with finance. In this regard, it has been rightly observed: "By properly deploying both incentives and nudges, we can improve our ability to improve people's lives, and help solve many of society's major problems. And we can do so while still insisting on everyone's freedom to choose" (Thaler and Sunstein 2008: 8). It is useful to provide a default option of financial products for those large sections of society that have neither the inclination nor the tools to make those choices. It could be argued that a competitive financial system which is well-regulated, keeping in view the needs for stability and consumer protection, would automatically ensure inclusive finance. Experience so far does not support such a view. Public policy in relation to the financial sector therefore needs to consider the expectations of large sections of the community, typically those of a common person. They are bound to be different depending on the society, but a few broad generalisations may be attempted.

First, common people need a place to keep financial savings in safe custody (e.g., wives often need to keep them safe from wayward husbands in rural areas in developing countries). They should be able to place and withdraw such savings with ease and at minimal cost. While a range of instruments with a host of risk-reward profiles may be provided by the financial sector, access to one safe and simple instrument is essential for a common person. Often, this is a deposit in a recognised deposit-taking institution, traditionally a retail bank-branch in the neighbourhood. The edifice of trust in the financial system, including leverage, is built primarily at this level.

Second, reasonable demand for credit for smoothing consumption between days/periods of income and of expenditure has to be met by the financial system at a reasonable cost. Smoothing of consumption may also be longer-term, including over lifetimes.

Third, remittances or payments may have to be made within families over different locations or for various other purposes, and such services should be available and accessible at affordable cost. These services are often a monopoly of the officially recognised or regulated banking or payment system, and hence regulators need to accept some responsibility for delivery of such services.

Finally, from a common person's point of view, public policy should ensure the easy availability of simple-to-understand instruments in credit, capital and insurance markets. Consumer protection is important in the financial sector, but ensuring the supply of simple-to-understand products should be an obligation of regulators; it is an essential step to gain the trust of the common person.

In some advanced economies, regulators are already paying attention to excessive charges on retail financial services, in particular credit cards. Experience in some developing countries indicates that the involvement of public policy in expanding coverage of finance among the general public has had a beneficial impact. It is true that public policy experience with subsidised credit in some developing economies, and with housing credit in some advanced economies, has not been good. But inclusive finance emphasises affordable access to simple products, and not excessive leverage or at the cost of prudence. Inclusive finance is not a substitute for the primacy of fiscal policy with regard to social welfare.

I would say that we are in a world of expanded mandates for central banks, and inclusive finance should not be excluded from such mandates. Perhaps central banks could satisfy themselves and the society at large that, between the markets and regulations, finance is serving the minimum needs of most common people while maintaining efficiency and stability. That would be the cornerstone for restoring trust and confidence in the financial sector. Central banks could explore avenues for using technology and financial innovations that meet the needs of common people.

Economic Policies and the Financial Sector

Experience with the crisis has brought into focus three interconnected complexities that have to be continuously addressed by the financial sector. These are: the balance between state and market as appropriate to the financial sector; the balance between real and financial sectors, where the latter should enable the real sector to perform; and, finally, balancing the conduct of macroeconomic policy at the national level with the dynamics of the global macroeconomic environment. Public policy is conducted at the national level, but at the same time, globalisation of economies, often driven by technology, is a reality and the global macroeconomic environment is an outcome of national policies in a framework of nebulous global governance arrangements. The challenge for national central banks is to find space for the conduct of their own policies in an increasingly interdependent global economy.

Macroeconomic Policies and the Financial Sector

It is tempting to debate the pros and cons of developments in the financial sector without full recognition of the macroeconomic environment and of the functioning of product and factor markets. The right balance between free markets and appropriate financial sector regulation is ideally explored in the light of the significant role of macroeconomic policies in maximising benefits and minimising costs of the financial sector to development and welfare. During the "Great Moderation", low and stable inflation was attributed to the success of monetary policy, ignoring the impact of the globalisation of trade and, to some extent, immigration in some economies. There was admittedly a spillover effect of monetary policies on stability in the financial sector. There is a realisation that, ideally, counter-cyclical monetary and fiscal policies should supplement counter-cyclical policies in the regulation of the financial sector in a variety of ways to ensure financial stability. For instance, consideration is being given to taxation of the financial sector, on institutions and on transactions, as a supplement to regulation of the financial sector in the interest of stability, and possibly growth and equity. Further, policies relating to management of public debt have a bearing on the functioning of the financial sector. For example, financial sector entities, particularly banks, either as part of portfolio management or through statutory pre-emption, hold significant government debt as assets. There is a recognition that large swings in capital flows could have an adverse impact on the financial sector. There is also awareness of the potential use of prudential regulation to manage capital accounts. Persistent and unsustainable current account deficits or surpluses may have the potential for destabilising the financial sector.

The macro policy framework at the national level, which is admittedly critical for good finance, is determined by the sovereign with legitimacy and accountability to its citizens. But macro policies at the national level have to take account of the deep and growing linkages between national economies and the global economy. An important issue, therefore, is the scope and limits for international coordination of national economic policies.

It is instructive therefore to briefly analyse the evolution and efficacy of the most recent efforts at global coordination of the macroeconomic environment through the mechanisms of the summits of the G-20. The initial stage of coordination through the G-20 summits was to avoid collapse in the financial system and to moderate the slide in the global economy through macroeconomic responses, in both monetary and fiscal areas. There were simultaneous actions. The uneven recovery that followed led to differences in short-run policy actions among countries, but this was recognised as inevitable under the circumstances. However, there was an effort to identify long-term structural issues and attempt to address them. There was some agreement in very broad terms, but differences persist on the sources of global imbalances and the appropriate correctives at the national level.

More recently, country-specific commitments to correct some imbalances have been attempted, but differences on the measurement of needed correctives and the timeliness of actions are stark. A possible reason for these differences is that short-term motivations at the national level seem to run counter to the longer-term interests of the global economy. There are unmistakable signs of diminishing returns from the G-20, despite initial achievements and the promise of greater coherence in future.

One positive development has been that the democratic deficit at the level of global financial architecture has been somewhat narrowed. But there is, as yet, no coherent global macroeconomic policy. The global macroeconomic environment is the result of the interaction between macro policies at the national level and national markets that are at different stages of development and that have differing degrees of integration into global markets.

It is true that successful arrangements for global coordination while retaining space for national public policies are working well in certain sectors, such as aviation, telecoms and the internet. But they seem to get into difficulties in regard to macroeconomic policies and finance. Clearly, there is a need to explore why global agreements work reasonably well in some sectors, leading to acceptable and assured outcomes, while when it comes to macro policies and finance such agreements appear difficult to arrive at—and what we can learn from them.

Global Finance and Global Governance

The basic assumption underlying the benefits of globalised finance is the existence of competitive efficiency in global financial markets. The assumption can be, and has been, questioned on several well-known grounds, namely: the lack of a sound international reserve currency system; the absence of credible lender-of-last-resort facilities at the global level; and the dominance of a handful of rating agencies and accounting firms without adequate evidence of market discipline or effective rules for their functioning. The leading rating agencies and accounting firms, along with few leading business news agencies, have continuous dealings with each other, which tends to reinforce the exercise of their oligopolistic power over markets. Further, operations of international banks/conglomerates specialising in cross-border flows, combining traditional banking and risky investment banking operations, have close business and operational links with rating agencies, accounting firms, etc. The concentration of global financial power in a few entities with close mutual connections has considerable potential to undermine competitive forces.

In assessing the competitive efficiency of global financial markets, it may be useful to make a distinction between the role of multinational banks which have subsidiaries or branches in different countries but predominantly operate in domestic markets, and that of international banks which specialise in crossborder financial activities, especially flows on capital accounts, both short-term and long-term. Experience has shown that multinational structures that relied less on wholesale funding and forex swap markets have been less vulnerable to crises. International banks are able to operate across different financial markets and countries with significant divergence in fiscal regimes as well as regulatory regimes. They have often been found to deal in financial flows of suspect legality in one country, though not always in both countries involved. International banks have the opportunity and incentive to conduct operations involving tax avoidance. Because of these operations, international banks enjoy significant influence over the political economy in several countries. In the prevailing environment of global financial markets, some large global financial conglomerates are larger and, perhaps, more powerful than some of the central banks.

It is clear from the experience of the euro area that, in effect, the sovereign becomes the source of extraordinary intervention as the ultimate risk-bearer in times of crisis. The problem arises when the sovereign's capacity for such intervention is constrained by globalisation: this may be beneficial in many respects, but it could undermine the capacity of the sovereign to tackle the financial sector problems that arise. The conduct of fiscal policy itself is dominated by consideration of the view of global financial markets on the sovereign's solvency and its capacity to support the financial sector under distress. Extraordinary intervention by the sovereign and related fiscal measures are thus subject to the credit rating agencies' appraisal of their solvency (Sen, 2012). These considerations may have a bearing on the conduct of both financial sector regulation and macro policies at the national level.

In brief, the prospects for credible and acceptable global governance arrangements to ensure a workable global economic policy and environment within which global finance could contribute to growth and stability, do not appear very bright. I am not addressing a more fundamental issue: whether global economic governance, ensuring common economic policies for all nations, would eliminate the benefits of diversity. Too much global policy coordination might lead to the universalisation of risks of policy mistakes. The main contention is that good finance is essentially a function of good economic policies, and such good policies are primarily national, though significantly affected by the global macroeconomic environment—which, as already mentioned, is not a product of design. Approaches to regulation of the financial sector will, therefore, continue to be national, in a global environment that is not necessarily favourable.

Regulation of the Financial Sector

There is a recognition that policies relating to regulation of the financial sector must optimise the benefits of the financial sector while minimising the costs or risks associated with it. There are several dimensions to striking this balance. I select three themes for consideration: the optimal level of financialisation, appropriate innovation in the financial sector, and the effectiveness of financial sector regulation.

Optimal Financialisation

Not long ago, many countries recognised the costs of excessive regulation of finance and of financial repression. More recent events seem to indicate that excess financialisation of an economy may also contribute to the crises. It may be that finance is good for economic d evelopment over a certain period, but only if practised in moderation. The idea of optimal financialisation seems to have been accepted implicitly by the financial sector reform measures being contemplated in many advanced economies. At the same time, several developing and emerging economies are considering measures to develop the financial sector, in particular financial markets. In their quest for optimal financialisation, the countries that are attempting further deregulation and development of financial markets would benefit from an understanding of how excess financialisation manifests itself. However, the manifestation of excessive financialisation may not be confined to finance, and may extend to commodity markets, corporates and households.

The financialisation of commodity markets happens both by virtue of deregulation of trade in commodity market exchanges and by virtue of the excessive liquidity that happens to be readily available. The correctives in public policy with regard to excessive financialisation of commodity markets may be at times beyond the scope of financial sector regulation.

During recent years, there has been a significant financialisation of household budgets, particularly in advanced economies. The changes in demand for certain goods are often dependent on credit conditions. Future cash flows are often determined by the market value of pension funds and other sources of social security over a lifetime. It is not clear whether limiting the leverage of financial intermediaries would by itself constrain the excess leverage in household budgets.

There has also been financialisation of corporates. Corporates are not only exposed to the financial markets in relation to their underlying operations in terms of what they produce or sell, but also in terms of treasury operations.

This excessive financialisation occurred in many advanced economies for other reasons. Incentives were created to multiply the transactions in the financial sector in the form of income from commissions related to transactions. Further, complexity was introduced with regard to some of these innovations, often to undermine the regulatory prescriptions regarding transparency or capital adequacy, or to mislead the counterparty. Shadow banking enabled undermining of regulatory prescriptions. Most recent initiatives with regard to reforms in regulation address these issues.

For many developing and emerging economies that are progressing on the path towards optimal financialisation, it is necessary to avoid excessive financialisation, and more importantly to explore the impact of finance on growth, ideally on the basis of empirical evidence. Research has associated higher growth with the development of the financial sector, but more recent evidence on trade-offs between growth in the real sector and the financial sector is equivocal. The experience of Asian emerging economies so far indicates that the beneficial effects of deregulated finance relative to free trade may be overstated. Further, institutional rigidities and the state of factor and product markets vary between countries, and they do interact with the level of financialisation.

This subject is explored in a recent paper of Cecchetti and Kharroubi (2012). It investigates how financial develop ment affects growth at both the country and the industry level. The paper shows, based on a sample of developed and emerging economies, that the level of financial development is good only up to a point, after which it becomes a drag on growth. It also shows that a fast-growing financial sector can be detrimental to aggregate productivity growth. This is a line of enquiry which should be further explored to arrive at what constitutes the optimum level of financialisation.

A recent working paper of the International Monetary Fund entitled "Too Much Finance?" (Arcand *et al.*, 2012) seems to confirm some of the broad conclusions of the BIS paper I referred to. Let me summarise the main findings.

First, there is a positive and robust correlation between financial depth and economic growth in countries with a small and intermediate financial sector. Second, beyond a threshold there is a negative effect of the financial sector; that threshold is when credit to the private sector reaches 100 per cent of GDP. Third, the negative effect is not confined to crisis periods, but extends to tranquil conditions also, possibly leading to misallocation of resources. Fourth, it is possible but not clear that bank lending and asset-based lending components of credit will have positive effects. Finally, analysis suggests that there are several countries for which a smaller financial sector would be desirable.

The global financial crisis also brought into focus the downside of excess debt, but then the issue is: what is excess debt? Debt sustainability in terms of sovereign debt has been analysed extensively in the past, but the issue is the real effect of debt—not only of sovereign debt but also other elements of the national economy. This has been explored by an interesting paper which poses the question, "When does debt go from good to bad?" Using a data set of member-countries of the Organisation for Economic Co-operation and Development (OECD) over 30 years, it concludes that the threshold is around 85 per cent of GDP for government debt, 90 per cent for corporate debt, and 85 per cent for household debt (Cecchetti, Mohanty and Zampolli, 2011). The subject should be researched further, since the issue of excess debt is closely related to excess financialisation, and the thresholds for excess debt may be lower for developing and emerging economies than for the advanced economies.

Excessive financialisation can also occur due to public policy failures in achieving socioeconomic development, resulting in the passing of an undue burden to the financial sector in the form of generating a range of quasi-fiscal activities. Improvements in overall governance structures and efficiency in the provision of public services can also contribute to limiting excessive financialisation outside the fiscal ambit.

More research is needed on what constitutes the optimum financialisation and leverage, which could be different for developing and emerging economies than for advanced economies, despite signs of some convergence in macroeconomic and financial sector issues. In any case, the direction of public policy relating to the financial sector in the near future will be characterised by increasing financialisation in some countries which have less developed finance, and restraining financialisation in others where it has gone too far.

Appropriate Innovation in the Financial Sector

Operationally, an important issue is the point at which an innovation requires the regulators' attention. Should it be before introduction in the market, or after receiving complaints from an affected party? Or should it rely on monitoring of every innovation and assessing *suo motu* whether there are harmful effects? Often, many innovations look attractive in the short run because risks are backloaded on some and rewards are frontloaded on others. In finance, pressure on regulators to regulate is also back-loaded, and is often too late. Different industries have different approaches and tools to regulate, and the point at which regulators' jurisdiction is activated varies across industries. For example, in pharmaceuticals, the regulator has to approve a product *ex ante*, while in regard to restrictive trade practices it may be *ex post*.

In many industries, regulations address issues relating to innovations. For example, in the pharmaceutical industry, considerable experimentation is demanded and *ex ante* approvals are required for marketing. In engineering systems, the consistency of innovations with the network in which they are to be applied is often required to be certified, either by an industry body or the regulator. In many others, innovations are left to the market test, unless they happen to have *ex post*, negative effects, in which case public policy may consider intervening. In brief, there are several industries which have been subject to different systems of regulation, and they have stood the test of time. The financial sector should be able to draw lessons from such experiences, recognising the unique characteristics of the financial sector. Such lessons will also help in differentiating between technological, process and product innovations.

Markets are, indeed, a source of many innovations, but there are examples in many industries where the public sector has been active in promoting innovations. There is merit in central banks encouraging innovations in the financial sector that have the potential to serve the public. I agree with the US Federal Reserve chairman, Ben Bernanke (2009), when he said, referring to striking the right balance between consumer protection and responsible innovation, "our goal should be a financial system in which innovation leads to higher levels of economic welfare for people and communities at all income levels."

Central banks in particular, and regulators in general, could be more proactive in promoting and incentivising appropriate innovations in the financial sector, and drawing on the experience of other industries may be of considerable value in evolving policies towards financial innovations.

Effectiveness of Regulation

There is considerable agreement that better and more effective regulation is of vital importance to the financial sector, and that more regulation is not necessarily better. At the same time, self-regulation, principles-based regulation, and the use of internally generated models of risk management have proved to be suboptimal. Hence, there is a need to consider mechanisms to make regulation more effective, to limit unnecessary regulatory burdens or to contain the cost of compliance with regulators' prescriptions. I wish to explore some practical ways of enhancing effectiveness.

A possible reason for deficiencies in regulation in the pre-crisis period may have been the loss of information as part of a process of deregulation and a lack of mechanisms to monitor events in the fast-changing world of finance. Regulatory effectiveness can be improved by enhancing the monitoring of transactions, and analysing them rigorously. No doubt, technology enables market participants to operate in a fraction of seconds, but the same technology is available for regulators too, to collect information, monitor and analyse in an equally fast manner. Modern technology minimises the costs of reporting and, to some extent, analysis by regulators. Close monitoring by regulators may enhance compliance with regulations and help in fine-tuning the regulatory prescriptions on ongoing and timely basis.

In debates relating to public policy on public utilities, issues of regulation, competition and ownership were considered in an integrated manner. That used to apply to the finance industry also, before deregulation and privatisation became the preferred policies. The global financial crisis is leading to a serious reconsideration of the extent, nature and effectiveness of regulation. There may be merit in considering, in an integrated fashion, appropriate regulation and its effectiveness in relation to competition and public ownership.

First, there is a recognition of the danger of 'too big to fail' and 'too powerful to regulate' financial conglomerates. Resolution regimes and the adoption of living wills are being considered to address this issue. It is often argued that it is difficult to unbundle them in a nondisruptive fashion. Under the circumstances, the option of public ownership of those too-big-to-fail institutions could also be reopened, keeping in view the advantages of diversity. Second, the crisis necessitated an increase in public sector ownership in the banking industry, mainly due to large bail-outs. The exit from this unintended expansion in state ownership of banks ought to consider the costs and benefits of options that may include divestment or continuing with state ownership along with appropriate participation in management. Third, a case for an approximate mix of public and private sector banks in a financial system could be examined. Such a mixed model for the structure of the banking sector or financial sector in general would lend stability through diversity. Differing priorities and practices enabled public sector institutions to retain a public sector character and not merely to replicate the functioning of private sector counterparts. The problem of information asymmetry may be moderated if public sector banks coexist, assuming that they have fewer incentives to withhold information from regulators and are often subject to legislation relating to the right to information. It is not necessary that a bank or a non-bank financial entity should be owned entirely by the government or only by private shareholders. A variety of combinations of public and private ownership and control can be considered.

In revisiting the issue of regulation in conjunction with competition and ownership, it is necessary to recognise the lessons from public sector banking in the 1970s and 1980s, particularly in developing and emerging market economies. The problems in the past with public sector banking were due to financial repression attributable to macroeconomic policies, the lack of appropriate global standards of regulation, the existence of monopoly status and technological obsolescence, in addition to standards of governance in public systems in general, and public ownership in particular. In the context of the global financial crisis, the practices of some entities that were virtually in the public sector, such as Freddie Mac and Fannie Mae, do not provide reassurance that a public sector character would in itself be benign. Experiences with some banks in the public sector in Europe may also be instructive. The temptation to politicise public sector banking may persist, but the need for professionalisation in the public sector should not be underestimated. The new realities consequent upon the crisis indicate the potential for a redefined role for public sector financial institutions, provided that the experience prior to deregulation and privatisation as well as select cases related to the global financial crisis, are also kept in mind.

The use of fiscal and related instruments to supplement regulatory effectiveness could be considered in earnest. Information generated for purposes of taxation is likely to be of great practical use for regulators in monitoring financial sector activities. Levying financial transaction taxes could be considered with rates that discriminate against excessive speculation. The cross-border activities of financial intermediation could be brought within the tax net, and thus the regulatory ambit by adopting the issuance principle (financial institutions located outside the country would be obliged to pay the tax if they traded securities originally issued within the country) and the residence principle (instruments issued outside the country but subsequently traded by at least one institution within the country would be liable). Further, evasion could be discouraged by adopting the example of stamp duty in United Kingdom, and of Brazil, where non-payment of the tax makes legal enforcement of such contracts difficult.

There is also significant merit in considering anti-avoidance rules in taxation for regulation of the financial sector as well. Thus, if the sole purpose of an instrument or institution in the financial sector is to avoid regulation, such transactions can be considered void for the purposes of regulation. Thus, a distinction can be made in financial sector regulation, as in the case of taxation, between planning, avoidance and evasion. Above all, taxation and the use of information thus acquired for regulation of financial sector would considerably enhance the effectiveness of both fiscal and financial management.

Conclusions

I believe that society expects central banks to ensure trust and confidence in money and finance, and hopes that they avoid the pitfalls of capture, while the common person seeks inclusive finance. It is not easy for central banks to deliver all this, but they should not ignore society's expectations.

In these efforts, central banks need to preserve space for public policy at the national level consistent with their obligations to the global economy. The financial sector may draw lessons from global coordination in other industries, especially in managing networks.

Global trends in financial sector regulation may see simultaneous re-regulation in some countries and deregulation in others. Innovations, by definition, are difficult to put into preconceived straitjackets, and a disaggregated contextual approach would be appropriate. Above all, better regulation warrants effective regulation. Consideration of regulation, competition and ownership in an integrated manner, enhanced monitoring of financial market activities and the use of fiscal tools to supplement regulation could be helpful in this regard.

Society has put its trust in central banks. Central banks have to ensure that bank managements and the financial sector in general serve the masses, and not merely the elite or the financially active. In the ultimate analysis, central banks are trustees, agents to look after the interests of the masses.

References

Arcand, Jean-Louis, Enrico Berkes and Ugo Panizza (2012). "Too Much Finance?", *International Monetary Fund* WP/12/161. June. *www.imf. org/external/pubs/ft/wp/2012/wp12161.pdf*

Bernanke, Ben S (2009). "Financial Innovation and Consumer Protection", Speech at the Federal Reserve System's *Sixth Biennial Community Affairs Research Conference*, Washington DC, April 17. available at *http://www.federalreserve. gov/newsevents/speech/bernanke 20090417a.htm*

Blanchard, Olivier, David Romer, Michael Spence and Joseph Stiglitz (2012). *In the Wake of the Crisis.* Cambridge Massachusetts: MIT Press.

CAFRAL-BIS (2011). Proceedings of a Conference on *Financial Sector Regulation for Growth, Equity and Stability in the Post Crisis World*, Conference jointly organised by the Centre for A dvanced Financial Learning and Research (CAFRAL) and BIS in Mumbai on November 15-16.

Cecchetti, Stephen and Enisse Kharroubi (2012). "Reassessing the Impact of Finance on Growth", Paper presented at the *Second International Research Conference*, Organised by the Reserve

Bank of India, February 1-2. available at *http:// sirc.rbi.org.in/downloads/4Cecchetti.pdf*

Cecchetti, Stephen, Madhusudan Mohanty and Fabrizio Zampolli (2011). "The Real Effects of Debt", *BIS Working Papers* No 352. http:// www.bis.org/publ/work352.htm

Chittenden, Oliver (ed.) (2010). *The Future of Money.* London: Virgin Books.

Crockett, Andrew (2011). "What Financial System for the 21st Century?", Per Jacobsson Lecture delivered on June 26. available at *http:// www.bis.org/events/agm2011/sp110626.htm*

Ferguson, Niall (2009). *The Ascent of Money (Afterword: The Descent of Money)*. London: Penguin Books.

Levine, Ross (2012). "The Governance of Financial Regulation: Reform Lessons from the Recent Crisis", *International Review of Finance* 12(1): 39-56.

Pringle, Robert and Claire Jones (2011). *The Future of Central Banking.* London: Central Banking Publications.

Roubini, Nouriel and Stephen Mihm (2010). *Crisis Economics: A Crash Course in the Future of Finance.* London: Penguin Books.

Sen, Amartya (2012). "Europe's Crisis: of Democracy", op ed in the *Business Standard*, May 25.

Sheng, Andrew (2009). *From Asian to Global Financial Crisis.* Cambridge University Press.

Shiller, Robert J. (2012). *Finance and the Good Society*. Princeton: Princeton University Press.

Thaler, Richard and Cass R. Sunstein (2008). *Nudge: Improving Decisions about Health, Wealth and Happiness:* New Haven: Yale University Press.

Turner, Adair and others (2010). *The Future of Finance: The LSE Report*. London: London School of Economics and Political Science.

Economic & Political Weekly XLVII(33), August 18, 2012. Per Jacobbson Foundation Lecture 2012 delivered at BIS, Basel Switzerland, June 24, 2012.

8

JOSEPH E. STIGLITZ

A Revolution in Monetary Policy

Lessons in the Wake of the Global Financial Crisis[1]

It is understandable that the global financial crisis should give rise to considerable reflection among macroeconomists, and especially monetary theorists and policy makers. After all, their models didn't predict the crisis—the most important economic event in three quarters of a century. Economics is supposed to be a science, and the test of any science is its ability to predict; and if a sub-discipline can't predict something of this importance, then it suggests something is wrong.

I say suggests because devotees of the model claim that there are always random exogenous shocks that cannot be anticipated. But this crisis was not an exogenous shock: the credit bubble that brought the economy down was endogenous. It was a shock created by the market itself. And it was the kind of shock that the theory said couldn't happen: for if markets are rational, there won't be bubbles.

This is but one example of the many flaws in the prevalent paradigm that were exposed by the crisis. In this paper, I do not want to dwell so much on the flaws in the economic theories and models that dominated mainstream thinking, including thinking inside many central banks, but on the central policy stances that

1. This lecture was given in Mumbai on January 3, 2013, to commemorate C.D. Deshmukh, who capped his 21 years in the Indian Civil Service with an outstanding stint as Governor of the Reserve Bank of India from 1943-1949. During his tenure, he oversaw the Bank's transformation to a nationalised institution, promoted regulation of banks, and established India's first financial institution for the provision of long-term credit to industry. He later served as Union Finance Minister, India's Special Financial Ambassador to America and Europe, and among many other notable achievements, made his mark in academia and public service. It is my honour to give this lecture in recognition of his deep contributions to India and to his field.

typically followed—sometimes quite loosely—from those theories and models.

These theories and models not only contributed to the failure to see the crisis coming, but led some leading central bankers to argue that its effects were contained, even after the bubble broke.[2] They were also extra ordinarily influential in shaping the policies that both contributed to the crisis and to its rapid spread around the world, and have contributed to the lack of effectiveness in responding to the crisis. A half decade after the beginning of America's recession, more than six years after the breaking of the bubble, unemployment in Europe and America remains unacceptably high, the GDP in many countries is still below the level attained before the crisis, a few countries are mired in depression, and the global economy is on the verge of another recession.

In this paper, then, I will enunciate 14 lessons for monetary policy that I believe emanate from the recession. Some are controversial. Most reflect a marked departure from the stances taken by at least many monetary authorities.

Self Regulation Does Not Work

The notion that financial markets are self-regulating seems slightly quaint now, but we should not forget how widespread and deeply believed that doctrine was. That that was so is testimony to the ability of ideology to prevail over the lessons of history and theory. Financial markets have repeatedly been prone to bubbles, which when they burst would bring havoc in their wake.[3] Conflicts of interest and predatory and abusive practices had repeatedly marked financial markets. These were among the reasons that the sector had become highly regulated. To think that somehow, things would have suddenly changed, beginning around 1980, was sheer fantasy.

---

2. Bernanke said, as late as March 2007, that "the impact on the broader economy and financial markets of the problems in the subprime market seems likely to be contained." Statement of Ben S. Bernanke, Chairman, Board of Governors of the Federal Reserve System, before the Joint Economic Committee, U.S. Congress, Washington, DC, March 28, 2007.

3. See, for example, Kindleberger (1978).

Indeed, advances in economic theory had explained why unfettered markets—and unfettered financial markets in particular—were likely not to be efficient or stable, and why they were likely to be marked by abuses and exploitation.

The general theory of imperfect and asymmetric information, developed in the 1970s and 80s, had shown that whenever information is imperfect and asymmetric (that is, some individuals know things that others do not) and risk markets incomplete—that is, always—the economy is not likely to be (constrained) *Pareto* efficient,[4] (Greenwald and Stiglitz, 1986). Adam Smith's invisible hand was invisible because it was not there. The theory also explained why risk markets are likely to be incomplete—why key risks could not be insured against.

The theory explained too why markets in which information was important were not likely to be fully competitive—for instance, someone who offered the same product at a lower price would not attract the entire market, as assumed in the conventional theory, simply because not everyone would know about the offer.

Moreover such markets could well be characterised by rationing—unemployment and credit rationing were real phenomenon, with important economic consequences.

Finally, markets in which information problems were important were likely to be marked by severe agency problems—where those making decisions might not fully reflect the interests of those on whose behalf they were supposed to be acting. Managers might not maximise shareholder value, let alone societal welfare.

These issues are of particular relevance to financial markets, precisely because information is at the centre of what financial markets do. They are supposed to allocate scarce capital resources and manage risk, but what makes these tasks difficult and interesting are information imperfections, ascertaining the returns and risks associated, for instance, with different assets, determining which risks are best suited for different individuals, etc. That

4. The term "constrained *Pareto* optimal" refers to the fact that the costs of creating new markets and obtaining more information are included in the analysis: information is not a free good.

America's financial markets did an abysmal job in this, their central function, should be obvious. The failures were not, however, that of a single bank, or an isolated banker: they were systemic, suggesting that the problems that gave rise to them were systemic, as indeed they were.

Further, the reason that we care so much about failures in the financial system (or even of a single large bank) is that there are systemic consequences—there are large externalities on the rest of the economy.

The implication is that there is a need for strong governmental regulation of financial institutions. Much of the rest of this paper will be concerned with the design of a good regulatory system.

This brings me to the second important lesson:

Regulation is Needed for a Well-functioning Market and Economy

Financial sector regulation is required both because it is a sector characterised by large market failures, and where there are systemic consequences (large externalities) arising from these market failures. Regulators need to bear this in mind, as they think both about the need for regulation and its design. In subsequent sections, I touch on the multifaced nature of this regulation, a long list that includes ensuring the safety and soundness of individual banks and systemic stability; maintaining competition; promoting access for all; protecting consumers and investors from exploitation, predation, manipulation, and a wide range of abusive practices that have become part of every-day business in the sector; and enhancing transparency. While regulations and regulators may be imperfect, the track record of success—in India, and even in the US in the decades after the last great crisis, the Great Depression—shows that good regulation is both possible and can make a difference.

In the aftermath of the financial collapse in 2008, Alan Greenspan, the chairman of the Federal Reserve, lamented about the flaw in his reasoning.[5] He was surprised that the banks had not

5. In Congressional testimony on October 23, 2008, Greenspan described being "in a state of shocked

managed their risk better. I was surprised at his surprise: after all, banks had repeatedly not managed risk well. Why did he think they would do so in the 21st century, when they had done such a bad job in previous centuries? Moreover, anyone looking at the incentive structures facing banks and bankers should have understood that they had incentives to engage in excessive risk taking and short sighted behaviour. They acted as any economist should have predicted that they would.

Even if there had not been such perverse incentive structures, those in the financial sector have often been prone to irrational exuberance. Even Greenspan had commented on this. History was replete of instances of such irrational exuberance. What distinguishes banks from other institutions is that in this sector, irrational exuberance has systemic consequences—there are large externalities. Bankers with irrational exuberance are gambling with other people's money,

But the problems go deeper. Bank managers and industry leaders often seem to show remarkable ignorance of some of the basic principles of risk—including the Modigliani-Miller theorem, which asserts that increasing leverage doesn't increase market value—it doesn't create wealth, it simply shifts more risk upon the residual equity base. (Of course, there could be an increase in value because of market imperfections, either because (a) market participants are irrational, and don't fully understand the increased risk imposed on equity; (b) shareholders as a whole may gain because of the shift of risk to the government, resulting from an increase in what might be termed the "bail-out subsidy"; or (c) distortions in the tax code. But none of these are reasons to countenance an increase in leverage.)[6]

disbelief" that the lending institutions' self-interest had not protected shareholders' equity. Testimony available at *http://democrats.oversight.house.gov/images/stories/documents/20081023100438.pdf* (accessed December 14, 2012).

6. For a more extensive discussion of these issues see "On the Need for Increased Capital Requirements for Banks and Further Actions to Improve the Safety and Soundness of America's Banking System", witness testimony of Joseph E. Stiglitz to the Senate Banking Committee, August 3, 2011, available at *http://banking.senate.gov/public/index.cfm?FuseAction=Files.View&FileStore_id=97cec3e1-2d1d-44fa-acd9-a0a1bc640bc4* (accessed December 14, 2012), and Admati *et al.* (2010).

Thus, the widely held notion in the banking community that increased capital requirements (say under Basel III) will increase the cost of borrowing either reflects a profound misunderstanding of risk among those in the banking community; and/or their understandable desire to increase the subsidy the sector gets from the public, disguising this in terms of the benefits to their customers; and/or their understanding of risk, but their understanding that other market participants don't understand risk.

This implies that there should be strong regulations on the incentive structures of banks—it is not just the size of the bonuses that should be of concern, but the design. Higher deposit insurance fees levied on banks engaged in higher levels of risk taking might also discourage excessive risk taking, offsetting the implicit subsidy associated with government bailouts. But because of pervasive irrationalities, we cannot rely on incentive structures to curb excessive risk taking. There have to be strong restrictions on the risk taking, including the degree of leverage. Excessively rapid expansion of a bank's assets, particularly within a given area, are almost a sure sign of excessive risk taking. There need to be 'speed bumps.' The costs of such restriction—a slight postponement of perhaps some socially profitable lending—is far less than the benefit—avoiding the kind of financial collapses that have occurred repeatedly.

It is natural to ask why so many financial institutions chose to adopt incentive structures that seem so perverse. Traditionally, one of the purported virtues of the market economy is that it provides not just strong incentives but well designed incentive structures. That has obviously not been the case. The explanation lies in deep rooted failures in corporate governance. Much of our thinking about the market economy is based on simple models of Marshallian 19th century economics, with little relevance to understanding the functioning of managerial and corporate capitalism of the 21st century. (This illustrates a more general theme, to which we return later in this paper: The financial sector cannot be viewed as separate from the rest of the economy. It is affected by the laws and mores that affect other sectors—laws like those related to bankruptcy and corporate governance, and mores such as those that affect the acceptability of exploitation and the primacy of material values and incentives. I will have little to say about these issues of social mores, except to note that as trust and social capital weakens, the need for public regulation is enhanced.)

There needs to be deep reform of corporate governance laws, providing in particular better provisions for say in pay.

The problems of distorted incentives are especially important with financial institutions which cannot be allowed to fail because of the systemic consequences. This brings me to the third major lesson:

Banks that are 'too big to fail', 'too interconnected to fail', and/or 'too correlated to fail' Present a Real Danger to the Financial System and the Economy

Financial institutions which are too big to fail, too interconnected to fail, or too correlated to fail have an incentive to gamble: if they win, they walk off with the profits, if they lose, the public picks up the losses. But the problems are deeper: banks have an incentive to become too big, too intertwined, and too correlated to fail; and because of the implicit guarantee that is provided to such institutions, they have an advantage over other institutions. The private returns to growth in size and to interconnectedness exceed by a large measure the social returns (which may, in fact, be negative.)

One aspect of 'correlated' risk taking is the herding behaviour that marks credit bubbles. Such irrational bubbles are a major source of macroeconomic volatility. In the past, regulation has typically focussed on the safety and soundness of individual banks, but once we recognise the central role of the correlated behaviour of banks in causing macroeconomic fluctuations, we have to ask how can we design a regulatory structure to reduce the scope and severity of such finance induced fluctuations.

There should be strong regulations restricting the size and interconnectedness of banks. Taxes on large banks should be levied to 'level the playing field.'

Reducing the risk of 'too correlated to fail' is more complex, and requires ensuring a diversity of financial institutions, with different ownership, incentives, and objectives.[7] This argues strongly against the universal bank model. While more specialised financial institutions may face a greater risk of bankruptcy, the risk of systemic failure is greater where all banks are universal banks, and the social costs of systemic failure is an order of magnitude greater than the costs of the failure of individual institutions. (Much of that cost can be handled through diversification of the ownership shares.)

Macroprudential regulation is essential to prevent the growth of credit bubbles and other forms of macroeconomic volatility. Of particular concern is collateral based lending—where the value of the collateral, and thus the magnitude of lending, increases in a bubble, thus reinforcing the bubble. By demanding high lending standards and increased collateral in boom periods, the financial system can act as an automatic stabiliser, rather than the automatic destabiliser that it is under current arrangements.

The Pervasive Imperfections in Competition Need to be Curbed

In most countries, the financial sector is far from perfectly competitive. In many markets, even in advanced countries, there are only one or two lenders to small businesses. In many countries, banks have acted collusively to obtain outsized returns from their control of the payments mechanism. In most countries, the persistence of returns that are far higher than could be justified by effective competition in certain lines of business are suggestive of limitations of competition.

Imperfections of information naturally give rise to imperfections in competition, so we should not be surprised that even in countries where there are many banks, markets are far from competitive. Because markets that are fully transparent are more competitive, and less profitable, there are strong market incentives for reducing

7. This was a key point emphasised in *The Stiglitz Report: Reforming the International Monetary and Financial Systems in the Wake of the Global Crisis*, with Members of the Commission of Experts of the President of the United Nations General Assembly on Reforms of the International Monetary and Financial System. New York: The New Press. 2010.

and impeding transparency. That is just one of the reasons that we need strong regulation ensuring transparency, including—and especially—for derivatives (see the discussion below).

But even with reasonable laws governing transparency, effectively enforced (not the situation today), in many areas within the financial markets competition is likely to remain limited. We can however circumscribe the worst practices. Modern technology has, for instance, made it possible to have an efficient electronic payments mechanism, where it would cost but a fraction of a cent to transfer money from a customer's bank account to the merchant from which he has purchased a good. But the banks, in their attempt to extract monopoly rents out of their control of the payments mechanism, have resisted the creation of this kind of an electronic transfer mechanism.

There need to be strong restrictions on credit card fees, interchange fees charged merchants, and other anti-competitive practices. Restrictions on the size and ranges of bank activities and the interconnectness of banks would not only increase systemic stability, it would also enhance competitiveness.

Consumer and Investor Protection: Information Asymmetries and Exploitation

In most countries, the financial sector has been actively engaged in exploiting poorly educated and financially uninformed users. They have engaged in deceptive practices, and even in market manipulation and fraudulent practices with seemingly sophisticated customers. They have demonstrated a remarkable level of moral turpitude. This has contributed not only to creating high levels of inequality—moving money from the bottom and middle of the pyramid to the top—but also to a lack of trust in markets and the market economy. Markets cannot function well without such trust—and this is another way in which the banks have exhibited enormous adverse externalities. More generally, there are large costs to the sector's rent seeking activities—money doesn't move from the bottom to the top costlessly; the benefits to those at the top are less than the losses to the rest.

There needs to be strong consumer protection legislation, a regulatory framework along the lines of the US Consumer Financial Protection Bureau. There need to be strong restrictions on usury, overdraft fees, credit card fees and penalties, predatory lending, etc.

But the consumer protection agency needs to do more than just protect against abuses of the private financial sector. It needs to innovate—to design, for instance, mortgage products that help ordinary citizens manage the risks of home ownership.

The London Interbank Offered Rate (LIBOR) scandal illustrates the potential depth of the consequences of unfettered markets: there is a $350 trillion derivative market and somewhat smaller loan market indexed to a number that we now know is manipulatible and manipulated, that doesn't represent what the words seem to suggest it represents.

The continuation of the market linked to LIBOR is itself scandalous. There is ample evidence that even today it does not reflect any true lending rate: is it conceivable that interbank lending rates for a particular bank whose CDS's spread have soared barely move?

Contracts should be indexed to T-bill rates, which are less manipulable, and may be even more linked to the kinds of risks which these indexed contracts are suppose to handle.

But even if the T-bill rate is less correlated with the risks that individuals care about, the advantages in the reduction of potential for manipulation and exploitation make the movement away from LIBOR desirable.

Derivatives and CDS's: We Need to Make Markets Work Like Markets

Derivatives and CDS's bring together many of the issues discussed so far: the market is far from competitive, with a few big banks deriving significant returns (in the billions) from these activities, making it understandable why they resist regulation so strongly. The lack of transparency facilitates market manipulation and a lack of competition, enhancing bank profits, but at the same time posing significant systemic risk, which became so evident in the 2008 crisis. There is also an element of regulatory arbitrage, or what might more accurately be described as regulatory deception. If regulators treat a bank's holding of a risky bond combined with a CDS (supposedly an insurance policy on the bond) as if the bank were holding a safe asset, it allows the bank to lend more money—to leverage its portfolio even more. But the insurance may be phony insurance—sold at a low price because the benefits would never be paid by the insurance company because in the event of the insured against event occurring, the insurance would default: this was precisely what happened with AIG.

Moreover, by failing to net out their positions and by not trading through exchanges, the banks increase systemic risk and reduce transparency, another instance of externalities imposed upon others. Indeed, they reduce the overall efficiency of the market, since the standard arrangements undermine principles of market decentralisation. For example, with large credit default swaps not cleared through an adequately capitalised clearing house, knowing the risk of default of any one firm required knowing the risk position of every firm with which it was financially interlinked—in a vast, difficult, simultaneous equation system.

Transparency and the Euro-Crisis

The euro crisis has once again brought out the consequences of the lack of transparency in derivative positions. No one knew for sure the full consequences of a Greek restructuring, partly because no one knew who bore the risks, or what banks may have taken a speculative positioning. One of the explanations for the ECB's hard-to-justify position that the restructuring should be done in a way that was not a credit event—that is, so that the banks who had bought insurance would not be repaid—was that they were more concerned with the banks who had taken a speculative position.

Government insured financial institutions (whether the insurance is explicit, or implicit—as a result of being too big to fail) should not be allowed to issue derivatives. While it is not clear whether such financial products are insurance products or gambling instruments, they are not loans, there is no justification for government encouraging them through implicit or explicit insurance. There is no evidence of compelling economies of scope to offset the market distortion arising from such subsidies.

Derivatives should be traded over adequately capitalised exchanges and positions should be transparent. Some critics have worried that trading over exchanges will concentrate risk; there could be systemic consequences to the failure of an exchange. The response is to increase capitalisation and to require all those who make use of the exchange to be jointly and severally liable for the losses. The rest of society should not have to bear the consequences of their failure at risk management.

It should be clear that Dodd-Frank went only a little way towards addressing the problems posed by derivatives. A fundamental flaw of Dodd-Frank was that it did not recognise the deep disparity between private rewards and social returns; it did not recognise that market participants had incentives to design transactions in ways that increased systemic instability and decreased the economy's efficiency, either in gathering and disseminating information or in assessing or distributing risk.

Derivatives and other new financial productions were championed as part of financial innovation. But as Paul Volcker pointed out, it was hard to see that any of this financial innovation had led to faster real economic growth. It had contributed to more inequality—to greater wealth for the bankers—but it was hard to see societal benefits. Indeed, it has been associated with more instability.

We now understand better why that is the case. Much of the financial innovation was not directed at improving the efficiency of the economy and enhancing the ability of ordinary Americans to manage the risks which they faced. Some of the innovations were directed at improved ways of exploiting poor Americans; some at regulatory arbitrage; some at new forms of market deception. In each of these cases, there were marked discrepancies between social and private returns. Whenever there are such discrepancies, not only will markets not be efficient, innovation will not be directed at enhancing societal welfare.

The one part of the agenda that seemed to have some rationale was called 'completing the market.' Since the earlier work of Arrow and Debreu, one of the widely recognised market failures was the absence of key risk markets. The notion was that the new products enabled individuals to manage risks better. Ironically, they were typically priced by using 'spanning' theorems—the new products were viewed as a linear combination of existing products, or at least near enough so to be able to base prices on these related products. In this view, the real advantage of the new products was the lower transactions cost. But as those in the financial sector heralded these benefits, total transactions costs soared—to the point that just profits in the financial sector amounted to 40 per cent of all corporate profits.

But there is a basic result called the theory of the second best, which says that when there are many market distortions, eliminating one of them may actually make matters worse. In the presence of imperfect risk markets, for instance, removing trade barriers may make everyone in both countries worse off (Newbery and Stiglitz, 1984). In the presence of imperfect risk markets, capital market liberalisation may increase volatility in consumption and make the economy worse off (Stiglitz, 2008).

In this case, matters may be even worse. When individuals have different assessments of risk (the probability of a given event), they can through buying and selling derivatives create pseudo-wealth—both parties believe that they will win the bet, and hence both believe that they are well off. In reality, of course, this is just a zero sum game, and next period, one will be proven right, the other wrong. But at that point, there can be large destruction of this pseudo-wealth, with severe macroeconomic consequences. Of course, if only two individuals engaged in such bets, the macroeconomic consequences would be negligible. But when they are engaged in by large numbers, there can be severe consequences.

This provides a still further reason for restricting derivatives—or at the very least, making sure that they are not facilitated and subsidised, implicitly or explicitly, by government policy.

Unfortunately, not only do we encourage the derivatives through allowing them to be sold by government-insured institutions, we implicitly encourage them through bankruptcy laws that give them priority in bankruptcy.

It is imperative for government to try to correct discrepancies between social returns and private rewards because in the presence of such distortions, not only will markets be inefficient, but innovation will be misdirected.

Legal frameworks—corporate governance laws, competition laws, bankruptcy laws, financial sector regulations—provide the rules of the game, affect the distribution of income and the relationship between social and private returns, and can be thought of as providing (implicitly) the basis of industrial policy, encouraging some sectors at the expense of others. The legal framework in some countries, such as the US, has resulted in a distorted and bloated financial sector. For example, among the reforms needed in our bankruptcy law are the following:

Bankruptcy law should treat derivatives junior to workers and senior creditors. Bankruptcy law should be used to encourage transparency: any derivative not registered would be junior to all other claimants; and losses on derivatives that are not fully disclosed would not be tax deductible.

The Shadow Banking System

Prior to the crisis, many thought that the shadow banking system did not pose systemic risk. An investment bank that failed would (some believed) have no systemic consequences. We now know that that is not true. Even a large insurance company can pose systemic risk.

Much of the shadow banking system arose to circumvent regulations imposed on commercial banks. And much of the theory providing justification for the shadow banking system has been put into question by the crisis. For instance, while the benefits of risk diversification through securitisation are well recognised, the crisis has exposed the downside to securitisation.

One of the arguments for institution- (bank-) based lending is the internalisation of information externalities. Securitisation offered advantages in risk diversification, but these advantages were more than offset by the attenuation of the quality of information. A great deal of attention has been focused recently on the failures of the rating agencies; but the problems associated with the inadequacy of incentives for gathering good information are partially inherent and have long been recognised: if markets perfectly conveyed information (as the advocates of informationally efficient markets claimed), then there would be no incentives to gather information (Grossman, *et al.*, 1976; Grossman and Stiglitz, 1980). Earlier, we noted that private decisions with respect to sharing and transferring risk are not, in general, socially optimal. Even worse, the way private markets balance risk and information efficiency is not, in general, optimal. Systems that disperse risk inherently weaken 'accountability' and incentives not just for gathering information, but for ensuring the 'quality' of the financial products being produced.

If diversification leads to an attenuation of incentives for obtaining good information (Calvo and Mendoza, 2000), it can lead not only to poorer overall performance, but more instability. Hence, the trade-off is markedly different than has traditionally been envisaged in the securitisation literature, where it was presumed that securitisation would lead to enhanced systemic stability. Different policy frameworks (rules of the game) can lead to different financial architectures; and different financial architectures balance the trade-offs differently, some better than others, some enhancing the ability to absorb small risks, but making the economy more prone to systemic risk in the event of a large shock, or a set of correlated smaller shocks.

The shadow banking system has to be tightly regulated, e.g., with tight leverage (capital and liquidity) requirements—and because wholesale deposits may be even more fickle that consumer deposits in commercial banks, the requirements may even have to be higher. Originators of securities have to have 'skin-in-the game,' i.e., they have to retain at least a 10 per cent stake in the security.

There need to be deep reforms in the credit rating agencies. The quasi-public role (delegating responsibility in ascertaining which securities are safe enough to be held by a pension fund) needs to be reexamined. There needs to be standardisation of the ratings. There needs to be a rating of the rating agencies performance. They need to be held more accountable. (Litigation in Australia where the credit rating agencies were found culpable is a beginning in doing so.)

The Centrality of Banks and the Necessity of Central Banks Using a Full Range of Instruments

Banks, and their failures, were central to the crisis of 2008. But curiously, banks play little role in standard macroeconomics models, in which the financial sector is often summarised in a money demand-and-supply equation. These models typically didn't model the banking sector carefully—or at all. Such a reduced-form approach may suffice in normal times, but not now, or in other times of crisis, such as the East Asia crisis.[8]

The importance of banking (including the shadow banking system), as opposed to the provision of credit through markets, is rooted in information economics. In particular, they are the repository of institutional knowledge (information) that is not easily transferred, and the internalisation of information externalities provides better incentives for the acquisition of information, but, as we have noted, at the cost of a lack of direct diversification of risk.[9]

It should now be clear why an analysis of banking has to be central in any macroeconomic analysis: A key channel through which monetary policy affects the economy is the availability of credit and the terms at which it is available. It is the lending rate that firms can borrow at that they care about—not the interest rate at which the government can borrow. The spread between the two can and does vary greatly; banks are central to the setting

8. The irony is that many of the proponents of these models made a great fuss over the fact that they were structural, i.e. deriving savings behaviour from intertemporal utility maximising bhaviour.

9. Though shareholder risk diversification can still occur. The fact that this is so raises questions even about the validity of the risk arguent for diversification through securitisation.

of the lending rates at which small and medium sized enterprises can borrow. Government policy can affect the spread through both conventional monetary instruments and a variety of regulatory policies, and monetary authorities need to be sensitive to the various market forces which might affect the spread, so that they could take offsetting actions.

If we are to understand the impact of monetary policy, we must better understand how what central banks do (either in conventional open market operations, reserve requirements, interest provided on reserves, or regulatory requirements) affects the behaviour of banks and the shadow banking system. This is especially so because banks are still the locus of most SME borrowing, and because variability in SME investment and employment is central to understanding macroeconomic variability.

Greenwald and Stiglitz (2003) provide a beginning of a research programme of creating macroeconomic models where banks play a central role and are explicitly modelled. Credit availability too plays a central role—rightly so, because credit markets are often characterised by credit rationing. If there were no credit rationing, there would be no liquidity crises.

Already, though, there are clear policy prescriptions both about policies aimed at macro-stability (preventing crises) and in restoring the economy after an economic crisis—prescriptions that may differ markedly from those arising out of the standard conventional (DSGE) models.

Quantities (credit availability) and liquidity can be as, or more important, than interest rates.

The interest rate that matters is the lending rate, not the T. bill rate, and this should be the focus of attention.

Credit availability and the terms at which banks lend money is affected by the T-bill rate (which in turn is affected by open market operations) but also by a host of regulatory measures, such as capital requirements. These regulatory instruments have first order macroeconomic consequences and should be treated as macroeconomic instruments. In some cases, they can be far more effective. Increasing margin and down payment requirements would have been far more effective in curbing the tech and housing bubbles than just adjusting interest rates.

Changes in technology and market structure and some regulations can affect the effectiveness of other instruments. In particular, the elimination of regulation Q has meant that changes in T-bill rates have a smaller wealth-effect on banks, so that much of the effect of conventional monetary policy is through substitution effects, which typically are far weaker.

Most importantly, central banks need to use all of the instruments at their disposal. The artificially self-imposed constraint adopted by many central bankers influenced by neo-liberal doctrines—that central bankers should limit themselves to adjusting short term interest rates—has been costly. It was predicated on the false notions that markets were always efficient, and therefore central banks should minimise their interventions. But all central banks intervene—that is why they were created. And there is no theorem that says that optimal intervention should be limited to short term rate setting. Indeed, in other contexts, such as tax policy, we know that optimal intervention (taxation) involves imposing a multiplicity of interventions (taxes)—it is better to have a large number of small interventions than one large intervention (Ramsey, 1927).

The crisis has forced many central banks to rethink their doctrinaire policies. Even the Fed has become more active in the use of alternative instruments. I should say a few words later about one such instrument, quantitative easing.

Broader Objectives—Beyond Inflation—As Well As More Instruments

In the aftermath of the crisis, it is evident that the single-minded focus of some central banks on inflation was misplaced. The losses in welfare from low to moderate inflation were of orders of magnitude smaller than the losses from the financial collapse. But the underlying hypothesis, held by many central bankers, that keeping inflation low was necessary, and almost sufficient, for stable and strong growth has been shown to be wrong—and was never really justified by sound economic models. By diverting attention from what was really important, inflation targetting may accordingly not only have failed to enhance macro-stability, it may actually have contributed to instability. (Of course, high levels of inflation are a problem, but they are often symptomatic of other more general problems in the economy.)

The period immediately before the crisis showed another aspect of the destabilising effects of inflation targeting: developing countries exposed to an adverse supply shock which results in 'imported' inflation increased interest rates, slowing the economy down even more, and imposing even greater costs on workers already suffering from high food and energy prices. The only way that the increased interest rate would have had a significant effect on inflation was by imposing such stress on the non-traded sector and on wages that prices of non-traded goods and labour declined enough to offset the rising international prices. But then the cure would have been worse than the disease.

The more general point is that the response to any shock to the economy should depend on the nature of the shock. If it is, for instance, a demand shock, then it may be appropriate to curb demand through interest rate policy.

This and the preceding point illustrate another more general one: for years, Tinbergen's approach to policy has been extremely influential. If the number of instruments equals the number of objectives, it has been argued that one should 'match' instruments with objectives, and different institutions should be assigned an instrument and a target for which they are responsible. The central bank should be responsible for inflation, using its instrument of choice, the interest rate. Tinbergen focused on controllability, but this system has been argued for on the basis of accountability: there is a simple metric (the level of inflation), in this view, by which central bank performance can be judged.

But Tinbergen's analysis was conducted in a highly stylised linear model, in which with n instruments one could control n objectives. In a complex non-linear system with risk—including instrument uncertainty[10]—and where one is concerned not just with the ultimate equilibrium (which in practice may never be attained) but with real-time performance—one should use all the instruments at one's disposal, and coordination among policy makers is essential. There are no general theorems on decentralisation—to the contrary, what theorems we have relate to the dangers of decentralisation.

In practice, this means that monetary and fiscal policy needs to be coordinated, and it makes no sense for the body controlling one of these to be allegedly independent, while the one responsible for the other is politically accountable, a point to which I shall return shortly.

Central banks should broaden their objectives beyond inflation. They need to focus too on employment, growth and financial stability. And monetary policies need to be coordinated with fiscal policies.

The Complex Effects of Monetary Policy: Asymmetries, Irreversibilities, Sectoral Effects, Distributional Effects

Monetary authorities need to be especially sensitive to asymmetries in 'controllability' and the costs associated with the conduct of monetary policy. While monetary policy may be an effective instrument in constraining output, it may be far less effective in stimulating the economy in a deep downturn. This, in turn, implies asymmetries in the conduct of monetary policy. There is always going to be uncertainty, for instance in judging the level of employment or growth at which inflation starts to increase or in Judging whether there is a bubble. But a slight restraint on the economy in dampening a potential bubble has a miniscule cost relative to the costs imposing by the breaking of a bubble.

This is an example where there are long-term, hard-to-reverse effects of mistakes. There are other examples: prolonged high unemployment gives rise to hysteresis effects, as skills atrophy.

10. That is, one cannot be sure about the consequences of any action. See, e.g. Greenwald and Stiglitz (1989).

So too, advocates of monetary policy as a control instrument (over fiscal policy) stress its flexibility, the ability to fine tune policies as new information comes in. But they fail to note that some parts of the economy are more interest-sensitive than others, and some parts are more sensitive to the availability of bank credit than others. Hence loosening and tightening of credit induces more volatility in some sectors than others, and because of imperfections in risk markets, this imposes significant costs on these sectors. In a sense, the way monetary policy is conducted distorts the economy.

At the same time, the way monetary policy is conducted can have significant distributional effects. While it is often asserted that inflation is the cruelest tax, in advanced countries at least we have protected the poor against much of the consequences, since social security and other programmes are often indexed to inflation. With competitive labour markets, wages tend to rise with inflation, and so even workers are protected. (Sometimes it seems that this is not the case, but that is because the shocks to the economy that set off inflationary episodes often are shocks that affect labour productivity; we confuse correlation with causation.) Inflation has redistributive effects—against holders of long term bonds. But fighting inflation by raising interest rates and increasing unemployment also has distributive effects—not only is the cost of the higher unemployment borne directly by workers, but workers suffer doubly as the higher unemployment exerts downward pressure on wages, and triply, as lower GDP leads to lower tax revenues and cutbacks of public programmes aimed at the bottom and middle.

Not only have monetary authorities often failed to note the significant distributive effects of their policies, the models on which they rely have not given them the prominence that they should. Even if one did not put much weight on inequality, inequality can have large macroeconomic effects. My own work (summarised in my recent book *The Price of Inequality*) highlights this (Stiglitz, 2012; 2011). So too did the International Commission of Experts appointed by the President of the UN General Assembly examining the causes of the 2008 crisis.[11] And so too has the IMF, which has noted the systematic relationship between inequality and instability (Berg and Ostry, 2011).

While I can't in this brief paper go into all the channels through which this occurs, let me note one that was evident in the run up to this crisis. As incomes of most Americans stagnated and declined, they incurred greater indebtedness as they strived to maintain their standards of livings and to keep up with those at the top who were doing so well. Had monetary authorities not offset the effects of growing inequality (because the marginal propensity to consume of those at the top is so much lower at the top than at the bottom and middle, as income shifts from the middle and bottom to the top total consumption demand is lowered) by lowering interest rates and relaxing regulations, thereby helping create a housing bubble, aggregate demand would have been lowered, and unemployment would have increased. But such actions provided only a temporary palliative. The temporising was sowing the seeds of destruction: it was simply a matter of time before the bubble which sustained the economy, offsetting the effects of the growing inequality, broke. But the period of recovery, during which actual output remains substantially below potential output, may be longer and the costs far greater than the benefits and duration of the bubble. And this is especially so when the underlying problem is not addressed; for the downturn itself gives rise to adverse distributional effects which weaken the economy further.

Monetary authorities need to be more sensitive to the distributive and sectoral consequences of their policies, and to the fact that some mistakes—letting bubbles grow, or allowing unemployment to rise in an excessive zeal for fighting inflation—have long term consequences which are hard to correct.

Limited Effectiveness of Monetary Policy and the Channels of Monetary Policy: Exploiting Market Imperfections

This discussion has highlighted one of the lacuna in the models used by many monetary authorities—the lack of attention to

11. Available as *The Siglitz Report: Reforming the International Monetary and Financial Systems in the Wake of the Global Crisis*, op.cit.

distribution. Earlier remarks highlighted other lacuna—the lack of attention to banks and the details of the financial system more broadly. But these are not just mistakes of modelling, about which I have written more extensively elsewhere (Stiglitz, 2011a; 2010), but they lead to misguided views about the channels through which monetary policy affects the economy, and indeed, the very reasons that monetary policy affects the economy. And without understanding these channels, one can't understand why sometimes monetary policy is less effective than at other times, nor can we design policies to maintain stability or restore the economy to full employment.

The effectiveness of monetary policy hinges critically on certain market imperfections.[12]

Some years ago, I proved a generalisation of the Modigliani-Miller (MM) theorem, which had shown the irrelevance of corporate financial policies, for the public sector.[13] I showed that, under the idealised conditions under which the MM theorem held, public financial operations, such as a change in the maturity structure of government debt, should have no effect. (The result could also be thought of as a generalisation of the Barro-Ricardo theorem, suggesting that government debt itself had no effect.) In a simple model with infinitely lived individuals, putting aside any distributive effects, we owe money to ourselves, so government debt is simultaneously a liability and an asset. That that is so provides an important critique to those excessively worried about government debt, at least when it is internally held (it's another matter when the debt is held by foreigners, because then the debt amounts to a diminution in the country's 'net worth.')

The intuition, of course, is simple, and it is the same that underlies the Barro-Ricardo analysis (in its general equilibrium form): if the government borrows more now (say, instead of paying

12. This section of my lecture is adapted from my paper, "Monetary Policy in a Multi-PolarWorld," presented to an *IEA Roundtable on Capital Flows* at Izmir, Turkey on November 1-2, 2012

13. That work itself was based on my generalisation of the MM theorem (Stiglitz, 1969) , work which itself, together with (Stiglitiz, 1982), explained the limitations on the theorem . For instance, in Stiglitz (1974), I showed the irrelevance of corporate financial policies in a general equilibrium model, under much more general conditions than those that Modigliani and Miller had established the result. I subsequently extended these results to the public sector in Stiglitz (1981; 1983; 1988)

for current expenses by raising taxes), to be repaid at some later date, the effect can and will (in general equilibrium) be precisely offset by the representative consumer saving more, and using the funds to repay the government debt later. But in the general equilibrium formulation, there can be multiple heterogeneous individuals, and the result holds, assuming, of course, that those who would have paid the taxes now pay the 'equivalent' amount later, i.e., that there are no distributive consequences to the postponement of the taxes. And the same holds if the government decides to raise more funds by a sequence of short-term borrowings, rather than by long-term debt.

The empirical evidence is overwhelming that the Barro-Ricardo theorem, and my generalisation of it, are wrong.[14] The question is not the validity of the proposition, but why it fails. And what insights does this provide us into capital markets and the workings of monetary policy?

Distributive effects, capital constraints, and seeing through the public veil

It should be obvious, as we have already noted, that it is hard to avoid distributive effects and political economy considerations (the absence of which are essential to the validity of the Barro-Ricardo result). In the limiting case, with an overlapping generations model, the decision to postpone financing for current expenditures through taxes has potentially important intergenerational effects. To be sure, there may be partially offset through changes in intergenerational transfers, but the fact is that most individuals do not leave any significant bequests to their children,[15] in which case there can't and won't be such offsetting bequests.

---

14. See for example, Johnson *et al.* (2006). Anecdotally, when Bush cut taxes dramatically in 2001 and 2003 the average savings rate fell to near zero—it did not increase as the Barro-Ricardo analysis would have suggested. Of course, there were many other things going on, and defenders of the theory might argue that were it not for the tax cut, savings would have been even lower, i.e. minus 2 or 3 per cent of GDP. But with credit constraints already binding for so many individuals—and with the bottom 80 per cent of America already consuming 110 per cent of their income—it is hard to believe that in the absence of the tax cuts, the savings rate would have been that low.

15. In fact, most individuals have almost no wealth--and hence no bequests of significance. See, for example, Wolff and Gittleman (2011), who find that between "1989 to 2007, 21 per cent of American households at a given point of time received a wealth transfer and these accounted for 23 per cent of their net worth."

A variety of capital market imperfections provide the basis of the strongest theoretical critique. If, for instance, individuals would have want to have borrowed more, but are constrained from doing so, the existence of an incremental future liability will not induce them to start saving. The borrowing constraint will simply be less binding than it was before. By the same token, were the government to decide to tax more and borrow less, the individual facing a borrowing constraint won't be able to offset the effect through increased borrowing.

In reality, most individuals do not fully incorporate future tax liabilities into their budget constraints—and even less so, do they incorporate the 'risk pattern", so that changes in the risk pattern, as a result of a change in say the maturity structure of debt (or a shift from unindexed debt to indexed debt) are not offset by corresponding changes in their portfolios. (As another example: as the Fed bought long term bonds, there was the obvious risk that should it reverse the purchases as the economy recovers, there would be a capital loss.[16] The expectation of such a capital loss, with full integration of the public and private budget constraints, should have had a contractionary effect on consumption, offsetting the intended expansionary effect. The Fed suggested it might hold the bonds to maturity, using other ways of tightening credit, e.g., by paying interest on deposits at the Federal Reserve, in effect enabling it never to realise the capital losses. But these only mask the reality that (the present discounted value of) government revenues are less than they otherwise would have been; they don't change the predicted adverse effect on consumption, assuming full integration of public and private budget constraints and full rationality.[17])

16. The general point that it is hard to explain why temporary interventions (such as associated with IMF short term loans to a country) should have long term effects in models with rational expectations was made in Stiglitz (1999).

17. The irony is that government insists that banks use mark to market accounting, but the central bank doesn't do so for itself.

Monetary Policy in a World of Interest Bearing Money

It is clear that the idealised world of Modigliani-Miller provides an inadequate description of the economy.[18] There is a widespread assumption that monetary policy has some effects.

But modern monetary theory lives in a half-way house of incompletely articulated assumptions of imprecisely defined market imperfections and distributive effects, leading to speculative observations about possible channels through which monetary policy might yield effects, with ambiguous quantitative significance.

Today, for instance, with cash management accounts, T-bills can, in effect, be used as money for purposes of transactions. In the standard model in which interest rates are determined by the demand and supply for money, an open market operation entailing an exchange of T-bills for, say, 'money', doesn't change the effective supply of money, since T-bills themselves can be used for transactions, and so such an exchange (open market operations) shouldn't have any effect on interest rates. And this is especially so in a world in which T-bills are yielding close to zero nominal interest rates.

Institutional Constraints, Credit Availability, Profit Maximising Risk-averse Firms and the Liquidity Trap

But it is possible in a world of banks with institutional rigidities that such open market operations could have an effect. For an increase in deposits held by the banking system in the Federal Reserve ('base money') can, through the credit multiplier, lead to increased lending. I say, can, not necessarily will. For banks are (for the most part) profit maximising risk averse firms,[19] and they may decide the best way to allocate their portfolios is not to issue

---

18. My own earlier work on asymmetric information and stressing the importance of bankruptcy provided part of the critique. Higher debt ratios may entail higher (expected) losses from bankruptcy and may have signaling/screening effects. (Stiglitz, 1969; 1982, *op.cit* . But these 'limitations' are not relevant, at least for countries like the United States, where there is essentially no risk of soverign default.

19. I should be more cautious: given the agency issues that were revealed so vividly in the crisis, they might be better described as managerial enterprises, maximising the well-being of the managers, subject to certain constraints on the access to credit. In either case, we have to describe the behavioural responses to a change in, say, base money or T-bill interest rates.

new loans to, say, SME's, but to buy government bonds from the household sector or from abroad, or simply to hold the excess liquidity at the Fed. This can give rise to a liquidity trap, though one that is distinctly different from that discussed by Keynes (where it arises because the demand function for money becomes infinitely elastic at low interest rates) and some more recent commentators focusing on the zero lower bound on the interest rate.

We have already referred to one reason that today, monetary policy may be much less effective than in the past: with the abolition of Regulation Q, restricting competition in the setting of deposit rates, the wealth-effects of monetary policy are largely eliminated, implying that monetary policy exerts its effects through much weaker substitution effects.

But in deep downturns, there are two further reasons for the inefficacy of monetary policy: the interest insensitivity of investment (and consumption) and the blocking of credit channels, so that the impact of monetary policy on the flow of credit is diminished.

The distinction between the situation confronting Keynes in the Great Depression and that of today is important: Keynes was confronting a situation where prices were falling at 10 per cent a year, so real interest rates remained in excess of 10 per cent, so it was plausible that the inability to lower real interest rates represented a constraint on the ability of monetary authorities to ignite the economy. Today, however, there is moderate inflation, of say 2 per cent, so that real (T-bill) interest rates are negative. To be sure, at a sufficiently negative real interest rate, individuals might be spurred to consume more and firms to invest more, but within reasonable ranges, further lowering (expected) real T-bill interest rates, to say -4 per cent—even were that feasible— is unlikely to spur much further investment or consumption.

There are some obvious reasons for this interest inelasticity: with firms sitting on excess capacity, even large changes in interest rates are not likely to induce much more investment. Why would firms acquire even more excess capacity, just because the interest rate is lowered? Moreover, as Greenwald and I have explained in our earlier work (Greenwald and Stiglitz, 1993; 2003) because of information imperfections, capital markets are imperfect; and because of capital market imperfections, firms act in a risk averse manner. In deep downturns, firms are likely to be particularly risk averse, and so particular unresponsive to even moderate changes in interest rates.

Today, large firms are sitting on some $2 trillion dollars of cash. It is hard to believe that small changes in T-bill rates are going to result in large changes in their willingness to convert those cash holdings into real investments.

For many smaller businesses, however, the real constraint is the lack of availability of credit (a problem that simply cannot be analysed in a model with perfect capital markets). For these firms, credit availability is far more important than interest rates. Providing more liquidity to banks does not necessarily lead either to more lending or to lower lending rates (Greenwald and Stiglitz, 2003).

The Ineffectiveness of Temporary Interventions: QE as an Example

One of the arguments often put forward in favour of monetary policy is its flexibility—the ability to change interest rates quickly up and down. But while that is undoubtedly an advantage (over the much slower process of adjustments of tax rates or government expenditures—though not of well-designed automatic stabilisers built into sound fiscal and financial frameworks), there has been a long standing theoretical conundrum: why should policy measures that are seen to be (and often announced to be) temporary have much of an effect?[20]

Consider, for instance, the temporary intervention of quantitative easing—buying long term bonds now, under the presumption that the economy will recover in say a couple of years, in which case the action will be reversed. Apart from slight

20. Temporary interventions can have long term effects if (a) they move the economy from one equilibrium to another, in a model in which there are multiple equilibria; (b) there are large substitution effects, so that, for instance, investment that might have occurred in a later period occurs earlier; or (c) it can generate large 'permanent' income effects, with longer last effects on the evolution of the economy. Many of the interventions associated with monetary policy have none of these characteristics. See, for instance, Stiglitz (1998).

changes in endowments (increases in the levels of state variables like human and financial capital) that might have been induced by the temporary intervention, at the later date, asset prices will be the same as they would have been before the intervention. Knowing this, it is hard to see why there should be large changes in asset prices (share prices) today. With lifetime budget constraints essentially unchanged, it is hard to see why there should be any significant changes in consumption during the period of the temporary interventions, even if there should be some changes in asset prices during that period.

Moreover, as we noted earlier, the capital gain on long term government bonds that individuals might enjoy today as long term interest rates fall will be offset either by a capital loss on their holdings when the intervention is reversed and/or by the capital loss that the government will realise when it sells back the long term bonds back to the public at a time when long term interest rates are lower. If public and private life-time budget constraints are largely integrated, then these effects are offsetting, and it is hard to believe that there will be large effects on aggregate demand.

Market Imperfections and Why QE may have Some Effects

Of course, in models with less than perfect rationality, high degrees of risk aversion, and significant capital market imperfections, such temporary interventions can have some effects.

The financial press continually describes the response to low interest rates as leading to a 'drive for yield.' There is, of course, no general theory that would suggest that as yields go down, individuals act in a less risk-averse manner; quite the contrary, the adverse wealth effects might more plausibly lead to more risk-averse behaviour. But such behaviour, if widespread, could in turn lead to an increase in the price of stocks—even if 'rationally' the forces leading to this increase (above what the prices would otherwise be) are just temporary. The standard wisdom from the advocates of QE are that the higher stock prices will lead to more consumption. We have questioned, though, whether that is so, if they rationally expect the intervention to be temporary.

But there is a more fundamental problem: if the reason for the increase in stock prices is the 'drive for yield,' then it reflects a worsening of the life-time budget constraint as a result of lower interest rates, and net, that should have ambiguous effects on consumption, with wealth and substitution effects operating in opposite directions.

But there is another set of effects that may be operating that may also imply that QE can have an adverse effect on consumption (and aggregate demand). The standard model ignores the effects of distribution, including across generations. Those that go into retirement at, say, t, and had been planning to sell their assets, will, if QE results in an increase in stock or bond prices, now receive more from them that they otherwise would have received, and this group may consume more than they otherwise would have.[21]

But once we start focusing on distributive effects, we need to take into account other effects associated with the lowering of interest rates: those prudent older people who had invested in say government bonds will find their incomes lowered as interest rates are reduced, and for many of these, a lowering of income translates quickly into a lowering of consumption. Their consumption is cash-constrained, and their cash flows will be diminished.

There are many other potentially significant effects that are typically ruled out in the 'standard' model: lower interest rates lead to more capital intensive technologies, laying the seeds for a 'jobless' recovery; lower interest rates can lead to asset price booms, increasing the prices of oil and other commodities which act much like a tax on consumers.

Market Imperfections and the Ineffectiveness of QE

While capital market imperfections help explain why monetary interventions like QE might have larger effects than one would have expected in a 'perfect markets' model, capital market imperfections also help explain why QE may have less of an effect than expected. (The most important reason for the limited effect of QE in the US is

---

21. But those among the elderly who expect to live long will obtain lower yields as they re-invest the proceeds, and this will largely cancel out these benefits.

globalisation of financial markets, and that is discussed in the next part of this paper.)

As we noted earlier, what matters for aggregate demand is the availability of credit and short and long term lending rates, and even with quantitative easing, credit availability and the spread between T-bill rate or other rates set by the Fed and the lending rate are endogenous variables. In deep downturns, changes in conventional monetary policies may have limited effects, especially if the monetary authorities have not done what they should have done to ensure the health of the institutions responsible for the flow of credit.

One of the hoped for effects was that lower long term interest rates would lead to lower mortgage rates, which in turn would lead to large numbers of Americans refinancing their mortgages, and the lower interest rates would effectively put cash in the pockets of households, leading to more consumption.

Note that underlying this analysis are implicit assumptions about distributive effects of interest rate changes. Lower interest payments by households corresponds to lower receipts of interest by lenders. In representative agent models, the effect would be a wash. More realistically, given large differences in the marginal propensities to consume of creditors and debtors, the redistribution from creditor to debtor should increase consumption (as the advocates of QE hoped. In the presence of capital constraints (limiting borrowing by households), the effect is even stronger.

However, in more general models focusing on capital and institutional constraints, the effects are more complex and ambiguous. For instance, in the presence of institutional constraints on banks, lower revenues/profits for the banks translates into less lending, an effect which could be stronger than that generated by differences in marginal propensities to consume.

The many and growing imperfections in the mortgage market help explain the ineffectiveness of monetary policy, including quantitative easing. There has been increasing concentration[22]—to the point where no one would describe the market as a competitive one. Without precisely specifying the appropriate model of tacit collusion or oligopoly, it is certainly conceivable that the banks would not pass on to consumers the full benefits of the lower long term government rates; they would limit the supply of mortgages so much as to increase their spread, their profit margins. And this is precisely what has happened. (This is especially the case because of the multiplicity of conflicts of interests that have been creating under existing institutional arrangements. The banks also derive large revenues as 'service providers,' from servicing existing mortgages, and the contracts as service providers also provide them with incentives not to refinance.) The result is that the consumer benefits (and thus the increase in aggregate demand through that channel) have been less than had been touted. Critics suggest that, like so many of the Fed's programmes, the real beneficiaries are the banks, especially the large banks that control the lion's share of the mortgage market. If that is the case, the short run benefit to the economy, at least through this channel, will be limited.

Another market imperfection may have reduced the benefits derived from QEIII even more. Mortgages that could easily be refinanced have already been refinanced; borrowers who have not have either insufficient income or are 'underwater.' The mortgage could be refinanced only if there were a principal write down. In a standard model with rationality, it would pay both lenders and borrowers to engage in debt restructuring. Foreclosures are expensive for everyone involved, including the communities in which they occur. There is enormous dead weight loss. But principal write downs entail a recognition of losses faster than would otherwise be the case, especially since the change in accounting regulations in 2009 that allowed even impaired mortgages not to be written down.

---

22. William C. Dudley (2012), President of the Federal Reserve Bank of New York, noted in a recent speech, "Federal Reserve MBS purchases have succeeded in driving down mortgage rates to historically low levels. But these purchases would have had still more effect on the economy if pass-through rates from the secondary market to the primary market had been higher [...]The incomplete pass-through from agency MBS yields into primary mortgage rates is due to several factors—including a concentration of mortgage origination volumes at a few key financial institutions and mortgage rep and warranty requirements that discourage lending for home purchases and make financial institutions reluctant to refinance mortgages that have been originated elsewhere."

That would make the seeming profits in the short run lower, even if it would make long run profits higher. But agency problems pervade the banking system, and bank management has incentives to focus on the short run. Moreover, some banks may face high costs in raising funds (a natural capital market constraint, arising in part from the high level of non-transparency of the banks.)[23]

In short, the level of refinancing may be far smaller than would be the case if financial markets were perfect, but analysing the extent to which there will be refinancing, and the impact on banks and aggregate demand, entails a complex analysis of institutional constraints and imperfections.[24] Monetary policy ignores these at its peril.

Balancing

Here, I do not wish to argue for the quantitative importance of any of the effects that I have described. What I do contend is that once one moves away from the 'perfect markets' model, or the 'almost perfect markets model' in which we know that monetary policy should have no (or negligible) effects, we have to be careful in thinking through the source of 'imperfections' and their consequences.

Too much reasoning on the impacts of monetary policy interventions has been based on an almost incoherent pastiche of analyses based on 'rationality,' 'rational expectations,' and 'well functioning markets' overlaying a variety of forms of imprecisely specified and explained market imperfections. I've alluded to some examples already: while there is ample discussion of markets

23. 34 Still further problems are posed by the conflicts of interest between the holders of the first and second mortgages. See Stiglitz, (2010a). Still further problems have resulted from the put-backs of flawed mortgages and the surrounding litigation: risk-averse banks now realise that there is more risk associated with the process of mortgage origination and securitisation than they had realised.

24. The list of imperfections in the mortgage market is not meant to be exhaustive. Institutional arrangements, for instance, make it difficult for lender A to refinance a mortgage held by lender B, and lender A often has little incentive to refinance the mortgage—it will simply lower his revenues. More broadly, the mortgage servicers have little incentive to facilitate mortgage restructurings. There is Congressional legislation under consideration as this paper goes to press attempting to deal with some aspects of these issues.

'discounting' future actions, temporary measures, it is still believed, can have significant effects.[25]

Some of the disappointments with QEII and QEIII would not have come as a surprise, if monetary authorities had grasped better the nature of market imperfections as they existed at the time of the implementation of these policies. Given the role that local (community) and regional banks play in the provision of credit to SME's, given the weaknesses that persist in these banks, given the role that collateral plays for such lending, given that real estate is the predominant form of collateral, and given that real estate prices remain persistently and markedly below the level before the crisis, it should be no surprise that QE would have limited effects on SME lending.

Given that large firms were sitting on large amounts of cash, it should be no surprise that QE might have little effect on lending to large firms and/or investment by these firms.

It is at least conceivable in a situation where there is excess capacity in industry and real estate and excess leverage in households, that the adverse effects of QE described earlier (including the adverse consumption effect among the elderly) could outweigh any inducement towards more investment or consumption among firms or households, and so lowering interest rates could have an adverse affect on aggregate demand.

The realisation that it is partly because of—and in some cases mainly because of—market imperfections that monetary policy has the effects it does (or does not have the effects it is supposed to have) complicates monetary policy in many ways.

It means that the simplistic notion, current in recent years, that all one needs to focus on is the real interest rate is simply wrong—even if one could figure out which real interest rate one should focus on.

---

25. They can, but typically only through substitution effects (a temporary investment tax credit or VAT tax), or through redistributive effects (e.g., the recapitalisations of the banking system, transferring, often in a non-transparent way, resources to the banks at the expense of others.)

It implies too that the current fad to suggest that the reason that monetary policy is ineffective today is the zero lower bound is misguided. We are not in a Keynesian liquidity trap.

It implies too that the effectiveness of monetary policy can be increased if monetary authorities work on increasing the effectiveness of the credit channel—strengthening the banks that are responsible, for instance, for SME lending and eliminating blockages in the mortgage market.

These insights help us understand why QEII and QEIII have not been effective—and are not likely to be.

Access to Credit

These experiences also highlight a point which is especially important in developing countries: lower T-bill rates do not necessarily translate into more access to credit. Access to credit for SME's is especially important for growth; and private financial systems, on their own, may not provide adequate access. (Emran and Stiglitz (2009) provide a partial explanation for why this is so: it is difficult to ascertain who will be good entrepreneurs, and repay their loans; those who prove themselves good get poached away by others. It is thus difficult for those providing capital to appropriate the full value of the information associated with their lending activities.)

Governments and central banks need to have explicit programmes to encourage lending to certain groups/sectors that are underserved.

This may entail partial government guarantees and direct government lending programmes and specialised institutions (like development banks) as well as regulatory interventions (like CRA lending requirements in the US and geographical requirements.)

It is important that such requirements be imposed not only on domestic institutions but also on foreign banks.

International Finance

Globalisation has changed the way that monetary policy operates, and its effectiveness. Capital and financial market liberalisation was supposed to help stabilise financial markets, but the evidence is to the contrary: it has brought new and higher levels of instability, without bringing the promised growth.

Even the IMF, long the champion of capital market liberalisation, has suggested that capital account interventions may be desirable (See, e.g., Ostry *et al.*, 2010).

These changes in view are not a surprise. Liberalisation/globalisation played a central role in the rapid movement of the 2008 crisis from the US around the world. The world of liberalisation has been one marked by far higher levels of volatility—and in the advanced countries far lower rates of growth—than the era before liberalisation. Closer studies of financial market liberalisation have shown that the flow of funds to SME's is often reduced, with consequent adverse effects on economic growth.

QEII too has heightened these concerns. In a world of globalisation, money goes where the returns are highest—and not necessarily to the country increasing liquidity. Thus, some argue that the major impact of the increased liquidity by the Fed has been to increase demand in emerging markets (and perhaps to support asset price increases globally); and in response to the overheating to which it has contributed in the emerging markets, the central banks there have tried to undo the effects of what they view as the US competitive devaluation and have constructed impediments to the free flow of capital. In effect, they have tried to offset, in their country, the expansionary effect of US Fed policy. In short, money has been going where it's not needed, and not going where it's needed. Why should an investor with access to funds invest them in the US or Europe, where there is excess capacity and a long term slump, rather than in the high return booming emerging markets? In the older, closed economy models, they had no choice: but in a globalised world with free capital markets, they do. From a global point of view, one needs to ask: of what value is there for the Fed to increase liquidity, which then moves to other parts of the world, and the Central Banks in these countries then take largely offsetting actions?

(One of the effects of that policy that may have increased US aggregate demand is a lowering of its exchange rate. But this attempt at competitive devaluation is a beggar-thy-neighbour policy, one to which emerging markets have rightly responded, suggesting that the US policy of quantitative easing has let loose a 'currency war.')

Advances in economic theory have helped us to understand what was wrong with earlier models, which assumed that risk diversification associated with liberalisation would obviously enhance stability and efficiency; and why the promised gains have not been materialised. The standard models made strong assumptions not only about perfect markets (including the absence of information imperfections and asymmetries) but also about the absence of non-convexities, so essentially by assumption, risk diversification worked. But as I showed in some recent papers, in the presence of such non-convexities, financial market integration may increase risk (Stiglitz, 2010a; 2010b). A host of papers have now shown that greater interlinkages (among financial institutions, across countries) may lead to a greater risk of systemic failure (See e.g., Battiston *et al.*, 2012; Gallegati *et al.*, 2008; Battiston *et al.*, 2012a; Haldane, 2009; Haldane and May, 2010).

Advances in economic theory have also highlighted some of the reasons that foreign banks are different from domestic banks: their risk profile is different, and they face greater asymmetries of information (e.g., about which small firms are likely to be good). Imperfections and asymmetries of information help also explain the high level of volatility associated with foreign capital flows (Greenwald and Stiglitz 2003).

There is now an emerging consensus among economists on several aspects of policy concerning cross border capital flows:

(a) Just as there is a need for financial sector regulation, there is a need for regulation of cross-border flows—countries should be cautious both about capital and financial market liberalisation.[26]

(b) Cross-border flows and foreign banks behave differently in important respects from domestic sources of funds and domestic banks, and therefore there is a need for a different regulatory regime. Of course, foreign financial institutions will oppose these regulations.

(c) Of particular concern is that many international agreements, signed in the hey-day of neoliberalism, restrict the ability of governments to impose adequate regulatory regimes, and these need to be changed.

(d) There is a need for closer cooperation among monetary authorities around the world, and

(e) Larger central banks, the Fed and ECB in particular, need to recognise that they can impose large externalities on other countries; by contrast, the externalities imposed by any small country are limited.

Institutional Design: The Failure of Independent Central Banks

Modern development economics has stressed the importance of good institutions (See for instance, World Bank, 2002). Before the crisis, American financial institutions and American regulatory institutions (including the Fed) were often held up as models for others to imitate. The crisis has not only undermined confidence in these institutions, but has also exposed deep institutional flaws. It has shown that one of the central principles advocated by Western central bankers—the desirability of central bank independence—was questionable at best. In the crisis, countries with less independent central banks—China India, and Brazil—did far, far better than countries with more independent central banks, Europe and the US. Elsewhere[27] I have provided part of the explanation. There is no

---

26. Reflective of this new trend, the IMF has recently supported the imposition of capital controls in certain instances, a major change in their stance, since 1997, when they tried to change their charter to give them a mandate to impose capital market liberalisation. See Ostry *et al.*, *op. cit.* For a discussion of that older debate, see Stiglitz (2002).

27. Stiglitz (2010a; 2010b).

such thing as truly independent institutions. All public institutions are accountable, and the only question is to whom. America's central bank was captured by Wall Street: it came to reflect the ideology and interests of the financial sector, which it was supposed to regulate. As we saw earlier in this paper, it glossed over central issues like externalities and agency problems, as it came to believe in self-regulation. The pervasive conflicts of interest—with the New York Fed President being at the centre of bailouts of the very banks that had played a role in his appointment—were a model of bad governance. The Fed had allowed the development of a financial structure that was rife with conflicts of interests, and had turned a blind eye to practices that not only exploited the poor, but put into jeopardy the American and global financial system.

The notion of the desirability of an independent central bank was predicated on the belief that monetary policy was a technocratic matter, with no distributional consequences. There was a single policy that was best for all—a view to which the simplistic models that the central banks employed may have contributed, but which was not supported by more general models. There does not, in general, exist a Pareto superior monetary policy.

That in turn implies that delegating the conduct of monetary policy and regulations to those who come from and reflect the interests of the financial market is going to result in policies that are not necessarily (and weren't) in society's broader interests.

Even if one wanted independence, one could have combined independence with broader representativeness—making sure that consumers who were hurt by banks' predatory and exploitive behaviour, merchants who were hurt by banks' anti-competitive behaviour, or workers who were hurt by higher levels of unemployment—had a greater voice in the conduct of monetary policy and regulation (Stiglitz, 1998).

The crisis has called into question the notion of independence on other grounds: monetary authorities have been engaged in quasi-fiscal operations, giving away tens of billions of dollars, in ways that are non-transparent, and often seem capricious. The Fed saved some banks, throwing tens of billions of dollars at them, but let other banks go. It saved some bondholders, but not others. The loans by the Fed and ECB to banks at low interest rates—which they could then use to buy higher yielding bonds—was, in effect, a gift worth tens of billions of dollars, a gift from the public, but which circumvented the usual public appropriations process. It is unconscionable that such power over the purse be given to a non-elected body.

Monetary authorities need to be held more accountable, especially when they are engaged in policies with strong distributive consequences and which are quasi-fiscal in nature. Monetary institutions need to be designed to ensure that they are more reflective of societal interests.

Concluding Comments

Some years ago, in joint work with my colleague Bruce Greenwald, we provided a critique of traditional models in which the effects of monetary policy are mediated just through interest rates, and interest rates reflect the balancing of the demand and supply of money. We pointed out that with most 'money' being interest bearing, the traditional view that the interest rate is the opportunity cost of holding money is just wrong; furthermore, most transactions are not income generating, but rather the exchange of assets, so even if money were required for transactions, there would still be no simple and stable relationship between money and the level of economic activity (since the ratio of asset transactions to income can be highly variable.) Further, most transactions do not require money; credit is typically an effective substitute, and when it is not, one needs to explain why not.

Over the past 30 years, macroeconomics has made a valiant struggle to place itself on firm micro-foundations, but it chose the wrong micro-foundations—that based on the perfects markets models that were just then becoming discredited, as the economcs profession gained deeper insights into the related effects of transactions costs, imperfections of competition, absence of risk markets, and imperfections and asymmetries of information. Most disappointing, the standard models for the most part didn't even provide structural foundations for the financial sector. (And when they attempted to do so, it was as a result of peculiar and unconvincing assumptions. For instance, cash-in-advance models simply assume that credit is not an effective substitute for cash.)

In the 1930s there was an active debate between two approaches to the determination of the interest rate, the Keynesian approach, based on the demand for money used for transactions purposes, and that of Robertson (1951), based on the demand and supply of loanable funds. In some ways, our approach represents a further development of the work of Robertson, with two important changes.

First, in his model, the supply of loanable funds was based just on savings. In ours, there is a critical role for banks, who make assessments of the credit worthiness of potential borrowers. Imperfect and asymmetric information is central. (Such information tends to be local and specialised; foreign lenders (suppliers) of funds have different information than domestic lenders, so that their allocation of funds is markedly different. This is one of the reasons that there is a need for special regulation of cross-border capital flows and foreign banks.)

Secondly, in both Keynes and Robertson, demand always equals supply; yet in models with imperfect and asymmetric information, there can exist rationing equilibrium. Indeed, such equilibria are pervasive.

Thus, traditional models (of both the Keynesian and Robertsonian version) have little to say about the determination either of credit availability or of the spread, the difference between the T-bill rate and the lending rate. If there is a difference, it only reflects a difference in (objectively determined) risk. With risk neutral lenders, the expected payments are the same. In the absence of a theory of credit rationing, it is hard to explain a liquidity crisis—and without a theory of liquidity (credit availability) it is hard to know how to respond to a liquidity crisis.

In the Greenwald-Stiglitz models, monetary policy is largely mediated through the banking system. The lowering of interest rates may (or may not) be reflected in a commensurate lowering of lending rates or a commensurate increase in credit availability. Indeed, there is a new version of a liquidity trap—not caused (as Keynes suggested) by a high elasticity of the demand for money, but by a low responsiveness of bank lending, even as the central bank provides the banking sector with more liquidity. This is precisely what has been happening in the US and Europe; and the theory developed by Greenwald and Stiglitz anticipated and predicted this kind of liquidity trap well before it became evidenced in the aftermath of this crisis.

Keynesian models of monetary economics came into fashion in the last great crisis, the Great Depression. The world has changed much since then; and our understanding of economics too has advanced. And yet, in some circles, we are wedded to ways of thinking that have not kept pace. Worse, in the interlude between the Great Depression and the Great Recession, some were lulled into believing that markets normally worked well; and the old classical model, slightly modified, came back into fashion. There was, as I have already noted, an irony in this, for among the advances in economics (game theory and theories of imperfect and asymmetric information) was an enhanced understanding of what was wrong with that model, and why it provided such a poor description of what was going on, both in normal times and even more so in times of crises.[28]

These alternative theories provided the foundations of a new theory of financial markets—an understanding of why financial markets are typically not perfectly efficient, and of how imperfect financial markets actually work. The effects of monetary policy are, of course, mediated through financial markets, so this new theory of financial markets is central to monetary theory. Modern monetary policy has to be based on these foundations.[29]

---

28. For a broader discussion of the evolution of these two strands of thinking, see Greenwald and Stiglitz (1987) Within the so-called New Keynesian tradition, there have also been two traditions. One following Keynes ignored the details of financial markets, and, following Hicks' interpretation of Keynes, focussed on wage and price rigidities. The other focuses explicit on financial market imperfections (e.g. Minsky (1972); as well as the work of Greenwald and Stiglitz to which I referred earlier), and encompasses an analysis of the consequences of deflation (following the work of Fisher (1933). See Greenwald and Stiglitz (1993).

29. See Greenwald and Stiglitz (2003) *op. cit.*

Monetary policy (understood broadly, to include financial regulatory policy) is of such importance in part because the financial sector is so important: the financial sector has been likened to the brain of an economy, and if the financial sector does not work well, the economy does not work well. In many countries around the world--including the US and the EU—the financial sector has not done what it should have done and done what it shouldn't have done; the costs of their failures in the US alone amount to trillions of dollars.

In this paper, I hope I have tried to describe what monetary policy based on a deeper understanding of the functioning of financial markets might look like. Most of the propositions that have been at the centre of monetary policy for the past quarter of a century need to be rethought. Monetary policy has not served our economies and societies well. It has arguably contributed to the growing inequality that has marked most countries around the world.[30] But of this there can be no doubt: It has not only failed to stabilise the economy in the way that was hoped; but the way that some central banks have conducted monetary policy and regulation has been at the centre of our greatest crisis in three quarters of a century.[31] This should be the grounds for a revolution in monetary policy.

References

Admati, A.R., P.M. DeMarzo, M.F. Hellwig and P. Pfleiderer (2010). "Fallacies, Irrelevant Facts, and Myths in the Discussion of Capital Regulation: Why Bank Equity is Not Expensive", *Stanford University Working Paper* No. 86.

Battiston, S., D. Delli Gatti, M. Gallegati, B. Greenwald and J.E. Stiglitz (2012). "Default Cascades: When Does Risk Diversification Increase Stability?" *Journal of Financial Stability* 8(3): 138-149.

Berg, Andrew G. and Jonathan D. Ostry (2011). "Inequality and Unsustainable Growth: Two Sides of the Same Coin?", *IMF Staff Discussion Note*, April 8. available at *http://www.imf.org/external/pubs/ft/sdn/2011/sdn1108.pdf* (accessed December 14, 2012).

Bernanke, Ben (2010). "On the Implications of the Financial Crisis for Economics", address delivered September 24, 2010 at Princeton University, available at *http://www.federalreserve.gov/newsevents/speech/bernanke20100924a.htm*, (accessed July 28, 2011).

30. See, in particular, Chapter 9 of Stiglitz (2012). *The Price of Inequality, op. cit.*

31. Thus, I take strong issue with Bernanke (2010) who has tried to suggest that there was nothing wrong with standard macroeconomic and monetary theory; there were only some minor flaws in its implementation.

Battiston, Stefano, Domenico Delli Gatti, Mauro Gallegati, Bruce Greenwald and J.E. Stiglitz (2012). "Liaisons Dangereuses: Increasing Connectivity, Risk Sharing and Systemic Risk", *Journal of Economic Dynamics and Control*, 36, pp. 1121-1141.

Calvo, Guillermo A. and Mendoza, Enrique G. (2000). "Rational contagion and the globalisation of securities markets", *Journal of International Economics*. 51(1): 79-113, Elsevier.

Emran, S. and J.E. Stiglitz (2009), "Financial Liberalisation, Financial Restraint and Entrepreneurial Development", *working paper*, Columbia University, available at *http://www2.gsb.columbia.edu/faculty/jstiglitz/download/papers/2009_Financial_Liberalisation.pdf* (accessed December 14, 2012).

Gallegati, M., B. Greenwald, M. Richiardi, and J.E. Stiglitz (2008). "The Asymmetric Effect of Diffusion Processes: Risk Sharing and Contagion", *Global Economy Journal*, 8(3), Article 2.

Greenwald, B. and J. E. Stiglitz (1993). "New and Old Keynesians," *Journal of Economic Perspectives* 7(1): 23-44. Winter.

———. (1986). "Externalities in Economies with Imperect Information and Incomplete Markets," *Quarterly Journal of Economics* 101(2): 229-64. May.

———. (2003). *Towards a New Paradigm in Monetary Economics*. Cambridge: Cambridge University Press.

———. (1989). "Toward a Theory of Rigidities", *American Economic Review* 79(2): 364-69, May.

———. (1987). "Keynesian, New Keynesian and New Classical Economics", *Oxford Economic Papers* 39: 119-133. March.

Grossman, Sanford and J.E. Stiglitz (1976). "Information and Competitive Price Systems", *American Economic Review* 66(2): 246-53, May

———. (1980). "On the Impossibility of Informationally Efficient Markets", *American Economic Review* 70(3): 393-408, June.

Haldane, A.G. (2009). "Rethinking the Financial Network", address to the Financial Students Association, Amsterdam, April, available at *http://www.bankofengland.co.uk/publications/speeches/2009/speech386.pdf*

Haldane, A.G. and R.M. May (2010). "Systemic Risk in Banking Ecosystems", University of Oxford mimeo.

I. Fisher, "The debt-deflation theory of great depressions," Econometrica1 (1933), pp. 337–357)].

Johnson, D.S., J.A. Parker, N.S. Souleles (2006). "Household Expenditure and the Income Tax Rebates of 2001", *The American Economic Review* 96(5): 1589-1610.

Jonathan, D. Ostry *et al.* (2010). "Capital Inflows: The Role of Controls", IMF Staff Position note 10/04, February 19, 2010, available at *http://www.imf.org/external/pubs/ft/spn/2010/spn1004.pdf* (accessed December 14, 2012).

Kindleberger, Charles (1978). *Manias, Panics, and Crashes: A History of Financial Crises.* New York: Basic Books.

Minsky, H.P. (1992). "The Financial Instability Hypothesis," The Jerome Levy Economics Institute of Bard College, Working Paper No. 74, May

Newbery, D. and J.E. Stiglitz (1984). "Pareto Inferior Trade", *Review of Economic Studies* 51(1): 1-12. January.

Ramsey, P.P. (1927). "A Contribution to the theory of Taxation", *Economic Journal*: 47-61.

Robertson, D. (1951). "Some Notes on the Theory of Interest", a contribution to *Money, Trade and Economic Growth, Essays in Honor of Professor J. H. William* (New York: Macmillan, 1951); reprinted in Sir Dennis Robertson, *Essays in Money and Interest* (Manchester: Collins, 1966), pp.203-22.

Stiglitz, J.E. (2012). *The Price of Inequality: How Today's Divided Society Endangers Our Future.* New York: W.W. Norton.

———. (2011). "Macroeconomic Fluctuations, Inequality, and Human Development", *Journal of Human Developmentand Capabilities* 13(1): 31-58.

———. (2011a). "Rethinking Macroeconomics: What Failed and How to Repair It", *Journal of the European Economic Association* 9(4): 591-645.

———. (2010). *Freefall: Americ, Free Markets, and the Sinking of the World Economy*. New York, W.W. Norton.

———. (2010a). Freefall: America, Free Markets, and the Sinking of the World Economy, New York: W.W. Norton.

———. (2010a). "Contagion, Liberalisation, and the Optimal Structure of Globalisation", *Journal of Globalisation and Development* 1(2) (Article 2, 45 pages).

———. (2010b). "Risk and Global Economic Architecture: Why Full Financial Integration May be Undesirable", *American Economic Review* 100(2); 388-92, May.

———. (1998). "Knowledge for Development: Economic Science, Economic Policy, and Economic Advice", in B. Pleskovic and J. Stiglitz (eds.), *Annual World Bank Conference on Development Economics.* Washington: World Bank. pp.9-58.

———. (2002). Globalisation and its Discontents, New York: WW Norton, 2002.

———. (1998). "Central Banking in a Democratic Society", *De Economist* (Netherlands), 146(2): 199-226. (Originally presented as 1997 Tinbergen Lecture, Amsterdam, October).

———. (1969). "A Re-Examination of the Modigliani-Miller Theorem", *American Economic Review* 59(5): 784-793, December; Stiglitz, J.E. (1974). "On the Irrelevance of Corporate Financial Policy", *American Economic Review* 64(6), December)

———. (1982). "Information and Capital Markets", in Financial Economics: Essays in Honor of PaulCootner, William F. Sharpe and Cathryn Cootner (eds.), Prentice Hall, New Jersey, pp. 118-158; reprinted in The Selected Works of Joseph E. Stiglitz, Volume II: Information and Economic Analysis: Applications to Capital, Labor, and Product Markets, Oxford: Oxford University Press, 2013, pp. 55-84)

———. (1974). "On the Irrelevance of Corporate Financial Policy," American Economic Review, 64(6), December 1974, pp. 851-866,

———. (1981). "On the Almost Neutrality of Inflation: Notes on Taxation and the Welfare Costs of Inflation," in M. June Flanders and Assaf Razin (eds.), *Development in an Inflationary World.* New York: Academic Press. pp.419-57.

———. (1983). "On the Relevance or Irrelevance of Public Financial Policy: Indexation, Price Rigidities and Optimal Monetary Policy," in Inflation, Debt and Indexation, R. Dornbusch and M. Simonsen (eds.), MIT Press, 1983, pp. 183-222 and of Economic Education, 19(2), Spring 1988, pp. 171-177.

———. (1988). "On the Relevance or Irrelevance of Public Financial Policy," in The Economics of Public Debt, Proceedings of the 1986 International Economics Association Meeting, London: Macmillan Press, 1988, pp. 4-76.

Stiglitz, J.E., "Capital Market Liberalisation, Globalisation, and the IMF", in J.E. Stiglitz and J.A. Ocampo (eds.), *Capital Market Liberalisation and Development.* New York: Oxford University Press, pp.76-100.

William C. Dudley, "The Recovery and Monetary Policy", Remarks at the National Association for Business Economics Annual Meeting, New York City, 15 October 2012, available at *http://www.newyorkfed.org/newsevents/speeches/2012/dud121015.html.*

Wolff E.N. and M. Gittleman (2011). "Inheritances and the Distribution of Wealth Or Whatever Happened to the Great Inheritance Boom?", *BLS Working Paper* 445, January,

World Bank (2002). *Building Institutions for Markets: World Development Report 2001-2002*, Washington, D.C.: The World Bank.

RBI Bulletin February 2013.

9

DEEPAK MOHANTY

Price Stability and Financial Stability

An Emerging Market Perspective

> A system of credit which has slowly grown up as years went on, which has suited itself to the course of business, which has forced itself on the habits of men, will not be altered because theorists disapprove of it, or because books are written against it. (Walter Bagehot, Lombard Street, 1873).

The recent global financial crisis has generated an intense debate on the role and responsibility of central banks in maintaining financial stability. Over the centuries, the world has experienced periodic financial crises, prompting changes in the way we think about monetary and financial stability. Yet, we are not immune from crisis.

In the present context, several questions arise. What ought to be the objectives of central banks or more specifically that of monetary policy? Is there a trade-off between price stability and financial stability? Were central banks blindsided by the success of price stability to the neglect of financial stability? Do central banks have the necessary mandate and instruments to handle multiple objectives and at the same time maintain credibility? How does one ensure accountability with multiple objectives? Is there a need to revisit the best practice in monetary policy? While we currently grapple with these issues, they are by no means new.

Against this background, I sequence my paper as follows. First, I briefly trace the evolution of central bank objectives over the centuries. Second, I review central bank objectives and

---

The assistance provided by J.K. Khundrakpam and Rajeev Jain is acknowledged.

practices in emerging market economies (EMEs). Third, I highlight our experience in India in the conduct of monetary policy and how we have combined it with financial stability. Finally, I conclude by drawing three practical lessons in central banking in terms of monetary policy framework, institutional design and communication in pursuit of both monetary and financial stability.

Evolution of Central Bank Objectives

Let me first turn to central banking history for some insights. What was the motivation for setting up central banks in the 17th century? While the early central banks were set up for issuance of currency and financing governments, financial stability considerations got embedded as trade expanded and the banking and financial sectors developed. For instance, the Swedish Riksbank, the first central bank, was set up in 1668 as a joint-stock bank to lend funds to the government and to act as a clearing house for commerce. The Bank of England (BoE) was set up in 1694 to act as the government's banker and debt-manager.

How did central bank objectives change in the 19th century? Most central banks began assuming financial stability function though it was not articulated the way we understand it now. Drawing from the criticism on its functioning during the panics in 1825, 1837, 1847, and 1857, the BoE adopted the 'responsibility doctrine' proposed by Walter Bagehot. The doctrine required the BoE to subsume its private interest to that of public interest of the banking system as a whole. As per the Bagehot's rule, the BoE was to lend freely on the basis of any sound collateral offered, but at a penal rate to prevent moral hazard. Thus, the role of the central bank as the lender of last resort (LOLR) as espoused by Bagehot remains the cornerstone of financial stability function even today.[1]

How did central banks change in the 20th century? The functions of central banks came to be further aligned with public policy objectives. Frequent bank panics in the US led to the creation of the Federal Reserve in 1913 with LOLR as one of its

---

1. The term was first used by Francis Baring (1797) but systematically explained by Thornton (1802) who first identified it as a function of Bank of England. Thornton, H. (1802). .

main functions. However, the Fed could not prevent the Great Depression as monetary policy followed the "Principle of Real Bills Doctrine".[2] After the Great Depression, central banks transformed themselves as growth and employment facilitators and put in place deposit insurance. This kept the world economy insulated from any major banking crisis from the late 1930s until the mid-1970s. But fiscal activism and the belief that employment can be permanently increased at the cost of inflation, supported by the early version of the Phillips Curve (1958), led to accommodative monetary policy. This manifested in high inflation in the 1970s.

In order to address the inflation surge and the accompanying economic stagnation, intellectual opinion swung in favour of price stability supported by the work of economists like Milton Friedman (1968), which advocated a dominant role for monetary policy. Thus, price stability emerged as a primary objective of most central banks during the 1980s. How did financial stability fit into this framework? The understanding around that time was that monetary policy directed at maintaining price stability would lessen both the incidence and the severity of financial instability. The argument was that price stability obviates the information problems for both borrowers and lenders and ensures financial stability through efficient allocation of resources. Studies based on the experience of advanced countries such as the US, the UK, Canada and Japan also concurred with the view that price instability contributed to financial instability (Bordo and Wheelock, 1998).

Did the financial crisis of the 21st century with its epicenter in the advanced countries change the world view of central bank objectives? The dominant view, particularly among the advanced economies, was that monetary policy should ideally have a single objective, a corresponding single tool, and an operationally independent and accountable central bank. In fact, following this wisdom, many countries, both advanced and emerging markets, set explicit inflation targets and mandated inflation control as the paramount objective of monetary policy since the 1990s. Explicit emphasis on price stability often came with certain legislative

---

2. If only real bills are discounted by banks, the expansion of bank money will be in proportion to the needs of trade. It was assumed that monetary system will be self regulating.

changes in central banks and emphasis on fiscal rules in many countries. Although central banks were cognisant of the importance of financial stability for conduct of monetary policy, a distinction between monetary policy and financial stability policy was generally maintained.

The current global crisis seems to have undermined the view that monetary policy should only have a single objective of price stability. The pre-crisis view, also called the "Jackson Hole Consensus", was that central banks should respond to asset prices and financial imbalances only to the extent that they affect the shorter term inflation forecast. However, such perception was belied by the recent crisis (Gali, 2011). It became clear that financial stability can be jeopardised even if there is price stability and macroeconomic stability (Subbarao, 2009). Consequently, post-crisis assessment increasingly veered towards explicit recognition of the financial stability objective. But there are unsettled issues and the jury is still out.

First, should financial stability be considered as an explicit objective of the central bank or, more specifically, as an additional objective of monetary policy? It has been argued that central banks are not only the LoLR, but also better equipped to look at both financial system and economic cycles. In this context, Eichengreen, Prasad and Rajan (2011) suggest a dual mandate of price stability and financial stability so that "monetary policy is recognised as a legitimate element of the macroprudential supervisor's toolkit." Similarly, Woodford (2012) argued that monetary policy might indeed lessen the severity of risks to financial stability. Gokarn (2010) was of the view that broader mandates for central banks will need to be made explicit and conditional on the priority of the core mandates. In contrast, Svensson (2010) argued that it was important to distinguish financial stability policy from monetary policy to avoid conceptual and practical confusion between the two policies. Using monetary policy for the financial stability objective can lead to poor outcomes.

Second, how compatible is inflation targetting framework with financial stability as an additional objective? The views are quite diverse. While some recommend eschewing of inflation targetting altogether, Woodford (2012) suggested modifying inflation-targetting practice for making interest rate policy a more effective tool for financial stability. In contrast, Svensson (2010) opined that flexible inflation targeting remains the best-practice monetary policy before, during and after the financial crisis.

Third, should financial stability be the sole or shared responsibility of the central bank? A BIS survey shows that in practice an overwhelming majority of central banks have either full or shared responsibility for financial stability, but the mandates are rarely explicit. Similarly, Čihák (2010) found that the remit for central bank's role in financial stability was weaker than in the case of price stability. The dominant view, however, seems to be that financial stability should be a shared responsibility, as monetary policy instruments of central banks can only have a partial impact on the ultimate objective of financial stability.

Fourth, do central banks have the instruments to ensure both price stability and financial stability? Central banks functioning with a single instrument of short-term interest rate, particularly those with inflation targetting framework may not be equipped to achieve multiple objectives following Tinbergen's (1952) assignment rule. In this context, many have argued that interest rate is too blunt an instrument for dealing with overall financial stability issues (for example, Bernanke, 2011). Goodhart (2008) opined that many central banks with only one instrument of monetary policy may find these two objectives often conflicting with each other. In contrast, it is argued that though identifying the bubble is difficult, and therefore a risky strategy, the cleaning up cost after the bubble burst may be costlier than leaning against the bubble (Stark, 2010).

Finally, there are additional complexities in the context of EMEs as asset price bubbles are often accompanied by exchange rate appreciation emanating from large capital inflows or trade surplus. Therefore, raising interest rate in an attempt to burst asset bubble may engender further capital inflows aggravating the bubble itself. Thus, it has been emphasised that even if monetary policy is used to lean against the wind, it needs to be supplemented by counter-cyclical instruments. Some economists believe that combining financial supervision with monetary policy tasks, as indeed the case in many EMEs, can lead to synergies and a more effective conduct of monetary policy (Borio, 2009), and it can be usefully connected to the central banks' LoLR function (Blinder, 2010). Danthine (2012) suggested that central banks should be endowed with macroprudential instruments that directly target the root causes of the problems generated by excessive risk taking in times of low interest rates.

In this regard, Mohanty (2011) argued that while interest rate continues to be the dominant instrument for implementing monetary policy, supplementing it by other quantity or macroprudential instruments even in normal times will enhance the flexibility of monetary policy to attain multiple objectives. Therefore, post-crisis, there has been greater emphasis on introducing additional instruments for central banks to deal with aspects of financial stability. In short, the role of central banks in ensuring overall stability of the financial sector has now got a fresh impetus. Against this background, I turn to the experience of EMEs.

Central Bank Objectives in Emerging Markets

How have the central bank objectives in EMEs been different? Historically, price stability has been a key objective for central banks in EMEs as in the case of advanced economies. However, given the level of financial market development and institutional structure, financial stability has been important to policymaking, considering the greater incidence of financial crises in EMEs in the 20th century. Moreover, many of them were also responsible for macroprudential regulation even though only a few of them directly derive it from the explicit mandate (Table 9.1).

Table 9.1

Financial Stability as Objective in Central Banks

(Per cent of total number of central banks)

	Central Bank	All Economies	Advanced Economies	Others
1.	Explicit Mandate for Financial Stability	3	9	2
2.	Derives Responsibility for Financial Stability from Interpretation of Law	34	89	18
	(i) from monetary policy objectives	10	26	5
	(ii) from payment system tasks	8	20	4
	(iii) from banking supervisory tasks	12	26	8
	(iv) other interpretations	5	17	1
3.	Oversees Payments system(s)	100	100	100
4.	Supervises banks	47	34	51
5.	Supervises all financial institutions	16	11	18
6.	Publishes a financial stability report	29	77	15
7.	Separate organisational unit for financial stability	32	83	17
8.	Has clear general accountability (to shareholders/government/public)	45	63	40
9.	Has clear accountability for financial stability	2	6	1

Source: A survey of 157 central banks by Čihák, 2010.

Indeed, the resilience of the financial systems in the emerging markets during the recent global financial crisis owes to financial stability already being an important monetary policy objective (De Gregorio, 2011). Even as many EMEs formally adopted inflation targeting (e.g., Chile, Brazil, South Africa, Indonesia, Thailand and Mexico), in practice they followed a 'flexible inflation targeting' framework, as discretion was used to respond to shocks and also to pursue other objectives.[3] EMEs which did not formally adopt inflation targetting (e.g., China, Nigeria, Malaysia and India) have price stability as one of the key objectives of monetary policy (Table 9.2).

3. Flexible inflation targeting (IT) framework which requires achievement of the desired inflation target over the medium-term makes it easier for central banks to look not only for price stability, but also consider other variables, such as the output gap or the exchange rate. In a sense, flexible IT also implies a departure from the corner solutions of the 'Impossibility Trinity' of fixed exchange rates, independent monetary policy and perfect capital mobility.

Table 9.2

Emerging Market Economies: Central Bank Objectives and Policy Tools

Country Objectives	*Mission/Main Instruments*	*Policy Inflation*	*Trend*	*Other Functions*
1. Brazil (IT since 1999) 4.5% since 2005	Currency stability and financial stability	PR OMO RR	5.3% (2005-11)	• Bank Regulation Regulation • Payment System
2. Chile IT (1991) 3% since 2007	Currency stability	PR OMO RR	3.9% (2007-11)	• Payment System • Financial System • Fiscal Agent • Foreign Exchange
3. China	Currency stability and growth	PR OMO RR	3.1% (2005-11)	• Payment System • Financial Markets • Debt Manager
4. India	Currency and financial stability and growth	PR OMO RR	6.6% (2005-12)	• Payment System • Bank Regulation • Debt Manager • Money Market
5. Indonesia IT since 2005 5% in 2010-11	Currency stability	PR OMO RR	5.2% (2010-11)	• Bank Regulation • Payment System
6. Malaysia	Currency and financial stability	PR OMO RR	2.8% (2005-11)	• Bank Regulation • Banker to Government • Financial Inclusion
7. Mexico IT (3% medium-term since 2003)	Currency stability	PR OMO RR	4.3% 2003-11)	• Bank Regulation • Payment System
8. Nigeria	Currency stability and management of the financial sector	PR OMO RR	11.5% (2005-11)	• Banker to Government • Payment System • Bank Regulation
9. Russia (Moving towards IT)	Currency stability	PR OMO RR	10% (2005-11)	• Bank Regulation • Foreign Exchange
10. South Africa Flexible IT (2000) 3-6%(y-o-y) since 2009	Currency and financial stability	PR OMO RR	5.5% (2000-11)	• Bank Regulation • Payment System • Banker to Government • Exchange control

Note: PR: Policy Rate; RR: Reserve Requirement; OMO: Open Market Operations

Source: Author's own compilation and *World Economic Outlook*, International Monetary Fund.

Multiple instruments, including quantitative tools such as the cash reserve ratio (CRR), were used to moderate the pace of domestic credit growth as well as monetary impact of large capital inflows in China, India and Russia. In the East Asian EMEs, the importance of financial stability and the need to prevent financial imbalances by active use of macroprudential policy measures was emphasised after the Asian crisis. Accordingly, central banks were given either the sole or shared responsibility in pursuing financial stability in addition to the traditional mandate of monetary stability (Watanagase, 2012). In South Africa, the prudential regulation and supervision of banks assisted and complemented the central bank in its pursuit of financial system stability. Similarly, the Central Bank of Brazil actively used macroprudential measures to deal with emerging financial risks, particularly from excess capital flows in the economy. According to a BIS survey (2010), EMEs significantly outnumbered advanced economies as users of some type of macroprudential instrument.

Global financial crisis highlighted the importance of using a broader set of instruments for financial stability. In this regard, most central banks in EMEs where monetary policy and prudential supervision were within their purview seem to have been better equipped to address financial stability issues as compared to advanced economies. Now, I turn specifically to our experience in India.

Financial Stability: Indian Framework

The core functions of the Reserve Bank of India (RBI) are enshrined in the preamble to the RBI Act, 1934 as, "to regulate the issue of bank notes and keeping of reserves with a view to securing monetary stability in India and generally to operate the currency and credit system of the country to its advantage." In addition, the RBI is also microprudential regulator as the Banking Regulation (BR) Act, 1949 entrusts it with the power to regulate and supervise commercial banks and cooperative banks. The RBI also regulates and supervises non-banking financial companies (NBFCs) under the RBI Act, 1934. Similarly, the Foreign Exchange Management Act (FEMA), 1999 empowers it to regulate the foreign exchange market and the oversight of the payment systems is derived from the Payment and Settlement Systems Act, 2007.

Drawing from a wider mandate, monetary policy in India has evolved to have multiple objectives of price stability, financial stability and growth. These objectives are not inherently contradictory, rather mutually reinforcing. The Reserve Bank's approach recognises that price and financial stability are important for sustaining high levels of growth which is the ultimate objective of public policy. The Reserve Bank's approach to financial stability has been proactive and preventive rather than reactive. Its role as monetary policy authority, well integrated with macroprudential regulation and microprudential supervision, with an implicit mandate for systemic oversight has enabled the Reserve Bank to exploit the synergies across various dimensions (Subbarao, 2011).

Even before the crisis, the institutional arrangement in the financial sector was already in place for inter-regulatory co-ordination to monitor financial stability in the economy. A High Level Coordination Committee on Financial Markets (HLCCFM) was set up in 1992 with the Governor of the Reserve Bank as Chairman, and the chiefs of the Securities and Exchange Board of India (SEBI), the Insurance Regulatory and Development Authority (IRDA) and the Pension Fund Regulatory and Development Authority (PFRDA), and the Finance Secretary to Government of India as members. However, post-crisis, the collegial approach to financial stability has been further strengthened by constituting the Financial Stability and Development Council (FSDC).

The FSDC, headed by the Finance Minister, was set up in December 2010 in the wake of the global financial crisis with a specific mandate, inter alia, for systemic financial stability. The FSDC is expected to deal with issues relating to financial stability, financial sector development, inter-regulatory coordination and macroprudential supervision of the economy including the functioning of large financial conglomerates. A sub-committee of the FSDC, headed by the governor of the Reserve Bank, replaced the HLCCFM and is the primary operating arm of the FSDC. This sub-committee has also set up a dedicated crisis management framework.

In addition, various committees of the Reserve Bank's Central Board monitor financial stability issues: the Board for Financial Supervision reviews the Reserve Bank's supervisory and regulatory initiatives and the Board for Payment and Settlement Systems oversees the overall functioning of the payment system.

Another development signifying the Reserve Bank's role in the context of financial stability is the setting up of Financial Stability Unit (FSU) in the Bank in July 2009 with a mandate to conduct effective macroprudential surveillance of the financial system on an ongoing basis and enable early detection of any incipient signs of instability. The Reserve Bank also brings out biannual Financial Stability Reports. Incidentally, the IMF has just concluded a Financial Sector Assessment Programme, which in fact comes close on the heels of a comprehensive self assessment of financial sector carried out by the Reserve Bank. Thus, the RBI is one of those central banks to recognise financial stability as one of the objectives of monetary policy even before the crisis.

Lessons for Central Banks

In my opinion, the global financial crisis has fundamentally altered the way we used to view monetary policy and financial stability and the interface between them. However, there are issues which entail further work in three key areas. First, a relook at monetary policy framework in terms of both objectives and instruments towards a clear recognition of financial stability. Second, to put in place an appropriate institutional mechanism drawing upon countries' own experience and history for better co-ordination among the concerned regulatory entities to deliver on financial stability. Third, address the communication challenge of multiple objectives to preserve central bank credibility to ensure price and financial stability. Let me now elaborate on each of these three aspects.

Monetary Policy Framework

The view that monetary policy framework should allow policymakers to lean against the build-up of financial imbalances, even if near-term inflation expectations remain anchored, is gaining importance. While there is little doubt that monetary policy framework of central banks needs to change, the moot point is what should be the ideal monetary policy framework for better analysis of the macroeconomic effects of financial imbalances? One approach could be to formally broaden the set of information variables for monetary policy decision-making: in a way, for example, the two pillar approach of the ECB or the multiple indicators approach of the Reserve Bank of India that factors in financial considerations into monetary policy.[4] The multiple indicators approach has the advantages of broad-basing monetary policy operations on a large set of information such as money, credit, asset prices, interest rates and exchange rate and providing flexibility in the conduct of monetary management. Such approach, however, may involve a greater element of judgement.

At an operational level, the most widely accepted presentation of monetary policy reaction function that combines both inflation and growth objectives is the "Taylor Rule". The Taylor rule can be augmented by adding financial variables to the standard monetary reaction function based on inflation and the output gap so as to enhance central banks' ability to react to financial stability concerns. However, efficiency of such a formulation needs to be tested. Whichever framework is adopted, there should be flexibility for the central bank to respond to potential imbalances and the risks, apart from growth and inflation control.

Institutional Design for Better Coordination

The recent crisis and the subsequent response have shed new light on the critical role of central banks in promoting financial stability. However, it needs to be recognised that this added responsibility should not come at the cost of their conventional role for price stability. This is more relevant particularly for central banks in EMEs which admittedly, are yet to achieve that level of credibility as their advanced economy counterparts. For many EMEs, exchange rate stability is an important objective,

4. For discussion on multiple indicators approach, please see: Mohanty (2010).

and without price stability it is not possible to maintain exchange rate stability. Furthermore, the financial markets and institutions have grown in complexity, the oversight and regulation of which could be beyond a single entity such as the central bank. Hence, financial stability would have to be a joint responsibility, though the central bank could have a dominant role by virtue of it being the natural LoLR. However, there is a need to explicitly incorporate the financial stability role of the central bank into its statute to establish an accountability framework.

The challenge for a central bank is to achieve multiple objectives without losing credibility as a monetary authority solely responsible for price stability. This would be possible only if policies implemented by various stakeholders in financial stability are coherent. Accordingly, an appropriate design for coordination mechanism is required to derive synergies between monetary policy and macroprudential policy and make more effective use of policy tools available with multiple bodies having the mandate of financial stability.

The design of coordination mechanism may, however, vary across countries depending on the nature and size of their financial systems and their own historical experience. In fact, efforts towards greater institutionalisation of coordination mechanism have already begun. Most prominent examples are the newly created bodies, both in advanced countries and EMEs, like the Financial Stability Oversight Council in the US, the Financial Policy Committee (Interim) in the UK, the European Systemic Risk Board for the European Union, Financial Regulation and Systemic Risk Council in France, Financial Stability Council in Chile, Council for the Stability of the Financial System in Mexico and Financial Stability and Development Council in India (Table 9.3). In some other countries, financial stability framework has been strengthened by setting up committees in central banks to gauge systemic risk (e.g., Brazil in 2011).

Table 9.3

Financial Stability Framework after the Crisis

Country/ Institution	*Objective and Functions*	*Structure*
1. Belgium Committee for Systemic Risks and System-Relevant Financial Institutions (CSRSFI), July 2010	• To be responsible for the prudential supervision of systemic financial institutions	Chairman: Central Bank Governor; Members: • Central Bank's Board of Directors • Management Committee of the Commission • Management Committee of the Commission Bancaire Financière et des Assurances • One member from Ministry of Finance as an observer
2. Chile Financial Stability Council, July 2011	• To oversee the integrity and solidity of the financial system, providing the mechanisms for coordinating and exchanging the information necessary to ensure the adequate management of systemic risk and the resolution of critical situations involved in the carrying out of the functions and powers of the superintendents in the economic area	Chairman: Treasury Minister; Members: • Superintendent of Securities and Insurance • Superintendent of Banks and Financial Institutions • Superintendent of Pensions (In addition, the Central Bank is invited for meeting)
3. EU The European Systemic Risk Board ((ESRB), November 2010	ESRB is part of the European System of Financial Supervision (ESFS). It • ensures supervision of the Union's financial System; • is responsible for the macroprudential oversight of the financial system within the European Union and contributes to the	Chairman: President of the ECB; Members: • Vice-President of ECB • Governors of the member national central banks • One member of the European Commission • Chairperson of the European Banking Authority (EBA) • Chairperson of the

contd...

.contd...

	prevention or mitigation of systemic risks to financial stability in the Union that arise from developments within the financial system • presents Annual Report to the European Parliament and the Council	European Insurance and Occupational Pensions Authority (EIOPA) • Chairperson of the European Securities and Markets Authority (ESMA) • Chair and the two Vice-Chairs of the Advisory Scientific Committee (ASC) • Chair of the Advisory Technical Committee (ATC)
4. France Financial Regulation and Systemic Risk Council (FRSRC)	• To foster cooperation and information exchange and consider French market/ institution developments from a macroprudential perspective	Chairman: Finance Minister; Members: • Governor of the Banque de France • President of the Financial Markets Authority • President of the Accounting Standards Authority
5. India Financial Stability and Development Council (FSDC)	• To strengthen and institutionalise the mechanism for maintaining financial stability and strengthen the institutional framework for coordination among all regulators and the Government.	Chairman: Finance Minister Sub-Committee under the Chairmanship of Governor of the Reserve Bank Member of the Council: • Reserve Bank of India • Securities and Exchange Board of India • Insurance Regulatory and Development Authority • Pension Fund Regulatory and Development Authority • Finance Secretary and/or Secretary, Department of Economic Affairs • Secretary, Department of Financial Services • Chief Economic Adviser
6. Mexico Council for the Stability of the Financial System (CESF), 2010	• To analyse risks and identify opportunities that may disrupt the functioning of the financial system, and thus reduce the impact on the economy	Chairman: Secretary, Secretariat of Finance and Public Credit; Members: • Under Secretary, Secretariat of Finance and Public Credit • President, National Banking and Securities Commission

contd...

...contd...

		• President, National Insurance and Surety Commission • President, National Commission for the Pension System • Executive Secretary, Institute for the Protection of Banking Savings • Governor, Central Bank • Two Deputy Governors, Central Bank
7. US Financial Stability Oversight Council (FSOC), October 2010	• Identifying and mitigating risks to the stability of the US financial system. To publish Annual Report which covers: • the activities of the Council • significant financial market and regulatory developments • potential emerging threats to the financial stability of the US	Chairman: Secretary of the Treasury; Member Agencies: • Board of Governors of the Federal Reserve System • Commodity Futures Trading Commission • Federal Deposit Insurance Corporation • Federal Housing Finance Agency • National Credit Union Administration Board • Office of the Comptroller of the Currency • Securities and Exchange Commission • Treasury Department • Consumer Financial Protection Bureau
8. UK Interim Financial Policy Committee (FPC), February 2011	• As per the Financial Services Bill (January 2012), a Financial Policy Committee (FPC) will be charged with identifying, monitoring and taking action to remove or reduce systemic risks with a view to protecting and enhancing the resilience of the UK financial system • Responsible for the Bank of England's bi-annual Financial Stability Report	Structure of Interim FPC Chairman: Governor of the Bank of England (BoE) Members: • BoE's Deputy Governor for Financial Stability • BoE's Deputy Governor for Monetary Policy • Chief Executive of the Financial Services Authority • Chairman of the Financial Services Authority • BoE's Executive Director for Financial Stability • BoE's Executive Director for Markets

contd...

...contd...

	• External Members: Four • Non-Voting members: One member each from the Financial Conduct Authority and a representative of the Treasury.

Source: Compiled from respective central banks' website.

Under the new institutional design, as shown in Table 9.3, though financial stability has been recognised as a shared responsibility, central banks have been assigned the lead role in most of the countries. Even as details of the newly created bodies differ, the thrust is the same, i.e., better coordination to gauge systemic risks and plan an appropriate response. Furthermore, with increasing sovereign risk concerns in a number of economies, particularly the advanced economies, better policy response is expected as fiscal authorities are also a part of the new institutional framework for financial stability. However, even under the more collegial approach to financial stability, policy coordination is not going to be so easy, especially when there is a problem of time-inconsistency and the objective functions of the authorities may not always be the same (Praet, 2011). It is also important to guard against the risk that active involvement of governments should not bring back fiscal dominance and compromise the autonomy of each regulator and the central bank.

Central Bank Communication

In a market-determined system, central banks have placed a greater reliance on transparency and communication to enhance monetary policy transmission and establish accountability to the public for their decision-making. So far the experience shows that communication on monetary policy issues has moved from complete secrecy, to constructive ambiguity to transparency. For instance, the Fed and the ECB have in recent years frequently provided fairly direct indications about future interest-rate decisions in their official statements. We, in the RBI, have also started giving forward guidance since September 2010. However, there are several challenges.

It is not easy to communicate clearly on a single objective. Going forward, as central banks broaden their mandates and institutional design grows in complexity, so also will the communication challenges. For example, if a central bank were to ease monetary policy on financial stability concerns even when inflation is high, it risks unhinging of inflation expectations, which in turn could complicate financial stability.

During the recent crisis, there were many instances of communication challenges faced by central banks. For instance, the US Fed faced communication challenge with regard to quantitative easing and the exit policy of its unconventional measures. We, in the RBI, had to face communication challenge when we reduced CRR of banks in January and March 2012 on liquidity concerns even when inflation was above our tolerance level. While some interpreted it as premature reversal of tight monetary policy stance, others saw this as a pure liquidity action not inconsistent with our monetary stance.

If the policy measures are not properly guided and not understood as intended, they may not transmit the right signal and eventually prove to be a noise to financial market entities. Guidance by central banks, at best, could be conditional because of the provisional nature of immediate available information set, limitations of macro models, incomplete knowledge and uncertainties about the evolution of the economy and periodic unanticipated shocks. Thus, transparency in communication is a double-edged sword which at times could produce unintended consequences. As central banks broaden their objectives so also they have to hone their communication skills.

Conclusion

Financial stability as an objective of central banks has turned a full circle from being the predominant objective, to a virtual neglect to being reinstated recently as an important objective drawing on the lessons of global financial crisis. However, financial markets and institutions have grown in complexity making it difficult for a single entity to deliver on financial stability. Therefore, financial stability has to be a shared responsibility wherein central banks have a predominant role. This necessitates a fresh look at monetary policy framework, institutional design for policy coordination and effective communication. Moreover, there is a need for explicit recognition of financial stability objective, particularly in the statute of the central bank, to establish an accountability framework. While it is not very apparent whether price stability can ensure financial stability, it is clear that price instability could jeopardise financial stability. Financial stability objective, therefore, cannot or should not override the price stability objective, which should continue to be the predominant objective of monetary policy.

References

Bank for International Settlements (2009). *Issues in the Governance of Central Banks: A Report from the Central Bank Governance Group. www.bis.org/publ/othp04.htm.*

Bank for International Settlements (2010). "Macroprudential Instruments and Frameworks: A Stocktaking of Issues and Experiences", *CGFS Papers* No. 38.

Bernanke, B. (2011). "The Effects of the Great Recession on Central Bank Doctrine and Practice," Speech at the Federal Reserve of Boston *56th Economic Conference.*

Blinder, A. (2010). "How Central Should the Central Bank Be?", *Journal of Economic Literature.* 48(1): 123-33.

Borio, C. (2009). "Implementing the Macroprudential Approach to Financial Regulation and Supervision", *Banque de France Financial Stability Review* No. 13: 31-41.

Bordo, Michael D. and David C. Wheelock (1998). "Price Stability and Financial Stability: The Historical Record", *Federal Reserve Bank of St. Louis Review.* September/October.

Čihák, Martin (2010). "Price Stability, Financial Stability, and Central Bank Independence", *38th Economics Conference* at the Oesterreichische Nationalbank, Vienna.

Danthine Jean-Pierre (2012). *Reconciling Price and Financial Stability.* Speech at the University of Zurich, Zurich. January 24.

De Gregorio, José (2011). "Price and Financial Stability in Modern Central Banking", Keynote Speech, Governor of the Central Bank of Chile, at the joint Latin American and Caribbean Economic Association (LACEA)-Latin American Chapter of the *Econometric Society (LAMES) Conference 2011.* Santiago: University Adolfo Ibáñez. November 11.

Eichengreen, Barry, Eswar Prasad and Raghuram Rajan (2011). "Central Banks Need a Bigger and Bolder Mandate", *Opinion.* Brookings Institution. October.

Friedman, Milton (1968). "The Role of Monetary Policy", AEA Presidential Speech, *Amercian Economic Review*, Vol LVIII, No.1.

Gali, Jordi (2011). "Monetary Policy and Rational Asset Price Bubbles", *Barcelona GSE Working Papers Series* No.592.

Gokarn, Subir (2011). "Monetary Policy Considerations After the Crisis: Practitioners' Perspectives", *RBI Bulletin*, January.

Goodhart, Charles A.E. (2008). "Central Banks' Function to Maintain Financial Stability: An Uncompleted Task", *http://www.voxeu.org/index.php?q=node/1263.*

Mohanty, Deepak (2010). "Monetary Policy Framework in India—Experience with Multiple-indicators Approach", *RBI Bulletin*, March

——. (2011). "Lessons for Monetary Policy from Global Financial Crisis: An Emerging Market Perspective", Paper Presented in the Central Banks Conference of the Bank of Israel, Jerusalem, *RBI Bulletin*. April.

Phillips, A.W. (1958). "The Relationship Between Unemployment and the Rate of Change of Money Wages in the United Kingdom 1861-1957", *Economica* 25 (100): 283–99.

Praet, Peter (2011). "The (Changing) Role of Central Banks in Financial Stability Policies", Speech at the *14th Annual Internal Banking Conference*, Organised by the Federal Reserve Bank of Chicago and the European Central Bank, Chicago. November 10.

Stark, Jürgen (2010). "In Search of a Robust Monetary Policy Framework", Keynote Speech at the 6th ECB Central Banking Conference *Approaches to Monetary Policy Revisited: Lessons from the Crisis*. Frankfurt am Main. November 19.

Subbarao, D. (2009). "Financial Stability: Issues and Challenges", *RBI Bulletin*, October.

——. (2011). "Financial Stability Mandate of Central Banks: Issues in the International and Indian Context", *RBI Bulletin*, July.

Svensson, Lars E.O. (2010). "Monetary Policy After the Financial Crisis", Speech at the Second International Journal of Central Banking (IJCB) Fall Conference, Tokyo, September.

Thornton, H. (1802). *An Inquiry into the Nature and Effects of the Paper Credit of Great Britain*. Edited with an Introduction by F.A. von Hayek (1939). New York: Rinehart and Co.

Tinbergen, J. (1952). *On the Theory of Economic Policy*. 2nd Edition. Amsterdam: North-Holland.

Watanagase, Tarisa (2012). "Remarks" at Monetary Policy Workshop on *Strengthening Macroprudential Frameworks*. Organised by IMF Regional Office for Asia and Pacific (OAP). March 22–23. Tokyo, Japan.

Woodford, Michael (2012). "Inflation Targeting and Financial Stability', *NBER Working Paper 17967*, National Bureau of Economic Research.

Address in the 2012 Central Bank of Nigeria (CBN) Board Retreat, Cape Town, South Africa, June 27, 2012. RBI Bulletin July 2012.

10

DUVVURI SUBBARAO

Price Stability, Financial Stability and Sovereign Debt Sustainability

Policy Challenges from the New Trilemma

The global financial crisis followed by the euro zone debt crisis has changed the theology of central banking in a fundamental way. The orthodoxy of central banking before the 2008 crisis was: single objective—price stability; single instrument—short-term interest rate. Although most central banks deviated to different extents from this minimalist model, this came increasingly to be considered the holy grail.

The crisis came as a powerful rebuke to central banks for having neglected financial stability in their single-minded pursuit of price stability. Two years ago, a consensus was developing around the view that financial stability has to be within the explicit policy calculus of central banks, although opinion was divided on the precise nature of institutional arrangements for maintaining financial stability.

Fast forward to 2011-12. Even as central banks are grappling with balancing the demands of price stability and financial stability, there is now yet another powerful assault on central bank orthodoxy arising from the big elephant in the room—the Euro zone sovereign debt crisis. The European Central Bank (ECB) is being called upon to bend and stretch its mandate to bail out sovereigns who have forfeited the confidence of markets. Actually that is an understatement. In reality, the ECB is being challenged on why it is, to use an Indian word, being so *brahminical* about its mandate when the world around it is collapsing. The argument, in its essence, is that if a central bank is committed to financial stability, it cannot ignore the feedback loop between financial stability and sovereign debt sustainability, and by extension therefore, it has to be mindful of sovereign debt sustainability concerns.

What do these trends engendered by the crisis indicate? In particular, is it the case that the mandate of central banks is set to expand from the single objective of price stability to multiple objectives of price stability, financial stability and sovereign debt sustainability? Can central banks simultaneously support all these three objectives and do so efficiently? That in essence is the new trilemma.

The new trilemma triggers several questions. How do the three objectives underlying the trilemma reinforce each other, and in what ways do they conflict with each other? What is their impact on growth? Is the trilemma an exclusive phenomenon of crisis times, or does it manifest in normal times as well? What is the nature and extent of the responsibility of central banks for each of these objectives? Are central banks equipped to handle these additional responsibilities? And finally, what does this expanded mandate mean for the effectiveness and autonomy of central banks?

That indeed is a long list of questions. The purpose of this paper is to think through these weighty questions centred around this new trilemma.

Is this Indeed a Trilemma?

We deliberated internally on whether this evolving challenge for central banks would indeed qualify as a trilemma. One view was that this is not strictly a trilemma as there is no theory which says that we cannot simultaneously obtain price stability, financial stability and sovereign debt sustainability. The opposing view was that what central banks have at hand is indeed a trilemma in as much as there can be clear tensions between the objectives underlying the new trilemma, and central banks may not be able to determine, with any degree of exactitude, what *inter se* priority must be accorded to each of the three objectives under different sets of circumstances. So, is this a trilemma or not? To compound the search for an answer, the word 'trilemma' has not made it to all standard dictionaries yet. So, permit me a little indulgence into the world of trilemmas.

The World of Trilemmas

Epicurus, the Greek Philosopher who lived around 300 BCE, was possibly the first to use the concept of a trilemma to reject the idea of an omnipotent God. The distinction of being the first to actually use the word 'trilemma' goes perhaps to the 17th century English non-conformist clergyman, Philip Henry, who recorded in his diary, "We are put hereby to a Trilemma, to turn flat Independents, or to strike in with the conformists, or to sit down in former silence." Arthur C. Clarke, the British science fiction writer, cited a trilemma in trying to achieve production quickly and cheaply while also maintaining high quality, leading to the quip: "quick, cheap, good: pick two." In public choice theory, there is the trilemma of juggling three priorities—coverage, cost and choice—when offering a public service.

If we turn to economics, we will see that trilemmas have indeed proliferated. Rodrik (2007) argued that if a country wants more of globalisation, it must either give up some democracy or some national sovereignty. Ferguson (2009) highlighted the trilemma of a choice between commitment to globalisation, to social order and to a small state (meaning limited state intervention). In one of his FT columns, Martin Wolf spoke about the US Republican Party's fiscal policy trilemma: the belief that large budget deficits are ruinous; a continued eagerness to cut taxes; and an utter lack of interest in spending cuts on a large enough scale. Then we have the Earth Trilemma (EEE), which posits that for economic development (E), we need increased energy expenditure (E), but this raises the environmental issue (E).

The trilemma more directly relevant to this theme is a financial stability trilemma put forward by Schoenmaker (2009), explaining the incompatibility within the euro zone of a stable financial system, an integrated financial system, and national financial stability policies. By far the most high profile current trilemma, as per some analysts, is the euro zone trilemma: the seeming irreconcilability between its three wishes: a single currency, minimal fiscal contribution to bailouts, and the ECB's commitment to low inflation.

The Old Trilemma

Even as I have spoken about more recent trilemmas in economics, the *prima donna* of all of them is Mundell's 'impossible trinity'. This old trilemma asserts that a country cannot simultaneously maintain all three policy goals of free capital flows, a fixed exchange rate and an independent monetary policy. The impossible trinity, as students of economics have learnt for over a half century, has a strong theoretical foundation in the Mundell-Fleming model developed in the 1960s.

Figure 10.1

Impossible Trinity

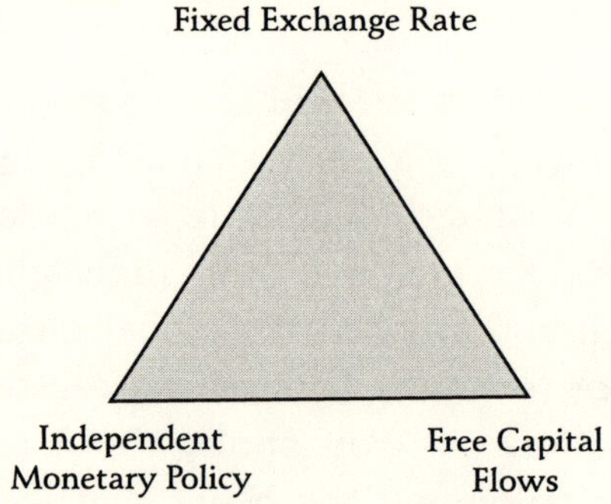

The choices the world made under the impossible trinity varied over time. Under the gold standard, exchange rates were fixed and capital could move around, but central banks were forced to adjust interest rates to ensure they did not run out of reserves. This could lead to pressure on the real economy, and a lot of booms and busts.

Under Bretton Woods, we had fixed exchange rates (with occasional adjustments) and independent monetary policy, but capital mobility was highly restricted; when I first went abroad over 30 years ago, Indians couldn't take out more than $20, no matter the purpose of the trip. The Bretton Woods system broke down under the weight of fixed exchange rates, and the world moved to largely floating exchange rates. Capital has flowed freely round the world.

In the post-Bretton Woods era, countries have made different choices. The most common case, typical across advanced economies, is to give up on a fixed exchange rate so as to run an open economy with an independent monetary policy. On the other hand, economies that adopt a hard peg give up on independence of monetary policy. Examples include the currency boards set up by Hong Kong and, for a time, Argentina. More recently, responding to a rapid appreciation of the Swiss Franc as a result of the safe haven effect, Switzerland declared its commitment to defend a pre-announced exchange rate.

History is replete also with examples of countries aiming to achieve all three goals at the same time, and failing to do so, often in a disorderly way. Thailand's decision to abandon the hard peg against the US dollar in July 1997 is a classic example.

Notwithstanding its real life validation, it is not as if Mundell's 'Impossible Trinity' is inviolable. Many of the assumptions underlying this model do not often hold; indeed the new open economy macroeconomy models that build in price rigidities and monopolistic competition demonstrate policy dynamics quite different from those built in the Mundell-Fleming tradition. It is also not the case that countries are forced into corner solutions at the nodes of the impossible trinity triangle. As it happens, reflecting the forces of globalisation and their asymmetric impact, many emerging economies have opted for middle solutions.

Impossible Trinity to Holy Trinity

In the context of this paper, is the new trilemma—the simultaneous pursuit of price stability, financial stability and sovereign debt sustainability—a new impossible trinity? Possibly not. There is no theory which says that these objectives are inconsistent with one another. It can even be argued that the three objectives reinforce each other, and that together they sustain growth, thereby constituting not an impossible trinity, but actually a holy trinity of objectives.

Figure 10.2

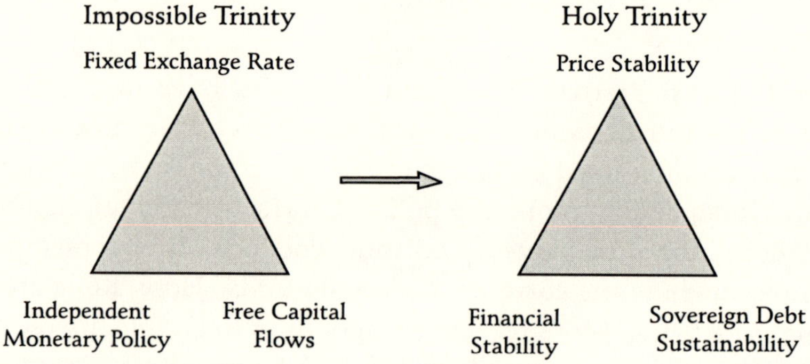

That does not by any means imply that the holy trinity of objectives can always be achieved simultaneously, or once achieved, can be maintained as such indefinitely. There would be tensions and trade-offs, especially in the short-term. In particular, the tensions materialise with brutal force in a state of disequilibrium—when inflation is off target, the financial system is fragile and public debt is ballooning. To the extent we have to manage these tensions, the policy problem qualifies as a trilemma.

The Many Ways in which the New Trilemma Plays Out

Policies in pursuit of the three objectives under the trilemma interact in complex, and often unintended ways. Sometimes they are supportive of each other; at other times, they may run counter to each other. More perplexingly, the tensions and trade-offs may be different in crisis times from normal times.

Let me attempt to illustrate this by citing some examples from global experience, including recent experience. Given the three objectives underlying the new trilemma, and the two-way directions in which they can interact, we have a total of six 'cause and impact' bilateral interactions. I will consider them one by one.

Figure 10.3

New Trilemma

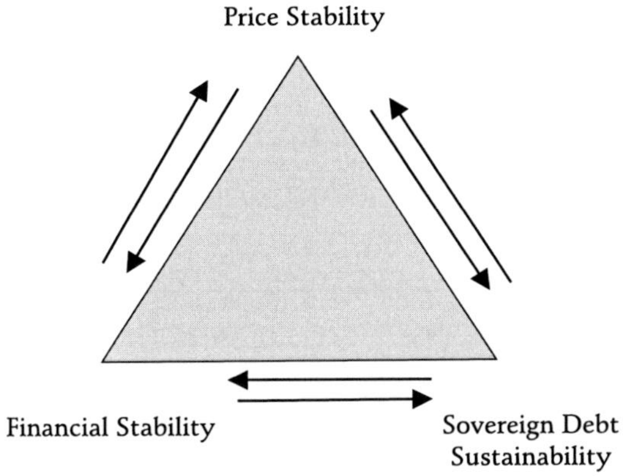

Price Stability→Financial Stability

Before the global financial crisis, the stereotype view was that price stability and financial stability complement each other i.e., monetary policy and policies for financial stability are mutually reinforcing. The crisis has proved that wrong. Note that we saw the global financial sector come to the brink of collapse in the midst of a period of extraordinary price stability.

Indeed the experience of the crisis has prompted an even stronger assertion—that there is a trade-off between price stability and financial stability. In other words, the more successful a central bank is with price stability, the more likely it is to imperil financial stability. The argument goes as follows. The extended period of steady growth and low and stable inflation during the 'great moderation' lulled central banks into complacency. Only with the benefit of hindsight is it now clear that the prolonged period of price stability blindsided policy makers to the cancer of financial instability growing in the underbelly.

An even more recent example of a conflict between policies for financial stability and price stability is of the ECB reversing its crisis-driven expansionary stance by raising interest rates twice during April-July 2011. The ECB justified this on the argument of stemming the underlying inflationary pressures, but many criticised this move as being premature and as clearly unhelpful to restoring financial stability. Of course, we all know that the ECB reversed these hikes during November-December 2011 in response to the euro zone slowdown.

Financial Stability→Price Stability

Let us now see the interaction in the reverse direction. Whether policies aimed at financial stability can affect price stability is a debate that has stayed with us all through the period of management of the crisis. Many analysts have argued that the extraordinary monetary expansion, especially by the Fed, to bring interest rates to the zero lower bound (ZLB) and following it up with two rounds of 'quantitative easing' (QE), all aimed at restoring financial stability, may actually be sowing the seeds of inflation. The argument goes that since the inflationary impact of easy monetary policies is difficult to see real time, the Fed risks going overboard with monetary easing thereby jeopardising future price stability.

We also have an illustration from emerging economies of policies for financial stability affecting price stability. During the crisis, EME central banks eased monetary policy to provide relief to the financial sector, but this also saw inflation quickly resurging when recovery started.

Financial Stability→Sovereign Debt Sustainability

The management of the crisis offered an important lesson on how policies aimed at restoring financial stability could impair sovereign debt sustainability. By far the most obvious illustration of this link is the cost of bailouts of failing financial institutions, accompanied by 'fiscal stimulus', to prevent the financial sector problems from causing overall economic activity to collapse. The fiscal action was unquestionably necessary to restore financial stability. But the net impact need not always be benign. There are circumstances under which fiscal expansion in support of financial stability can threaten sovereign debt sustainability. That will happen if the sovereign is already highly indebted, and the recovery is not quick enough or robust enough. Governments will then see their revenues falling, will need to borrow to bridge the fiscal gap, and can potentially get trapped in a self-reinforcing adverse fiscal feedback loop eventually jeopardising their sovereign debt sustainability.

Sovereign Debt Sustainability→Financial Stability

For transmission of shocks from the sovereign to the banking system, the evolving situation in the euro zone is clearly the most glaring example. Consider Greece, where banks are being asked to share the burden of bailing out the government, the so called private sector involvement—(PSI), so that sovereign debt could be brought down to sustainable levels. But this will affect their collective viability and potentially threaten broader financial stability. There has been acrimony over whether the PSI is voluntary or involuntary. For the purpose of this issue, that debate is a technicality; it does not alter the basic contours of contagion from sovereign debt to financial stability.

The ECB's new term repo longer-term refinancing operation (LTRO) window offers another example of how sovereign debt sustainability concerns can affect financial stability. This new window offers banks three-year money at the repo rate to encourage them to use that money to lend to sovereigns, taking advantage of the arbitrage opportunity. But this financial engineering is a fragile and potentially problematic arrangement. Banks will need to post additional collateral with ECB if the bonds they offered fall in value or suffer a credit downgrade. For precisely the same reasons—fall in value and credit downgrade—banks will need to provide additional capital against monies they have lent to sovereigns. This could put banks on a collateral spiral and erode overall financial stability.

Sovereign Debt Sustainability→Price Stability

The most obvious route for sovereign debt concerns impinging on price stability is through the monetisation of government debt. Central banks do, of course, resort to open market operations (OMOs)—buying and selling government paper—for purposes of liquidity management. But if the motivation for the OMO is to help out a fiscally vulnerable sovereign or to reduce the cost of borrowing for the sovereign, central banks could end up holding price stability hostage to sovereign debt concerns.

Fiscal concerns can dominate monetary policy in other less dramatic ways. In the years before the crisis, an increasing number of governments were voluntarily adopting fiscal responsibility rules, thereby allowing room for autonomous monetary policy. These rule-based fiscal regimes unravelled during the crisis as both governments and central banks implemented expansionary policies in close coordination. While such coordination during the crisis was not questioned except by extreme purists, now in the recovery period, several fundamental concerns are resurfacing.

At the heart of these concerns is whether monetary policy is once again becoming hostage to fiscal compulsions. The specifics of the debate vary but the basic issues are similar. In the US, the debate is over the trade-off between short-term fiscal stimulus and long-term fiscal consolidation. In the euro area, the question is about the shared benefits of a monetary union without the shared responsibilities of a fiscal union. In India, the question has been whether the OMOs conducted by the Reserve Bank to manage systemic liquidity are acting as a disincentive for fiscal discipline. The questions all around are: are central banks being forced beyond their comfort zone to subordinate their monetary policy stance to the government's fiscal stance? Aren't the so called unconventional measures, in reality, quasi-fiscal measures? Are central banks, in the process, compromising their basic commitment to price stability?

Price Stability→Sovereign Debt Sustainability

There are several ways in which policies aimed at price stability can influence sovereign debt sustainability. Higher interest rates, necessitated to combat inflation, raise the costs of debt to the government. Also, if the government has large subsidies on its budget, as do many emerging and developing economies, inflation could raise the cost of subsidies thereby raising the borrowing need of the government. On the other hand, governments with large debts may not actually mind a bit of inflation as it affords them an opportunity to inflate away some of the debt.

I have spoken about the tensions and trade-offs between the three objectives underlying the new trilemma. The examples that I have given are by no means exhaustive but are intended to illustrate the complex policy challenges they pose to central banks.

Four Questions Underlying the New Trilemma

Now let me turn to some important questions that central banks will confront in managing the new trilemma. In particular, I will raise four questions.

Are We Seeing a Return of Fiscal Dominance of Monetary Policy?

This question has surfaced with vigour in the context of the euro zone crisis. The ECB claims that its bond purchase programme is aimed at restoring liquidity and improving monetary transmission. But many analysts believe that this is a thinly veiled attempt to shore up sovereign borrowing and that the ECB is actually acquiescing in fiscal dominance.

Although this tension between the central bank mandate and sovereign debt sustainability is presently being played out in Europe, it is not new; nor is it unique to Europe. The 70 odd years since the Great Depression saw a famous rivalry between fiscal and monetary policies for influence. Historically central banks suffered from fiscal dominance since they had to acquiesce in governments 'borrowing as much as required at as low a cost as possible'.

This state of affairs started changing in the 1980s, with a wave of support for central bank independence arising largely in response to the damage inflicted by the stagflation of the 1970s and the clear lesson that high inflation is detrimental to sustainable growth. So, fiscal dominance gradually yielded to independent central banks, free of short-term compulsions, targetting largely, and in some cases exclusively, price stability. Now it seems we are seeing a reversal of that trend with central banks being called upon to mind sovereign debt sustainability concerns.

Fiscal dominance manifests through the central bank acquiescing in the fiscal stance of the government. This usually happens through monetisation of debt through the central bank's bond buying programme. Central banks typically conduct OMOs more as reverse transactions (repos) for liquidity management purposes in line with their monetary policy stance and intermediate targets. In that case, they should be seen as pure monetary policy operations. But at times, OMOs could be motivated by the objective of providing liquidity to support government borrowing or of reducing the yield on treasury bonds to enhance debt sustainability. It then becomes a case of acquiescence in fiscal dominance. There is often only a thin line, and the interpretation of the motivation for outright OMOs could vary depending on the circumstances.

In the presence of large sovereign borrowing that makes the government's fiscal stance unsustainable, central banks typically have little choice. If they do not conduct OMOs to bring systemic liquidity within reasonable limits, they risk losing control over financial stability. If they do conduct OMOs, they risk losing control over price stability. What this really says is that fiscal responsibility is much more than a question of whether monetary policy is independent or not. It is a question of sustaining macroeconomic stability.

Will the Management of the New Trilemma Erode the Autonomy and Accountability of Central Banks?

The much prized autonomy of central banks has come under assault post-crisis with an influential view gaining ground that one of the principal causes of the crisis was the unbridled autonomy of central banks. The standard argument for central bank autonomy is that autonomy enhances the credibility of the central bank's inflation management credentials. Monetary policy typically acts with a lag, and price stability therefore has to be viewed in a medium-term perspective. Having autonomy frees the central bank from the pressure of responding to short-term developments, deviating from its inflation target and thereby compromising its medium-term inflation goals.

Now that the importance of central bank autonomy in monetary policy has come to be largely accepted, the question is: will additional responsibilities underlying the new trilemma affect that autonomy? And how will this new situation also affect the accountability structures of the central banks? It may be useful to take stock of the apprehensions in this regard.

For overseeing systemic stability, new governance structures have emerged after the global crisis. These include the Financial Services Oversight Council (FSOC) in the US, the Financial Policy Committee (FPC) in the UK and the European Systemic Risk Board (ESRB) in the EU. Here in India, we have the Financial Stability and Development Council (FSDC). The precise institutional arrangements vary, but across all of them, central banks have a lead responsibility.

With these new institutional arrangements for financial stability in place, the autonomy question has acquired an additional dimension. Note that central bank autonomy has worked because they could keep at arm's length from the governments. But once a coordination mechanism is in place, these barriers may melt away. Also, even if that is what the book says, it may be difficult to straitjacket the discussion at the coordination forum to financial stability. As we have seen, there are no 'pure' financial stability issues; they are all inter-connected. A discussion on financial stability could very well lead to a discussion on monetary policy. What then of the autonomy of the central bank? This apprehension, as all of you will appreciate, is non-trivial.

If we now add responsibility for sovereign debt sustainability to this already complex situation, the reason for apprehension about the threat to the autonomy of central banks becomes more obvious. Sovereign debt is a quintessentially political subject, and as we noted earlier, the very foundation of central bank autonomy is justified on the need to free monetary policy from fiscal dominance. By requiring central banks to be mindful of sovereign debt sustainability concerns as part of the 'new trilemma', is the hard won gain of freedom from fiscal compulsions being compromised? But look at it also from the opposite perspective. Given that investor trust in public debt is part of the foundation of a nation-state, is it realistic for a central bank to remain indifferent to sovereign debt sustainability?

The new trilemma also poses questions for central banks on the accountability front. With a single objective of price stability, the deliverable could be precisely defined, the outcome accurately measured, and accountability clearly extracted. Multiple objectives, and as we have seen, with tensions and trade-offs between them, can diffuse and erode this accountability mechanism. The central bank can always explain away any failure on one front as a result of policies to defend another front.

There are no easy answers to these apprehensions about the impact of the new trilemma on central bank autonomy and accountability. Governments and central banks in each jurisdiction will have to define the nature and extent of the latter's responsibility for financial stability and sovereign debt sustainability. I can only lay down certain tenets that must inform this process. First, the fundamental responsibility of central banks for price stability should not be compromised. Second, central banks should have a lead, but not exclusive, responsibility, for financial stability. Third, the boundaries of central bank responsibility for sovereign debt sustainability should be clearly defined. Fourth, in the matter of ensuring financial stability, the government must normally leave the responsibility to the regulators, assuming an activist role only in times of crisis.

Does the Pursuit of the New Trilemma Militate against Growth?

My short answer to this question is 'no'. Let me elaborate. It is possible that in the short term, policies aimed at price stability, financial stability and sovereign debt sustainability could, at times, run counter to policies required for promoting growth. But growth achieved at the cost of the objectives of the new trilemma cannot be sustained. What can be sustained is only growth that is consistent with these objectives. So, some sacrifice ratio may be operative in the short term, but in the medium term, there is no trade-off between sustainable growth and maintaining the objectives of the new trilemma.

Let me illustrate this with reference to the debate that played out quite actively in India all of last year around the growth-inflation trade-off. We had inflation ruling all through the year in the range of 9-10 per cent. To combat this, the Reserve Bank has had to tighten monetary policy—raising rates, as all our critics are fond of saying repeatedly—a record total of 13 times. While inflation did not show any downward trend till late in the calendar year 2011, growth has certainly moderated. The Reserve Bank's latest projection for growth for FY12 is 7 per cent, down from 8.4 per cent last year. The criticism has been that we could not bring inflation down but only ended up hurting growth. This is not the occasion to enter a defence of our position. But the criticism throws up an important issue on the growth-inflation trade-off.

Evidence from empirical research suggests that the relationship between growth and inflation is non-linear. At low inflation and stable inflation expectations, there is a trade-off between growth and inflation. But above a certain threshold level of inflation, the trade-off disappears, this relationship reverses, and high inflation actually starts taking a toll on growth. Estimates by the Reserve Bank using different methodologies put the threshold level of inflation in the range of 4 per cent-6 per cent. With WPI inflation ruling above 9 per cent till recently, we were way past this threshold. At this high level, inflation is unambiguously inimical to growth; it saps investor confidence and erodes medium-term growth prospects. The Reserve Bank's monetary tightening all through last year was accordingly geared towards safeguarding medium-term growth even if it meant some sacrifice in near-term growth.

The debate on the trade-off between financial stability and growth runs along roughly similar lines. Post-crisis, regulation of financial institutions is being tightened. In particular, under the Basel III package, banks will be required to hold higher capital, better quality capital and also buildup capital and liquidity buffers. What does this mean for growth?

A BIS study, undertaken by a group led by Stephen Cecchetti, estimates that a one percentage point increase in the target ratio of tangible common equity (TCE) to risk-weighted assets (RWA) phased in over a nine-year period reduces output by close to 0.2 per cent. The study argues though that as the financial system makes the required adjustment, these costs will dissipate and then reverse after the adjustment period, and the growth path will return to its original trajectory. A Basel Committee study estimates that there will be net positive benefits from Basel III because of the reduced probability of a crisis and reduced volatility in output in response to a shock. An IIF study, however, estimates a higher sacrifice ratio—that the G3 (US, Euro area and Japan) will lose 0.3 percentage points from their annual growth rates over the full 10-year period (2011-2020).

What are the implications of these numbers relating to growth sacrifice for emerging market economies (EMEs)? Let me take the example of India. Admittedly, the capital to risk weighted asset ratio (CRAR) of our banks, at the aggregate level, is above the Basel III requirement although a few individual banks may fall short and may have to raise capital. But capital adequacy today does not necessarily mean capital adequacy going forward. As the economy grows, so too will the credit demand, requiring banks to expand their balance sheets, and in order to be able to do so, they will have to augment their capital.

In a structurally transforming economy with rapid upward mobility like India, credit demand will expand faster than GDP for several reasons. First, India will shift increasingly from services to manufactures whose credit intensity is higher per unit of GDP. Second, we need to at least double our investment in infrastructure which will place enormous demands on credit. Finally, financial inclusion, which both the Government and the Reserve Bank are driving, will bring millions of low income households into the formal financial system with almost all of them needing credit. What all this means is that we are going to have to impose higher capital requirements on banks as per Basel III at a time when the economy's credit demand is going to expand rapidly. How best can we resolve this tension between the demands of growth and the demands of financial stability is a question that we in India and several other EMEs will have to address.

I have gone at some length on this not to argue that the costs of financial stability outweigh the benefits, but to argue that the cost-benefit calculus will vary from country to country, and will vary for a given country over time. So, the challenge for every country, advanced, emerging and developing, is to tailor its financial stability policies to maximise the benefit cost ratio on a dynamic scale.

Now let me come to the third leg of the equation—the link between growth and sovereign debt sustainability. Like with the other two legs of the new trilemma, even in the case of sovereign debt, there is an inflexion point beyond which fiscal deficits militate against growth. Government borrowing is not bad *per se*, but excessive borrowing is. There is, therefore, a need to cap total public debt as a proportion of GDP.

What is equally important in respect of fiscal management is the quality of public expenditure. If the government borrows and squanders that money away on unproductive current expenditure, both fiscal sustainability and growth would be jeopardised. Governments need to spend on merit goods and public goods, in particular on improving human and social capital and on physical infrastructure.

So, after all this discussion, what is the answer to the question: does the pursuit of the new trilemma militate against growth? No. It does not. But there could be some trade-offs and governments will have to tailor their policies to ensure that the benefit-cost calculus is always maximised.

What are the Limits to Unconventional Policy Measures?

As the crisis exploded with brutal intensity and depth, central banks around the world acted with an unusual show of policy force, ferociously cutting policy rates to near zero or even zero. Realising soon that this was not sufficient to restore calm and confidence to the markets, they had to follow up the conventional measures with a slew of unconventional measures variously described as quantitative and credit easing.

The first wave of unconventional measures was aimed at providing liquidity to the system either by way of collateralised loans through the repo window or outright purchase of bonds. Liquidity management is of course standard monetary policy procedure. What made this unconventional were mainly two things. The first was the quantum of operations. The volumes were large, and were aimed at flooding the market with liquidity, much beyond what is expected in normal times.

The second characteristic that made liquidity infusion unconventional was the relaxation of standards regarding the type of bonds bought under the OMOs. In this regard, different central banks relaxed regulations to different extents. While the Bank of England stuck to treasuries, the Fed bought federally backed mortgage bonds in addition to treasuries. The Bank of Japan went further buying also corporate bonds, commercial paper, exchange traded funds and real estate investment trusts.

The second wave of unconventional measures went beyond repo operations and OMOs. The Bank of Japan extended targetted loans to banks to spur long-term investment. The Fed supplemented two rounds of QE with 'operation twist'—of purchasing longer-term treasuries against sale of short-term treasuries in an effort to depress the entire yield curve rather than just its short end. Last week, it also began publishing the expected interest rate path for the coming years. The ECB, as noted earlier, is providing three-year loans to banks.

What of emerging economy central banks? They too had resorted to unconventional measures although their policy rates did not hit the zero lower bound. In the Reserve Bank, for example, at the height of the crisis, we operated a term repo window to enable banks to meet the liquidity requirement of mutual funds and non-bank finance companies (NBFCs). We relaxed the statutory liquidity ratio (SLR) prescription for banks by up to 1.5 percentage points of their net demand and time liabilities (NDTL) for this purpose. The risk weight on banks' exposure to NBFCs, which was raised earlier, was rolled back. The restriction on commercial banks in buying back the CDs held by mutual funds was lifted. We also instituted a foreign currency swap facility for banks.

Unconventional measures have been contentious. Central banks have largely maintained that the unconventional measures they deployed are a part of the monetary policy arsenal, and that the intent behind them is to improve monetary transmission. Their critics have argued that central banks have actually stepped beyond their mandates to accommodate extraneous compulsions.

All in all, the global financial crisis and the ongoing Euro zone crisis have raised important questions about the unconventional measures that central banks can resort to—their range, intent and the way the intent should be communicated to the markets.

Conclusion

Let me now conclude by summarising what I have said. I explained the rationale behind the theme: Price Stability, Financial Stability and Sovereign Debt Sustainability: Policy Challenges from the New Trilemma. I then illustrated how the three legs under the new trilemma interact with one another. Thereafter, I raised the following four questions that central banks need to address in the context of the new trilemma:

(i) Are we seeing a return of fiscal dominance of monetary policy?

(ii) Will the management of the new trilemma erode the autonomy and accountability of central banks?

(iii) Does the pursuit of the new trilemma militate against growth?

(iv) What are the limits to unconventional policy measures?

To what extent are the old and new trilemmas similar? Under the old trilemma—the impossible trinity—countries had to sacrifice one of the three objectives—fixed exchange rate, independent monetary policy and free capital flows. Under the new trilemma—the holy trinity—no country can afford to sacrifice any of the objectives as the feedback loops can quickly shift the economy from an equilibrium to a disequilibrium. The issue really is of managing the *inter se* prioritisation among the objectives and of determining the role of the central bank in this management.

So, how best can we manage the new trilemma? The crisis has given us valuable lessons from practice. We also have assorted bits of theory. The task ahead is to put them together into a coherent, workable theory of the new trilemma. I hope this paper will take us closer to that.

A final thought. In his best-selling book, *The Ascent of Money*, Niall Ferguson says that sometimes the most important historical events are the non-events: the things that did not happen. From that perspective, that the Great Recession did not turn into the second Great Depression, as we had feared, will count as a major non-event, notwithstanding the depth and duration of this recession. If the euro survives the sovereign debt crisis, as we hope, it will be another spectacular non-event. Non-events they may be, but they have changed our thinking on central bank mandates in a powerful way. How influential that thinking will be on the way forward will depend on how firmly central banks embrace the new trilemma.

References

Chancellor, Edward (2011). "Germany's Eurozone Trilemma", *Financial Times*. November 6.

Ferguson, Niall (2009). "Conservatism and the Crisis: A Transatlantic Trilemma", *Centre for Policy Studies Ruttenberg Lecture*. March 24.

Rodrik, Dani (2007). "The Inescapable Trilemma of the World Economy", June 27. *rodrik.typepad.com/dani_rodriks_weblog*

Schoenmaker, Dirk (2009). "A New Financial Stability Framework for Europe", *The Financial Regulator* 13(3).

Wolf, Martin (2010). "The Political Genius of Supply Side Economics", *Financial Times*. July 25.

Inaugural speech at the Second International Research Conference of the Reserve Bank of India, Mumbai, February 1, 2012. RBI Bulletin February 2012.

11

K.C. CHAKRABARTY

Crisis Preparedness in Interconnected Markets

Prevention is Better than Cure

Crises and their Origin

Let me begin first by attempting to define a crisis. The word crisis originates from the Greek word *krisis*—which means 'decisive moment'. The Oxford dictionary defines a crisis as "a time of intense difficulty or danger" while the Cambridge dictionary describes it as "a situation that has reached an extremely difficult or dangerous point; a time of great disagreement, uncertainty or suffering." The term financial crisis, to be more specific, is broadly applied to a range of situations which encompass banking panics, disorderly functioning of markets, stock market collapses, bursting of asset price bubbles, currency collapses, sovereign defaults, amongst others.

Crises can happen anywhere, at any time, and often occur when they are least expected. History is peppered with crises that have varying origins—starting from the Tulips mania of the 17th century to the dotcom bubble of the 2000s and to the 2007 subprime crisis and the latest brouhaha over the sovereign debt crisis.

Origins of a crisis are hard to pinpoint. They can be caused by an act of nature—an earthquake or a tsunami (as seen recently in Japan), for instance, which, within a very short span of time, can cause untold damage to the real economy, which can, in turn, affect the financial sector and governments. The origins of crises can also

Assistance provided by Ms Dimple Bhandia in preparation of this address is gratefully acknowledged.

play out over a relatively longer period of building up of systemic risks in the macrofinancial system, as the recent global financial crisis demonstrated, shattering belief in what are now believed to be 'myths'—the 'Great Moderation' and the 'Goldilocks Economy'.

As central bankers and policy makers tasked with fostering financial stability, we are interested in both kinds of crisis. Both have the potential to cause financial instability. Both will need swift action if the fallout has to be managed and the collateral damage contained. But what interests us most are the crises which are a result of build-up of risks over time and which we can take policy initiatives to influence and, perhaps, avert.

Each crisis has certain unique features and there is a tendency to consider each crisis as different. This illusion is furthered by the fact that each crisis originates in different markets, through varied products and is propagated through different sets of economic agents. But there are always similar strands which cut across these superficial differences. In any case, the cornerstone of any crisis is the same—aptly summed by Mahatma Gandhi who stated, albeit in a different context, that "There is enough in the world for everybody's need, but not enough for anybody's greed." When 'greed' takes over 'need' and a group of 'mischievous elements' are able to hold the 'good' to ransom, the seeds of a crisis are sown.

Each crisis is preceded by excesses, e.g., excessive credit growth or excessive asset price spirals. Each crisis leaves behind its own set of lessons. And as the dust settles on each crisis, these lessons are forgotten by all concerned. As Hyman Minsky aptly remarked, "As a previous crisis recedes in time, it's quite natural... to believe that a new era has arrived. Cassandra-like warnings that nothing has changed, that there is a financial breaking point that will lead to a deep depression, are naturally ignored in these circumstances."

Crisis and Interconnectedness

This global financial crisis has brought to the fore the importance of interconnections—amongst the banking system, financial markets and payment and settlement systems. It has underlined the fact that focussing on only one part of the financial system can obscure vulnerabilities that may prove very important from the perspective of systemic stability.

Concomitant with the rapid financial globalisation of the past three decades—reflected in the manifold increase in the external assets and liabilities of nations as a share of GDP—there has been an increase in the degree of financial interconnectedness. According to BIS (Bank for International Settlement) data, consolidated banking assets have risen from US $13.2 trillion in 2002 to over US $ 30 trillion. Financial linkages between countries have been increasing exponentially, especially since the mid-1990s, through an intricate web of claims and obligations which link the balance sheets of sovereigns, financial institutions and corporations. The trend has only been reinforced by rapid growth in cross border capital flows. In the last decade or so, the proliferation of sophisticated financial products has further heightened the complexity of these balance sheet connections.

A highly interconnected world tends to increase both the probability and the impact of crisis. The potential for systemic risks increase, for example, due to potential build-up of leverage and liquidity mismatches at the same time or due to exposures to common networks of intermediaries. This leaves the financial system vulnerable to adverse changes in the macrofinancial environment, on the one hand, while, on the other, pervasive interconnections can result in a rapid transmission of adverse shocks across the global financial system at an amplified speed. The system dynamics of a set of networked markets and institutions can, thus, play a critical role in the amplification as well as the propagation mechanisms of shocks.

The potential of interconnected markets to render more severe the reach and impact of financial crisis through contagion has been demonstrated time and again. In the case of the Mexican crisis, a number of other Latin American countries felt pressures and were forced to intervene and/or raise interest rates. This, despite the fact that they had virtually no trade and investment links with Mexico. In East Asia, the crisis that began in Thailand spread throughout the region and reverberated as far away as South Africa, the Czech

Republic and South America. The financial crisis of 2007-2009 began in the subprime market in the US but had soon engulfed the global economy through real, trade and financial channels. The European debt crisis is proving to be no different. The crises in the 1990s originated in the emerging market economies but affected the advanced economies. In the 2000s, the crises originated in the developed economies but soon engulfed the developing world.

Management of Crises

The recent financial crisis has emphatically demonstrated the potential impact of a crisis. The subprime crisis, which originated in the financial sector, left deep scars on the real economy affecting growth in advanced and emerging nations alike. The buck, not surprisingly, stopped at the common man, especially in emerging markets such as ours, who was left to bear the brunt of any crisis. The potentially devastating impact of financial crises gave rise to a felt need to manage such crises, in particular, to put in place a framework to manage crisis, if and when they arise.

A key attribute of the crisis situation is that it calls for decision and action with a view to managing and containing the fallout of the consequences of the crisis. Management of financial crisis typically involves some basic phases, as discussed in the case of the 2007 global financial crisis in a Congressional Research Service Report (Nanto, 2009). Management of crisis would involve intervention to contain the contagion and restore confidence in the system in the first phase. The second phase would typically involve coping with the secondary effects of the crisis, for example, recession, if any, flight of capital, etc. The third phase of this process would involve affecting changes in the financial system to reduce risk and prevent future crises.

Simultaneously, the other key features of a crisis situation, *viz.*, the unpredictability associated with the event, the speed with which it typically unfolds and the uncertain but dangerous outcomes that it can spawn, suggest that it is necessary to lay down a comprehensive contingency plan which envisages, in a given context, all possible crisis situations of varying gravity and possible decisions and actions as well as the framework under which decisions can be taken and implemented.

A Crisis Management Framework

Evolving events since August 2007 have put to test arrangements for crisis management and financial stability across the globe. Swift and proactive action was indeed taken once the contours of the crisis started becoming clearer. Once the crisis broke, central banks, governments and other regulators across the globe, including in India, managed to coordinate effectively to improvise solutions to the problems they faced. The experience, however, also revealed several shortcomings in the arrangements in place to manage the crisis, ahead of the crisis.

Drawing from the lessons learnt during this crisis, let me lay down some broad attributes, which I believe, are key to the design of an effective crisis management framework. Let me confess at the very outset, however, that this list is far from exhaustive. Crisis management remains an inexact science and I, along with all of you in central banks and other policy making institutions, continue to learn.

- First, there should be a clear assignment of responsibility for financial stability. Where this responsibility is shared amongst different agencies, roles and responsibilities need to be clearly delineated and the protocol for coordination during crisis clearly spelt out.
- Crisis management plans need to be flexible. The characteristics of a crisis can always differ from earlier crises, so authorities need to be prepared to apply flexibility rather than working from a set framework.
- Effective crisis management hinges on the authorities identifying and addressing problems at an early stage implying that the processes that enable early identification of emerging systemic risks need to be strengthened.
- The framework for crisis management needs to strike an appropriate balance between rules and judgement. While

rules foster transparency and aid in avoiding moral hazard, use of judgement is critical as crises or crisis like situations differ from one another and warrant suitably 'customised' solution.

- Availability of accurate, relevant and timely information is key for any effective framework for financial stability. It is even more critical for crisis management where time is of the very essence. A framework for managing crises must, therefore, take cognisance of need to ensure availability of timely and relevant information by addressing legal and other hurdles to information collection and obstacles to information sharing among the agencies.
- A crisis management framework needs to be dynamic and responsive to the evolving macrofinancial environment and developments in the financial markets. Most importantly, the framework should be, and should continue to remain, commensurate to the degree of complexity in the financial system.
- The crisis management framework needs to take cognisance of global interdependence and integration. Certain crisis actions may need to be internationally coordinated and without adequate preparation and groundwork, efforts to manage crises by authorities in different countries could become a demonstration of the Prisoners' Dilemma where each country looks out for itself.
- Above all, a crisis management framework must enable nimble footed decision-making. This will necessitate the creation of a framework which involves all the agencies that will be involved in the decision-making process, with clearly defined responsibilities and mechanism for information exchange and coordination.
- Also critical for the management of crises, would be an effective strategy for communication. Measured transparency, especially during a crisis, can help prevent panic and also add to credibility of policy initiatives.

- Finally, the framework should include a continuous programme of work on crisis preparation including ensuring that effective coordination and information sharing arrangements are in place and that crisis management tools remain up to date and are tested to meet any potential risks to financial stability.

There are two further points I would like to make in respect of some of the tools which form a critical part on any crisis management framework. The first is the lender of last resort function of the central bank and the second relates to the recovery and resolution planning of financial institutions in distress.

The first important tool at the disposal of crisis management is the role of the central banker as a lender of last resort. The recent financial crisis, during which central banks in the advanced economies used tools through a series of conventional and unconventional measures, underscored the importance of the lender of last resort function of the central bank for crisis management. Going forward, it would be important to clearly define principles for access to emergency liquidity assistance from the central bank. The principles will need to balance the imperatives of ensuing capacity to provide adequate liquidity support during the crisis while ensuring that perverse incentives for lax liquidity management are not built-up in the banking system. The principles may also need to address issues relating to collateral standards, given the experiences of recent crises.

The spectre of 'too big to fail' institutions raised its ugly head during the 2007 global financial crisis focussing attention on the lack of the necessary arrangements for orderly resolution of such institutions. A crisis management framework will need to be alive and open to the possibility of failure, if only to prevent the associated moral hazard problems. For the 'no-failure' perception to be altered, robust arrangements, which allow orderly resolution and mitigate systemic consequences of such failures will need to be put in place, especially for the resolution of cross border financial firms. The Financial Stability Board has recently released the 'Key Attributes of Effective Resolution Regimes' that would lay down the essential features and tools that national resolution regimes for financial institutions, including non-bank financial institutions, should have. For the large and complex financial institutions, *ex-ante* resolution plans, or 'living wills' are one solution being contemplated internationally in this regard. Recent initiatives towards introducing contingent capital instruments may also potentially play an important role in banks' recovery and resolution plans, going forward.

Crisis Prevention

While the subject of this paper is crisis management, let me emphasise that the most preferable approach to fostering financial stability is crisis prevention.

A series of reforms to the regulatory architecture and plethora of reforms are underway globally which seek to reduce the probability of a crisis occurring. The Basel III reforms aim at increasing the resilience of banks through prescription of a higher quality, quantity and consistency and better risk coverage of capital. The set of reforms for systemically important financial institutions are aimed at reducing the probability of failure of these large and complex financial institutions and at putting in place a robust resolution framework so that the institutions can be winded down in an orderly manner, should they fail. Regulatory perimeter issues are being addressed by putting in place a regulatory framework for the shadow banking system. Another set of reforms are aimed at addressing issues in the over-the-counter (OTC) derivatives markets by ensuring that the transactions in these markets are reported, centrally cleared and, where possible, settled through a central counterparty. Compensation structures are being streamlined to ensure that compensation is aligned to the risks assumed. Financial market infrastructures are being strengthened and deposit insurance systems reformed to take cognisance of the lessons of the crisis. A macroprudential overlay to the entire regulatory framework is being proposed to address issues related to procyclicality and the cross-sectional dimensions of systemic risks. Most importantly, organised frameworks for pursuit of financial stability and crisis management, which promote inter-agency cooperation, are being put in place both nationally and internationally.

Notwithstanding the improvements in the regulatory framework, putting in place a robust system for the assessment of systemic risks which enables identification of emerging excesses and facilitates timely intervention to prevent such risks from materialising, is critical for an effective crisis prevention framework. In order words, putting in place a robust early warning system is a *sine quo non* for any effective crisis prevention framework.

Frameworks for systemic risk identification are taking place around the world as part of an overall framework for macroprudential framework even as there is a growing realisation that systemic risks are complex and measuring them with precision may be challenging exercise of judgement is hence critical. Notwithstanding the complexities, there is a need for the framework for systemic risk assessment to be comprehensive; to take cognisance of interconnectedness, risk concentrations and the channels for cross-sector and cross-border spillovers; to identify key risk drivers; and to conduct periodic stress tests to check the capacity of financial institutions to withstand severe shocks.

Central banks around the world are engaged in developing tools and techniques to accurately assess such risks to the financial system. In India too, upgrading technologies and adding to its existing toolkit for identifying and measuring systemic risks is a continuing endeavour.

Concomitantly with the setting up of an early warning system, an early action system also needs to be put in place. There is, thus, a need for greater emphasis on remedial measures e.g., through pre-resolution and supervisory intervention to ensure that identified risks are managed well before they reach their respective tipping points.

A number of countries are in the process of introducing a framework for such early intervention, especially in case of financial institutions. Denmark, for instance, proposed to introduce the 'diamond framework' from 2013. Under this framework, a set of five quantitative indicators relating to, *inter alia*, credit growth, lending to real estate, large exposures, funding ratio and liquidity coverage, have been defined and the supervisor will take remedial action in case the limits are breached by any financial institution. The Canadian framework consists of five stages *viz.*, a 'normal' stage, an 'early warning' stage, a 'risk to financial viability or solvency' stage, a 'future financial stability in serious doubt' stage and a 'non-viability/insolvency imminent' stage. Each stage is identified by a set of conditions and a number of options for supervisory measures. In India, an early intervention system in the form of a prompt corrective action based on three indicators—capital to risk weighted assets, non-performing advances and return on assets, has existed since 2002. Threshold values for each of the indicators have been defined along with associated structured and discretionary actions.

Interconnectedness as a potential source of crisis was recognised in India much before the onset of the crisis and, as a result, in March 2007, Reserve Bank of India (RBI) limited a bank's inter bank liabilities (IBL) to twice its net worth. A higher IBL limit of 300 per cent of net worth is allowed for banks whose capital to risk (weighted) assets ratio (CRAR) is 11.25 per cent. Further, crisis prevention has been an integral part of regulatory framework in India.

More recently, we set up the Financial Stability Unit (FSU) within the Reserve Bank to *inter alia* carry out macroprudential surveillance. Since its formation in 2009, the FSU has published four Financial Stability Reports (FSRs) on a biannual basis. In the most recent report published in December 2011, we introduced the financial stability indicator based on a combination of financial market stability, macroeconomic stability and banking stability indicators. We also introduced new tools for risk assessment such as the systemic risk survey and the systemic liquidity indicator in addition to improving the coverage of the network model analysis introduced in the previous FSR.

Most people are aware of RBI's counter cyclical policies that won us accolades in our management of the crisis. However, we have also taken several measures to address systemic risk arising out of interconnectedness amongst financial institutions such as placing prudential limits on call borrowing and lending, limits on banks cross holdings of bank's ownership, limits on exposure to single and group borrowers, etc. The further use and development of a macroprudential policy toolkit to manage systemic risk is actively being pursued within the bank.

Concluding Remarks

Recent experiences have clearly demonstrated that resolving a financial crisis is complex and costly. This holds true regardless of what caused the crisis, and regardless of the solution. The best crisis management framework is one that prevents crises. Having said this, no financial system can be completely immune from episodes of financial instability from time to time and there will be a need to manage crisis. As central bankers and regulators carrying the responsibility of fostering financial stability, the best service we can do to our objective, therefore, is to remain prepared to manage crisis. There are important lessons to be learnt from each crisis. Yet, we can count on each crisis to be sufficiently different from every other crisis so as to make their identification a challenge. We can, but, be alert and flexible to evolving risks. Let me conclude with an extract from Carmen M. Reinhart & Kenneth S. Rogoff's book *This Time is Different: Eight Centuries of Financial Folly*

> This time may seem different, but all too often a deeper look shows it is not. Encouragingly, history does point to warning signs that policy makers can look at to assess risk—if only they do not become too drunk with their credit bubble-fueled success and say, as their predecessors have for centuries, "This time is different".

References

Nanto, Dick K. (2009). *The Global Financial Crisis: Analysis and Policy Implications*. October 2.

Keynote address delivered at the Programme held jointly by CAFRAL and Toronto Centre, Canada, January 16, 2012. RBI Bulletin February 2012.

12

ANAND SINHA

Financial Stability: 2007 to 2012

Five Years On

Global financial markets froze abruptly following collapse of Lehman Brothers on September 15, 2008, and have never fully recovered since then. While there have emerged signs of hope, of 'green shoots', from time to time, they too have been quickly dashed. While it was the financial sector which triggered the instability at the outset, it is now the high debt burden in advanced economies which threatens the safety of the financial system and continues to be a drag on economies. The financial system is far from being sound as banks in several advanced economies, particularly in the Eurozone remain vulnerable. Structural imbalances, predating the crisis, persist. The room for fiscal and monetary manoeuvre has shrunk drastically due to the burden of rescue shared by these policies in the aftermath of the sub-prime crisis of 2007. Central bank balance sheets across the world have grown in size and have almost doubled in the last decade and now amount to about 30 per cent of world GDP. Central banks have quickly emerged as the single largest creditors of governments, especially, in the beleaguered Eurozone. Interest rates too have been slashed in a bid to stimulate the sagging economies and the rates are either zero or nearly zero in advanced economies. The expanded balance sheets of the central banks and the near zero policy rates have raised concerns that financial imbalances may buildup all over again.

It is now five years since the outbreak of the global financial crisis. The developments during these years have thrown the global

Inputs provided by Ms Dimple Bhandia are gratefully acknowledged.

economy off balance and seriously challenged the intellectual framework and traditionally held beliefs about the functioning of the financial system, theory and practice of monetary policy and macroeconomic modelling. In the new order of things, financial stability has come to the centre stage of policy making across the globe.

Against this backdrop, I will focus on three sets of developments. First, I will present a brief synopsis of the regulatory changes which have been effected in the years since the financial crisis first broke out. Second, I will present a snapshot of the attempts being made to assess and measure systemic risk, in its many facets. Third, I will discuss the institutional arrangements made to manage financial stability in different countries. I will then present the Indian approach to financial stability and conclude with some of the challenges that confront us in the days to come as we strive together to put in place a healthier and more resilient financial system.

Financial Stability: Pre and Post Crisis

The global financial crisis of 2007 was caused by a combination of macroeconomic and, regulatory and supervisory factors and their interaction. At the core of the crisis lay an interplay between macro imbalances which had grown rapidly in the last 10 years, and the financial market developments and innovations which accelerated over the last 10 to 15 years, partly under the stimulus of the macro imbalances (The Turner Review, 2009). In the years leading up to the financial crisis, policy framework for the financial sector globally was guided by a few doctrines. One, monetary policy should focus only on price stability (the inflation targetting framework). Second, price stability ensures financial stability, the latter being pursued through microprudential regulatory and supervisory framework. Third, the approach towards asset price bubbles, when they are building up, should be one of 'benign' indifference and central banks should 'mop the dust' when bubbles burst, with aggressive easing of monetary policy—the now infamous Greenspan orthodoxy. Fourth, light touch regulation is the way forward in a 'free market' environment where markets self correct in the larger interest and welfare of the economy. Fifth, a set of individual financial institutions constitutes a healthy and robust financial system.

The overall policy framework, prior to the crisis, reflected these doctrines. The policy approach comprised inflation targetting to ensure price and macroeconomic stability and prudential regulatory and supervisory policies focused on the health and stability of individual institutions. Systemic concerns, especially contagion risks, were sought to be contained through a robust financial infrastructure.

In this scheme of things, liquidity risk did not receive the serious consideration that it was entitled to and there was a glaring conceptual flaw inasmuch as there was no framework to address systemic risks. The experiences during the crisis drove home the fact that the risk of financial system disruptions that can destabilise the macroeconomy were not correctly understood and that the impact of interlinkages and common exposures across the financial system were not fully appreciated. The critical lesson which has emerged from the crisis is that financial stability needs to be pursued as an explicit policy objective, and the pre-crisis notion of mopping up the debris from financial bust is not a viable policy as it can have huge macroeconomic costs which we are witnessing today.

The crisis also brought to the fore the role of the sovereign in financial stability—first as a lender of last resort (LoLR) in case of bankruptcy and then as the harbinger of financial instability. The burden of past fiscal indiscretions in several advanced economies, coupled with the stimulus measures taken as part of the crisis management has returned to haunt policy makers. Global instability acquired a new 'avatar'—that of a sovereign debt crisis.

To address the deficiencies which led to the global crisis, the international standard setters—Basel Committee on Banking Supervision (BCBS) and Financial Stability Board (FSB)—have undertaken a massive overhaul of the regulatory framework. The comprehensive reform package known as Basel III framework is designed to address both firm specific risk and broader systemic risk. Basel III essentially enhances the regulatory framework introduced by Basel II at the level of individual banks. It also sets up a macroprudential overlay to limit systemic risk. The measures relate to enhancing the quality and quantity of capital, liquidity risk management, valuation practices, dealing with procyclicality issues and with systemically important banks. It also encompasses resolution mechanism, compensation practices, stress testing, disclosures to enhance transparency and moving OTC derivatives to central clearing and settlement mechanisms for reducing the systemic risk in derivative markets.

Systemic Risk: The Elephant in the Room

Measuring and analysing systemic risk is at the core of ensuring financial stability. It is, therefore, important to understand what systemic risk is. While there is no single universally accepted definition of systemic risk, it is now commonly accepted that these are risks which affect large chunks of the financial system and which have the potential to adversely impact the real economy. A comprehensive definition of risk as defined by the IMF, FSB and BIS is "a risk of disruption to financial services that is caused by an impairment of all or parts of the financial system and has the potential to have serious negative consequences for the real economy." There is also a broad agreement that there are two facets to systemic risk. In its first dimension, systemic risk evolves over time. This time dimension of systemic risk is also called procyclicality and it deals with the buildup of risks through financing imbalances. The imbalances i.e., high leverage, rapid credit growth and compressed risk premia build up during the expansionary phase of a business cycle due to the inherent procyclicality of the financial system and through the risk taking channel. These imbalances interact with macroeconomy amplifying the booms and busts. Larger booms lead to larger busts and larger damage to macroeconomy. The second dimension, interconnectedness, relates to systemic risks being distributed across the financial system at any given point in time. These risks relate to common exposures, entangled balance sheets, common business models or profiles and interconnectedness amongst financial institutions.

The set of policies which deal with managing the systemic risk is known as macroprudential policy. Macroprudential policy tools are essentially microprudential tools i.e., capital provisioning, loan-to-value ratios, debt to income ratios, etc., which are applied both at the institution level as well as at the system level as an overlay to microprudential requirements in a countercyclical way. These tools are used to limit systemic risk and thereby minimise disruptions in the provision of key financial services that can have serious consequences for the economy by: (i) dampening the buildup of financial imbalances; (ii) building defences that contain the speed and sharpness of subsequent downswings and their effects on the economies; and (iii) identifying and addressing common exposures, risk concentrations, linkages and interdependencies that are sources of contagion and spillover risks that may jeopardise the functioning of the system as a whole. While the third objective of macro-prudential policy [(iii) above] is concerned with the cross-sectional dimension, the first two objectives [(i) and (ii) above] are concerned with the procyclicality issues. Reserve Bank of India (RBI) has been using macroprudential policies, more notably the countercyclical policies, since 2004 as a toolkit for ensuring financial stability though it had used them sporadically even earlier.

While there is credible evidence regarding the ability of countercyclical policies to enhance the resilience of the financial system, the evidence regarding their ability to dampen the buildup of financial imbalances is not unequivocal and credible. RBI had countercyclically raised risk weights and provisioning for certain sectors during the expansionary phase of 2004-2008. While these policies could dampen the rapid credit growth of the commercial real estate sector, they were not as effective for other sectors. Spain's case is another example, which had pioneered dynamic provisioning, a countercyclical tool. Dynamic provisioning had significantly enhanced the resilience of the Spanish banking system but it could not dampen the credit boom in the housing sector. The inability of macroprudential policies to dampen the buildup of financial imbalances would leave the system still vulnerable despite building up the resilience. It is thus evident that macroprudential policies would need support from other policies, more notably monetary policy. The question of monetary policy having a role in containing the buildup of financial imbalances by leaning against the wind has thus got reopened. There is still a lack of consensus on this issue but increasingly an opinion is gaining ground that monetary policy should complement the macroprudential policies for dampening the upswing by leaning against the wind. In effect, it means that when the financial imbalances are building up in the system threatening financial stability, the policy rates could be raised above what would, otherwise, be warranted for achieving the inflation target within the defined time horizon. In this framework, the monetary policy response to financial cycles would be more symmetric during the expansionary and recessionary phases unlike under the Greenspan doctrine which prevailed earlier. The coordination between the two policies and with other policies is important. Generally the two i.e., monetary policy and macro-prudential policy would operate in the same direction. However, there could be situations where the two may be pulling in opposite directions and that is where the hierarchy of policy objectives will have to be determined and acted upon.

Measuring Systemic Risk

Over the last five years, as our understanding of systemic risks has increased, so has our realisation that assessment of such risks is far from straightforward. Systemic risks per se are typically complex, encompass multiple facets of the financial system, and are very often opaque. It became clear during the crisis that no single measure or tool would be sufficient to cover all the different aspects of systemic risks. Assessment of systemic risks necessitated development of diagnostic tools that simultaneously trace the changes in macrofinancial conditions which pose risks to financial stability, identify 'point in time' risk conditions, while also assessing the potential future impact of all these risk factors, jointly, on systemic stability. The tools, thus, needed to take simultaneous cognisance of various facets of the financial system with their myriad correlations and intersections and also peep through the proverbial 'crystal ball' (Schwaab *et al.*, 2011) into the future as to how these facets may evolve.

These challenges have spurred a great deal of research within central banks, in academia, and elsewhere leading to the development of a host of new quantitative measures of systemic risk. The models variously attempt to measure the systemic risk in the financial system, quantify the contagion, capture distress dependencies amongst financial institutions, measure the systemic importance and the resilience of the financial system. Other class of models relates to stress tests while yet another class aims to develop coincident indicators of systemic stress and attempt to develop early warning indicators. Let me discuss some of these emergent techniques.

Measuring Systemiticity and Assessing Resilience

The first set of quantitative techniques, which I am going to touch upon, deals with the systemic importance of institutions. The experience during the global financial crisis brought to the forefront, the concept of 'too-big-to-fail' and 'too-connected-to-fail' institutions and raised a whole range of questions. Why are these entities important? How do they affect the risks of the overall financial system? How does distress in any financial firm and especially in a 'too big to fail' financial institution, affect the rest of the financial system? There are, in fact, several ways in which this can happen and understanding each of these, is the key to designing prudential policies to address such risks (Tarullo, 2011).

First is the domino effect—a distressed financial institution may be unable to meet its liabilities to other financial institutions, resulting, in turn, in these counterpart financial institutions failing to meet their liabilities to others. If the distressed firm is significantly large, the overall contagion impact of its failure can severely strain the financial system.

Second is the potential market impact of the fire sale of assets, by the distressed financial institutions which may affect asset prices, margin calls and mark-to-market losses for other financial sector entities holding similar assets. These entities may, in turn, be forced to sell their own assets to meet their liquidity requirements. As the financial crisis showed, the adverse impact of such collective sales by financial institutions could result in a significant dislocation of asset markets.

Third, the impact of a 'too-big-to-fail' financial institution is further aggravated if the entity is also a provider of a critical service in financial markets, such as payment and settlement systems, as would typically be the case with most large financial institutions.

Fourth, there is also the reputational impact that the failure of a financial institution has on other financial institutions, especially those with similar business profiles. Failure of an institution may reinforce and magnify the adverse feedback loop leading to a chain of failures. This contagion impact is, however, not necessarily a function of the size of the financial institution. Indeed, the failure of even a relatively small financial entity could cause widespread systemic concerns if it highlighted a hitherto unrealised source of risk.

Given the potential of large or systemically important financial institutions to cause system-wide distress in the event of their failure, there have been concerted efforts to develop models/ techniques for the measurement of, first, the systemic risk of the financial system and, second, methodologies through which such systemic risks could be attributed to individual financial institutions. These models attempt to quantify or assess the role that the bank's/financial institution's size, its risk profile, the degree of exposure to a risk factor, etc., play in determining the institution's contribution to systemic risks.

Traditional attempts to measure systemic risk have focused on banks' balance sheet information, such as non-performing assets (NPAS), earnings, liquidity and capital adequacy ratios (CARs). Post crisis, the focus has increasingly moved to market based measures both because of the availability of higher frequency data and the fact that such data is usually forward looking and reflects the market expectation of the future performance of the underlying institutions.

Different sets of models have been developed using equity prices, CDS prices, CDO indices, LIBOR spreads, etc., as proxies for systemic risks, employing techniques such as econometric analysis including principal component analysis (PCA) to derive the systemic risk measure. Another set of techniques use the Merton model to estimate the asset portfolio of banks and to derive a systemic risk measure which is based on the probability of default of a given proportion of banks in a given financial system. Another set of measures assesses systemic risk by computing the multivariate density of a portfolio of banks. For example, these models propose a set of banking stability measures based on distress dependence, which is estimated by the banking system multivariate density (BSMD). Another set of systemic risk measures are based on the traditional risk management tools such as value-at-risk (VaR) and expected shortfall (ES).

Stress Testing Measures

Stress testing has assumed great importance as a risk management tool, particularly because it helps in overcoming limitations of models and historical data. Stress tests evaluate the potential impact of an extreme event on a financial firm or financial sector. Stress testing exercises, especially macro stress testing, are increasingly becoming an important component of a macroprudential policy framework. These tests provide a thorough assessment of what could happen if the identified risks materialise.

A wide variety of stress tests are employed to assess the resilience of financial institutions and of the financial sector. The methodology employed varies from 'top down' approaches (which are typically implemented by regulators/supervisors by applying uniform stress scenarios to the balance sheets of all financial institutions) to 'bottom up' approaches (where the stress tests are conducted by individual institutions themselves, relying on a common set of assumptions and/or scenarios determined by regulators/supervisors) and also a combination of both.

The adverse scenarios that underpin the stress tests typically encompass both sensitivity tests and scenario analysis. In the first case, only a single key variable, e.g., interest rates or exchanges rates, is shocked. Such single factor sensitivity tests are typically the starting point of stress testing exercises as they are relatively simpler to implement. These tests, however, lack plausibility as, in the event of the shock materialising, it is unlikely that only a single variable will be affected.

In contrast, scenario analysis based stress tests examine the impact of simultaneous changes in a number of key economic variables. These tests, based on historical or hypothetical stress scenarios, lend greater plausibility to the stress testing exercise and also yield a more accurate assessment of total losses under adverse developments. Not surprisingly, they are relatively more difficult to implement as it is difficult to anticipate the manner in which different macro variables would move together, especially under conditions of stress.

Of late, there is an evidence of the increased use of macroeconomic models to design stress tests. Economic models are being used to examine the linkages between the health of financial institutions and underlying driving factors (macrofinancial variables or latent factors). Often, these models also incorporate the feedback effect from the banking system to the rest of the economy. Some models also use the joint vector auto regression (VAR) systems to incorporate financial market variables into a framework for stress testing the stability of the banking system. The attempt is to design an integrated micro-macro model that takes into account dynamic linkages between the health of the financial system and macro-financial conditions (Huang *et al.*, 2009).

Coordinated stress tests are, thus, being used to estimate the losses that a group of financial institutions, typically the banking system, could suffer under adverse macroeconomic developments. Such stress tests offer an overall assessment of the vulnerability of the banking system over a defined time period. They are also important tools for the individual banks themselves and for their microprudential supervisors e.g., from the perspective of capital planning and ensuring the resilience of individual financial institutions.

In the aftermath of the global crisis, financial sector regulators initiated various types of coordinated disclosures of bank exposures, stress test results and similar metrics to rebuild trust in the financial sector. Prominent examples of such disclosures are the 2009 Supervisory Capital Assessment Program in the US, followed by the disclosure of the stress scenario projections of the Comprehensive Capital Analysis and Review in 2012. Similarly, the European Banking Authority and its predecessor, the Committee of European Banking Supervisors, conducted EU-wide stress tests from 2009, disclosing the disaggregated results. The stress testing exercises focused on assessing the resilience of both individual banks and the EU banking system as a whole to possible adverse economic developments, while the capital exercise estimated banks' recapitalisation needs to meet a target capital ratio. These initiatives marked the beginning of disclosures of firm level data on stress tests in contrast to the disclosure of sectoral or aggregate data as has been the earlier practice. The aim was to enhance market transparency at a time of prevailing uncertainty and to provide market participants with the necessary information to conduct their own risk assessments.

Developing Early Warning Framework

The third set of models I will now discuss relates to the coincident stability indicators which are used to evaluate prevalent conditions of financial stability. These indicators assess the movements in a range of factors which could have a bearing on financial stability and aid in measuring how risks develop over time and in putting in place an early warning framework.

Several types of indicators are being developed in this context. Macroeconomic indicators are typically compiled at the country level and measure changes in macroeconomic data. These include measures such as GDP growth, growth in total credit, inflation, unemployment, measures of external sector balance such as the current account deficit (CAD) and measures of fiscal imbalances. Another class of indicators uses aggregated data pertaining to financial institutions representing developments in the financial sector's assets and earnings. Banking sector indicators examine the risks emanating from the banking sector, given the typical importance of this sector for financial stability. These indicators examine the movements in financial soundness indicators of the banking system to assess how risks posed by the banking system are evolving. Another set of indicators examine conditions in financial markets.

Five years on, there is clearly no widely accepted single indicator or model capturing systemic risks and instabilities comprehensively. Most models/techniques that have been developed cover one or a few specific aspects of systemic risk. Each measure is an approximation and each has its own strengths and weaknesses. No single measure is complete in all aspects in a macroprudential context and policy makers need, therefore, to rely on a wide range of measures and tools, covering various segments of financial systems and various types of shocks and transmission mechanisms. The challenge remains of constructing a comprehensive systemic risk surveillance and assessment system which serves as an effective early warning system.

Institutional and Governance Arrangements

Institutional and governance arrangements for ensuring financial stability is another critical issue. The overlap between macroprudential and monetary policies raises questions about the role of central banks in financial stability both in peace as well as crisis time. The broad consensus which has emerged is that central banks must be involved in the formulation and execution of financial stability policy, exclusively or as part of a collegial arrangement.

Much work has been undertaken over the last two years on the design of financial stability policy and related governance arrangements in some of the world's major jurisdictions. Abstracting from details, the amendments to the regulatory and oversight architecture made in different jurisdictions have, inter alia,

- designated the central bank as the systemic regulator with accountability;
- placed central banks in charge of microprudential regulation, where not already so responsible, in addition to macroprudential regulation, especially with respect to systemically important financial institutions;

- set up financial stability councils/commissions to provide high level focus on financial stability.

Let me recapitulate some of these changes. The reform of supervisory arrangements in the European Union (EU) drew largely upon the report of the de Larosière Group. In the second half of 2009, the European Commission presented two sets of legislative proposals that saw the creation of two new pan-European authorities for microprudential and macroprudential supervision. For microprudential supervision, the European System of Financial Supervisors (ESFS) was established which brings together the national supervisors and three new independent supranational European Supervisory Authorities (ESAs) set up replacing the former European committees for the banking, securities, and insurance and occupational pensions sectors. With respect to macro-prudential oversight, a European Systemic Risk Board (ESRB) was created and tasked with detecting risks to the financial system as a whole. Though the ESRB has no formal directive power, it can issue recommendations and risk warnings to EC member states, to national supervisors and to the ESAs, all of which will be expected to comply or else explain.

In Mexico, a Financial Stability Council (FSC) was established. The FSC comprises the Bank of Mexico, the Finance Ministry and the country's other principal regulatory agencies and is tasked with the identification of potential risks to the country's financial stability, recommending appropriate policies and actions, and coordinating their implementation by member agencies.

The Bank of Korea Act was amended in August 2011. The amendment, inter alia, granted the Bank of Korea a financial stability mandate that calls on it to play a more proactive role in financial stability

With the introduction of the Central Bank of Malaysia Act 2009, the 1958 version of the Act was repealed. The 2009 Act provides greater clarity on the Bank Negara Malaysia's mandate for financial stability and granted it specific powers for macroprudential financial stability, including for crisis prevention, management and resolution.

In the UK, the Banking Act 2009 introduced a new special resolution regime and entrusted the Bank of England with a statutory objective for financial stability. The financial sector reforms envisaged replacing the United Kingdom's current tripartite institutional framework by a new framework integrating macro- and microprudential oversight within the Bank of England. The reforms focus on three key institutional changes: Creation of a Financial Policy Committee within the Bank of England as a formal committee of its Court of Directors and tasked with responsibility for delivering systemic financial stability through macroprudential regulation. Second, an operationally independent subsidiary of the Bank, the Prudential Regulation Authority (PRA), will be responsible for day to day supervision of financial institutions that manage significant risk on their balance sheet. Third, a new specialist regulator, the Financial Conduct Authority (FCA), which will have responsibility for conduct of business issues across the entire spectrum of financial services.

The Dodd-Frank Wall Street Reform and Consumer Protection Act of 2010 was passed by US Congress with the objective of promoting financial stability by improving accountability and transparency in the financial system, ending 'too-big-to-fail', protecting the American taxpayer by ending bailouts, and protecting consumers from abusive financial services practices. Under the Act, the extant American system of multiple supervisors continues. However, a new Financial Stability Oversight Council (FSOC) under the chairmanship of the treasury secretary was created to identify systemic risks and gaps in supervision, and to recommend regulatory enhancements. Though the Federal Reserve's role in the FSOC is not apparently very prominent, it has become the primary regulator for systemically important entities, thus expanding its supervisory role beyond large bank holding companies.

In India, the Financial Stability and Development Council (FSDC) has been set up but I will discuss this a little later.

Financial stability would require governance arrangements to ensure independence of the macroprudential regulator, clarity of objectives and mandates and accountability.

Financial Stability: The Indian Context

In India, prior to the crisis, no agency had explicit mandate for financial stability though the Reserve Bank acted as the implicit systemic regulator for the country. The Reserve Bank of India (RBI) Act, 1934 provides a broad legal mandate to the Reserve Bank to secure monetary stability and generally to operate the currency and credit system of the country to its advantage. In practice, this meant the dual objective of growth and price stability, the relative emphasis being dependent on the context. In 2004, the Reserve Bank formally added financial stability as an additional objective in view of the growing size and importance of the Indian financial sector. The broad compulsions of financial stability had, however, underlined all major policy initiatives of the Reserve Bank especially since the balance of payment crisis of the early 1990s—much ahead of the articulation of financial stability as an objective. Manifestation of the focused attention of the Reserve Bank on financial stability is evidenced in its approach towards financial sector regulation over the last couple of decades. Let me touch upon some of these.

The Banking Sector

The gradual process of introducing structural reforms in the banking sector was undertaken with the key objective of strengthening the banking sector balance sheets and governance frameworks in a non-disruptive manner. The reforms were carefully sequenced with prudential norms and supervisory strengthening introduced early in the reform cycle, followed by interest rate deregulation and gradual lowering of statutory preemptions. The more complex aspects of legal and accounting measures were ushered in subsequently. The regulatory framework has also focused on ensuring good governance through 'fit and proper' owners, directors and senior managers of the banks.

The Non-banking Financial Sector (NBFC)

India is unique with respect to the NBFC being within the regulatory perimeter, in sharp contrast to many jurisdictions which are grappling with the very complex issue of regulating the shadow banking sector. Regulation of Non-Banking Finance Companies in India was considered necessary as far back as the sixties as a corollary to the monetary and credit policy of the country and protection of depositors' interest. Statutory powers for the regulation of the segment were given to the Reserve Bank through the RBI (Amendment) Act in January 1997. The initial focus of the Reserve Bank was on depositor protection and stringent regulatory requirements were put in place for deposit taking entities. With the growth of the financial system, the focus shifted to non-deposit taking entities which could pose systemic risks on account of their interaction with the formal banking system and market based financing. A gradually calibrated regulatory framework was created for these entities.

Large and Complex Financial Institutions

As liberalisation led to the emergence of financial conglomerates cutting across sectors and geographical boundaries, a need for a framework for monitoring of Systemically Important Financial Intermediaries (SIFIs) or Financial Conglomerates (FC) was seriously felt. Accordingly, a FC monitoring mechanism was put in place in India since June 2004 and is being continuously upgraded.

Macroprudential Regulation: Addressing Systemic Risks

The Reserve Bank has, over the years, attempted to address both aspects of systemic risks—the time dimension (which essentially refers to procyclicality) and the cross sectional dimension (which refers to interconnectedness) within a macroprudential framework, without christening these policies as macroprudential policies. Operationally, India being a bank-dominated economy, the bank credit and credit growth have always formed important variables in the conduct of monetary and countercyclical policies.

In addressing systemic risks in the time dimension, Reserve Bank's countercyclical policies have aimed at increasing the resilience of the banking system. The instruments used have been time varying risk weights and provisioning norms on standard assets for certain specific sectors wherein excessive credit growth, led to apprehension about potential build-up of systemic risk. A slew of regulatory measures, including prudential exposure limits, address systemic risks arising out of inter-connectedness among banks and between banks and NBFCs and from common exposures.

Financial Markets

The development of financial markets was pursued by the Reserve Bank in the broader context of financial stability. A calibrated approach to financial sector development was adopted based on the level of maturity of the financial system and the needs of the real economy. Delicate balance between fostering growth by encouraging financial innovation *vis-à-vis* the impetrative of containing excesses that could lead to instability was meticulously observed. The approach was to ensure that finance remains firmly wedded to the real sector and does not assume dynamics of its own. New products were permitted after due deliberations and wide consultations so as to take into account both the requirements of the participants as also the preparedness of the system for managing the risks.

OTC Derivative Markets

The regulatory stance is of a cautious approach to introduction of complex financial products. Structured derivative products are permitted only as long as they do not contain any derivative which is not allowed on a standalone basis. In India, a CCP (central clearing party) existed, even prior to the crisis, for the critical interest rate and foreign exchange markets. Reporting arrangements are in place for other OTC derivative products. This approach has been appreciated globally and the RBI was recently awarded the 2012 Dufrenoy Prize for its precautionary approach to the regulation of derivatives market, thus facilitating financial innovation in a responsible manner.

Capital Account Management

The approach of the Reserve Bank to the management of the capital account also evolved from the broader objective of maintaining financial and macroeconomic stability. The policy framework included an explicitly stated active capital account management framework, based on the policy stance of encouraging non-debt creating and long-term capital inflows and discouraging debt flows. At the same time, there was significant liberalisation of permissible avenues for outward investments for domestic entities.

Organisational Arrangements for Financial Stability

Organisational developments within the Reserve Bank, over the last couple of decades, have also reflected the Bank's commitment to maintaining financial stability. Two separate Committees of the Reserve Bank's Central Board, *viz.*, the Board for Financial Supervision (BFS) and the Board for Payment and Settlement Systems (BPSS), are responsible for focused regulation and supervision of financial institutions regulated by the Reserve Bank and the payment and settlement infrastructure, respectively. Towards ensuring a coordinated approach to the supervision of the financial system, a High Level Coordination Committee on Financial Markets (HLCCFM) was functional since 1992 with the Governor of the Reserve Bank as Chairman, the Finance Secretary, Government of India and the heads of other regulatory authorities such as the Securities and Exchange Board of India (SEBI), the Insurance Regulatory and Development Authority (IRDA) and the Pension Funds Regulatory and Development Authority (PFRDA) as members. Post crisis, a Financial Stability and Development Council (FSDC) has been set up to provide focused attention to the pursuit of financial stability. The Council is chaired by the finance minister and has representation from all the financial sector regulators. However, the oversight of systemic risk in normal times is with a Sub-Committee of the FSDC (which replaced the HLCCFM) chaired by the Governor, RBI and having, as members, heads of other regulatory agencies as well as all the deputy governors of Reserve Bank of India and the finance secretary.

In July 2008, the Reserve Bank set up a Financial Stability Unit (FSU) with a mandate to, inter alia, conduct effective macro-prudential surveillance of the financial system on an ongoing basis to enable early detection of any incipient signs of instability. With the establishment of the FSU, the Reserve Bank started publication of half yearly Financial Stability Reports (FSRs)—which now forms a critical tool for the Reserve Bank in its attempt to communicate the potential systemic risks facing the financial system.

Financial Stability Analytics

A number of initiatives have been taken to improve the financial stability analytics to take full account of the different sources of systemic risk. A series of indicators and indices have been developed to assess the health and resilience of the financial system on an ongoing basis.

A Banking Stability Indicator is being used by the Reserve Bank to monitor the dimensional riskiness of the banking system in the country. It presents an overall assessment of changes in the underlying conditions and risk factors having a bearing on the stability of the banking sector based on the five dimensions of, soundness, asset quality, liquidity, profitability and efficiency. A financial stress indicator—a contemporaneous indicator of conditions in the equity, foreign exchange and interest rate markets and in the banking sector—has been developed to assess the degree of stress in the financial system and to forecast market conditions in the near term.

Imbibing the lesson from the global financial crisis about the importance of interconnectedness in the financial system, a model of the bilateral exposures in the banking system and the broader financial system has been developed with a view to assess the degree of interconnectedness in the system and to analyse the possible contagion impact of the idiosyncratic failure of a bank. The model uses cutting edge techniques in analysing the network of the Indian financial system and identifying, on a real time basis, buildup of excesses and risk concentrations, if any.

Advanced stress testing techniques are being used to assess the resilience of the financial sector. A series of banking stability measures (in the form of Banking System's Portfolio Multivariate Density), including a 'Toxicity Index', a 'Vulnerability Index' and 'Cascade' effects have been developed for the purpose of assessing the systemic importance of individual banks (Caruana, 2012). Also, the impact of macroeconomic shocks on the stability of the banking system is being assessed based on the vector autoregression (VAR) approach.

Thus, in the case of the RBI, the focus on financial stability from the policy perspective attempts to put in place a prudential framework aimed at strengthening the resilience of the financial sector while also ensuring that the financial sector development is designed to correspond to the level of maturity of the financial system and the needs of the real economy. Simultaneously, advanced tools and techniques are being employed to put in place an effective system of macroprudential surveillance of the financial system.

In discharging its function towards maintaining financial stability, the Reserve Bank derives considerable systemic advantage from its roles as the monetary authority, LoLR regulator of the banking and non-banking system and of key financial markets—money market, government securities market, forex market and credit market. From a financial stability perspective, the above framework has proved to be a sound model as evidenced by the resilience of the Indian financial system during various episodes of systemic instability in the global economy.

Challenges: Going Forward

It would perhaps be a truism to state that the last five years have been challenging. Challenging in terms of the continuing instability which has dogged the global financial system with barely a respite. Challenging in terms of the sheer breath of regulatory changes which have taken place over a relatively short span of time—changes which are far reaching, changes which encompass a wide span, changes which are historic. I strongly believe that the next five years will be equally exciting though, I hope, less stressful for the global financial system.

The last few years have also been defining moments in the history of central banking. The crisis has raised questions about the functioning of central banks leading up to the crisis and has presented tough challenges in steering the global financial system out of the crisis. For central banks, just as managing the crisis was difficult, managing the recovery is going to be equally, if not more, difficult. One of the most important challenges I see in the days to come is that of exit from accommodative policies adopted during the crisis management phase and to ensure that the financial imbalances which led to crisis do not build up again. But the policies that are most suited to crisis management are not necessarily the best for crisis resolution (Caruana, 2012). In recent periods, the extraordinarily easy monetary policies in advanced countries have provided some relief, but, sooner or later, central bank balance sheets will have to be repaired. The main challenge for policy makers will then be to prevent such balance sheet recession/repair from spilling over to protracted economic weakness.

When the dust from this crisis has settled, the biggest challenge, going forward, would remain preventing the buildup of financial instability when there would be stability, as risk is highest in the system when the perceived risk is lowest. Tough decisions are difficult to sustain and to implement, when memory recedes—and human memory is notoriously fickle.

An impressive range of regulatory reforms have been set in motion in the five years since the crisis first unfolded. But there are formidable implementation challenges ahead which will need to be carefully managed. The progress in certain areas of reforms, notably OTC derivative market reforms and measures to put in place robust resolution regimes, has been slow. There are apprehensions about the impact of the Basel III capital measures on credit offtake as well as on investor interest in the banking system. There are also concerns about the impact of the Basel III liquidity measures on the functioning of the markets for such securities. The potential unintended consequences of the reform measures, especially for emerging markets, will need to be carefully monitored and managed, should they emerge.

The years ahead will also be very exciting in terms of development of financial stability analytics. While we have made progress, financial system modelling is still in its infancy and the critical lesson that the crisis has taught us is that understanding, preventing and reducing systemic risks, as we seek to preserve financial stability, deserve our full-fledged attention.

Let me conclude. There is a downside risk to global financial stability. In India though the financial system remains robust, the downside risks to financial stability have increased due to several global and domestic factors. As I said earlier, financial stability is a shared responsibility and therefore, Indian banks have a major role to play because while strong financial institutions need not necessarily make up a strong financial system, for a strong financial system we would need strong banks. Indian banks are facing several challenges in the current scenario—implementation of Basel III and for some, implementation of 'advanced approaches' of Basel II—in a situation where there is increasing pressure on asset quality.

While the macroeconomic situation would certainly have an impact on NPAs, this can still be contained by substantially upgrading the credit management systems so as to be able to contain slippages and improve recovery. Overall, improvement in risk management systems, upgradation of technological platforms and building up of specialised skills in the banking system are the challenges which will distinguish the more successful ones from the others. It is important and this is a lesson from the recent crisis that the competitive pressures are not allowed to override basic prudence. I am sure that our banking system will rise above the formidable challenges and emerge stronger and more efficient.

References

Caruana, Jaime (2012). "Central Banking in a Balance Sheet Recession", Panel remarks at the Board of Governors of the Federal Reserve System 2012 conference on *Central Banking: Before, During and After the Crisis*. Washington. March 23-24.

Huang, Xin, Hao Zhou and Haibin Zhu (2009). "A Framework for Assessing the Systemic Risk of Major Financial Institutions", *BIS Working Papers* No. 281 April.

Schwaab, Bernd, Siem Jan Koopman and Andre Lucas (2011). *"Systemic Risk Diagnostics, Coincident Indicators and Early Warning Signals", ECB Working Paper Series* no 1327/April.

Tarullo, Daniel K. (2011). "Regulating Systemic Risk", Remarks at the *Credit Markets Symposium*. Charlotte, North Carolina, March 31.

The Turner Review (2009). *A Regulatory Response to the Global Banking Crisis.*

Special address at the FIBAC 2012 organised by FICCI and Indian Banks' Association at Mumbai, September 6, 2012. RBI Bulletin October 2012.

13

B. MAHAPATRA

Implications of Basel III for Capital, Liquidity and Profitability of Banks

The Context

Basel III is the regulatory response to the causes and consequences of the global financial crisis. So, what were the causes of the crisis and the consequence?

Causes of Global Financial Crisis

From the macroeconomic perspective, the crisis has been attributed to the persistence of global imbalances. It is often said that the solution to a previous crisis becomes the cause for the next crisis. You may recall that the previous crisis was the Asian crisis of 1997-98, and one of the important lessons learnt by the Asian countries was to build a war chest of foreign exchange reserves to fight against the attack on the country's currency. Therefore, Asia and in particular, China and some other emerging economies produced goods at a cheaper rate and pursued a policy of export-led growth and accumulated huge foreign exchange reserves. As a corollary, the USA and Europe consumed that produce and became net importers. The foreign exchange reserves accumulated by the Asian and other emerging economies were necessarily to be invested in advanced economies which have deep markets.

The huge amount of capital that flowed from the emerging economies to the advanced economies, depressed yields in the financial markets of advanced economies. In the 'search for yield' to

---

The contributions made by Shri Rajinder Kumar and Shri Rajnish Kumar are gratefully acknowledged.

improve returns on investment, market players indulged in financial innovation and engineering. They developed structured financial products like securitisation and resecuritisation based on subprime mortgage backed securities (MBS), collateralised debt obligations (CDOs) and CDO squared etc. Credit default swaps (CDS) were also used to create synthetic structures which increased their illiquidity and complexity. Oblivious of the inherent risks created by these features, securitisations continued to grow by leaps and bounds leading to the spiraling of subprime lending with impending disastrous consequences.

Another cause of the crisis was attributed to the socioeconomic and political factors in the USA. Dr Raghuram Rajan in his book *Fault Lines* has highlighted that the income of average American was stagnant for quite some time and poverty and inequality were increasing. The politicians could not improve the income of the people but devised policies to encourage them to fulfill the dream of owning a house by taking loans from banks and financial institutions (FIs) at the prevailing low interest rates. Thus, the birth of the toxic product 'subprime mortgage' took place. It was said if the poor people cannot have income for consumption, "let them eat credit."

At the micro level, the business models of banks and FIs also contributed to the fermentation of the crisis. The 'originate-to-distribute' model of subprime mortgages did not create any incentive for banks for better appraisal and supervision of such mortgages. Their reliance on wholesale funding markets created gaps in liquidity risk management. Short term funds were used for creating long term assets. The availability of plenty and cheap funds encouraged banks to be highly leveraged, that too by borrowing short term funds.

The crisis has also been attributed to the inadequate corporate governance and inappropriate and perverse incentive system in the financial sector. There were several weaknesses in corporate governance in the run up to the crisis. Corporate governance arrangements failed to curb excessive risk taking in banks and FIs. Studies have shown that risk management systems failed in many cases more due to poor corporate governance than due to the inadequacy of the mathematical models used. The board and even senior management, in some cases, failed to establish an informative and responsive risk measurement and management reporting framework. The institutional arrangements in many instances conferred importance and status on the risk takers at the expense of independent risk managers and control personnel. Where strategy was in place, boards did not establish suitable metrics to monitor implementation.

Out of the many issues that have arisen in the context of the global crisis, executive pay and compensation practices in the financial sector have perhaps invoked the maximum public outrage. There has been wide spread criticism that incentives and pay packages were set inappropriately, encouraged irresponsible risk taking, were inconsistent with the firm's capital bases and focussed on short-term profit maximisation. Compensation for senior executives has been perceived to be excessive with little correlation to the long term performance of the institutions concerned. Particularly glaring was the multimillion dollar payments and bonuses to the executives of failed firms which had received public funding. It is now widely acknowledged that the flawed incentives framework underlying banks' compensation structures in the advanced countries fuelled the crisis.

Banks entered the crisis with inadequate capital. The Basel requirement of common equity was as low as 2 per cent of risk-weighted assets (RWAs). Banks did not calculate the risk-based capital properly. The Basel capital rules favoured lower capital for the trading book and higher capital for the banking book. Banks exploited this loophole and parked banking book assets in the trading book, indulging in capital arbitrage. Similarly, capital requirement for mortgage loans was higher than capital requirement for mortgaged backed securities MBS. This encouraged banks to securitise their mortgage loans through a special investment vehicle (SIV) set up by them. Banks offered liquidity supports to their own SIVs which securitised the mortgage loans and enhanced the credit rating of such instruments. Enhanced ratings require less capital. Banks invested in such products requiring less capital. Thus, there was an 'incestuous' relation in keeping banking book assets in trading book, for which liquidity support was given by the bank to enhance its rating and reduce capital requirement.

The growth of 'shadow banking' system in the run up to the crisis was unprecedented. One estimate suggests that the size of shadow banking system was almost three times the formal banking system. This coupled with their dependence on the wholesale funding market compounded the crisis.

Supported by unprecedented innovation and engineering, the financial sector became too big in relation to the real economy, but the regulatory and supervisory system was found wanting. The regulators and supervisors did not look at system-wide build up of risk. They reposed faith in free markets and believed in self-correction of market excesses. But that did not happen. 'Leaning against the wind' was considered inappropriate. The credit rating agencies also did not perform their role as envisaged and junked themselves.

Every banking crisis has some common elements. But every time, experts say, "this time is different." Then what was different this time? Probably, the phenomenal growth of shadow banking system, most of which was outside the regulatory purview, and the excessive dependence of banks and FIs on the wholesale funding markets, are the 'different' factors behind this crisis.

At a more philosophical level, what the crisis highlighted was the massive breakdown of trust—trust in banks, in financial system, in rating agencies, in investment advisers and in politicians. Trust, which takes time to build up is an important element in the functioning of financial markets as the very nature of financial contracts requires a high level of trust. Several questions come to mind in this context during the crisis. Was the behaviour of the players across the chain of the financial system fair and ethical or was it influenced by the greed to make quick profits and fat bonuses? Did the bankers and investment advisers explain the risks in the complex financial products they sold to their clients? And what about the credit rating agencies? Did they compromise on their standards?

The crisis has triggered an interesting, if also a soul searching debate on the role of leadership. Leaders at the helm of affairs probably let us down. They were lulled by the phenomenal success of modern financial engineering and the 'great moderation' and got carried away by 'irrational exuberance' and could not see the 'black swan'.

Consequences of the Global Financial Crisis

The consequences of the crisis are there for all of us to see. What started as a contamination of subprime mortgage loans and the securitised products based on that, led to an illiquidity spiral and soon became a solvency issue for the financial sector. The interconnection between banks in the financial system propagated it into a systemic crisis. Banks, starved of liquidity, started to deleverage and stopped lending to the real sector. The financial crisis, thus, became a full-scale economic crisis. Since banks are essential to an economy and their failure affects the real sector, particularly when they are too big, the public authorities had no alternative but to rescue the banks by injecting capital, guaranteeing their liabilities and purchasing their toxic assets. This created the moral hazard issue of 'privatisation of profits but socialisation of losses'.

However, one unintended but interesting aspect of the rescue programme was that non-equity capital providers to the banks escaped scot free as they were required to absorb losses only in the event of liquidation of banks and not otherwise.

There are several estimates of the cost of the crisis to the public exchequer. The amount of support to the systemically important financial institutions (SIFIs) during the crisis was about 25 per cent of GDP. Capital injection and asset purchase for G-20 countries was US $ 653 billion or 2.1 per cent of GDP. Fiscal cost of direct support for G-20 countries averaged 2.8 per cent of GDP, with UK at 6.1 per cent, Germany at 4.8 per cent and USA at 3.6 per cent. The government debt of these countries is projected to rise by 40 per cent of GDP during 2008-2015. Cumulative output loss in these countries is estimated to about a quarter of their GDP.

Enhancement to Basel II or Introduction of Basel II.5

Post-crisis, the global initiatives to strengthen the financial regulatory system are driven by the political leadership of the G-20 under the auspices of the financial stability board (FSB) and the Basel Committee on Banking Supervision (BCBS). Immediately after the crisis, the Basel Committee, in July 2009, came out with certain measures, also called enhancement to Basel II or Basel II.5, to plug the loopholes in its capital rules which were exploited to arbitrage capital by parking certain banking book positions in the trading book which required less capital.

These measures, under Pillar 1, include introduction of an incremental risk charge (IRC) for specific risk or credit risk in trading book under the internal models approach (IMA). Capital charge for securitisation of commercial real estate was increased and that for resecuritisation introduced. The value-at-risk (VaR)-based measure for capital charge for market risk under IMA has been substantially enhanced by including a stressed-VaR element. The overall capital requirement for the trading book is expected to rise by about 3 times. Pillar 2 has been strengthened by issuing guidance on firm-wide risk management; managing reputation risk and liquidity risk; improving valuation practices; and implementing sound stress testing practices. Appropriate additional disclosures complementing enhancements in Pillar 1 and 2 have also been introduced.

The Basel III

The Basel Committee published its Basel III rules in December 2010. I propose to discuss the major features of Basel III in a little more detail. Learning the lessons from the crisis, the objectives of Basel III are to minimise the probability of recurrence of a crisis of such magnitude. Towards this end, the Basel III has set its objectives to improve the shock absorbing capacity of each and every individual bank as the first order of defence and in the worst case scenario, if it is inevitable that one or a few banks have to fail, Basel III has measures to ensure that the banking system as a whole does not crumble and its spillover impact on the real economy is minimised. Therefore, Basel III will have some microprudential elements so that risk is contained in each individual institution; and a macroprudential overlay that will 'lean against the wind' to take care of issues relating to the systemic risk.

Microprudential Elements of Basel III

The microprudential elements of Basel III are: (i) definition of capital; (ii) enhancing risk coverage of capital; (iii) leverage ratio; and (iv) international liquidity framework.

Definition of Capital

The existing rules require a capital adequacy ratio of 8 per cent to the RWAs. Rules allow Tier 1 capital at a minimum of 4 per cent of RWAs and Tier 2 capital comprising debt instruments of medium term maturity of at least 5 years at a maximum of 4 per cent of RWAs. Tier 3 capital with short maturity of at least 2 years can also support Tier 2 capital to some extent. Common equity in Tier 1 capital can be as low as 2 per cent of RWAs. Innovative features such as step-up option are allowed in capital instruments. The regulatory adjustments to capital are effected both at Tier 1 and Tier 2 capital in equal measure.

The existing definition of capital is, thus, flawed. Capital is not only deficient in quality equity capital but also contains elements of debt which do not support the bank as a going concern. As I have stated earlier, big banks entered the crisis with insufficient level and quality of capital. Under Basel III, Tier 1 capital will be the predominant form of regulatory capital. It will be minimum 75 per cent of the total capital of 8 per cent, i.e., 6 per cent, as against 4 per cent now, i.e., 50 per cent of total capital. Within Tier 1 capital, common equity will be the predominant form of capital. It will be minimum 75 per cent of the Tier 1 capital requirement of 6 per cent, i.e., 4.5 per cent, from the existing level of 2 per cent. You may observe that the meaning of 'predominant' portion of common equity in Tier 1 capital and Tier 1 capital portion in total capital (Tier 1 plus Tier 2) as 50 per cent under Basel I and II has undergone a change to 75 per cent under Basel III, improving the overall level of high quality capital in the banks.

To my mind the most revolutionary feature of Basel III in this regard is to ensure that public sector rescue of non-viable, but still functioning banks, does not entail absorption of losses by the tax-payers while leaving the non-common equity capital providers unscathed. Therefore, under Basel III, the terms and conditions of all non-common Tier 1 and Tier 2 instruments issued by banks will have a provision that requires such instruments, at the option of the relevant authority, to be either written off or converted into common equity upon the bank being adjudged by the supervisory authority as having approached or approaching the point of non-viability.

Additionally, innovative features in non-equity capital instruments are no longer acceptable. Tier 3 capital has also been completely abolished. The regulatory adjustments or deductions from capital presently applied at 50 per cent to Tier 1 capital and 50 per cent to Tier 2 capital will now be 100 per cent from the common equity Tier 1 capital. To improve market discipline, all elements of capital are required to be disclosed along with a detailed reconciliation to the reported accounts. These requirements will be implemented uniformly across all jurisdictions and the consistency in application will be ensured by the Basel Committee through a peer review process.

Thus, the definition of capital in terms of its quality, quantity, consistency and transparency will improve under Basel III.

Enhancing Risk Coverage of Capital

In view of significant shortcomings noticed in the management and capitalisation of counterparty credit risk, measures have been introduced under Basel III, to strengthen the capital requirements for counterparty credit exposures arising from banks' OTC derivatives, repo and securities financing activities. These reforms will raise the capital set against these exposures, reduce procyclicality and provide additional incentives to move OTC derivative contracts to central counterparties, thus helping to reduce systemic risk across the financial system. They also provide incentives to strengthen the risk management of counterparty credit exposures.

Going forward, banks must determine their capital requirement for counterparty credit risk using stressed inputs. This will address concerns about capital charges becoming too low during periods of compressed market volatility and help address procyclicality. Banks will be subject to a credit valuation adjustment (CVA) capital charge to protect themselves against the potential mark-to-market losses associated with deterioration in the creditworthiness of the counterparty. The CVA is a measure of diminution in the fair value of a derivative position due to deterioration in the creditworthiness of the counterparty. Standards for collateral management and initial margining have been strengthened. Banks with large and illiquid derivative exposures to counterparties will have to apply longer margining periods as a basis for determining the regulatory capital requirement. Additional standards have been adopted to strengthen collateral risk management practices.

Thus, the Basel III framework will have enhanced risk coverage. This is necessitated due to the excessive exposures of banks to derivative products whose risks were not captured comprehensively under Basel I or Basel II framework.

Leverage Ratio

Pre-crisis, the leverage of some of the internationally active banks was at a high level of about 50 times of the capital, even though such banks complied with capital adequacy requirement. The risk of leverage, particularly when built up with short term borrowings, and the consequential impact of deleveraging during periods of stress by withdrawing credit to the real sector, accentuated the crisis. The Basel Committee has, therefore, introduced a simple, transparent, non-risk-based leverage ratio as a supplementary 'backstop' measure to the risk-based capital requirements. The leverage ratio has both microprudential and macroprudential elements. At the micro level, it serves the purpose of containing excessive risk, as a supplement to the risk-based capital ratio. The risk-based capital ratio does not capture the risk of excessive leverage on account of having low risk assets. The leverage ratio as a simple accounting measure will capture that. The Basel Committee has proposed testing a minimum Tier 1 leverage ratio of 3 per cent (33.33 times) to start with as a Pillar 2 measure which will eventually be made a Pillar 1 requirement.

International Liquidity Framework

Despite liquidity being central to the functioning of financial markets in general and banks in particular, liquidity regulation did not receive adequate attention until recently. There were no internationally agreed and harmonised liquidity standards. The regulation of banking sector during the past two decades largely revolved around Basel I and Basel II capital regulations. Nor were there any international standards to limit excessive maturity mismatch resulting in increasing proportions of long-dated assets being financed by short-term borrowings. The financial crisis has highlighted the importance of robust liquidity risk management by banks. It was observed during the crisis that even those banks which had sufficient capital base had experienced difficulties due to imprudent liquidity management practices by excessive dependence on wholesale funding markets. The crisis demonstrated that liquidity and solvency are quite deeply interrelated. Illiquid banks can become insolvent in no time and similarly an insolvent bank can become illiquid rapidly.

Basel III has introduced two new liquidity standards to improve the resilience of banks to liquidity shocks. In the short term, banks will be required to maintain a buffer of highly liquid securities measured by the liquidity coverage ratio (LCR). This liquidity buffer is intended to promote resilience to potential liquidity disruptions over a 30-day horizon. It will help ensure that a global bank has sufficient unencumbered, high-quality liquid assets to offset the net cash outflows it could encounter under an acute short-term stress scenario of 30 days. The scenarios may include a significant downgrade of the institution's public credit rating, a partial loss of deposits, a loss of unsecured wholesale funding, a significant increase in secured funding haircuts and increases in derivative collateral calls and substantial calls on contractual and non-contractual off-balance sheet exposures, including committed credit and liquidity facilities.

Another liquidity risk measure, the net stable funding ratio (NSFR), requires a minimum amount of stable sources of funding at a bank relative to the liquidity profiles of the assets, as well as the potential for contingent liquidity needs arising from off-balance sheet commitments, over a one-year horizon. The NSFR aims to limit over-reliance on short-term wholesale funding during times of buoyant market liquidity and encourage better assessment of liquidity risk across all on- and off-balance sheet items. The objective of the NSFR is to promote resilience over a longer time horizon by creating additional incentives for banks to fund their activities with more stable sources of funding on an ongoing basis.

Macroprudential Elements of Basel III

The changes in definition of capital and enhancements of capital requirement for trading book under Basel II.5 mentioned by me earlier would raise the collective resilience of banks and would in a way, contribute to reduction in systemic risk. However, in extreme situations this alone would be inadequate to ensure the financial stability. Therefore, ensuring financial stability would necessitate specific macroprudential elements. Basel III seek to address issues relating to systemic risk through various measures including: (i) leverage ratio; (ii) capital conservation buffer; (iii) countercyclical capital buffer; (iv) addressing procyclicality of provisioning requirements; (v) addressing interconnectedness; (vi) addressing the 'too-big-to-fail problem'; and (vii) addressing reliance on external credit rating agencies.

Leverage Ratio

The macroprudential element of leverage ratio under Basel III has the objective of protecting against system-wide build up of leverage that result in destabilising unwinding process during stress. It also protects against perverse incentive to pile on 'low risk' assets, which may not remain as such under extreme situations producing systemic risk.

Capital Conservation Buffer

Drawing lessons from the crisis that banks were distributing earnings even during periods of stress, Basel III prescribes that a capital conservation buffer of 2.5 per cent of RWAs, comprising common equity Tier 1 capital, over and above the minimum common equity requirement of 4.5 per cent and total capital requirement of 8 per cent, needs to be built up outside periods of stress. This can be drawn down as losses are incurred during periods of stress. When buffers have been drawn down, banks can build them up either through a reduction in distribution of dividend, share buyback and staff bonus payments or raising capital from the private sector.

Countercyclical Capital Buffer

The countercyclical capital buffer is aimed at ensuring that banking sector capital requirements take account of the macro-financial environment in which banks operate. National authorities will monitor credit growth and other indicators which may signal a build-up of system-wide risk and, accordingly, they will put in place a countercyclical capital buffer requirement as and when circumstances warrant. This requirement will be released when system-wide risk crystallises. The buffer will be implemented through an extension of the capital conservation buffer and vary between zero and 2.5 per cent of RWAs, depending on the extent of the build-up of system-wide risks. Banks are required to meet this buffer with common equity Tier 1 capital or other fully loss-absorbing capital. Furthermore, banks will be subjected to the restrictions on distributions also if the capital level (capital conservation buffer plus countercyclical buffer) falls below the required levels during the periods when the countercyclical capital buffer is in force. Banks will have to ensure that their countercyclical buffer requirements are calculated and publicly disclosed at least with the same frequency as their minimum capital requirements.

Addressing Procyclicality of Provisioning Requirements

Financial institutions are prone to business cycles. In good times, banks' borrowers do well and service the loans in time. In bad times, borrowers tend to default in servicing interest and principal payment. Banks' profits go down but at the same time they are required to make higher loan loss provisions for the non-performing loans. In order to address the procyclical issues, the Basel Committee is working closely with the International Accounting Standards Board (IASB) towards an expected loss approach to loan loss provisioning instead of the current practice of incurred loss approach.

Addressing Interconnectedness

Interconnectedness among banks, especially the large ones, is sought to be addressed through various measures such as enhanced regulatory framework for global systemic important banks (G-SIBs), prescription of higher asset value correlation under the internal ratings based (IRB) approach for exposures to large FIs with assets of US $ 100 billion and with unregulated institutions.

Addressing 'too-big-to-fail' Problem

The Basel Committee will group G-SIBs into different categories of systemic importance based on the score produced by the indicator-based measurement approach. G-SIBs will be initially allocated into four buckets based on their scores of systemic importance, with varying levels of additional loss absorbency requirements applied to the different buckets. Based on policy judgement derived from various empirical analysis, the Basel Committee has determined that the magnitude of additional loss absorbency for the highest populated bucket should be 2.5 per cent of risk-weighted assets at all times, with an initially empty top bucket (fifth bucket) of 3.5 per cent of risk-weighted assets. The magnitude of additional loss absorbency for the lowest bucket should be 1.0 per cent of risk-weighted assets. The magnitude of additional loss absorbency is to be met with common equity Tier 1 capital as defined by the Basel III framework. The G-SIBs will also be subject to tighter supervision. In addition, liquidity standards have been introduced to reduce excessive reliance on short term wholesale funding.

Addressing Reliance on External Credit Ratings

To reduce the reliance on external ratings of the Basel II framework, measures have been proposed that include requirements for banks to perform their own internal assessments of externally rated securitisation exposures, the elimination of certain 'cliff effects' (sharp increase in applicable risk weights) associated with credit risk mitigation practices, and the incorporation of key elements of the IOSCO Code of Conduct Fundamentals for Credit Rating Agencies into the Committee's eligibility criteria for the use of external ratings in the capital framework.

Transition and Phase-in

In view of the large scale reforms and their impact, Basel III will be phased in and implemented over a long period of time, staring from January 1, 2013 to January 1, 2019. Capital instruments that no longer qualify as non-core Tier 1 capital or Tier 2 capital, will be phased out over a 10-year period starting from 2013. The final calibration of liquidity ratios and leverage ratio will be made after further quantitative impact study and observation.

Macroeconomic Impact of Basel III

Assuming that banks may be able to raise the increased capital requirement under Basel III from the market, questions have been raised as to its impact on economic growth and profitability of banks. In general, the increase in equity capital requirement is likely to increase the weighted average cost of capital. Banks would partly pass on the increase cost of capital to the borrowers as higher lending rates. Thus, the equilibrium lending rates are likely to be marginally higher and as a consequence, credit growth could be a little lower than in the last few years.

However, the important question is how much? Also, after the steady state has been reached on full implementation of Basel III, whether the cost would come down? I would try to provide some answers to these questions based on the research done by the official sector including the Basel Committee, and non-official or private sector institutions.

The Bank for International Settlements (BIS) and the FSB, with a view to phase-in the new regulations in a manner that is compatible with the global economic recovery, undertook studies to assess the macroeconomic impact of the transition to higher capital and liquidity requirements. The Macroeconomic Assessment Group (MAG) set up by the Basel Committee and FSB has estimated that bringing the global common equity capital ratio to a level that would meet the agreed minimum and the capital conservation buffer, would result in a maximum decline in GDP, relative to baseline forecasts, of 0.22 per cent, at the end of Basel III implementation period. The estimated maximum GDP impact per percentage point of higher capital was 0.17 per cent.

In addition, the Basel Committee's study on the Long-term Economic Impact (LEI) of the stronger capital and liquidity requirements has suggested that the net benefits in terms of the gains from reduced probability of banking crises, and the consequential loss of growth, remain positive.

The estimates of the International Institute of Finance (IIF), a private sector body, is that level of GDP will be 3.2 per cent lower than it would otherwise be (i.e., relative to the baseline scenario) after five years with an output loss of 0.7 per cent per annum. This is several magnitudes higher than the MAG's estimate of an output loss of 0.03 per cent per annum. The wide difference in estimates is attributed to different assumptions and samples.

Implications of Basel III on Indian Banks

In general, higher capital and tighter liquidity requirements under Basel III will increase the capital requirements in Indian banks, as in other countries. However, the actual impact would vary in different countries depending upon the amount of exposures impacted under Basel III, existing capital structure of banks, i.e., extent of reliance on non-common equity capital elements, existing rules relating to regulatory adjustments, credit growth experienced by the economies and existing credit to GDP ratio. The impact of these requirements on the profitability of banks would depend upon sensitivity of lending rates to capital structure of banks and sensitivity of the credit growth to the lending rates.

Capital

Under Basel III, the trading book exposures especially those having credit risk and re-securitisations exposures in both banking and trading book attract enhanced capital charges. The CVA for OTC derivatives will also attract additional capital. Since the trading book and OTC derivative portfolios of Indian banks are very small and they do not have any exposures to re-securitised instruments, impact of these changes in capital regulation on their balance sheets is insignificant.

The average Tier 1 capital ratio of Indian banks is around 10 per cent with more than 85 per cent of it comprising common equity. The regulatory adjustments will reduce the available equity capital only marginally for various reasons. First, items such as goodwill, deferred tax assets (DTAs) etc., are already deducted from Tier 1 capital for Indian banks. Secondly, some other items which are subject to deduction such as mortgage servicing rights, treasury stocks, gains on account of fair valuation of liabilities which exist in other developed economies, do not exist in India. Thirdly, reciprocal cross-holdings of capital and other investments in the capital of banking, financial and insurance entities are insignificant because these investments are restricted due to existing regulatory limits. Thus, Indian banks will have high common equity capital ratio even under Basel III which will stand them in good stead. It is worth noting that more than 50 per cent of Indian banks have common equity ratio of higher than 8 per cent at present and can implement Basel III even today without any phase-in.

Bank credit to GDP ratio of India is around 55 per cent which is relatively lower as compared with that in many other countries. However, the past trend shows that it is likely to increase in future as the credit penetration in the economy has been steadily increasing. The Indian economy is also expected to grow at an annual growth rate of 8-9 per cent for next 10 years or so. This would undoubtedly necessitate a considerable growth in bank capital. However, we also know that many Indian banks have actually been operating with equity capital ratio of 7-8 per cent for last 5 years when the economy continued to grow at an average rate of about 8 per cent. This provides us comfort in terms of both the ability of banks to operate at higher equity capital levels required under Basel III and also the capacity of the Indian capital market to provide the required equity capital to banks.

Government of India has progressively reduced its shareholding in public sector banks and in the case of many of these banks, the government's shareholding is close to 51 per cent. This means that in the future, the Government of India would provide the matching contribution to meet the additional equity requirements of banks, in contrast to the past when it had allowed a large part of additional equity requirements to be met from the market by letting its shareholding fall from 100 per cent to 51 per cent. Thus, the demand for equity from the capital market would be less to that extent but public sector banks' dependence on the government for capital support will increase.

Liquidity-Issues Relating to SLR and LCR

In India, banks are statutorily required to hold minimum reserves of high-quality liquid assets. Currently, such reserves (statutory liquidity ratio–SLR) are required to be maintained at a minimum of 24 per cent of net demand and time liabilities (NDTL). Since these reserves are part of the minimum statutory requirement, RBI faces a dilemma whether and how much of these reserves can be allowed to be reckoned towards the LCR. If these reserves are not reckoned towards the LCR and banks are to meet the entire LCR with additional liquid assets, the proportion of liquid assets in total assets of banks will increase substantially, thereby lowering their income significantly. RBI is examining to what extent the SLR requirements could be reckoned towards the liquidity requirement under Basel III.

Profitability

Studies have suggested that internationally, Basel III requirements will have a substantial impact on profitability. One such study conducted by McKinsey & Company suggest that all other things being equal, Basel III would reduce return on equity (RoE) for the average bank by about 4 percentage points in Europe and about 3 percentage points in the US. The retail, corporate, and investment banking segments will be affected in different ways. Retail banks will be affected least, though institutions with very low capital ratios may find themselves under significant pressure. Corporate banks will be affected primarily in specialised lending and trade finance. Investment banks will find several core businesses profoundly affected, particularly trading and securitisation businesses. Banks are already seeking to manage RoE in the new environment by balance sheet restructuring and business model adjustments. The study suggests that the balance sheet restructuring and business-model adjustments could potentially mitigate up to 40 per cent of Basel III's RoE impact, on an average.

I would like to give you a sense of likely impact on the lending rates of banks. Suppose, a typical Indian bank has RoE of 15 per cent and interest paid on non-equity elements of capital is 10 per cent. Further, suppose that the equity to RWAs ratio of the bank is 6 per cent. Now if the bank is required to maintain an additional 1 per cent equity, the weighted average cost of funds would rise by 5 basis points only. If the equity capital required rises by 2 per cent, the increase in lending rate to pass on the full increase in cost of capital to borrowers would be 10 basis points. There is likely to be some increase in cost of non-equity capital as well. But, all this is unlikely to push the cost of lending significantly. And, Indian banks should keep in mind that their net interest margins (NIMs) are very high as compared with their counterparts in many other countries. This only indicates the need for improving efficiency and considerable scope for bringing down the cost of intermediation. I would also like you to appreciate the fact that while many large international banks are required to increase their equity capital by more than 100 per cent over the existing levels, many Indian banks would certainly not be required to increase their equity levels by that order. Therefore, the impact on their RoE is likely to be much less than 3 to 4 percentage points as observed in the case of US and European banks.

Benefits of Effective Implementation of Basel III

Effective implementation of Basel III will demonstrate to regulators, customers and shareholders that the banking system is recovering well from the global financial crisis of 2008 and has been developing the resilience to future shocks. A smooth implementation will also contribute to a bank's competitiveness by delivering better management insight into the business, allowing it to take advantage of future opportunities. At the same time, the challenges in implementation of Basel III should not be underestimated. For every bank, working out the most cost-effective model for implementing Basel III will be a critical issue. The comfortable capital adequacy levels at present for the Indian banking system do provide some comfort. However, as the economy grows, so will the credit demand requiring banks to expand their balance sheets, and in order to be able to do so, they will have to augment their capital; more specifically the equity capital.

While implementation of Basel III would undoubtedly imply some costs, this should not be the criterion to determine whether Basel III would add value to the financial system. The correct measure should be whether or not Basel III would deliver a much safer financial system with reduced probability of banking crises at affordable costs. I think Basel III passes that test. The impact of costs is minimised through long phase-in.

At times a question is asked whether it is appropriate for the countries which neither contributed to the crisis nor have exposure to the toxic assets need to implement Basel III. The answer is a clear 'Yes'. The reason is that in the present-day globalised world it is difficult for any local financial and economic system to completely insulate itself from the global economic shocks. The indirect effects of events happening in any part of the world can very well be transmitted throughout the world through various channels. In addition, many provisions of Basel III address the weaknesses in the measurement of risk under Basel II framework revealed during the crisis. Thus, Basel III would strengthen the financial system of both developing and developed countries. It needs to be appreciated that if the implementation of Basel III is not consistent across jurisdictions there would be a race to the bottom to make use of arbitrage opportunities, which nobody wins!

I feel Indian banks should minimise costs by retaining maximum amount of earnings in the initial years of implementation, even though they might meet the capital requirements at that point in time with smaller retentions. This would avoid costs involved in fresh issuances. Indian banks are also comfortably placed in terms of liquidity requirements as they have a large reservoir of liquid government securities to meet the SLR stipulation. RBI is considering how much of it can be allowed to be reckoned towards compliance with the LCR. It is also expected that as the proportion of equity in the capital structure of banks rises, it would reduce the incremental costs of raising further equity as well as non-common equity capital.

Banks will have to issue fresh capital particularly to replace the ineligible non-equity capital towards later years of implementation. Successful issuance of fresh capital would demand greater transparency and greater market discipline.

The Reserve Bank of India has issued the draft guidelines on capital and liquidity rules of Basel III on 30 December 2011 and 21 February 2012, respectively. The Reserve Bank's approach has been to adopt Basel III capital and liquidity guidelines with more conservatism and at a quicker pace. As I have discussed above, the impact of these rules is not going to be onerous and there will be considerable advantage in adopting Basel III by our banks.

Conclusion

Let me now sum up. I started with the context in which the Basel III was set up—the causes and consequences of the global financial, nay, economic crisis. I thereafter discussed the immediate response to the crisis in enhancing Basel II or introducing Basel II.5 capital requirement for the trading book, which was the epicenter of the crisis and capital arbitrage. Moving from there, I went in detail into the objectives of Basel III and the microprudential and macroprudential elements of Basel III in relation to its objectives.

I went on to describe how the definition of capital, its quality and quantity, and consistency and transparency, and risk coverage will improve microprudential regulation under Basel III. I also underscored that the new leverage and liquidity framework will not only enhance the risk absorbency of individual banks but also aid in stabilising financial system during periods of extreme stress. The other macroprudential elements of Basel III, such as, capital conservation buffer, countercyclical capital buffer, and too-big-to-fail problem, were also discussed.

I analysed the macroeconomic impact of Basel III and the various research that have observed that there could be some initial cost in implementation of Basel III, but the long term benefits will be immense as it would reduce the probability of banking crises. The implications of Basel III on capital, liquidity and profitability of banks, particularly Indian banks, were discussed.

I would also take this opportunity to apprise you that Basel III is just a part of the financial sector reforms agenda being pursued by G-20. While the immediate challenge is to ensure consistent implementation of Basel II and Basel III across banks and jurisdictions, other important issues such as strengthening the corporate governance, compensation practices, and resolution regimes; enhancing the regulatory and supervisory framework for global and domestic systemic important banks (SIBs); improving the OTC derivatives markets; and regulation of shadow banking system have also been addressed or are engaging the attention of FSB and Basel Committee. The macroprudential framework under Basel III is still untested and would need continuous research, monitoring, and experience sharing among the regulators to ensure its effectiveness.

Address at the National Conference on Emerging Macro Environment, Regulatory Changes and Bank Competitiveness, organised by the National Institute of Bank Management, March 3-4, 2012 at Pune. RBI Bulletin April 2012.

14

DUVVURI SUBBARAO

Basel III in International and Indian Contexts

Ten Questions We Should Know the Answers For

September 2012 marks the fourth anniversary of the collapse of Lehman Brothers which, in popular perception, was the trigger for the biggest financial crisis of our generation. Four years on, the crisis is still with us—only the geography and the main actors have changed a bit. What has not changed is that virtually every country in the world remains affected, and the toll on global growth and welfare continues.

Banks and bankers have been at the heart of the crisis. Quite understandably, enhancing the banking sector's safety and stability has been the thrust of the post-crisis policy reforms. Even as much of this reform is still work in progress, one segment of reforms that has taken a final shape is the Basel III framework for bank capital regulation. The final package was approved by the G20 and the roll out has begun. We in India issued the Basel III guidelines on capital regulations in May 2012 after extensive consultations with all stakeholders.

Now that we are shortly going to get into the implementation mode for Basel III, I would like to speak about some of the conceptual and implementation issues underlying Basel III. In particular, I will raise ten questions and attempt to answer them.

1st Question: There is a View that it was Actually the Risk Sensitive Framework of Basel II that Caused the Crisis. Is that View Valid?

This question does not admit of a binary answer. If I were to give a short answer, I would say that the view is valid, but only partly so. Let me explain.

What was the paradigm shift from Basel I to Basel II? The paradigm shift was that while Basel I had a 'one-size-fits-all' approach, Basel II introduced risk sensitive capital regulation. The main charge against Basel II is that it is precisely this risk sensitivity that made it blatantly procyclical. In good times, when banks are doing well, and the market is willing to invest capital in them, Basel II does not impose significant additional capital requirement on banks. On the other hand, in stressed times, when banks require additional capital and markets are wary of supplying that capital, Basel II requires banks to bring in more of it. As we saw during the crisis, it was the failure to bring in capital when under pressure that forced major international banks into a vicious cycle of deleveraging, thereby hurtling global financial markets into seizure and economies around the world into recession.

The second charge against Basel II was that even as it made capital regulation more risk sensitive, it did not bring in corresponding changes in the definition and composition of regulatory capital to reflect the changing market dynamics. The market risk models failed, in particular, to factor in the risk from the complex derivative products that were coming on to the market in a big way. These models demanded less capital against trading book exposures on the premise that trading book exposures could be readily sold, and positions rapidly unwound. This gave a perverse incentive for banks to park banking book exposures in the trading book to optimise capital. And as we now know, much of the toxic assets and their securitised derivatives, which were the epicenter of the crisis were parked in the trading book.

So, the second charge against Basel II was that even as it was supposedly risk sensitive, it failed to promote modelling frameworks for accurate measurement of risk and to demand sufficient loss absorbing capital to mitigate that risk.

The third charge against Basel II concerns leverage. Note that Basel II did not have any explicit regulation governing leverage. It assumed that its risk based capital requirement would automatically mitigate the risk of excessive leverage. This assumption, as it turned out, was flawed as excessive leverage of banks was one of the prime causes of the crisis. Similarly, Basel II did not explicitly cover liquidity risk. Since liquidity risk, if left unaddressed, could cascade into a solvency risk, this proved to be the undoing of virtually every bank that came under stress in the depth of the crisis.

Finally, Basel II was also seen to be guilty of focusing exclusively on individual financial institutions, ignoring the systemic risk arising from the interconnectedness across institutions which, as we now know with the benefit of hindsight, was the culprit for ferociously spreading the crisis across financial markets.

Is all this criticism against Basel II valid? As I said before, only partly valid. Note that Basel II, which became operational in June 2006, was still largely work in progress as the crisis began unfolding in August 2007. It is possible that the failure of the market risk framework underlying Basel II may have abetted the crisis, but to claim that the risk sensitivity of Basel II caused the crisis would be extreme.

2nd Question: How is Basel III an Improvement Over Basel II?

Basel III represents an effort to fix the gaps and lacunae in Basel II that came to light during the crisis as also to reflect other lessons of the crisis. What is important though is that Basel III does not jettison Basel II; on the contrary, it builds on the essence of Basel II—the link between the risk profiles and capital requirements of individual banks. In that sense, Basel III is not a negation, but an enhancement of Basel II.

The enhancements of Basel III over Basel II come primarily in four areas: (i) augmentation in the level and quality of capital; (ii) introduction of liquidity standards; (iii) modifications in provisioning norms; and (iv) better and more comprehensive disclosures. Let me discuss each of these briefly.

Higher Capital Requirement

Table 14.1

Capital Requirements Under Basel II and Basel III

		As a percentage of risk weighted assets	
		Basel II	*Basel III (As on January 1, 2019)*
A = (B+D)	Minimum Total Capital	8.0	8.0
B	Minimum Tier 1 Capital	4.0	6.0
C	*of which:*		
	Minimum Common Equity Tier 1 Capital	2.0[1]	4.5
D	Maximum Tier 2 Capital (within Total Capital)	4.0	2.0
E	Capital Conservation Buffer (CCB)	-	2.5
F = C+E	Minimum Common Equity Tier 1 Capital + CCB	2.0	7.0
G = A+E	Minimum Total Capital + CCB	8.0	10.5

As can be seen from the comparative data in Table 14.1, Basel III requires higher and better quality capital. The minimum total capital remains unchanged at 8 per cent of risk weighted assets (RWA). However, Basel III introduces a capital conservation buffer of 2.5 per cent of RWA over and above the minimum capital requirement, raising the total capital requirement to 10.5 per cent against 8.0 per cent under Basel II. This buffer is intended to ensure that banks are able to absorb losses without breaching the minimum capital requirement, and are able to carry on business even in a downturn without deleveraging. This buffer is not part of the regulatory minimum; however, the level of the buffer will determine the dividend distributed to shareholders and the bonus paid to staff.

There are also other prescriptions regarding the quality of capital within the minimum total so that capital is able to absorb

1. Basel II does not explicitly prescribe a minimum common equity Tier 1 capital. It is generally accepted that common equity should be the predominant part of Tier 1 capital i.e. 50 per cent.

losses, and calling upon taxpayers to bear the burden of bail out becomes absolutely the last resort.

In addition to the capital conservation buffer, Basel III introduces another capital buffer—the countercyclical capital buffer—in the range of 0-2.5 per cent of RWA which could be imposed on banks during periods of excess credit growth. Also, there is a provision for a higher capital surcharge on systemically important banks.

To mitigate the risk of banks building up excess leverage as happened under Basel II, Basel III institutes a leverage ratio as a backstop to the risk based capital requirement. The Basel Committee is contemplating a minimum Tier 1 leverage ratio of 3 per cent (33.3 times) which will eventually become a Pillar 1 requirement as of January 1, 2018.

As we noted earlier, Basel II failed to demand adequate loss absorbing capital to cover market risk. To remedy this, Basel III strengthens the counterparty credit risk framework in market risk instruments. This includes the use of stressed input parameters to determine the capital requirement for counterparty credit default risk. Besides, there is a new capital requirement known as CVA (credit valuation adjustment) risk capital charge for OTC derivatives to protect banks against the risk of decline in the credit quality of the counterparty.

To mitigate liquidity risk, Basel III addresses both potential short-term liquidity stress and longer-term structural liquidity mismatches in banks' balance sheets (Table 14.2). To cover short-term liquidity stress, banks will be required to maintain sufficient high-quality unencumbered liquid assets to withstand any stressed funding scenario over a 30-day horizon as measured by the liquidity coverage ratio (LCR). To mitigate liquidity mismatches in the longer term, banks will be mandated to maintain a net stable funding ratio (NSFR). The NSFR mandates a minimum amount of stable sources of funding relative to the liquidity profile of the assets, as well as the potential for contingent liquidity needs arising from off-balance sheet commitments over a one-year horizon. In essence, the NSFR is aimed at encouraging banks to exploit stable sources of funding.

Liquidity Standards

Table 14.2

Liquidity Standards

Ratio	*Basel II*	*Basel III*
Liquidity Coverage Ratio (LCR) (to be introduced as on January 1, 2015)	–	$\frac{\text{Stock of high-quality liquid assets}}{\text{Total net cash outflows over the next 30 calendar days}} \geq 100\%$
Net Stable Funding Ratio (NSFR) (to be introduced as on January 1, 2018)	–	$\frac{\text{Available amount of stable funding}}{\text{Required amount of stable funding}} > 100\%$

Provisioning Norms

The Basel Committee is supporting the proposal for adoption of an 'expected loss' based measure of provisioning which captures actual losses more transparently and is also less procyclical than the current 'incurred loss' approach. The expected loss approach for provisioning will make financial reporting more useful for all stakeholders, including regulators and supervisors.

Disclosure Requirements

The disclosures made by banks are important for market participants to make informed decisions. One of the lessons of the crisis is that the disclosures made by banks on their risky exposures and on regulatory capital were neither appropriate nor sufficiently transparent to afford any comparative analysis. To remedy this, Basel III requires banks to disclose all relevant details, including any regulatory adjustments, as regards the composition of the regulatory capital of the bank.

3rd Question: What is the Additional Capital that Indian banks have to Mobilise to Conform to Basel III? What are the Options for, and Challenges in, Raising this Size of Capital?

Admittedly, Indian banks already meet the minimum capital requirements of Basel III at an aggregate level, even though some individual banks may have to top up. But capital adequacy today does not mean capital adequacy going forward. Currently, the bank credit-GDP ratio in India is around 55 per cent. If we want growth to accelerate, this ratio will have to go up as a necessary pre-condition. Besides, as our economy goes through a structural transformation, as it should, the share of the industry sector will increase and the credit-GDP ratio will rise even further. What this means is that Indian banks would have been required to raise additional capital even in the absence of Basel III. In estimating the net additional burden on account of Basel III, we have to take this factor into account.

What is the size of the additional capital required to be raised by Indian banks? It depends on the assumption made, and there are various estimates floating around. The Reserve Bank has made some quick estimates based on the following two conservative assumptions covering the period to March 31, 2018: (i) risk weighted assets of individual banks will increase by 20 per cent per annum; and (ii) internal accruals will be of the order of 1 per cent of risk weighted assets.

Reserve Bank's estimates project an additional capital requirement of ₹ 5 trillion, of which non-equity capital will be of the order of ₹ 3.25 trillion while equity capital will be of the order of ₹ 1.75 trillion (Table 14.3).

The additional equity capital requirement of the order of ₹ 1.75 trillion raises two questions. First, can the market provide capital of this size? Second, what will be the burden on the Government in capitalising public sector banks (PSBs) and what are its options?

Table 14.3

Additional[2] Common Equity Requirements of Indian Banks under Basel III

(₹ billion)

		Public Sector Banks	*Private Sector Banks*	*Total*
A	Additional Equity Capital Requirements under Basel III	1400-1500	200-250	1600-1750
B	Additional Equity Capital Requirements under Basel II	650-700	20-25	670-725
C	Net Equity Capital Requirements under Basel III (A-B)	750-800	180-225	930-1025
D	Of Additional Equity Capital Requirements under Basel III for Public Sector Banks (A)			
	Government Share (if present shareholding pattern is maintained)	880-910	-	-
	Government Share (if shareholding is brought down to 51 per cent)	660-690	-	-
	Market Share (if the Government's shareholding pattern is maintained at present level)	520-590	-	-

Let us turn to the first question, whether the market will be able to provide equity capital of this size. The amount the market will have to provide will depend on how much of the recapitalisation burden of PSBs the Government will meet. Data in Table 14.3 indicate that the amount that the market will have to provide will be in the range of ₹ 700 billion-₹ 1 trillion depending on how much the Government will provide. Over the last five years, banks have revised equity capital to the tune of ₹ 520 billion through the primary markets. Raising an additional ₹ 700 billion-₹ 1 trillion over the next five years from the market should therefore not be an insurmountable problem. The extended period of full Basel III implementation spread over five years gives sufficient time to banks to plan the time-table of their capital rising over this period.

2. On top of internal accruals.

Moving on to the second question of the burden on the Government which owns 70 per cent of the banking system. If the Government opts to maintain its shareholding at the current level, the burden of recapitalisation will be of the order of ₹ 900 billion; on the other hand, if it decides to reduce its shareholding in every bank to a minimum of 51 per cent, the burden reduces to under ₹ 700 billion.

Clearly, providing equity capital of this size in the face of fiscal constraints poses significant challenges. A tempting option for the Government would be to issue recapitalisation bonds against common equity infusion. But this will militate against fiscal transparency. In the alternative, would the Government be open to reducing its shareholding in PSBs to below 51 per cent? If the Government decides to pursue this option, an additional consideration is whether it will amend the statute to protect its majority voting rights.

4th Question: Will Basel III Hurt Growth?

One major criticism against Basel III has been that it will hurt growth. Even though we do not have a precise quantitative estimate of the impact on growth, the main concern is that the higher capital requirements under Basel III will kick in at a time when credit demand in the economy will be on the rise.

In a structurally transforming economy with rapid upward mobility, credit demand will expand faster than GDP for several reasons. First, India will shift increasingly from services to manufactures, and the credit intensity of manufacturing is higher per unit of GDP than that for services. Second, we need to at least double our investment in infrastructure which will place enormous demands on credit. Finally, financial inclusion, which both the Government and the Reserve Bank are driving, will bring millions of low income households into the formal financial system with almost all of them needing credit.

What all this means is that we are going to have to impose higher capital requirements on banks as per Basel III at a time when credit demand is going to expand rapidly. A crucial question is this.

Will this raise the cost of credit and hence militate against growth? Put differently, how much growth are we willing to sacrifice in order to buy insurance against financial instability? At its core, this boils down to the tension between short-term compulsions and long-term growth prospects. Comfortingly, empirical research by BIS economists shows that even if Basel III may impose some costs in the short-term, it will secure medium to long term growth prospects.

5th Question: How will Basel III Affect the Profitability of Banks? Will it Alter their Incentive Structure?

Let me attempt an answer. As we noted, Basel III requires higher and better quality capital. Admittedly, the cost of equity capital is high. It is also likely that the loss absorbency requirements on the non-equity regulatory capital will increase its cost.

The average return on equity (RoE) of the Indian banking system for the last three years has been approximately 15 per cent. Implementation of Basel III is expected to result in a decline in Indian banks' RoE in the short-term. However, the expected benefits arising out of a more stable and stronger banking system will largely offset the negative impact of a lower RoE in the medium to long term. It is also fair to assume that investors will perceive the benefits of having less risky and more stable banks, and will therefore be willing to trade in higher returns for lower risks.

A related question is whether banks will bear the increased cost of capital themselves or pass it to their depositors and borrowers. This trade off has to be assessed in the context of the relatively higher level of net interest margins (NIMs) of Indian banks, of approximately 3 per cent. This higher NIM suggests that there is scope for banks to improve their efficiency, bring down the cost of intermediation and ensure that returns are not overly compromised even as the cost of capital may increase.

Having dealt with capital requirements, let us now turn to the liquidity standards under Basel III. Will the mandate to maintain a higher quantum of liquid assets encourage banks to resort to the passive option of lending to the Government, thereby crowding out credit to the private sector? Hopefully, this question will resolve itself as the savings rate of the economy improves and the fiscal deficit comes down.

A related question is about the extent of banks' holding of government securities that should be taken into account for assessing compliance with liquidity standards. One view is that since statutory liquidity ratio (SLR) securities are required to be held on an ongoing basis, they should not be reckoned for calculating liquidity requirements under Basel III. An alternate view is that since the Reserve Bank is expected to provide liquidity against these securities under stressed conditions as part of its lender of last resort (LoLR) obligation, at least a prespecified portion of these securities should be taken into account for assessing compliance with Basel III's liquidity standards. The Reserve Bank will take a view on this in due course.

So, the answer to the question of whether Basel III will affect the profitability of banks and alter their incentive structure is that the competitive dimensions of our banking sector should ensure that banks are able to deliver efficient financial intermediation without compromising the interests of depositors and borrowers.

6th Question: Does India Really Need Basel III? Don't the Costs Outweigh the Benefits?

The last three questions, if you noticed, dealt with the putative negative consequence of Basel III—the burden of raising additional capital and the costs of complying with the new liquidity standards, their impact on banks' profitability, and on the overall growth prospects of the economy.

One view, although not explicitly spelt out in that form, is that India need not adopt Basel III, or should adopt only a diluted version of it, so as to balance the benefits against the putative costs. To buttress this view, it is argued that Basel III is designed as a corrective for advanced economy banks which had gone astray, oftentimes taking advantage of regulatory gaps and regulatory looseness, and that Indian banks which remained sound through the crisis should not be burdened with the 'onerous' obligations of Basel III.

The Reserve Bank does not agree with this view. Our position is that India should transit to Basel III because of several reasons. By far the most important reason is that as India integrates with the rest of the world, as increasingly Indian banks go abroad and foreign banks come on to our shores, we cannot afford to have a regulatory deviation from global standards. Any deviation will hurt us both by way of perception and also in actual practice.

The 'perception' of a lower standard regulatory regime will put Indian banks at a disadvantage in global competition, especially because the implementation of Basel III is subject to a 'peer group' review whose findings will be in the public domain.

Deviation from Basel III will also hurt us in actual practice. We have to recognise that Basel III provides for improved risk management systems in banks. It is important that Indian banks have the cushion afforded by these risk management systems to withstand shocks from external systems, especially as they deepen their links with the global financial system going forward.

I must also add, as I complete my answer to this question, that some of the prescriptions of Basel III have already been in existence in India, and the net additional burden will be lower than we tend to imagine.

7th Question: The Reserve Bank has already Rolled out the Implementation of Basel III Even as Many Countries are Yet to do so. Why did you have to Frontrun and why are Some of your Regulations More Onerous than Required under Basel III?

The Reserve Bank issued final guidelines on Basel III capital regulation in May 2012 to be implemented from January 1, 2013 to March 31, 2018 even as many other jurisdictions have yet to do so. We have been criticised for being unduly proactive in this regard. Let me respond to this criticism.

First, on the start and end dates. We have not advanced the start date. It is the same as the internationally agreed date of January 1, 2013. However, we have advanced the end date from the internationally agreed date of December 31, 2018 by nine months to March 31, 2018. We did this to align our date with the close of the Indian fiscal year, which is March 31. We could have gone up to March 31, 2019, but that would have overshot the Basel III prescription by three months and would have attracted adverse notice. Our assessment is that the cost of that adverse notice will far exceed the marginal burden of a slightly earlier close date. So, we settled for March 31, 2018.

Third, major global banks often engage themselves in the Basel Committee's consultative process which is not the case with Indian banks. We moved early since we had completed the consultative process, and thought that we must give our banks a head start in transiting to Basel III.

Let me then move to the more weighty question of why the Reserve Bank has prescribed higher capital and leverage norms for Indian banks than the Basel III minimum. Table 14.4 summarises the Basel III (international) prescriptions alongside the current requirements in India under Basel II, and as required under Basel III when fully implemented.

What is the rationale for our more 'onerous' capital standards? Note that banks in India follow the standardised approaches under Basel II. The higher prescription is intended to address any judgemental error in capital adequacy *viz.*, wrong application of standardised risk weights, misclassification of asset quality etc. Also, while advanced approaches under Basel II have been strengthened, the calibration of standardised risk weights is yet to be comprehensively effected. And more importantly, Indian banks have not so far been subjected to Pillar 2 capital requirement under Basel II. Thus, the higher prescription addresses any potential concerns relating to undercapitalisation of risky exposures. It should also be noted in this context that even under the Basel I and Basel II regimes, the Reserve Bank's prescriptions were a percentage point higher than the international norms. Experience shows that this prudence on our part had been helpful and was positive on the cost-benefit calculus.

Table 14.4

Minimum Regulatory Capital Prescriptions
(As Percentage of Risk Weighted Assets)

		Basel III (As on January 1, 2019)	*Reserve Bank's Prescriptions*	
			Current (Basel II)	*Basel III (as on March 31, 2018)*
A = (B+D)	Minimum Total Capital	8.0	9.0	9.0
B	Minimum Tier 1 capital	6.0	6.0	7.0
C	Of which: Minimum Common Equity Tier 1 capital	4.5	3.6[3]	5.5
D	Maximum Tier 2 capital (within Total Capital)	2.0	3.0	2.0
E	Capital Conservation Buffer (CCB)	2.5	-	2.5
F = C+E	Minimum Common Equity Tier 1 capital + CCB	7.0	3.6	8.0
G = A+E	Minimum Total Capital + CCB	10.5	-	11.5
H	Leverage Ratio (ratio to total assets)	3.0	-	4.5[4]

Please note that India has not been an outlier in prescribing higher capital standards. Several other jurisdictions, particularly Asian countries, have proposed higher capital adequacy ratios under Basel III as may be seen from Table 14.5.

3. There is no direct prescription for minimum common equity. However, non-common equity elements in Tier 1 are restricted to a maximum 40 per cent of Tier 1 capital. Accordingly, indirectly minimum common equity is considered as 3.6 per cent of Tier 1 capital.

4. During the period of parallel run for Tier 1 leverage ratio beginning from January 1, 2013 to January 1, 2017, banks should strive to maintain the existing level of leverage ratio but, in no case it should fall below 4.5 per cent. Banks having leverage ratio below 4.5 per cent strive to achieve the target as early as possible. Under Basel III, the minimum Tier 1 leverage should be 3 per cent during the parallel run period.

Table 14.5

Sample of Countries with Higher Capital Adequacy Norms Than India

Country	*Minimum Common Equity Ratio (including capital conservation buffer) (percentage)*	*Minimum Total Capital Ratio (percentage)*
Basel III	7.0	10.5
India	8.0	11.5
Philippines, The	8.5	12.5
Singapore	9.0	12.5
China	7.5	10.5
South Africa	9.0	12.5

Similarly, a question has been raised about why the Reserve Bank prescribed a higher leverage ratio, 4.5 per cent, against the Basel III norm of 3 per cent. It is a matter of supervisory comfort that the Indian banking system is only moderately leveraged on an aggregate basis (22 times of Tier 1 capital approximately). We thought it prudent not to dilute this 'comfortable' position during the parallel run period of the leverage ratio. The Basel Committee is monitoring and analysing the potential impact of the leverage ratio. As indicated in our Basel III framework, we will finalise the leverage ratio requirement taking into account the final proposal of the Basel Committee.

8th Question: What are the Potential Challenges in Implementing the Countercyclical Capital Buffer?

As we noted earlier, a critical component of the Basel III package is a countercyclical capital buffer which mandates banks to build up a higher level of capital in good times that could be run down in times of economic contraction, consistent with safety and soundness considerations. This is conceptually neat, but is challenging in operational terms, as indeed evidenced by Spain's recent experience. The foremost challenge is identifying the inflexion point in an economic cycle which should trigger the release of the buffer. It is quite evident that both tightening too early or too late can be costly in macroeconomic terms. The identification of the inflexion point therefore needs to be based on objective and observable criteria. It also needs long series data on economic cycles. So, what we need is both a better database and more refined statistical skills in analysing economic cycles.

The countercyclical capital buffer as prescribed in Basel III was initially based on the credit/GDP metric. Is this a good economic indicator from the Indian perspective? A study undertaken by the Reserve Bank shows that the credit to GDP ratio has not historically been a good indicator of buildup of systemic risk in our banking system.

Furthermore, some economic sectors such as real estate, housing, microfinance and consumer credit are relatively new in India, and banks have only recently begun financing them in a big way. The risk build up in such sectors cannot accurately be captured by the aggregate credit to GDP ratio. The Reserve Bank has so far calibrated countercyclical policies at the sectoral level, and I believe we need to continue to use that approach. The Basel Committee also has now recognised that no single variable can fully capture the dynamics of the economic cycle. Appropriate calibration of the buffer requires country specific judgement backed by a broad range of other simple indicators used in financial stability assessments.

9th Question: What are D-SIBs? Will any Indian Bank be Classified as a D-SIB?

The moral hazard relating to too-big-to-fail institutions which encourages risky behaviour by larger banks has been a huge issue on the post-crisis reform agenda. Basel III seeks to mitigate this externality by identifying global systemically important banks (G-SIBs) and mandating them to maintain a higher level of capital dependent on their level of systemic importance. The list of G-SIBs is to be reviewed annually. Currently, no Indian bank appears in the list of G–SIBs.

Separately, the Basel Committee is working on establishing a minimum set of principles for domestic systemically important banks (D-SIBs), and also on the norms for prescribing higher loss absorbency (HLA) capital standards for them. Besides, it is also necessary to evolve a sound resolution mechanism for D-SIBs.

The moral hazard issue of too-big-to-fail and the regulatory endeavour to address that raise a question about the optimal size of a G-SIB, and the optimal size of a D-SIB relative to the size of the economy. Admittedly, larger banks offer certain benefits such as economies of scale in operation and capacity to finance large infrastructure projects which are typically considered more risky. In India, we also need large banks with potential capacity to become significant global players. Nevertheless, we have to balance the benefits that large banks extend with the moral hazard costs they entail.

10th Question: What Sort of Capacity Building is Required in the Implementation of Basel III, especially in the Area of Risk Management? What Should Banks do and What Should the Reserve Bank do in this Regard?

There are no two views about the need for building capacity within the banks, and also in the Reserve Bank which is the regulator, to efficiently implement Basel III.

By far the most important reform is that there should be a radical change in banks' approach to risk management. Banks in India are currently operating on the standardised approaches of Basel II. The larger banks need to migrate to the advanced approaches, especially as they expand their overseas presence. The adoption of advanced approaches to risk management will enable banks to manage their capital more efficiently and improve their profitability.

This graduation to 'advanced approaches' requires three things. First and most importantly, a change in perception from looking upon the capital framework as a compliance function to seeing it as a necessary prerequisite for keeping the bank sound, stable, and therefore profitable; second, deeper and more broad based capacity in risk management; and finally adequate and good quality data.

Conclusion

That brings me to the close of my list of ten questions and answers. Even as I have tried to be comprehensive, I am conscious that the list of questions I have raised is not exhaustive; neither are my answers complete. Under the circumstances, I believe I would have done a good job if this paper raises more questions in your minds, and sets you off on finding answers.

There may be many unanswered questions. What I am certain of though is that effective implementation of Basel III is going to make Indian banks more strong, stable and sound so that they can deliver value to the real sectors of the economy.

Inaugural Address at the Annual FICCI - IBA Banking Conference at Mumbai, September 04, 2012. RBI Bulletin October 2012.

15

DUVVURI SUBBARAO

G-20 and India

The G-20, as all of you know, has been in the forefront of battling the financial crises—the global financial crisis of 2008-09 and the eurozone crisis since 2010—that have taken a devastating toll on global growth and welfare. Indeed when the history of this crisis is written, the London G-20 Summit in April 2009 will be acknowledged as the clear turning point when world leaders showed extraordinary determination and unity. Sure, there were differences, but they were debated and discussed, and compromises were made so as to reach the final goal—of ending the crisis. This resulted in an agreed package of measures having both domestic and international components but all of them to be implemented in coordination, and indeed in synchronisation where necessary. The entire range of crisis response measures—accommodative monetary stance, fiscal stimulus, debt and deposit guarantees, capital injection, asset purchases, currency swaps, keeping markets open—all derived in varying degrees from the G-20 package.

Five years on the crisis is still with us; only its epicenter and the main actors have changed. During these five years, the world has also become privy to the differences on some vital issues within the G-20 membership. Understandably therefore, there are concerns and apprehensions that the vaunted unity and sense of purpose that the G-20 showed earlier on are dissipating.

My own view is that these differences should not be exaggerated. After all, in a world comprising nation states, there is no natural constituency for the global economy. There are bound to be differences when the agenda is so broad and country level compulsions are seen to be clashing with global interests. What is important is that we are able to resolve these differences with the realisation that in a globalising world, no country can be an 'island'. What happens anywhere affects economies everywhere. Global financial stability is a global public good, and there can be no more an effective forum than the G-20 to steer the world towards globally optimal solutions.

Having set that context, I will now address the following questions:

(i) What is the G-20 and how does it function?

(ii) Why is the G-20 important?

(iii) What have been/are the main issues on the G-20 agenda and India's concerns regarding them?

(iv) What are the future challenges for the G-20?

What is the G-20?

The G-20 is an informal club with 19 member countries and the European Union which together represent 90 per cent of global GDP, 80 per cent of global trade and two-thirds of the global population.

Contrary to popular belief, the G-20 is not a new international grouping triggered by the global financial crisis. It was, in fact, triggered by an earlier crisis, the Asian crisis of 1997. Although, it has been meeting regularly since 1997, it acquired a higher profile and credibility in the aftermath of the global financial crisis during which time it was elevated from a Finance Ministers' forum to a Leaders' forum.

The chair of the G-20 rotates every year from country to country. The chair country takes the lead in formulating and driving the agenda. The G-20 leaders meet at the summit level once a year.[1] Besides, the finance ministers and central bank governors of G-20 meet twice a year. All the meetings are typically held in, and hosted by, the chair country. The president of the World Bank and

1. During the crisis, the Leaders met twice a year. Now, the frequency has reverted to the standard pattern of once a year. Post-crisis, seven Leaders' Summits have been held: Washington (November 2008), London (March 2009), Pittsburgh (October 2009), Toronto (June 2010), Seoul (November 2010), Cannes (November 2011) and Los Cabos (June 2012).

the managing director of the IMF attend the G-20 meetings, thereby ensuring that the activities of the G-20 are integrated into the agenda of the Bretton Woods Institutions where necessary. There are also other invitees to the G-20 meetings such as the OECD, UNDP and the regional development banks.

Why is the G-20 important?

The G-20 can be seen as a watermark in international economic diplomacy in at least two ways.

First, it is a major step forward from the old divisive style of global governance of the Bretton Woods system characterised by little communication and much acrimony between major developed (G-8) who were largely seen as donors, and developing (G-77) countries that were seen as the recipients of bilateral and multilateral aid. Differences in perception remain, but there is now a paradigm shift in the donor-recipient equation, a better appreciation of each others' viewpoint, and an emerging consensus on what increasingly appears to be an incipient new international order through G-20 reports and declarations to which both sets of countries are committed.

This new style of international governance had been in the making for some time. The bigger EMEs, particularly the BRICS,[2] were growing at a much faster pace than OECD countries for a long time, and were becoming increasingly systemically important. It became clear that for any multilateral economic consultative process managing globalisation to be effective, their inclusion in the process was imperative. Even prior to the global crisis, the G-8 found it expedient to invite the big emerging economies—the G-5 (Brazil, India, China, Mexico and South Africa)—to their Summits as special invitees, but only to select sessions in what was termed the Heligandamm process. The global financial crisis has simply underscored the need to associate major emerging economies in global economic governance. From being the sources of constant instability in the global economy, some of the larger emerging

2. Brazil, Russia, India, China and South Africa comprise the BRICS.

economies are now increasingly seen as nodes of stability and growth.

The second factor that makes the G-20 unique is its attempt to coordinate the macroeconomic policies of systemically important economies to make them more effective in a world where national macroeconomic policy instruments are being blunted via rapid global integration through trade and financial markets. Following its concerted and coordinated policy response to the crisis, the G-20 set about the task of addressing reform of the global economic and financial architecture, and to remove long-standing structural impediments to strong, sustainable and balanced global growth going forward by launching its signature 'mutual assessment process' which is increasingly seen as the heart and soul of the G-20. The success of this process is important for global financial stability, as I will explain later.

Main Issues on the G-20 Agenda

In that context of the origins and importance of G-20, let me now turn to some of the main issues on the G-20 agenda after the world surfaced from the depth of the 2008-09 global financial crisis. I will also give the Indian perspective where appropriate.

Global Rebalancing

The first issue I want to address is global imbalances. Almost everyone is agreed that one of the root causes of the global financial crisis is the buildup of global imbalances. In as much as global imbalances—no matter whether they were caused by a 'consumption binge' in advanced economies or a 'savings glut' in EMEs—were the root cause of the crisis, reducing imbalances is a necessary condition for restoring global financial stability.

The post-crisis debate on global imbalances has three interrelated facets. The first is the role of exchange rates in global rebalancing. The second relates to capital flows into EMEs raising the familiar challenge of managing the impossible trinity. And the third facet is the framework for the adjustment process. Let me turn to these one by one.

First, on the role of exchange rates—a prime lever for redressal of external imbalances. Global rebalancing will require deficit economies to save more and consume less. They need to depend for growth more on external demand which calls for a real depreciation of their currencies. The surplus economies will need to mirror these efforts—save less and spend more, and shift from external to domestic demand. They need to let their currencies appreciate. The problem though is that while the adjustment by deficit and surplus economies has to be symmetric, the incentives they face are asymmetric. Managing currency tensions will require a shared understanding on keeping exchange rates aligned to economic fundamentals, and an agreement that currency interventions should be resorted to not as an instrument of trade policy but only to manage disruptions to macroeconomic stability.

That takes me to the second facet of global imbalances—capital flows. The problem of capital flows came centre stage in the aftermath of the quantitative easing by advanced economy central banks when the excess liquidity in the global system found its way into faster growing EMEs. The most high profile problems thrown up by capital flows, in excess of a country's absorptive capacity, are erosion of monetary policy effectiveness, currency appreciation and loss of competitiveness. Speculative capital flows could also lead to asset and commodity bubbles potentially threatening both financial and economic stability.

In the G-20 debate on capital flows, popularly but mistakenly referred to as 'currency wars', EMEs agitated mainly two points. First, that in as much as lumpy and volatile capital flows are a spillover from the quantitative easing of advanced economies, the burden of adjustment has to be shared. Second, that capital controls should be understood as legitimate and acceptable defence against speculative capital flows.

Global imbalances and their correction were the main concern in the G-20 Framework and Mutual Assessment Process (MAP) exercise. The MAP exercise is aimed at making countries commit to external sector policies that lead to strong, sustained and balanced growth at the global level. The understanding is that global imbalances, especially imbalances built on the strength of undervalued exchange rates accompanied by a build-up of reserves, threaten the stability of the global economy due to the possibility of disorderly unwinding.

China's exchange rate policies were at the centre of the debate in the G-20. As on date, China's current account surplus (in relation to its GDP) has declined from the pre-crisis peak, and China's real effective exchange rate has also appreciated since 2005, even though it is widely believed that it needs to appreciate further. In the meanwhile, however, the cumulative surpluses of oil producing countries (mostly OPEC, Russia and Norway) have increased and now account for the lion's share of global current account surpluses. While global imbalances have declined in the post-crisis period, their nature and composition continue to evolve. It is important that the MAP exercise in the G-20 keeps a watch on changes in the composition, nature and distribution of global imbalances and their implications, and to steer the work towards their underlying causes.

Now let me comment briefly on the India perspective on the global imbalance problem. India did not contribute to the generation or transmission of global imbalances. As much as we want to enhance our export competitiveness, we believe that it should come from improved productivity rather than an artificially calibrated exchange rate. Our exchange rate is largely market driven, and we intervene in the forex market only to manage volatility in the rate and to prevent macroeconomic disruptions. As a developing economy, we run a large current account deficit (CAD) that has in recent period expanded relative to our historical record. We need capital flows to finance the CAD. We have an express preference for equity flows over debt flows, for direct investment over portfolio investment and for long term over short-term flows. We are moving gradually towards opening our capital account along a roadmap, the roadmap itself being recalibrated to the evolving global situation. Our policy, in short, is *festina lente* which is Latin for 'make haste slowly'.

India co-chairs, along with Canada, the G-20 Framework 'MAP' Working Group (FWG). This provides India an opportunity not only to get an early preview of the macro and micro consequences of global initiatives, but also to actively contribute to such initiatives. India's suggestions on the role infrastructure investment can play in the global recovery and rebalancing is a case in point. As a co-chair, it may be important to ensure that the work of the FWG is not seen as merely a technical exercise but as an effort towards a genuine dialogue on macroeconomic policies of the 20 most significant economies and for engaging in a cooperative game that results in greater policy coordination which is a public good.

Global Reserve Currency

The global crisis has revived the familiar concerns about the robustness of the international monetary system, and in particular about the global reserve currency and the provision of liquidity in times of stress. The system we now have is that the US dollar is the world's reserve currency by virtue of the dominant size of the US economy, its share in global trade and the preponderant use of dollar in foreign trade and foreign exchange transactions. And as Barry Eichengreen (2012) told us in his book on the story of the dollar, the reserve currency status depends also on a host of intangible factors such as strategic and military relationships, laws, institutions and incumbency which he referred to as 'network externalities'.

In line with the Triffin paradox, the US has met the obligation of an issuer of reserve currency by running fiscal and external deficits while enjoying the 'exorbitant privilege' of not having to make the necessary adjustment to bridge the deficits. With no pressure to reduce the deficit, a dominant economy can potentially create imbalances at the global level as indeed happened in the build up to the crisis. An argument can be made that even in the context of a single reserve currency, global imbalances are not inevitable. The US could not have run persistent deficits had not the EMEs provided the demand side impetus by accumulating reserve assets either for trade advantage or as a measure of self-insurance against external shocks.

The problem with the world having only a single reserve currency came to the fore during the crisis as many countries faced dollar liquidity problems as a consequence of swift deleveraging by foreign creditors and foreign investors. Paradoxically, even as the US economy was in a downturn, and its central bank resorted to extraordinary quantitative easing, the dollar strengthened as a result of flight to safety.

Based on the experience of the crisis, several reform proposals have been put forward to address the problems arising from a single reserve currency. One is to have a menu of alternative reserve currencies. But this cannot happen by fiat. To be a serious contender as an alternative, a currency has to fulfill some exacting criteria. It has to be fully convertible and its exchange rate should be determined by market fundamentals; it should acquire a significant share in world trade; the currency issuing country should have liquid, open and large financial markets and also the policy credibility to inspire the confidence of potential investors. In short, the 'exorbitant privilege' of a reserve currency comes with an 'exorbitant responsibility'.

A second solution to the single reserve currency issue is to develop the SDR (special drawing right) as a reserve currency. This does not seem to be a feasible option. For the SDR to be an effective reserve currency, it has to fulfil several conditions: the SDR has to be accepted as a liability of the IMF, it has to be automatically acceptable as a medium of payment in cross-border transactions; it should be freely tradeable and its price has to be determined by forces of demand and supply.

Another option, a third possible solution, is to expand the SDR basket by including the currencies of countries that are increasingly important economically and politically. With the increasing economic weight of emerging markets, it seems inconceivable that emerging markets will not want to see their currencies play a greater role in international transactions. Recent initiatives by some EMEs, especially China and Russia, aim at facilitating international use of their currencies. The exclusion of emerging markets currencies makes emerging markets bystanders of the system rather than stakeholders. Integration of emerging markets into the international monetary system could increase their incentives to gear their policy conduct towards contributing to the stability of the system.

However, the pros and cons of this alternative have yet to be fully studied. In particular, we have to reckon with the question of whether emerging market currencies, not being fully convertible, can meet the demanding criteria required for inclusion in the SDR.

The fourth option is not actually an alternative, but is in part a solution. It aims at reducing the need for self-insurance and thereby the dependence on a reserve currency by supporting a multilateral option of a prearranged line of credit that can be easily and quickly accessed. The IMF has designed some line of credit specifically with this objective in view.

None of the above solutions fully addresses the problems arising from a single global reserve currency. What this underscores is that at the global level we need to explore these and other options for protecting ourselves from the vulnerabilities that we confront as a consequence of a single reserve currency.

India's own position on the global reserve currency is that the world will be better served by increasing the number of reserve currencies, but this has to happen in an organic way, not by fiat. Meanwhile countries need safety-nets to protect themselves against the vulnerabilities of the global currency system. Also, the US has the responsibility of ensuring that every country has access to dollar liquidity, especially in times of stress.

According to this view, countries cannot be asked to desist from building up reserves and depend entirely on external safety-nets. Foreign exchange reserves should invariably form the first line of defence. On top of that, they need currency swap arrangements. In fact, the US obligation, by virtue of its status as the issuer of the global reserve currency, to provide dollar swap facilities to all large economies, including India, is one of the issues that we discussed in the Ministerial Level Indo-US Dialogue last month.

Protectionism

In the post-crisis world, there may not actually be 'deglobalisation' but the earlier orthodoxy that globalisation is an unmixed blessing is being increasingly challenged. The rationale behind globalisation was, and hopefully is, that even as advanced countries may see some low end jobs being outsourced, they will still benefit from globalisation because for every low end job gone, another high end job—that is more skill intensive, more productive—will be created. If this does not happen rapidly enough or visibly enough, protectionist pressures will arise, and rapidly become vociferous and politically compelling.

Recent international developments mark an 'ironic reversal' in the fears about globalisation. Previously, it was the EMEs which feared that integration into the world economy would lead to welfare loss at home. Those fears have now given way to apprehensions in advanced economies that globalisation means losing jobs to cheap labour abroad.

Following the global financial crisis, the G-20 leaders were determined not to repeat the mistakes of the 1930s when the brunt of protectionism exacerbated the Great Depression. However, there is concern in some quarters that even as open protectionism has been resisted relatively well during the current crisis, opaque protectionism has been on the rise. Opaque protectionism takes the form of resorting to measures such as anti-dumping actions, safeguards, preferential treatment of domestic firms in bailout packages and discriminatory procurement practices. To strengthen multilateral trade discipline, the need for a quick conclusion of the Doha Round can hardly be overemphasised. In a world with growing worries about the debt creating stimulus packages, a Doha Round agreement should be welcomed as a non-debt creating stimulus to the global economy.

India opposes protectionism in all its forms. However, at the same time, we have to respect the WTO-consistent policy space available to the developing countries to pursue their legitimate objectives of growth, development and stability. We are encouraged by the analysis of the recent trade monitoring report jointly released by WTO, OECD and UNCTAD on G-20 economies which shows that majority of the trade measures taken by India in the review period were either trade facilitative or roll back measures.

IMF Quota and Governance

The global economic and financial crisis of 2008 exposed critical weaknesses in the structure of the International Financial Architecture (IFA) as well as in its governance. The G-20 has been trying to address these governance and structural weaknesses while at the same time endeavouring to stabilise the global economy through a process of mutual consultations and policy cooperation. An important motivation for these reforms is that the global economy has undergone fundamental changes in the past decade and a half and these changes have not been reflected appropriately in the IFA.

While agreement has been reached in the G-20 for effecting major reforms, implementation has so far has been disappointing. The agreement for IMF quota and governance reforms in 2010 has not yet been implemented. India's major concern is that we should adhere to the timeline for completing the IMF quota reforms by January 2013, so that it serves as the basis for the 15th General Review of Quotas to be completed no later than January 2014.

There has been some criticism that IMF quota and governance issues should be settled within the IMF management and not at the G-20. The dominant view though has been that the G-20 should continue to be the main forum for overall guidance not only on the direction that the comprehensive review of the formula should take but on continued reform of the IFA, as it may be difficult to reform this from the inside in view of its flawed and outmoded shareholding structure. The G-20 has played a crucial role in steering discussions on the quota formula in the past and it will be unfortunate if this aspect is diluted going forward.

Global institutions can only be legitimate and credible if their vote share and governance structure reflect members' share in the world economy. It is in this context that India and other emerging countries believe that GDP should have predominant weight in the quota formula as it is the most robust measure of relative economic weights in the global economy.

Financial Sector Reforms

Received wisdom today is that financial deregulation shares the honours with global imbalances as being one of the twin villains of the crisis. Not surprisingly therefore, reforms to the financial sector regulation have been on top of the G-20 agenda.

The broad contours of the international initiatives spearhead by the G-20 on financial sector reform rest on four broad pillars: regulation, supervision, resolution, especially in respect of global systemically important financial institutions (or SIFIs), and assessment of the implementation of new standards. So far, one pillar that has received substantial public attention is regulatory reform, where there have already been some notable achievements, including agreement on the new Basel III capital and liquidity standards.

However, the process of regulatory reforms that is proceeding across various jurisdictions has come to pose new challenges especially as the global economy continues to be marked by new risks. The uncertain and uneven recovery has led to calls in some quarters to dilute or slow the financial reform initiatives. While there may be a case for some back loading of difficult adjustments to strengthen the recovery of the financial sector, any weakness in our resolve or commitment to reform will sow the seeds for a fresh crisis down the line. The key task is therefore to fully implement what has been agreed in a cooperative manner.

All G-20 members have committed to the implementation of the Basel III package. However, major jurisdictions have come out with their own regulatory standards. It is important that there is no disharmony that could be confusing. We need to guard against the possibility of regulatory arbitrage. If comparable standards are not implemented in all jurisdictions simultaneously, financial activity will likely migrate to less regulated jurisdictions as well as into shadow banking with disruptive consequences for the entire global financial system.

As we move forward in the area of regulation, the investment needs of the emerging market and developing economies also deserve special attention. There are two important points in this regard. First, it is important to ensure that financial intermediaries in emerging and developing economies are not disadvantaged in the new regulatory framework, especially since the opportunities and challenges in their systems are quite different.

Second, the more demanding regulatory standards should not lead to deleveraging by global financial institutions out of emerging markets. It should be noted in this regard that the financial regulatory reform has so far focused on reducing systemic risks, and rightly so, but not much attention has been devoted to redirecting savings from investment in volatile financial assets to financing investment in the real economy, where the impact on growth and jobs is more tangible and direct. We need to recognise that it is income from the real sector that must ultimately pay for the profits of the financial sector. Standards setting bodies should design incentives in a manner that helps redirect global savings into investment in the real economy, particularly in infrastructure, supports demand and enhances long-term potential growth thereby fulfilling the original role of intermediating for growth and development of the real economy.

Collaboration between financial authorities on these issues is an important, albeit a difficult and painstaking task. Collaboration becomes difficult especially when it entails profound structural changes in the face of volatile financial markets and anaemic growth. Yet, it is precisely these challenges that make it so vital that the regulatory response in the G-20 should be well coordinated internationally to ensure that the new regulatory framework is effective and globally implemented and the follies of the past that led to the financial crisis are not repeated.

Future Challenges for the G-20

I have so far discussed some of the major items on the agenda of the G-20. Let me now look ahead to the challenges that confront the G-20 on the way forward.

The first challenge is drawing a balance between short term compulsions and medium term sustainability. A case in point is the intense debate in the advanced economies on fiscal austerity *versus* growth. Everyone is agreed that long term fiscal consolidation is critical to macroeconomic sustainability. At the same time, everyone is also aware of the pains of fiscal adjustment in the short-term. If fiscal profligacy is seen as consumption of future income and shifting the burden to a future generation, fiscal austerity should be seen as the price for the necessary correction so that burden sharing across generations is fair and optimal. If the compulsions of short-term and long-term policies point in different directions, how can these be harmonised, especially since the long-term is a stringing together of the short-terms? How can G-20 commitments and the 'Mutual Assessment Process' (MAP) commitments and assessments accommodate such dynamic policy shifts?

The second challenge for the G-20 is to nudge countries' policies in mutually agreed directions and hold sovereigns accountable for commitments given, especially since these are not legally binding and there is no enforcement mechanism. This is particularly difficult in vigorous democracies where the popular perception could be that national interests are being compromised for the sake of global stability. How can national leaders build and nurture, within their national boundaries, a constituency for the global optimal?

Seeking firm, forward looking commitments, or pointed criticism of policy frameworks of other countries, on the lines of the European Union, or even the OECD, style of functioning, may be difficult and divisive at this stage. A more ambitious style of global governance would understandably take some time to take shape. At this stage the issue really is monitoring and assessing whether the general direction of G-20 member country policies is heading in a mutually consistent and agreed fashion over the medium to long-term, and how the G-20 processes can help countries navigate their domestic legislative, regulatory and judicial processes such that commonly agreed policies are adopted.

The third challenge for the G-20 is that the success of domestic policy actions in an increasingly globalising world with growing policy and market spillovers is linked to global outcomes. If rebalancing is uncoordinated, the outcomes could be even worse. Policy cooperation is therefore potentially win-win, since economic integration has moved far ahead of political integration. While this is most clearly manifest in the case of the euro zone, to a great extent, the challenges ahead before the G-20 may be similar. In this sense, the G-20 can be seen as a brave new experiment to push the boundaries of globalisation to harvest this cooperation dividend.

Summary and Conclusion

Let me now conclude. I began with explaining the importance of G-20 and how it acquitted itself quite credibly in managing the global financial crisis. I have also dealt with some criticism of the G-20 for its seeming failure to address post crisis issues with the same alacrity and unity of purpose. I then went on to address some of the major items on the G-20 agenda, and where appropriate, indicated the Indian position on these issues. Finally, I listed the three big challenges on the way forward for the G-20 experiment.

The G-20 is by all accounts a bold initiative. It is unique from earlier international initiatives in the sense that it is not formed by a charter, has no mandate for global governance and its decisions are not legally binding and enforceable. In short it is based on the realisation that in a globalising world, our futures are all tied together and the only way we can all prosper is though policy cooperation and on the belief that the only way global governance can be pursued is through an honour code.

Can the G-20 survive? What would the late Shri Shroff have said? Pragmatist that he was, he would have said that the only way the G-20 can survive is by showing exemplary leadership in resolving our most pressing challenges at the global level.

References

Eichengreen, Barry (2012). *Exorbitant Privilege: The Rise and Fall of the Dollar and the Future of the International Monetary System.* New York: Oxford University Press.

46th A.D Shroff Memorial Lecture delivered in Mumbai, November 20, 2012. RBI Bulletin December 2012.

16

DEEPAK MOHANTY

Money Market and Monetary Operations in India

Over the last decade, there has been substantial development in the Indian money market in terms of depth, variety of instruments and efficiency. This has enabled the Reserve Bank to change its monetary operations from direct quantity based instruments to indirect interest rate based instruments to enhance the efficiency of monetary transmission consistent with international best practice. Against this background, I will briefly capture the developments in the money market and discuss the experience with the recently modified operating procedure of monetary policy before concluding with some thoughts on the way forward.

Role of Money Market

Money market can be defined as a market for short-term funds with maturities ranging from overnight to one year and includes financial instruments that are considered to be close substitutes of money. It provides an equilibrating mechanism for demand and supply of short-term funds and in the process provides an avenue for central bank intervention in influencing both the quantum and cost of liquidity in the financial system, consistent with the overall stance of monetary policy. In the process, money market plays a central role in the monetary policy transmission mechanism by providing a key link in the operations of monetary policy to financial markets and ultimately, to the real economy. In fact,

---

The assistance provided by Sitikantha Pattanaik, Jeevan Khundrakpam, Binod Bhoi and Rajeev Jain is acknowledged.

money market is the first and the most important stage in the chain of monetary policy transmission.

Typically, the monetary policy instrument, effectively the price of central bank liquidity, is directly set by the central bank. In view of limited control over long-term interest rates, central banks adopt a strategy to exert direct influence on short-term interest rates. Changes in the short-term policy rate provide signals to financial markets, whereby different segments of the financial system respond by adjusting their rates of return on various instruments, depending on their sensitivity and the efficacy of the transmission mechanism. How quickly and effectively the monetary policy actions influence the spectrum of market interest rates depends upon the level of development of various segments of financial markets, particularly the money market. Cross-country studies suggest that as domestic financial markets grow, transmission of monetary policy through various channels becomes better.

As a crucial initial link in the chain through which monetary policy aims at achieving ultimate goals relating to inflation and growth, money market developments are closely monitored and influenced by central banks. Besides expecting money market rates to respond to policy rate changes in a well anchored manner, central banks aim at ensuring appropriate liquidity conditions through discretionary liquidity management operations so that money market functions normally. Money market is also an important funding market for banks and financial institutions, and at times, even for corporates. Stressed conditions in the money markets could increase moral hazard with banks expecting a central bank to function as the lender of first resort. Following the recent global financial crisis, money market funding for the financial system effectively got replaced with central bank funding in advanced countries. Money market rates (like LIBOR and EURIBOR) are standard benchmarks for pricing of bonds, loans and other financial products. Market manipulation of this key benchmark—as reportedly happened to LIBOR recently—though undermined the faith in money market. A sound money market would have to ensure conditions where banks can conduct business safely.

Money market transactions could be both secured and unsecured, i.e., without collaterals. What does one expect from the secured and unsecured markets? The unsecured market should primarily promote market discipline. Loans being uncollateralised in this market, lenders are directly exposed to the risk of non-repayment. This works as an incentive for them to address information asymmetry by collecting information about borrowers. It is the constant peer monitoring that promotes market discipline. In the secured segment of the money market, the lender may address credit risk concerns by asking for sound collaterals and also applying some haircuts, but the peer monitoring could potentially then be less emphasised. Conditions of market stress can lead to collateral scarcity and falling value of collaterals could stifle even the secured money market. Illiquidity spiral from the financial markets, i.e., when financial instruments held as assets turn illiquid, may lead to a situation where central banks would be required to dilute the collateral standards for liquidity injection, and even exchange good quality securities against securities facing illiquidity risks. This becomes necessary to unfreeze the markets in general. After the global crisis, asset quality, particularly liquidity, has received greater policy focus.

Money market rates also reflect market expectations of how the policy rate could evolve in the near term. As per standard expectations hypothesis, money market rates for different time duration should equal expected future short-term rates, plus term premium and risk premium. Bernanke (2004) had examined how expectations of the likely future course of the federal funds rate respond to the Fed's policy actions and statements and noted that "...Our findings support the view that FOMC statements have proven a powerful tool for affecting market expectations about the future course of the federal funds rate."

Empirical research suggests that if the shortest end of the money market, which is influenced the most by policy rate, is stable, or less volatile, then it may help in keeping term premium lower, compared to a period when volatile short rates get transmitted to the entire money market and simultaneously the term premium rises.

With the sophistication of financial markets rendering the money, output and price relationship unstable, by the early 1980s, major central banks began to emphasise on the price channel, i.e., policy interest rate for monetary policy transmission. As a result, the role of money market became all the more important for signalling and transmission of monetary policy. Thus, the development of money markets across countries in terms of instruments and participants with varying risk profiles has necessitated changes in the operating procedures of monetary policy.

In the case of India, the ultimate goals of monetary policy, i.e., price stability and growth, have remained unchanged over the years. In the recent years, financial stability has been considered as an additional objective of monetary policy. However, operational and intermediate objectives of monetary policy have undergone periodic changes in response to changes in the economic and financial environment. The development of the money market over the years and relative stability in the call money market enabled the Reserve Bank to move away from quantity-based instruments to price-based instruments under its multiple indicators approach adopted since 1998. Accordingly, the overnight call rate, which was used implicitly as operating target since the institution of liquidity adjustment facility (LAF) in 2000, became explicit after the adoption of a new operating procedure in May 2011.

Money Market in India

Financial reforms in India began in the early 1990s. However, various segments of domestic financial markets, *viz.*, money market, debt market and forex market underwent significant shifts mainly from the 1990s. Earlier, the Indian money market was characterised by paucity of instruments, lack of depth and distortions in the market micro-structure. It mainly consisted of uncollateralised call market, treasury bills, commercial bills and participation certificates.

Following the recommendations of the Chakravarty Committee (1985), the Reserve Bank adopted a monetary targeting framework. At the same time, efforts were made to develop the money market following the recommendations of Vaghul Committee (1987). In this regard, important developments were: (i) setting up of the Discount and Finance House of India (DFHI) in 1988 to impart liquidity to money market instruments and help the development of secondary markets in such instruments; (ii) introduction of instruments such as certificate of deposits (CDs) in 1989 and commercial papers in 1990 and inter-bank participation certificates with and without risk in 1988 to increase the range of instruments; and (iii) freeing of call money rates by May 1989 to enable price discovery. However, the functioning of the market continued to be hindered by a number of structural rigidities such as skewed distribution of liquidity and the prevalence of administered deposit and lending rates of banks.

Recognising these rigidities, the pace of reforms in money market was accelerated. Following the recommendations of an Internal Working Group (1997) and the Narasimham Committee (1998), a comprehensive set of measures was undertaken by the Reserve Bank to develop the money market. These included: (i) withdrawal of interest rate ceilings in the money market; (ii) introduction of auctions in treasury bills; (iii) gradual move away from the cash credit system to a loan-based system. Maturities of other existing instruments such as CP and CDs were also gradually shortened to encourage wider participation. Most importantly, the ad hoc treasury bills were abolished in 1997 thereby putting a stop to automatic monetisation of fiscal deficit. This enhanced the instrument independence of the Reserve Bank (Table 16.1).

More importantly, efforts were made to transform the call money market into primarily an inter-bank market, while encouraging other market participants to migrate towards collateralised segments of the market, thereby increasing overall market stability and diversification. In order to facilitate the phasing out of corporate and the non-banks from the call money market, new instruments such as market repos and collateralised borrowing and lending obligations (CBLO) were introduced to provide them avenues for managing their short-term liquidity. Non-bank entities completely exited the call money market by August 2005. In order to minimise the default risk and ensure balanced development of various market segments, the Reserve Bank instituted prudential limits on exposure of banks and primary dealers (PDs) to the call/notice money market. In April 2005, these limits were linked to capital funds (sum of Tier I and Tier II capital) for scheduled commercial banks.

Table 16.1

Major Developments in Money Market since the 1990s

1. Abolition of ad hoc treasury bills in April 1997
2. Full-fledged LAF in June 2000.
3. CBLO for corporate and non-bank participants introduced in 2003
4. Minimum maturity of CPs shortened by October 2004
5. Prudential limits on exposure of banks and PDs to call/notice market in April 2005
6. Maturity of CDs gradually shortened by April 2005
7. Transformation of call money market into a pure inter-bank market by August 2005
8. Widening of collateral base by making state government securities (SDLs) eligible for LAF operations since April 2007
9. Operationalisation of a screen-based negotiated system (NDS-CALL) for all dealings in the call/notice and the term money markets in September 2006. The reporting of all such transactions made compulsory through NDS-CALL in November 2012.
10. Repo in corporate bonds allowed in March 2010.
11. Operationalisation of a reporting platform for secondary market transactions in CPs and CDs in July 2010.

In order to improve transparency and efficiency in the money market, reporting of all call/notice money market transactions through negotiated dealing system (NDS) within 15 minutes of conclusion of the transaction was made mandatory. Furthermore, a screen-based negotiated quote-driven system for all dealings in the call/notice and the term money markets (NDS-CALL), developed by the Clearing Corporation of India Limited (CCIL), was operationalised in September 2006 to ensure better price discovery.

Beginning in June 2000, the Reserve Bank introduced a full-fledged liquidity adjustment facility (LAF) and it was operated through overnight fixed rate repo and reverse repo from November 2004. This helped to develop interest rate as an important instrument of monetary transmission. It also provided greater flexibility to the Reserve Bank in determining both the quantum of liquidity as well as the rates by responding to the needs of the system on a daily basis (Figure 16.1).

Figure 16.1

Liquidity Adjustment Facility and Call Rate

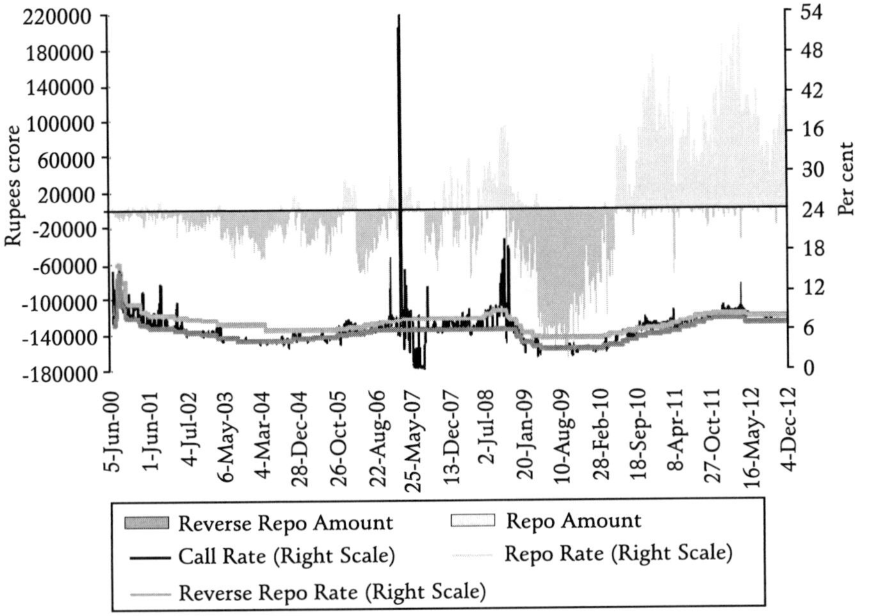

In the development of various constituents of the money market, the most significant aspect was the growth of the collateralised market *vis-à-vis* the uncollateralised market. Over the last decade, while the daily turnover in the call money market either stagnated or declined, that of the collateralised segment, market repo plus CBLO, increased manifold (Figure 16.2). Since 2007-08, both the CP and CD volumes have also increased very significantly (Figure 16.3). Furthermore, issuance of 91-treasury bills has also increased sharply (Figure 16.4). The overall money market now is much larger relative to GDP than a decade ago.

Figure 16.2

Average Daily Turnover in the Money Market has Moved Towards Collateralised Segment

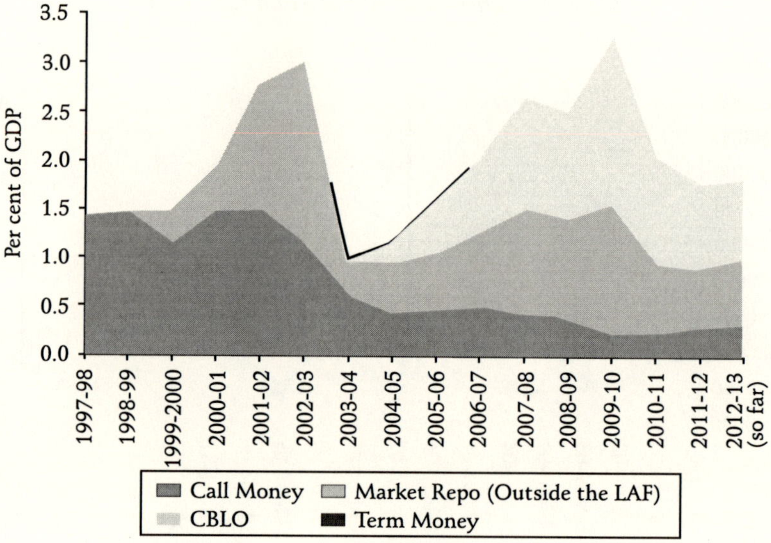

Figure 16.3

Outstanding CPs and CDs

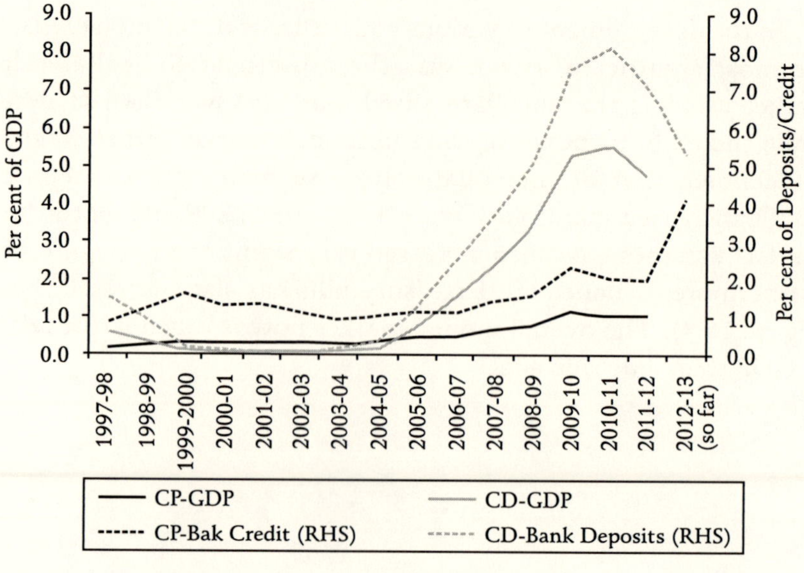

Figure 16.4

Issuance of 91-day Treasury Bills has Increased Sharply

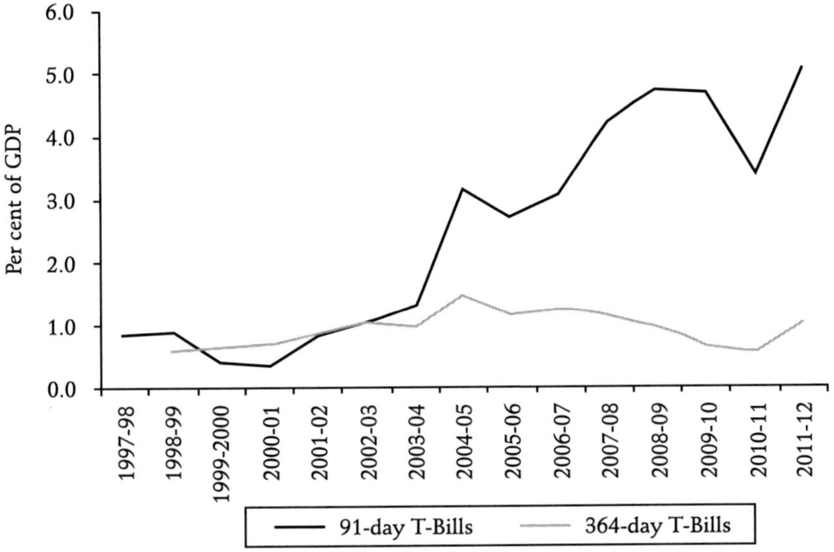

Alongside, the rates of return on various instruments in the money market have shown greater co-movement, especially since the introduction of LAF (Table 16.2 and Figure 16.5).

Table 16.2

Interest Rates in the Money Market

(Percent per annum: Annual Averages)

	Repo Rate	*Call Rate*	*CBLO Rate*	*Market Repo Rate*	*91 day T-Bills*	*364-day T-Bills*	*CP Rate*	*CD Rate*
1	*2*	*3*	*4*	*5*	*8*	*9*	*6*	*7*
2000-01	11.2	9.1	-	-	9.0	9.8	10.8	9.6
2001-02	8.5	7.2	-	-	7.0	7.3	9.2	8.0
2002-03	7.7	5.9	-	-	5.8	5.9	7.7	6.6
2003-04	7.0	4.6	-	-	4.6	4.7	6.1	5.3
2004-05	6.0	4.7	-	-	4.9	5.2	5.8	5.0
2005-06	6.2	5.6	5.3	5.4	5.7	6.0	6.7	6.1
2006-07	7.0	7.2	6.2	6.3	6.6	7.0	8.5	7.9
2007-08	7.8	6.1	5.2	5.5	7.1	7.5	9.3	9.1
2008-09	7.4	7.1	6.1	6.5	7.1	7.2	10.7	9.2
2009-10	4.8	3.2	2.7	2.8	3.6	4.4	5.3	5.4
2010-11	5.9	5.7	5.4	5.5	6.2	6.6	8.7	7.7
2011-12	8.0	8.1	7.8	7.9	8.4	8.4	10.1	9.6
2013-14 (so far)	8.0	8.1	7.9	8.0	8.2	8.1	9.3	9.0

Figure 16.5

Money Market Rates Show Greater Co-movement

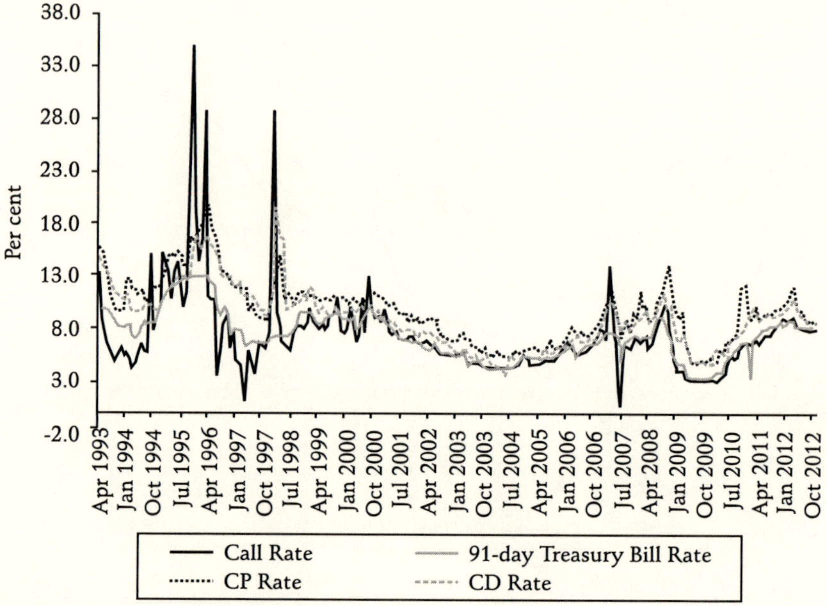

Monetary Operating Procedure

The development of money market as well as its growing interlinkages with other segments of financial markets enabled the Reserve Bank to alter the operating procedures of monetary policy consistent with the objectives of the monetary policy. Based on the recommendations of Chakravarty Committee (1985), a monetary targeting framework with feedback was introduced during the mid-1980s, under which reserve money was used as operating target and broad money (M3) as an intermediate target. By the mid-1990s, this framework was rendered increasingly inadequate due to several developments. Structural reforms and financial liberalisation led to a paradigm shift in the financing of government and commercial sectors with increasingly market-determined interest rates and exchange rate. Development in the various segments of the financial market led to deepening of the financial sector. This provided the Reserve Bank to effectively transmit policy signals through indirect instruments such as interest rates. On the other hand, increase in liquidity emanating from capital inflows raised the ratio of net foreign assets to reserve money and rendered the control of monetary aggregates more difficult. With financial innovations, the stability in the demand function for money also came under question.

Recognising these challenges and the growing complexities of monetary management, the Reserve Bank switched to a multiple indicators approach in 1998-99. Under this approach, a host of macroeconomic indicators including interest rates in different segments of financial markets, along with other indicators on currency, lending by banks and financial institutions, fiscal position, trade, capital flows, inflation rate, exchange rate, refinancing and transactions in foreign exchange available on high frequency basis are juxtaposed with output data for drawing implications for monetary policy formulation. However, the approach itself continued to evolve and was further augmented by forward-looking indicators drawn from Reserve Bank's various surveys and a panel of parsimonious time series models (Mohanty, 2011).

Along with the multiple indicators approach, operating procedure also underwent a change following the recommendation of Narasimham Committee II (1998). The RBI introduced the interim liquidity adjustment facility (ILAF) in April 1999, under which liquidity injection was done at the Bank Rate and liquidity absorption was through fixed reverse repo rate. The ILAF gradually transited into a full-fledged liquidity adjustment facility (LAF) with periodic modifications based on experience and development of financial markets and the payment system. The LAF was operated through overnight fixed rate repo and reverse repo from November 2004, which provided an informal corridor for the call money rate.

Though the LAF helped to develop interest rate as an instrument of monetary transmission, two major weaknesses came to the fore. First was the lack of a single policy rate, as the operating policy rate alternated between repo during deficit liquidity situation and reverse repo rate during surplus liquidity condition. Second was the lack of a firm corridor, as the effective overnight interest rates dipped (rose) below (above) the reverse repo (repo) rate in extreme surplus (deficit) conditions. Recognising these shortcomings, a new operating procedure was put in place in May 2011.

Let me elaborate on the key features of the new operating procedure. First, the weighted average overnight call money rate was explicitly recognised as the operating target of monetary policy.[1] Second, the repo rate was made the only one independently varying policy rate. Third, a new Marginal Standing Facility (MSF) was instituted under which scheduled commercial banks (SCBs) could borrow overnight at 100 basis points above the repo rate up to one per cent of their respective net demand and time liabilities (NDTL). This limit was subsequently raised to two per cent of NDTL and in addition, SCBs were allowed to borrow funds under MSF on overnight basis against their excess SLR holdings as well. Moreover, the Bank Rate being the discount rate was aligned to the MSF rate. Fourth, the revised corridor was defined with a fixed width of 200 basis points. The repo rate was placed in the middle of the corridor, with the reverse repo rate at 100 basis points below it and the MSF rate as well as the Bank Rate at 100 basis points above it (Figure 16.6). Thus, under the new operating procedure, all the three other rates announced by the Reserve Bank, i.e., reverse repo rate, MSF rate and the Bank Rate, are linked to the single policy repo rate.

The new operating procedure was expected to improve the implementation and transmission of monetary policy for the following reasons. First, explicit announcement of an operating target makes market participants clear about the desired policy impact. Second, a single policy rate removes the confusion arising out of policy rate alternating between the repo and the reverse repo rates, and makes signalling of monetary policy stance more accurate. Third, MSF provides a safety valve against unanticipated liquidity shocks. Fourth, a fixed interest rate corridor set by MSF

1. Even though the share of call money market in the overnight money market is lower than that of collateralised segment, the weighted overnight call rate is used as operating target. This is partly on account of high correlation between the overnight call money rate and the collaterallised money market rate at 0.9. The issue was examined in detail by the Working Group on Operating Procedure of Monetary Policy which observed that the transmission of policy rate to the overnight call money rate is stronger than the overnight money market rate. In addition, the call money market is a pure inter-bank market and, hence, better reflects the net liquidity situation.

Figure 16.6

Revised LAF Framework

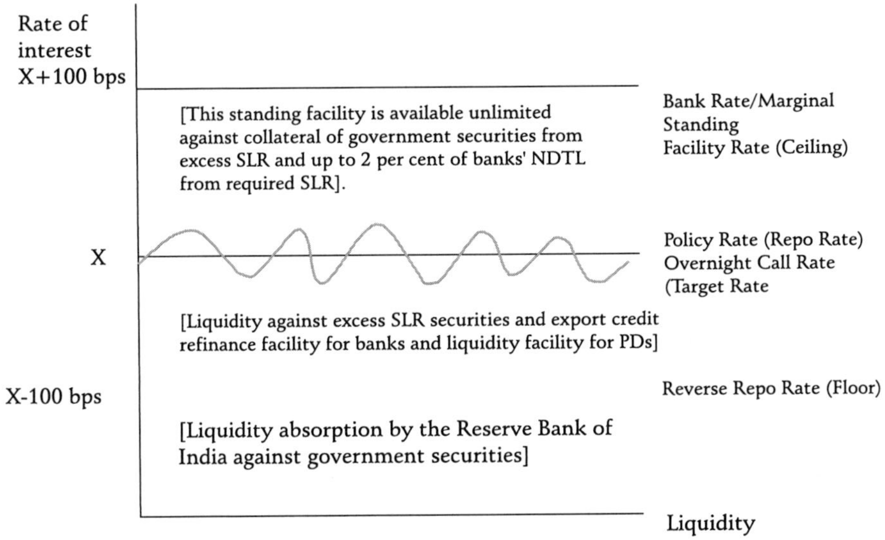

rate and reverse repo rate, reduces uncertainty and communication difficulties and helps keep the overnight average call money rate close to the repo rate.

Let me now turn to a brief evaluation of the experience with the new operating procedure. In the implementation of the new procedure, the Reserve Bank prefers to keep the systemic liquidity in deficit mode as monetary transmission is found to be more effective in this situation (RBI, 2011). The Reserve Bank also announced an indicative liquidity comfort zone of (+)/(-) 1.0 per cent of net demand and time liabilities (NDTL) of banks.

Since May 2011, the liquidity conditions can be broadly divided into three distinct phases. After generally remaining within the Reserve Bank's comfort zone during the first phase during May-October 2011, the liquidity deficit crossed the one per cent of NDTL level during November 2011 to June 2012. This large liquidity deficit was mainly caused by forex intervention and increased divergence between credit and deposit growth. The deficit conditions were further aggravated by frictional factors like the build-up of government cash balances with the Reserve Bank that persisted longer than anticipated and the increase in currency in circulation. Accordingly, the Reserve Bank had to actively manage liquidity through injection of liquidity by way of open market operations (OMOs) and cut in cash reserve ratio (CRR) of banks. This was supported by decline in currency in circulation and a reduction in government cash balances with the Reserve Bank. As a result, there was a significant easing of liquidity conditions since July 2012 with the extent of the deficit broadly returning to the Reserve Bank's comfort level of one per cent of NDTL (Figure 16.7).

Figure 16.7

Liquidity Conditions Ease following a Period of Tightness

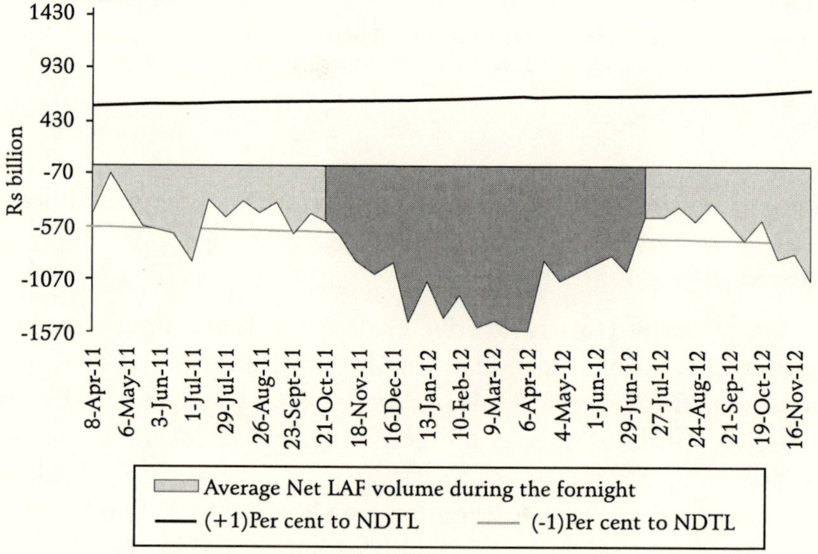

Since its implementation, the systemic liquidity has been in deficit mode, which has helped in better transmission of policy rate to various segments of money markets. First, the overnight interest rate has been more stable since its implementation (Figure 16.8).

Figure 16.8

Stability of Call Rate Improves under New Procedure

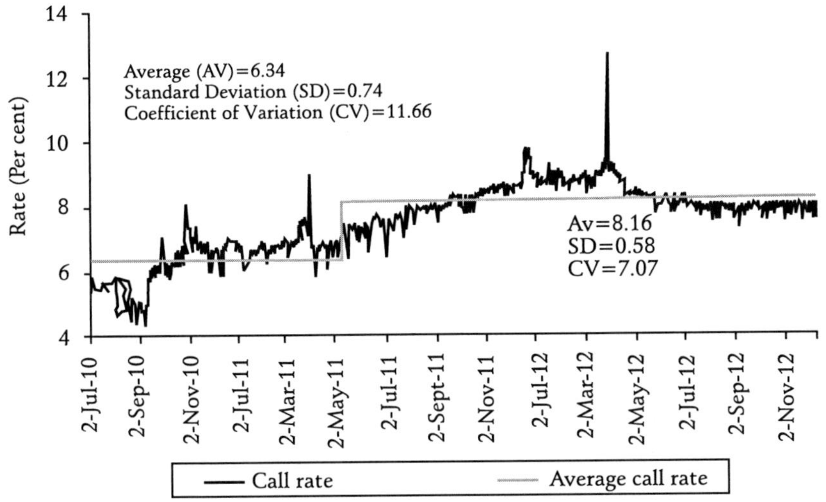

Second, the repo rate and weighted call rate are far more closely aligned under the new operating procedure than earlier; implying improved transmission of monetary policy in terms of movement in call money market interest rate (Figure 16.9).

Figure 16.9

Monetary Transmission Improves under Liquidity Deficit

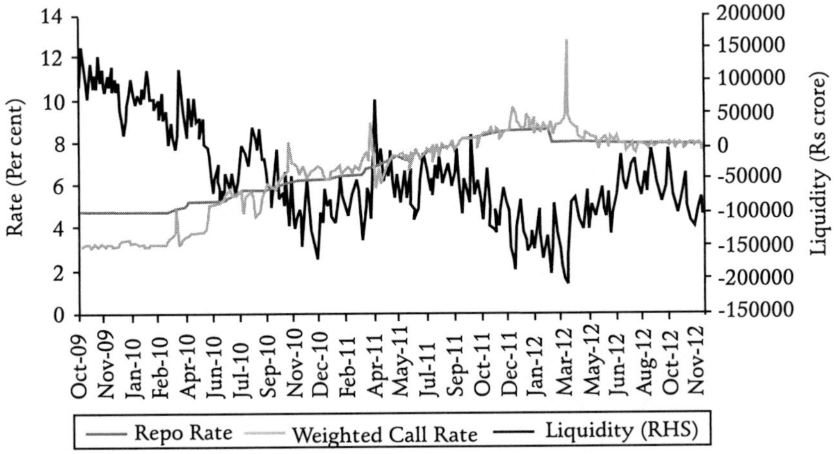

Third, the call money rate in turn is observed to be better aligned with other money market interest rates after the implementation of new operating procedure than before (Figure 16.10).

Figure 16.10

Call Rates Move in Tandem with other Money Market Rates

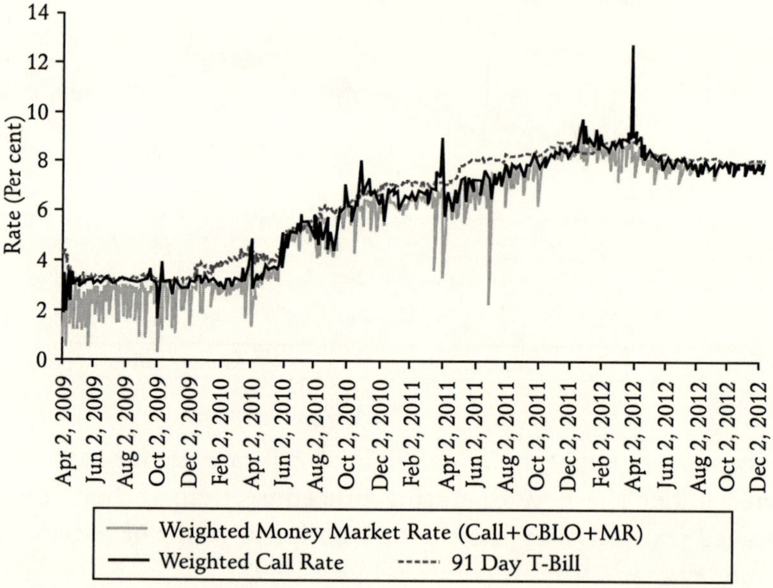

Conclusion

Let me conclude. Our experience shows that the development of money market and refinements in operating procedures of monetary policy have moved in tandem. Financial sector reforms along with Reserve Bank's emphasis on development of various segments of financial market enabled shifts in operating procedures based on direct quantity-based instruments to indirect interest rate-based instruments. The Reserve Bank has been able to better transmit monetary policy signals in the money market through a single policy repo rate. Evidence so far suggests a significant improvement in monetary policy transmission under the new operating framework. In order to reinforce this process, I make three suggestions.

First, there has been a swift transmission of policy rate at the short-end of money market, partly due to the prevalence of market liquidity in deficit mode. However, ensuring market liquidity in a deficit mode of desired level on a sustained basis is contingent on Reserve Bank's ability to effectively conduct OMOs and the market appetite for such operations. Hence, there is a need to develop the market micro-structure and further enhance secondary market transactions in government securities to facilitate smooth conduct of OMOs.

Second, the LAF is not the appropriate instrument for managing the liquidity of more enduring nature. As the system is expected to be in deficit, there is a need to develop term repo to minimise daily requirement of liquidity.

Third, notwithstanding significant advances in developing the market, the term structure in the money market is incomplete. It is, therefore, desirable to extend the yield curve beyond the overnight rate by developing a term-money market.

References

Bernanke, Ben S. (2004). *Central Bank Talk and Monetary Policy*. At the Japan Society Corporate Luncheon. New York. October 7.

Mohanty, Deepak (2010). "Monetary Policy Framework in India: Experience with Multiple-Indicators Approach", *RBI Bulletin*, March 2010.

Reserve Bank of India (2011). *Report of the Working Group on Operating Procedure of Monetary Policy* (Chairman: Deepak Mohanty), March.

Speech at the Seminar on Issues in Financial Markets, Mumbai, 15th December 2012. RBI Bulletin January 2013.

17

HARUN R. KHAN

Musings on Foreign Exchange Dealers Association of India (FEDAI), Forex Market and Indian Rupee

Evolution of FEDAI in the Changing Environment of Indian Forex Market

In the early post-Independence years, under the Foreign Exchange Regulation Act (FERA), 1947, a few foreign banks, designated as 'exchange banks' were permitted to transact foreign exchange business. The terms and conditions for undertaking such business were being laid down by the then Exchange Banks' Association. With the increase in India's foreign trade, several scheduled commercial banks (SCBs) were authorised by the Reserve Bank to deal in foreign exchange business. This led to the formation of FEDAI on August 16, 1958 with a mandate to lay down the terms and conditions which were mandatory in nature for the authorised dealers (ADs). With developments in the Indian foreign exchange market and growth in external trade, the role and responsibility of FEDAI underwent changes. I am happy to note that FEDAI, through its members, continues to play a pivotal role in dissemination of the foreign exchange related banking expertise across the country which has led to significant improvement in the customer service.

Let me now highlight two important milestones in the evolution of Indian forex market. In the year 1994, an Expert Group on Foreign Exchange Market in India was set up under the Chairmanship of O.P. Sodhani, the then Executive Director, Reserve

The author acknowledges the valuable contributions of G. Padmanabhan, G. Mahalingam, Chinmoy Kumar, Rakesh Tripathy, S.C. Rath and Surajit Bose.

Bank of India (popularly known as the Sodhani Committee). The committee had made wide ranging recommendations ranging from methodology for correct computation of open exchange position to introduction of rupee based options, and these suggestions had laid the foundation for a modern foreign exchange market in India. FEDAI played an important role in supporting the Reserve Bank in implementing these pioneering measures and suggestions aimed at major reforms in the market. The second milestone was the replacement of restrictive FERA with the Foreign Exchange Management Act (FEMA) in the year 2000. This provided further fillip to the development of the foreign exchange market which can be gauged from the rise in the average daily forex market turnover from approximately US$ 6 billion in 2000 to nearly US$ 60 billion in 2010-11. This figure excludes the daily turnover in the exchange traded currency futures market which would add up to another US$ 5 to 7 billion a day. The depth of the foreign exchange market can also be gauged from the fact that the bid offer spread in USD INR pair is now around half a *paisa*. The average daily foreign exchange turnover has, however, showed a dip since the second half of December 2011. One plausible reason for the decline could be the administrative measures taken by the Reserve Bank of India (RBI) to moderate the excessive volatile conditions prevalent in the foreign exchange market, but I will touch upon this issue a bit later in my address.

Future Role and Responsibilities of FEDAI

Having briefly touched upon the significant role played by the FEDAI so far, let me now turn to the possible future role and responsibilities of the FEDAI with special focus on should FEDAI become a full-fledged SRO (self regulatory organisation).

Many countries rely on self-regulation because expansive resources are required to regulate the financial markets effectively, especially in large and complex markets. With the existence of an effective SRO, often referred to as frontline regulator, the statutory regulator (the regulator) relies on the SRO to carry out supervision of operations and activities of the market participants. The supporters of the idea of self-regulation claim that it offers significant advantage over direct government/statutory regulation. This can be attributed to the fact that SROs have thorough domain knowledge of their respective area and regulatory framework within which they operate. Therefore, they are considerably more flexible, context-driven and are able to respond faster to the changes in market conditions. This also allows the regulator to spare its resources more on identifying and responding to major systemic risks and to other priorities outside the ambit of self-regulation. It is believed that self-regulation system works effectively because of the business incentive to operate in a fair, financially sound and competitive marketplace. The critics, on the other hand, argue that private profit seeking enterprises cannot be trusted to regulate their own activities as such self-regulation tends to create an illusion of regulation. In addition to the conflict of interest, critics of self-regulation point to certain other inefficiencies, such as, widespread collective action problems, lack of effective enforcement capabilities, inability to gain or maintain legitimacy and the failure of accountability.

Having weighed the views of the supporters and critics of the SRO system and in view of the increasing complexities of financial markets and activities, it is important to realise and emphasise that industry self-regulation cannot fully replace government regulation and supervision of the financial services sector. At the same time, it may not be out of place to say that cooperation amongst the statutory regulators and SROs in an increasingly complex financial environment is no longer an option but a necessity. Coordination and communication should be structured to address potential problems before they occur. One of the important regulatory lessons learnt from the recent global financial crisis is the need for a concerted response. The government or the regulator alone cannot provide an effective response. Active engagement of market participants, in particular through industry organisations, such as, SROs and other industry bodies with some self-regulatory capacity, is essential to craft practical regulatory responses and to act effectively on policy changes.

In this era of fast paced liberalisations and developments, FEDAI should gradually assume the role of a full-fledged SRO. Typically, a generic and effective SRO in its template of elements cover, inter alia, internal rulemaking process, authorisation and access to market-place, including fitness/qualification standards for market intermediaries, surveillance of market activities, administration of dispute resolution, sharing information and cooperating with other SROs and the regulators, etc. SROs enable members to exercise self-discipline, make regulations more responsive to market demand and also promote innovation and development in a market based approach. This is critical for the development of the financial markets in order to make them competitive, regionally and globally, and improve standards of conduct by self-regulation.

Developmental Role of FEDAI

When the Reserve Bank issues instructions, it is expected that the instructions are understood, interpreted and implemented in a uniform and customer friendly manner by all ADs without building up system level stresses. In the absence of unambiguous clarity of instructions to the base level official, the objectives of various measures initiated by the Reserve Bank may not yield the desired results. With the advent of FEMA which aims at facilitating external trade and payments besides promoting orderly development and maintenance of forex market in India, the economy has been witnessing rapid liberalisations. In such a scenario, FEDAI needs to monitor the level of customer service and consumer protection provided by its members and try to fill the gaps arising out of inadequate knowledge or operational bottlenecks. The Reserve Bank has been emphasising the need for designing some basic training module covering the rules and regulations, and also the operational guidelines for the frontline staff at the branch and corporate office levels. Such a module will help them in improving the foreign exchange related customer service, reduce incidents of complaints and bring down the level of correspondence seeking clarifications both within the bank and from the Reserve Bank. Member banks of FEDAI and the Reserve Bank have since formed a Group which is working to develop an e-learning module to address these concerns. Another related area where FEDAI is expected to play an important role is in framing of a 'Citizens' Charter' in the area of foreign exchange business.

Role of Market Participants: Freedom with Responsibility

The existing guidelines on OTC foreign exchange derivatives were revised in December 2010 in the context of developments in the international and as well as the domestic markets. The revised guidelines put more emphasis on the suitability and appropriateness aspects of products being offered. Market-makers have been advised to undertake derivative transactions with a sense of responsibility and cautioned to avoid, among other things, misselling. These products are to be offered to corporates who understand the nature of the risks inherent and have a well laid down risk management policy. Such policy must clearly lay down, inter-alia, guidelines on risk identification, management and control, prudent accounting and disclosure norms, and must be capable of ascertaining the mark to market positions on an ongoing basis. In fact, the Reserve Bank has made it mandatory for the market participants to offer a tool or a calculator which would enable the corporate to mark-to-market these products on a continuous basis. Though the objective of the policy is prudential in nature as it protects the market participant against the credit, reputation and legal risks, it is important to realise that the policy protects the interest of the corporates as well.

Banks need to closely monitor the unhedged foreign currency exposures of corporates as they had hedged approximately only 60 per cent and 38 per cent of their trade and non-trade related exposures respectively till December 2011. Excessive risk taking by corporates could lead to severe distress to them and large credit loss to the banks in event of sharp adverse movements in currencies. In 2008, it was conveyed to the banks that they should have a Board approved policy covering unhedged foreign exchange exposure of all the clients including small and medium enterprises (SMEs). Banks while extending fund and non-fund based credit facilities to corporate, should rigorously evaluate the risks arising out of unhedged foreign currency exposure of the corporates and price them in the credit risk premium as we have recently reiterated in our circular following the announcements made in the Second Quarter Review of the Monetary Policy 2011-12.

During the recent episode of excessive volatility leading to sudden and sharp depreciation of Indian rupee against US dollar, it was noticed that the flexibility given to banks for fixing their intra-day limits, which were in many cases, significantly higher than their net overnight open positions limits, were often being used for building up speculative positions and taking a directional bet on rupee. The facilities given to corporates by way of cancellation and re-booking of their forward contracts and booking of forward contracts under past performance criterion were also not being used in the right spirit. As you would appreciate such speculative forces tend to be self-reinforcing and often result in a situation where exporters keep on deferring their receipts and importers rush in to buy forwards, thus aggravating the situation in hand. The administrative measures undertaken by Reserve Bank in the month of December 2011 were aimed at curbing these speculative behaviour of such entities. The measures did achieve the intended policy objectives and also led to an immediate fall in the volumes of the markets. The actual hedging requirements of the real sector, however, were not left unattended as we subsequently relaxed some of the measures to accommodate customer needs. Within the overarching prerequisite of facilitating genuine hedging needs of the customers, Reserve Bank would consider relaxations, in particular those relating to intra-day position limits, in a calibrated manner at appropriate time.

Reserve Bank will continue with its calibrated and gradual approach towards liberalisation of the foreign exchange market in India but at the same time we will expect greater degree of responsibility and accountability from all the participants. In the context of our measured approach to market liberalisation, there has been a lot of debate on scope of wider usage of Indian rupee both in the region/abroad, or in other words, internationalisation of Indian rupee. I will now briefly touch upon the issue in the third and last part of my paper.

Challenges for Internationalisation of Indian Rupee

In view of the recent crisis in the financial market which resulted in a slowdown in the world economy, some views have emerged from various quarters on whether the Indian rupee could play a larger role as an international currency. This issue assumed a topical and, if I may add, patriotic significance when the symbol for Indian rupee was unveiled amidst huge media publicity. Proposals for use of local currencies of the EMEs under bilateral and multilateral arrangements including the initiatives taken by China for Yuan and the recent suggestions emanating from BRICS nations have provided renewed focus to this. It is a known fact that wide acceptance by participants in trade and financial markets makes a currency a popular option for trade settlement and for maintenance of reserves. The characteristics which a currency needs to possess before it could become popular as a transactions currency would include free convertibility, ability to invest, borrow, issue marketable instruments, significant volumes of international trade in different regions, stability of the exchange rate, the currency being a favoured choice for invoicing which would, inter-alia depend on the mutual negotiating strength of trading partners, availability of deep foreign exchange markets, cost-effective hedging facilities including forward cover, availability of efficient banking arrangement/market infrastructure, etc.

Based on the analysis of Prof Peter Kenen of Princeton University, we can lay down the following seven broad prerequisites for the process of internationalisation of a currency.

i. Domestic entities are permitted to invoice some of their exports in the country's currency, and similarly foreign entities are also allowed to invoice their exports in that country's currency.

ii. There should be no restrictions on any entity, domestic or foreign, to buy/sell its country's currency in the spot and forward markets. In other words, there should be freedom of foreign exchange trading by domestic and foreign entities and no limits be imposed on holding the domestic currency and derivative instruments denominated in it.

iii. Foreign entities/financial institutions/official institutions, and individuals, are permitted to hold the country's currency and financial instruments denominated in it as a part of prudent investment strategy/the official reserves.

iv. Foreign entities, including official institutions, are able to issue marketable instruments in the country's currency. These may include both equity and debt instruments, not only in the country's domestic markets but also in foreign markets, including, the home country markets of the foreign entities.

v. The issuing country's own financial institutions and other entities are able to issue in foreign markets instruments denominated in that country's currency.

vi. International and regional financial institutions are able to issue debt instruments in a country's market and use its currency in their financial operations.

vii. The currency may be included in the 'currency baskets' of other countries, in consideration of their own exchange rate policies.

Measured against the above prerequisites for internationalisation of currency, Indian rupee is certainly far away from any meaningful internationalisation. Of course, a few measures taken in the recent years deserve some attention. Since the introduction of FEMA, the Indian rupee invoicing is a permitted form of invoicing under the current trade and FEMA regulations. In order to facilitate greater use of Indian rupee in trade transactions, the RBI has now allowed non-resident importers and exporters to hedge their currency risk in respect of exports from and imports to India, invoiced in Indian rupees. In this regard, forward foreign exchange contracts with Indian rupee as one of the currencies and foreign currency—Indian rupee options are the available products for the purpose of hedging the risks. Non-resident exporter/importer can avail of the facility either directly from ADs in India or through their banker overseas. The AD, on the basis of the documentary evidence and undertakings provided by the non-resident, has to be satisfied of the bona fides of the customer as well as of the transaction. As with all other hedging facilities available to non-residents, these contracts once cancelled cannot be rebooked.

Eligible borrowers have been permitted to avail of ECBs designated in Indian rupee from their foreign equity holders under the automatic/approval route. In order to hedge the currency risk arising out of such ECBs, forward foreign exchange contracts with Indian rupee as one of the currencies, foreign currency-Indian rupee options and foreign currency-Indian rupee swaps have been permitted.

The debate on internationalisation of a currency often goes hand-in-hand with that on capital account convertibility. It is a known fact that capital controls can coexist with an international currency. Economic history is rich with examples of countries, especially advanced countries with an international currency, imposing a variety of capital controls to stem the depreciation/appreciation of their currencies and/or to regulate short-term capital flows. While internationalisation of a currency is not a pre-requisite for capital account convertibility, its large scale externalisation has the potential to impose significant costs, especially over the medium to long-term as the real and financial sectors of a country grow and develop strong linkages with the world economy.

The pace and the process of internationalisation of a currency is of course dependent on the acceptable degree of capital account convertibility. This, in turn, involves the extent to which non-residents are allowed to participate in the domestic forward foreign exchange markets to obtain cover and invest in the domestic markets for any Indian rupee balances that they may accumulate. At the same time, the benefits and costs of the Indian rupee becoming an international currency needs to be reckoned. The benefits broadly include reduction of exchange risk for domestic exporters/importers as risks would instead have to be taken by the overseas party and extensive use of Indian rupee by non-residents would mean increased seigniorage. Domestic entities can also access international financial markets without exchange rate risk and can avail of larger amounts of investment at a lesser cost than in the domestic market. Expanded investor base and reduction in the cost of capital may help both the financial sector intermediation and the real sector. Governments, particularly those with high fiscal deficit, may benefit by foreign participation in its debt market and get the benefit of higher flows to finance the current account deficits. The costs would include difficulty in managing the implications for monetary policy and exchange rate management besides the administrative costs. Under the 'Impossible Trinity' framework higher internationalisation would severely limit either the country's flexibility to influence the monetary condition, such as, interest rate, money supply, or manage exchange rate under stress situations. Coming to the issue of benefit to domestic entities/government by way of easy access to external resources, the huge risk in terms of increased vulnerabilities arising out of sudden stops, panic outflows unrelated to fundamentals of the economy, speculative bets by large pools of international funds, loss of confidence in the context of size of reserves in relation to external debt, particularly short term debt, have to be reckoned with. These vulnerabilities have now been accentuated in the context of the recent global financial crisis.

It is also imperative to understand that unlike countries with current account surpluses, India generally has a sizeable quantum of current account deficit. The exchange rate of Indian rupee remains susceptible to ebb and flow of external capital, especially outflows during periods of stress. Given the growing level of our twin deficits of fiscal and current account, hasty internationalisation could only add to our external sector vulnerabilities. As has been witnessed in the past, sudden reversal of capital flow imparts significant volatility to the exchange rate which at times needs to be curbed by the Reserve Bank. In the event of internationalisation of the Indian rupee, the exchange rate would be largely determined by the sentiments of the market forces and the present policy measures to curb such volatilities may not prove to be as effective as they are today.

Concluding Thoughts

Economy and financial markets of India are in the midst of rapid transformation due to its increasing linkages with the rest of the world. In keeping with the changing needs, RBI has been striving for more simplification, liberalisation and rationalisation of the policies and the processes in the area of foreign exchange administration without jeopardising the financial stability. Market-players, therefore, now have more freedom to undertake transactions as compared to the earlier days. These flexibilities, however, should be utilised in a responsible manner that is transparent, fair and beneficial to the customers and the economy as a whole and not misutilised for short term gains of a few market-players with adverse consequential effects on our financial sector. Therefore, the role of FEDAI assumes greater significance in the present context. There is, thus, a need to have a closer look at the working and functions of FEDAI and strategise on how to transform it to a full-fledged and responsive SRO. This would be a win-win proposition for all the stakeholders including the banks, customers and the regulators like the RBI.

Keynote address delivered at the 7th Annual Conference of FEDAI at Zurich on April 5, 2012. RBI Bulletin May 2012.

18

HARUN R. KHAN

Issues and Challenges in Financial Inclusion

Policies, Partnerships, Processes and Products

Importance of Financial Inclusion

In majority of the developing countries, access to finance is now being perceived as a public good, which is as important and basic as access, say, to safe water or primary education. A question that arises is whether financial inclusion can be interpreted as a public good. A good is considered a public good if it meets the conditions of 'non-rivalness' in consumption and non-excludability. I am sure you would agree that financial inclusion meets the two criteria. One of the important effects of financial inclusion is that the entire national financial system benefits by greater inclusion, especially when promoted in the wider context of economic inclusion. The concept of financial inclusion has a special significance for a growing economy like India as bringing the large segment of the productive sectors of the economy under formal financial network could unleash their creative capacities besides augmenting domestic demand on a sustainable basis driven by income and consumption growth from such sectors. Financial inclusion efforts do have multiplier effect on the economy as a whole through higher savings pooled from the vast segment of the bottom of the pyramid (BoP) population by providing access to formal savings arrangement resulting in expansion in credit and investment by banks. Deeper engagements of the BoP/under-banked population in the economy through the formal financial system could lead to improvement of

The author acknowledges the contribution of Rekha Mishra, Sushma Vij, Pankaj Ekka and Surajit Bose of Reserve Bank of India.

their financial conditions and living standards, enabling them to create financial assets, generate income and build resilience to meet macroeconomic and livelihood shocks. Government also immensely benefits by way of efficient and leakage-proof transfer of vast amounts of welfare benefits to the targetted, disadvantaged groups of population.

Concerns relating to Anti-Money Laundering/Counter Terrorist Funding (AML/CFT) get addressed through financial inclusion efforts without compromising the basic Know Your Customer (KYC) requirements. From the perspective of the Reserve Bank of India, (RBI) greater participation by all the economic agents in the financial system makes monetary policy more effective and, thereby, enhancing the prospects of non-inflationary growth. It also reduces reliance on the informal sector which tends to dent the impact of monetary policy decisions.

Financial Inclusion: India's Position Compared with Other Countries

The extent of financial exclusion in India is found to be higher as compared with many developed and some of the major emerging economies. The wide extent of financial exclusion in India is visible in the form of high population per bank branch and low proportion of the population having access to basic financial services like savings accounts, credit facilities, credit and debit cards. Table 18.1 summarises India's performance in the area of financial inclusion as compared with other developing as well as developed countries.

Measuring Financial Inclusion

One of the measures of the level of financial inclusion is the Financial Inclusion Index. This index is based on three basic dimensions of an inclusive financial system–banking penetration, availability of the banking services and usage of the banking system (Sarma, 2008). Banking penetration is definitely the most critical parameter for measuring the depth of financial inclusion and is measured as a ratio of bank accounts to the total population. The second parameter, availability of banking services provides an

Table 18.1

Select Indicators of Financial Inclusion: Cross Country Analysis

Country	*Number of Branches*	*Number of ATMs*	*Bank Credit*	*Bank Deposits*
	(per 0.1 million adults)		*(as per cent of GDP)*	
India	10.91	5.44	43.62*	60.11*
Austria*	11.81	48.16	35.26	32.57
Brazil	13.76	120.62	29.04	47.51
France	43.11	110.07	56.03	39.15
Mexico	15.22	47.28	16.19	20.91
UK*	25.51	64.58	467.97	427.49
United States	35.74	173.75*	46.04	53.14
Korea	18.63	250.29*	84.17	74.51
Afghanistan	2.25	0.50	11.95	21.40
Philippines	7.69	14.88	27.57	53.02

Note: Data pertains to 2010. For rows/cells indicated as '*' data pertains to 2009.
As at end of 2010-11, the number of ATMs per 0.1 million stood at 6.3, bank credit and bank deposit as a percentage of GDP stood at 50.10 per cent and 66.10 per cent respectively.

Source: World Bank, *Financial Access Survey*.

indication to the number of bank outlets available per 1000 people to deliver financial services. The bank outlets may include the brick and mortar branches, ATMs, business correspondents, etc. The third parameter seeks to determine the usage of banking services going beyond mere opening of accounts. Therefore, this is evaluated on the basis of outstanding deposits and credits. Accordingly, the volume of outstanding deposit and credit as proportion to the net district domestic product is used for measuring this dimension. According to the value of the index, Indian states can be classified into three categories, i.e., states having high, low and medium extent of financial exclusion. According to the empirical results, Kerala, Maharashtra and Karnataka are some of the states having wider extent of financial inclusion as compared to other states of India. Tamil Nadu, Punjab, Andhra Pradesh, Himachal Pradesh, Sikkim and Haryana fall under the category of medium financial exclusion.

Figure 18.1

State-wise Index of Financial Inclusion

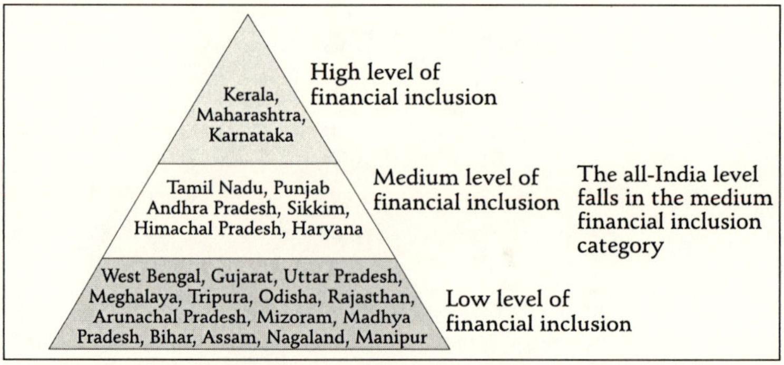

Source: Sadhan Kumar Chattopadhyay, "Financial Inclusion in India: A Case-study of West Bengal", *RBI Working Paper*.

The extent of financial inclusion is found to be significantly low in North-Eastern and Eastern States, i.e., Assam, Nagaland, Manipur, Odisha, Bihar, West Bengal, etc. Though the index and findings of the report in reference are based on empirical study, they are possibly not way off the ground realities.

Indian Approach to Financial Inclusion

Financial inclusion can be construed in two ways. One is countering the exclusion from the payment system, that is, not having an access to a bank account. The second is countering the exclusion from the formal financial services. The Indian approach in recent years has been to establish the basic right of every person to have access to a bank account. This approach is based on the fundamental principle of 5A's of ensuring adequacy and availability of financial services to all sections of the society through the formal financial system covering savings, credit, remittance, insurance, etc. and, at the same time, increasing awareness of such services and ensuring affordability and accessibility of the appropriate financial products through a combination of conventional and alternative delivery channels and technology enabled services and processes. Against this background, we can see large variance in the level of financial inclusion across the country. The Reserve Bank has therefore been pursuing a multi-pronged strategy for enhancing the outreach of financial services including the delivery channels across all sections. The entire spectrum of the financial system which comprises commercial banks, regional rural banks (RRBs), urban co-operative banks (UCBs), primary agricultural credit societies (PACS) and post offices is, therefore, geared for this purpose. Besides, self-help groups (SHGs) and micro finance institutions (MFIs) also meet the financial service requirements of the poorer segments. Furthermore, banks have been encouraged to use a combination of strategies which include provision of new products and relaxation of processes coupled with leveraging ICT for efficient handling of low ticket large volume transactions. Broadly, the policy approach adapted to financial inclusion in India can be divided in two categories—the minimalist approach and the expanded approach.

The minimalist approach for financial inclusion focuses on the provision of a bouquet of basic financial products and services, including thrift, credit, remittance and payment facilities for the vulnerable and financially excluded sections. Banks have been urged to include products, such as, savings cum overdraft product, remittance product, pure savings product and entrepreneurial credit product while pursuing the objective of greater inclusion. The expanded approach for financial inclusion, on the other hand, focuses not only on the provision of the basic banking products but also other important ancillary financial products, such as general insurance, health insurance, micro-pension, mutual fund, finance for affordable housing, etc. The expanded bouquet of financial inclusion would also entail focus on consumer protection and education, particularly financial literacy for the new entrants to the formal financial system. Sustainable and viable financial inclusion, which would be a win-win proposition for both those who supply financial services and those who demand the same, would also mean that financial inclusion in a sense forms a part of the broader context of economic inclusion.

Against this background, I shall now touch upon some of the major issues and challenges in relation to partnerships, processes, policies and products involved in Indian efforts at financial inclusion in the recent years.

SHG-Bank Linkage Programme

In the last two decades, the major institutional innovation in India for expanding financial system access and usage for the poor and marginalised sections of the population has been the SHG-Bank Linkage Programme (SBLP). This was an outcome of pilot projects during the 1980s for improving access of rural poor to formal institutional financial services. For the banks, it was a way of reducing their transaction costs by dealing with groups of people rather than individuals, reducing the credit risks through peer pressure and making people save. Subsequently in the year 1992, the National Bank for Agriculture and Rural Development (NABARD) started a pilot project of linking SHGs with branches of banks across the country. The project provided a cost-effective SBLP model for providing financial services to the underserved poor. Being a 'savings-first, credit later' model, credit discipline became a norm for SHGs and 'social collateral' made them bankable. The model was also successful in providing solution to the twin problems faced by banks, i.e., low recovery of loans in rural areas and high transaction costs in dealing with small borrowers at frequent intervals. One of the major positive impacts of the SBLP was social and economic empowerment of the membership.

Table 18.2

SHG-Bank Linkage Programme

(Numbers in millions, ₹ in billion)

Particulars	*2009-10*	*2010-11*
Total number of SHGs savings linked with banks	6.95	7.46
Total savings amount of SHGs with banks	₹ 61.98	₹ 70.16
Total number of SHG credit linked during the year	1.58	1.19
Total amount of loans disbursed to SHGs during the year	₹ 144.53	₹ 145.47
Total number of SHGs having loans outstanding	4.85	4.78
Total amount of loans outstanding against SHGs	₹ 280.38	₹ 312.21
Estimated number of families covered	97.00	97.00

Source: NABARD, *Status of Micro Finance in India.*

Despite the noteworthy accomplishments of SHGs (Table 18.2), certain issues, such as, inadequate outreach in many regions, delays in opening of SHG accounts and disbursement of loans, impounding of savings by banks as collateral, non-approval of repeat loans by banks even when the first loan was repaid promptly, multiple membership, borrowings by SHG members within and outside SHGs, adverse consequences of unhealthy competition between NGO promoted SHGs and Government promoted/subsidy oriented SHGs and limited banker interface and monitoring continued to affect the programme in many areas. While the basic tenets of the SHGs being savings led credit product remain true even today, recent developments have given rise to the need for crucial changes in the approach and design of SBLP to make it more flexible and client friendly. The revised NABARD guidelines, popularly known as SHG2 (version 2), have sought to address some of the shortcomings of the earlier version. The major features of SHG2 are : (a) more focus on voluntary savings; (b) cash credit system of lending over three to five years cycle to minimise the problem of inadequate finance and non-availability of repeat loans; (c) enabling creation of Joint Liability Groups (JLGs) within SHGs to scale up economic activities by more entrepreneurial members of the group; (d) improving risk mitigation systems by bringing in third party audit; (e) building second tier institutions; (f) strengthening the self-monitoring mechanism, and (g) meeting the training/capacity building requirements of the SHGs.

Microfinance Institutions (MFIs)

Given the limitation of scaling up SHG movement in the absence of human and financial resources and in the absence of deeper geographical penetration of formal banking system due to several demand and supply side factors, other intermediaries with a reach to the excluded segments of the society were required to augment the efforts. Semi-formal financial sector service providers like the MFIs fill this niche space and, to that extent, play a critical role in the financial inclusion. The MFIs have served the underserved/un-served populace in the last few years and improved access to credit though there have been quite a few debatable issues on the style of corporate governance and ethics of conducting business on part of some of the MFIs. Despite these debates, it has been realised that the MFIs do help in financial deepening and can remain an important segment of the Indian financial market keeping in view the present level of penetration of the banking system. Many of the MFIs have therefore been conduits of credit flows from the banks whose capacities for last mile reach are constrained under various forms of MFI-bank partnership model.

The conceptual framework underlying MFIs, however, requires a change, more so in the context of serious challenges the sector faces in the post Andhra crisis phase. These institutions have to revisit their business models to support the income earning ability of the borrowers and, at the same time, themselves remain economically viable. MFIs will have to work hard in pursuit of transparency and responsible finance, shaking off the perception that their motto is profiteering at the cost of the poor but not profitability for sustainable and viable growth. MFIs will also have to take initiatives to retool the product redesign for garnering new customers and acquiring more share of the market. At the same time they need to re-engineer the customer responsive processes so as to create a favourable climate for doing business. MFIs will have to revisit the mission and business strategy and reinvent the sector to remain relevant in the system. Creation of a new category of MFI-NBFC under the framework prescribed by the Malegam Committee, more nuanced appreciation by the financing banks of the difficulties being faced by some of the MFIs despite having responsible and sustainable business model, greater sense of responsibility in the sector as evident from the code of conduct being voluntarily accepted by the MFIs and the microfinance legislation which is in the offing, possibly hold key to future success and sustainability of the MFIs.

Business Correspondents (BCs)

Due to the constraints involved in going for a full-fledged brick & mortar branch model, the Reserve Bank, based on the recommendations of the Internal Group on Rural Credit and Microfinance, adopted the ICT based agent bank model through

Business Facilitators (BFs)/Business Correspondents (BCs) for ensuring door step delivery of financial products and services. In January 2006, the Reserve Bank permitted banks to engage BFs and BCs like NGOs/MFIs set up under the Societies/Trust Acts, Section 25 companies, post offices, etc., as intermediaries for providing financial and banking services, thus, addressing the proverbial last mile problem. The approach adopted has been technology and delivery model neutral. Initially, the BC retail outlets were being created by the banks themselves.

Over the last few years, however, a number of innovations, in particular with regard to the universe of entities that can work as agents of banks (individuals like retired bank/government employees, *kirana*/fair price shops, insurance agents, operators of common service centres, etc.), have been brought in under the BC model so as to scale up the financial inclusion drive in a sustainable manner, latest being the use of corporate entities as BCs of banks. The adoption of corporate entities as BCs has, however, raised a number of issues both for the partner banks and also for the regulators. On one hand, the corporates with a widespread retail network bring in larger resources, higher organisational strength and financial backing needed for a large network of BCs besides providing financial security to the bank. The outlets of corporates being familiar to the local populace are able to tap the benefit of 'one of us'.

On the other hand, the challenges arise in the event of failure of a large corporate BC as this would translate into a reputation risk to the banks and endanger their substantive business. From the perspective of a regulator, the major cause of concern is that banking and financial services should not be thrust on the uninformed customers. Corporates in the interest of revenue maximisation may use their resources and network to push banking and financial products, unmindful of whether they are suitable or appropriate for the targeted persons. There is also the issue of lack of grassroot level of experience of rural India and possibly lack of commitment to financial inclusion per se on the part of large corporates/technology service providers.

Business Correspondents bridge the connectivity gap between the service seekers, i.e., under-served populace, and the service providers, i.e., the banks. Banks, being regulated entities, are governed by prudential regulations and supervisory rules, e.g. adherence to KYC/AML, consumer protection laws, etc. In the BC-oriented model of financial inclusion, pursuit of higher volume of business for revenue maximisation may dilute prudential requirements exposing the banks concerned to whole host of risks like reputation risk, strategic risk, compliance risk, operations risk, besides the risk of contaminated asset portfolio. In case of a cluster approach where a common BC could work for many banks then there could be the issue of concentration risk. These risks may get further aggravated if the monitoring systems of the banks are not strong enough to detect these red flags. Given the lack of financial strength of the BCs, risk of inability to fulfil commitments arising due to shortfalls in cash due to frauds, errors, etc., is high. Banks engaging BCs may, therefore, have to put in place risk mitigants and adequate checks and balances to prevent such incidents and also ensure proper customer redressal. The sponsoring banks are expected to lay down processes, procedures and practices for the BCs, but there still exists a risk that some agents may end up pursuing activities or adopting processes which are inconsistent with the overall strategic goals of the bank concerned. Further, banks and their BCs are also exposed to huge risk of cash management, particularly as cash dependence of the economy continues to be very high. There is also huge requirement of hand-holding and training of the BCs to enhance the trust level of the end customers. In this context, the current thinking of having lean, brick & mortar outfits of the banks (e.g., ultra small branches) to provide support to and supervise work of certain number of BCs appears to be a step in right direction. The success of BC model also hinges on adoption of technology, which in turn, is dependent on the degree of compatibility and integration of technology being used by the banks and their BCs. Lack of integration of technology and processes may lead to delay in submission or submission of accurate information to the regulators or generating MIS for the internal use by the banks. There is a view that banks could also have their in-house BC outfits in the form of separate trusts/subsidiaries with separate recruitment and remuneration structure but under closer supervisory control. This idea is worth a trial.

Viability of the BC model in general has remained a critical issue for which the model has not taken off as expected. There is a mismatch between the revenues earned and costs incurred while undertaking the BC operations, resulting in non-viability of the model. Hence, attempts to employ large BCs under competitive L-1 (lowest one) bidding system without ensuring their financial and technical capabilities, and without assessing the performance of a large number of existing BCs who are yet to become viable, run the risk of creating huge uncertainty for the whole system of bank-BC partnership model. Many of the BCs became non-operational due to lack of timely payments by banks or inadequate commission paid by banks. It is extremely critical to ensure that the remuneration paid to the BCs is adequate to keep the model economically viable and attractive. A combination of fixed and variable pay would encourage BCs to strive harder for bringing in more business for the bank. Under the circumstances, it is imperative that the bank-BC partnership model is structured appropriately, supervised closely by the banks/regulators and scaled up in a calibrated manner after taking into account the problems encountered at the grassroot level. If this is not done, there is a huge risk of the entire model being discredited with all its adverse consequences for the financial inclusion efforts.

Having discussed the three important partnerships in the pursuit of financial inclusion, I would now turn towards products and technology enabled processes in the next part of my paper.

Product Initiatives

RBI has been providing policy impetus for introduction of new products and innovative intermediary channels to enable sustainable and meaningful financial inclusion. The 'no-frills account' (NFA) has been one of the landmark financial products which allowed financially excluded individuals to access banking services for the purpose of savings and also had credit feature in the form of overdraft facility. To ensure that more and more people come within the banking fold and realising that there is some stigma attached to the NFA, it is now felt that banks should offer all the customers a 'basic savings deposit account' with certain minimum common facilities and without the requirement of minimum balance. The services provided in this account should include deposit and withdrawal of cash at the bank branches as well as ATMs, receipt/credit of money through electronic payment channels or by means of deposit/collection of cheques drawn by Central/state government agencies and departments. The Reserve Bank is currently in the process of issuing guidelines on opening of such basic savings bank deposit account by banks. Another innovative product offered by the banking system is the General Credit Cards (GCCs). This was, however, preceded by Kisan Credit Cards (KCCs) which are likely to undergo major transformation when they become smart-card based cards. Innovation of products for the specific needs of the poor is necessary for achieving the ultimate objective of inclusive growth. A bouquet of products may be offered through the BCs instead of a single product to make the financial inclusion efforts viable.

Rural customers are looking upon banks for insurance products in view of their confidence in the banking system. Insurance is a useful way for households to protect themselves from financial shocks and other adverse events. Unfortunately, although a range of insurance products is available, very few of them have migrated successfully downmarket to serve the poor, whose need for such protection is arguably more acute. One plausible reason holding back the diffusion of micro-insurance is transaction costs, i.e., the cost of selling and underwriting insurance and evaluation of claims in a timely and efficient manner. Using traditional channels and processes, insurance companies simply cannot write policies with values below a certain floor without pricing them unrealistically. Moreover, micro-insurance is a low-cost, high-volume business; therefore, scale of economy is crucial for success. Currently, only insurance company agents, banks, MFIs, non-governmental organisations (NGOs) and SHGs are allowed to sell micro-insurance policies, while a BC is authorised to offer banking services, such as, cash transactions to customers. The BC network could be tapped to increase penetration of micro-insurance and take insurance to the uninsured segments of the country. The concern, however, remains on account of the possibility of mis-selling.

Tapping Technology Platforms

It has been observed that the product initiatives are usually scaled down versions of the existing products. To enable a successful financial inclusion, innovation of products for the specific needs of the poor is not only necessary but also an essential condition. Today, banks can provide a bouquet of financial services through the various networks of agents and branches by leveraging and fine tuning technology platforms. Technology holds the key to providing models for efficient delivery of small value transactions in large volumes while reaping economies of scale. The implementation of such effective, scalable and platform-independent technology will help drive down the cost of providing banking services to the poor. Further, technology helps in spreading financial literacy both as a delivery channel and as an intrinsic part of the learning process (e.g., instructional computer). Today, both the service providers and service seekers have a number of technology options, such as, smart cards, micro-ATMs, ATMs, mobile technology, Aadhaar Enabled Payment Systems (AEPS), etc., to choose from to provide/seek financial services irrespective of their geographic locations.

Mobile Banking

Mobile banking transactions have been defined as customers undertaking banking transactions using mobile phones involving credit/debit to their accounts. With the rapid growth in the number of mobile phone subscribers in India, banks in collaboration with telecom companies are seeking to develop an alternate channel of delivery of banking services. Keeping in view the issues relating to diversity of network providers in India, remittance centric approach of such model and KYC related concerns, the Reserve Bank has advocated bank-led mobile banking model and issued operative guidelines to banks for effecting mobile based banking transactions. As on May 31, 2012, the Reserve Bank had permitted 69 banks to provide mobile banking services to their customers. During May

2012, about 3.34 million transactions amounting to ₹ 2.86 billion as against 1.28 million transactions amounting to ₹ 0.91 billion in May 2011 were transacted through this channel. Even though the value and volume are increasing on month on month basis, the growth rate is low when compared with the number of bank accounts and the vast mobile subscriber base of more than 900 million. This indicates that banks are yet to fully exploit this technology even for their existing customers. While the Reserve Bank has provided the policy framework for a collaborative relationship between the banks and mobile network operators, the results of this collaboration are not yet fully visible. Some of the likely reasons which have been flagged relate to ownership of the customer, control of transactions and developing an appropriate revenue sharing model. The need of the hour, therefore, is that the banks and the mobile operators reach a workable understanding while protecting their mutual interests. Such an approach would result in a 'win-win' situation for both and, more importantly, serve the larger cause of public good of financial inclusion.

The Inter Bank Mobile Payment Service (IMPS), an instantaneous 24x7 electronic funds transfer system has been developed by the National Payment Corporation of India (NPCI). Despite tremendous potential of the product, the volumes are low, probably due to the reluctance of the telecom companies to offer the common Unstructured Supplementary Service Data (USSD) platform. The USSD platform is menu driven and can be invoked by dialling a number. Its main advantage is that even users with low-cost handsets can perform their banking transactions through the mobile phone. It is, however, gathered that the telecom companies prefer negotiating with individual banks on the issue rather than with NPCI in providing such a common USSD platform. Telecom companies, regulatory authorities, NPCI and all the stakeholders need to work together to draw up a roadmap for increasing the IMPS supported mobile banking transactions.

Mobile Based Remittance Services

Many countries have experimented with mobile based remittance services for reaching the unbanked population. The success story cited often is that of M-Pesa in Kenya. Several mobile based remittance services are operating in a few countries, e.g., Tigo Cash in Paraguay, Pago Movi in Peru, Nipper in Mexico and Oi in Brazil. The common thread running through all these examples have been the successful deployment of technology to service low income, financially excluded households. Most schemes use mobile phones for providing financial service platforms, others use point-of-sale (PoS) devices in conjunction with magnetic stripe cards (mostly in Latin America), some use both mobile phones and PoS devices (e.g., WIZZIT in South Africa and Smart in the Philippines). In Indian context, among others, money transfers through mobile wallets (up to ₹ 50,000 for the present) leveraging National Electronic Fund Transfer (NEFT) platform of RBI being promoted by a few telecom companies hold a great promise for facilitating small value remittances.

Aadhaar Enabled Payment Systems (AEPS)

The AEPS architecture designed by Unique Identification Authority of India (UIDAI) in collaboration with the NPCI is a platform which banks can leverage upon for expanding their financial inclusion initiatives. The basic premise of AEPS is that one BC Customer Service Point (CSP) will have the ability to service customers of many banks based on the unique bio-metric identification data stored in the Aadhaar database. The AEPS platform is expected to empower a bank customer to use Aadhaar as his/her identity to access the respective Aadhaar enabled bank account and perform basic banking transactions like balance enquiry, cash withdrawal and deposit through the BC. A pilot scheme in four districts of Jharkhand state is currently being carried out under which MGNREGA wages to labourers are credited to their Aadhaar enabled bank accounts. The beneficiaries withdraw the amounts through micro-ATMs which authenticate their Aadhaar number. There is a need to scale this up across the country.

Issues and Challenges in ICT—based Financial Inclusion

Use of Technology

For the success of the ICT-based models, resolving technology related issues is the key. One of the major constraints of the ICT—based BC model has been the technical problems associated with the model. It has been reported that devices, such as, hand held machines, smart cards, PoS terminals and utilities which are crucial to the functioning of the model are not properly functioning in many areas of the country. Limited number of technology service providers to cover the unbanked villages of all banks as well as limited service centres for servicing devices has resulted in banking operations coming to a halt in many villages. Given the literacy level of the rural population, availability of trained manpower in the villages to ensure that transactions are carried out in a user friendly manner in the local language and that the customers smoothly transit from assisted model to self-service model in using technology, wherever feasible (e.g., use of ATMs/mobile/internet banking). This could lead to erosion of confidence on the ICT-based BC model. Technical glitches, therefore, need to be addressed quickly. Banks also have to ensure that the turnaround time between account opening and account operationalisation has to be minimised so as to gain confidence of the customers in such models.

Security Concerns

Given the increasing reliance on technology to deliver banking services to customers, it is essential that adequate attention is paid to security, especially IT security. Security related issues resulting in frauds have the potential to undermine public confidence in the use of electronic payment products. Further, they could also lead to reputation risks. While preventing fraud through robust security measures, one should not lose sight of the fact that the ease and efficiency in operations for the customers is not unduly eroded. Cumbersome security procedures would deter customers from using the product and carrying out electronic transactions. Accordingly, a proper balance should be struck between such apparently conflicting objectives. The Reserve Bank has been taking several measures to strengthen the security for electronic transactions to prevent their misuse. For instance Second Factor Authentication has been made mandatory for all Card Not Present (CNP) transactions (e.g., requirement of PIN in addition to CVV (Card Verification Value) while putting through the transactions). Similar measures are going to be implemented for Card Present (CP) transactions (e.g., use of chip and PIN or Aadhaar cards) over a defined time period. SMS alerts now made mandatory for all card related transactions is another added security feature. Encryption of transactions for value above ₹ 5,000/- has also been mandated for all mobile based transactions as a better security protocol.

Infrastructural Limitations

Power supply and network connectivity are issues in most parts of the country, especially, so in the rural/remote areas. While banking transactions are enabled on a real-time basis in urban centres, it often takes more time to complete a transaction in remote areas due to poor internet connectivity and frequent power failures. To overcome this in the North Eastern states, the Reserve Bank had launched the Satellite Connectivity Scheme in 2009 to provide 100 per cent subsidy to bank branches in the North-East Region (NER) subject to a maximum of ₹ 12,000/- per month or the actual expenditure incurred by the bank, whichever is less, subject to the condition that the branches would offer services of electronic funds transfer free of charge to their customers. Of the total 1756 branches in the NER, 762 branches (43.4%) had taken satellite connectivity after the launch of the scheme. The scheme has since been extended by another year and Sikkim has also been brought under the ambit of the scheme.

Multiplicity of Models

Multiple technologies and delivery models could be used based on the geographical peculiarities, infrastructure availabilities, etc. Too many disparate technologies, however, may prove counter-productive as there will be several challenges like integration with CBS (Core Banking System), support issues and people at the operating level (i.e., at the level of BFs and BCs) may not fully apprehend all the products and technologies. So it may be a better idea to narrow down to a few stable and scalable technologies and delivery channels and build the financial inclusion products around them with inter-operability being the key theme.

Way Forward

Meaningful Collaborations

Financial inclusion calls for significant investment in technology based applications, related research and development efforts, comprehensive MIS and monitoring and evaluation systems. Banks, especially those who desire to have much longer exposure to under-banked/unbanked population could collaborate with technology service providers (TSPs), mobile network operators (MNOs), corporate houses and various categories of BCs to develop efficient delivery models. It is heartening to note that a few banks have also started taking initiatives with couple of them appointing mobile service providers (MSP) to act as their BC. The strategy should aim to create a facilitating eco-system, leveraging on technology and promote partnerships of brick & mortar branches including ultra-small branches with the ICT-based BC outlets for evolving an effective financial inclusion delivery mechanism.

Innovative Product Lines and Processes

Banks have to look at their policies and procedures to develop new product lines rather than merely adopting the complex products of urban India in the rural milieu. Providing simple and basic banking services in the form of deposit account with remittance services and small credit facility would ideally suffice for bringing the unbanked into the folds of banking system. This will require easy-to-understand documentation process, preferably in the vernacular language, sufficient to meet the legal requirements of the banking entity or the service provider. Innovations, however, should not be restricted merely to product designing. Given the fact that poor are generally susceptible to events that can adversely affect their already fragile livelihoods, more focus is required on enhancing the staying power of the poor. Here comes the importance of insurance which need to be enmeshed with banking products in a seamless manner. Banks should institute systems of reward and recognition for personnel initiating, ideating, innovating and successfully executing new product initiatives and services in the rural areas.

Financial Literacy and Awareness

Campaigns for spreading awareness about financial inclusion and financial literacy need to be intensified. This can be done through innovative dissemination channels including films, documentaries, pamphlets and road shows. Stakeholders, including the regulators and policy makers, may launch large scale awareness programmes. RBI is in the process of launching electronic Banking Awareness and Training (e-BAAT) programmes to increase awareness about technology-enabled financial services. Initiatives need to be taken for including financial literacy as a regular curriculum in school syllabus. Training programmes for bank staff, particularly for the frontline staff, should include aspects relating to financial education of the customers. There is also a great need for certain amount of standardisation of services/facilities extended by the Financial Literacy and Credit Counselling Centre (FLCC) being set up at several centre by the lead banks. Such facilities should cover the entire gamut of the requirements of the under-privileged/inadequately informed customers (e.g., basic financial concepts, appropriateness of savings ad credit products, use of credit cards, financial planning and debt management, retirement planning/micro-pension, insurance, investment, grievance redressal mechanism, awareness about electronic banking and the safeguards to be followed, etc.). It is hoped that the efforts to evolve a nationwide strategy of financial literacy involving all the financial sector regulators across banking, insurance, capital market and pension products would bear the fruits.

Customer Service and Consumer Protection

Along with financial literacy and education, customer service is another issue that needs closer attention. In recent years, the Reserve Bank has worked towards improving customer service through better dissemination of information to customers and also by improving the mechanisms for redressing the grievances. Mind-set, cultural and attitudinal changes at the grassroot levels and user friendly technology at the level of branches of banks and BC outlets are needed to extend holistic customer service to the new entrants to the banking system. Government, regulators like RBI, banks, service providers and consumers themselves have to play important role in developing a comprehensive approach to consumer protection.

Concluding Thoughts

Reserve Bank has been emphasising that the bankability of the poor holds a major business opportunity for the banks in developing a stable, retail deposit base and in curbing volatility in earnings with the help of a diversified asset portfolio. The recent crisis has, in fact, underscored the need for reducing banks' reliance on wholesale deposits and borrowed funds and cultivating a retail portfolio of assets and liabilities for financial stability. The current policy objective of inclusive growth with financial stability cannot be achieved without ensuring universal financial inclusion. Pursuit of financial inclusion by adoption of innovative products and processes does, however, pose challenge of managing trade-offs between the objective of financial inclusion and financial stability. In the Indian context, Reserve Bank has always sought to balance the risk of partnerships and product innovations with the ability to achieve greater penetration in a safe, secured and prudentially sound manner. The underlying belief is that only sound and strong institutions can promote financial inclusion in a sustainable manner and, towards this end, prudent regulations have to be in place to achieve inclusion while protecting financial stability and consumer interest. One such measure, for example, has been restricting deposit taking to banks and encouraging the non-bank financial companies (NBFCs) to focus on innovative approaches to lending under a lighter regulatory framework, with additional regulations for systemically important NBFCs. By adopting appropriate regulatory framework for innovations in policies, partnerships, processes and products meant for financial inclusion, Reserve Bank has sought to further the cause of inclusion without falling short of the policy goal of financial stability.

I am sanguine about rapid progress of financial inclusion efforts in India as the stakeholders have come to realise the need for viable and sustainable business models which focus on accessible and affordable financial services, products and processes, synergistic partnerships with non-bank entities including the technology service providers for efficient handling of low value, large volume transactions, particularly in remote, banking shadow areas and appropriate regulatory and risk management policies that ensure financial inclusion and financial stability move in tandem.

References

Sarma, M. (2008). "Index of financial inclusion", *Working Paper No.* 215. New Delhi: Indian Council for Research on International Economic Relations.

Based on the keynote address delivered at the symposium on "Financial inclusion in Indian Economy" organised by the Indian Institute of Public Administration, Bhubaneswar, June 30, 2012. RBI Bulletin August 2012.

19

DUVVURI SUBBARAO

Touching Hearts and Spreading Smiles

Mahatma Gandhi said, the test of every public policy decision should be, "how is this decision going to affect the poorest person in the country?", which is the same as asking yourself, "is this decision that I am taking 'going to touch hearts and spread smiles' among the less privileged people in the country."

The Reserve Bank's responsibilities include bank regulation and supervision and oversight of banks' customer service. Our endeavour in fulfilling these responsibilities is to support growth and enhance welfare—in other words 'touch hearts and spread smiles'. In this paper, I would be reviewing some of the important policy initiatives of the Reserve Bank over the last two years in the area of bank regulation and supervision and explain how they have been informed by the goal of touching hearts and spreading smiles. However, I will be restricting to just five of the several policy actions.

Micro-Finance

When it started off in the 1980s, the development of the micro-finance sector was primarily led by the bank-SHG (self-help group) model, with the SHGs operating as collective liability vehicles with responsibility for maintaining credit standards and enhancing credit discipline among the members.

The SHG model was handicapped by inherent scalability issues, and thereby yielded the 'last mile' space to microfinance institutions (MFIs) which represent a more formal, structured and profit oriented approach. In some ways, the growth of the microfinance sector has been a remarkable success story of recent years; in some other ways, that very growth has also raised concerns about the quality of income generation support MFIs were offering. In particular, allegations about usurious interest rates, coercive recovery practices and multiple lending led the Government of Andhra Pradesh, a state that accounted for as much as 40 per cent of the total microfinance activity in the country, to promulgate an ordinance in October 2010. The ordinance, subsequently converted into an act, requires all MFIs operating in the state to register on an annual basis with the state government. The law stipulates that the total interest cost cannot exceed the principal, and seeks to further protect borrowers from getting enticed into an unviable debt burden by restricting multiple lending by MFIs.

The Andhra Pradesh law brought the MFI activity in that state to a stand still; several other states began considering if they too should clamp down on the activities of the MFI sector. On the other side, both the MFIs and the banks that loaned funds to the MFIs were agitated about the security of the funds already lent, and more generally about the prospects for MFI activity in general.

In October 2010, the Central Board of the Reserve Bank discussed the policy impasse arising out of this situation and decided to constitute a sub-committee under the chairmanship of one of the Board members, Y.H. Malegam, to study the issues and concerns in the MFI sector. The Malegam committee submitted its report in January 2011; its important recommendations were: (i) creation of a separate category of NBFC-MFIs; (ii) continuation of priority sector status to bank loans to MFIs which comply with the regulation laid down for NBFC-MFIs; (iii) a margin cap and an interest rate cap on individual loans; (iv) transparency in interest charges; (v) lending by not more than two MFIs to individual borrowers; (vi) creation of one or more credit information bureaus; (vii) establishment of a proper system of grievance redressal by MFIs; and (viii) creation of one or more "social capital funds".

The Reserve Bank accepted the broad framework of recommendations by the Malegam Committee. A separate category of NBFCs—non-banking financial company—micro finance institution (NBFC-MFI)—was created. Further, regulatory instructions were issued mandating the following. For an entity to qualify as a MFI, the aggregate amount of loan extended by it for income generating activity should not be less than 75 per cent of its total loans. Bank credit to MFIs extended on or after April 1, 2011 for on-lending to individuals and also to members of SHGs/JLGs (joint liability groups) would be eligible for priority sector status only if not less than 85 per cent of total assets of MFI were in the nature of 'qualifying assets'. To qualify as an asset under priority sector lending, banks should ensure that the interest rate charged by MFIs on final borrowers is capped. Further, to protect borrowers from usurious rates of interest, the interest rate that a MFI can charge a customer has been pegged at 12 per cent over the rate at which it borrows from the bank subject to a maximum of 26 per cent.

The more effective regulation imposed by the Reserve Bank —particularly by way of a cap on interest rate and transparency in MFI operations—has restored calm to the MFI sector. The sentiment of investors too has improved, and some MFIs are also reportedly attracting venture capital funds.

Nevertheless, the roll out of the new regulatory regime has run into some bottlenecks. Some MFIs are unable to comply with the qualifying asset criterion for registering as a NBFC-MFI, and therefore banks are reluctant to make fresh loans to them as such loans do not qualify as priority sector lending. Small MFIs are also not able to meet the ₹ 50 million entry point capital to be eligible to register as NBFC-MFI. In particular, the Andhra Pradesh based MFIs, saddled with huge losses, large NPAs and eroded capital, are facing an especially acute problem in complying with the capital and provisioning norms. The Reserve Bank is working on resolving these issues so that MFI operations can get back on track.

Reflecting the lessons of the agitation in the microfinance sector, Government of India is considering a central legislation to comprehensively cover the regulation of the MFI sector. The important features of the Micro Finance Institutions (Development & Regulation) Bill 2011 are: (i) the Reserve Bank will be the regulator of all MFIs irrespective of their size and organisational structure; (ii) the minimum entry point capital for a MFI will be ₹ 500,000; (iii) MFIs will be permitted to collect thrift; (iv) both Government of India and the Reserve Bank will enjoy concurrent power to frame rules; and (v) there will be an ombudsman for the MFI sector.

Even as MFIs should be brought back on track, albeit under more effective regulation, there is another issue that banks need to ponder. By and large banks have largely outsourced the 'last mile' to intermediaries such as MFIs, SHGs, etc. This is a model that has worked, and one that we should pursue, and refine. Nevertheless, the question is, "is there a business case for banks to do some of the last mile themselves?" Can banks rely entirely on outsourcing? Isn't there valuable experience to be gained by banks by 'dirtying their hands' more and reoccupying the last mile?

Priority Sector Lending

The second issue I want to address is 'priority sector lending' (PSL). PSL is by far the longest standing affirmative action programme pursued by the Reserve Bank. The objective of the programme, as is obvious, is to ensure flow of credit to certain productive sectors of the economy which may, in the normal course, be handicapped in accessing such credit. The current stipulation is that all domestic banks must ensure that at least 40 per cent of their total advances go to the priority sectors. The prescription in respect of foreign banks is 32 per cent.

Is such 'directed lending' good? Evidence from development experience from around the world is mixed. From a purely efficiency point of view, it can be argued that the decision on where to lend and at what interest rate should be left to the banks, and that superimposition of a regulatory prescription on top of that would lead to misallocation of resources. On the other hand, the argument in support of directed lending is that given information asymmetries, a *laissez faire* regime will not necessarily guarantee efficiency. Besides, the pursuit of inclusive growth demands that public policy must manage the balance between equity and efficiency.

Even as the Reserve Bank remains committed to the broad objectives of PSL, it nevertheless received suggestions and requests from several quarters on the need to revisit the guidelines on PSL, especially as banks are increasingly using intermediaries in directing credit to the priority sector, and there is growing incidence of misclassification of non-priority sector accounts as priority sector. The Malegam Committee on Microfinance had also recommended a review of the PSL guidelines on the arbitrage argument—that tightened regulation on microfinance without corresponding tightening of other intermediaries that route priority sector credit may bias the flow towards the lightly regulated sectors.

In response, the Reserve Bank appointed a Committee under the chairmanship of M.V. Nair, former Chairman of the Union Bank of India, to reexamine the existing classification and suggest revised guidelines with regard to PSL classification. In its report submitted in February 2012, the Nair committee reaffirmed the need to continue with the PSL scheme on the argument of lack of access to credit for a vast segment of the society. The committee advised that the PSL target for domestic commercial banks be retained at 40 per cent of their adjusted net bank credit (ANBC) and that the positive bias in favour of foreign banks be done away with by raising the target for them too from 32 to 40 per cent.

The thrust of the Nair committee report was to recommend changes in the allocations to various sectors within the aggregate target. Important among these recommendations are the following:

(i) The distinction between direct and indirect agricultural lending be done away with by making 'agriculture and allied activities' a composite sub-sector within the priority sector.

(ii) A sub-target for small and marginal farmers 'within agriculture and allied activities', equivalent to 9 per cent of ANBC or credit equivalent of off-balance sheet exposures (CEOBE), whichever is higher, be achieved in stages by 2015-16. Similarly, within the MSE sector, a sub-target for micro enterprises equivalent to 7 per cent of ANBC or CEOBE, whichever is higher, be achieved in stages by 2013-14.

(iii) Loans for construction/purchase of one dwelling unit for an individual up to ₹ 2.5 million may be treated as PSL.

(iv) Limits under PSLs for studies in India be increased to ₹ 1.5 million from the existing limit of ₹ 1 million, and for studies abroad to ₹ 2.5 million from the existing ₹ 2 million.

(v) Bank loans to non-bank financial intermediaries (NBFI) for on-lending to specified segments may be reckoned for classification under priority sector up to a maximum of 5 per cent of ANBC or CEOBE, whichever is higher.

(vi) The interest rate on the PSL shortfall amount deposited by defaulting banks in specified funds with NABARD/SIDBI/NHB be benchmarked to the reverse repo rate.

The Nair committee report has since been placed on the Reserve Bank's website for feedback and comments. Pending that, a decision has been taken to index both the interest paid to banks on the deposits they make into specified funds on account of PSL shortfall and the interest charged to states on their borrowing from the RIDF to the Bank Rate which, in turn, is indexed to the repo rate.

There are two open ended issues relating to PSL that I want to raise. The first relates to a scheme of Priority Sector Lending Certificates (PSLCs) recommended by the Raghuram Rajan committee. The idea is to allow banks to fulfill their PSL target by buying off PSL assets from other institutions through a PSLC. It is argued that the PSLC system will enhance efficiency as it will allow banks with a comparative advantage in PSL to exploit that advantage by overachieving on their target and selling the 'surplus' to other banks which have a comparative disadvantage.

The PSLC scheme has some merits. The most obvious is that since it is a market based mechanism that leverages on comparative advantage, it could be efficiency enhancing. Second, it could lower interest rates for final borrowers provided the efficiency gains on account of PSLCs are passed on to them. However, on the flip side it is argued that there may likely be reduction in aggregate PSL from the banking system and of its contribution to the RIDF to the extent PSLCs are acquired from non-bank institutions such as MFIs, NBFCs which currently have no PSL obligation.

The Nair committee accepted the concept of PSLC, but recommended that in the first instance only a restricted PSLC, non-tradable and open only to commercial banks and RRBs, be introduced. A more broad based PSLC, tradable and open to all institutions involved in PSL, the committee felt, could be considered on the experience of the pilot experiment.

The second issue relates to the expansion of the list of eligible sectors under the PSL scheme. Almost every interest group in the economy wants its sector to be accorded priority sector status in the hope and expectation that this will provide easier access to credit at a lower cost. The lower cost issue is a clear misunderstanding since there is no regulatory interest rate ceiling on PSL. Expectation of easier access too is misguided. The more sectors we include in PSL, the more they will compete for the same fixed pool of resources and crowd each other out. Priority sector can deliver on its promise only if the eligible sectors are restricted to a select few which are important from the perspective of improving livelihoods.

Lending Interest Rate System

Let me now move on to the Reserve Bank's policy initiative on the lending interest rate system. The benchmark prime lending rate (BPLR) was introduced by the Reserve Bank in 2003 to serve as a benchmark rate for pricing of loans. It was expected that this method of determining interest rate with reference to a benchmark will make loan pricing fair, transparent and contestable. In the event, the BPLR system failed to fulfil these objectives.

Under the BPLR system, banks were allowed to lend at rates below the BPLR, but such lending was expected to be at the margin. However, in actual practice, banks started doing the bulk of their business below the BPLR. In 2009, as much as 65 per cent of the advances were made at sub-BPLR rates; for private sector banks, the proportion was as high as 83 per cent. The lack of transparency in the system encouraged some perverse cross-subsidisation. Loans to priority sectors such as agriculture and SME sectors were overpriced so as to lend below the BPLR to presumably preferred customers such as large corporates. The lack of transparency in the operation of the BPLR also made it difficult to assess the effectiveness of monetary transmission from the policy rate of the Reserve Bank to lending rates by banks.

In order to correct the situation, the Reserve Bank appointed a committee under the chairmanship of Deepak Mohanty, Executive Director. As per the recommendations of the committee, the BPLR system was replaced by a base rate system effective July 1, 2010.

Under the new system, each bank is mandated to determine a base rate of interest to include those cost elements which can be clearly identified and are common across all borrowers—cost of deposits, cost of maintaining the statutory liquidity ratio (SLR) and cash reserve ratio (CRR), cost of operations, and the profit margin. Banks are allowed to determine the actual lending rate they charge on loans and advances by topping up the base rate with other customer specific charges such as product specific operating costs, credit risk premium and tenor premium. Since the base rate is the minimum rate for all loans, banks are not permitted to do any lending below the base rate, save for specified exceptions such as DRI advances, loans to banks' own employees, loans to banks' depositors against their own deposits and loans where borrowers enjoy subvention. As banks, in general, are not allowed to lend below the base rate, the stipulation of BPLR as the ceiling rate for loans up to ₹ 200,000 was rescinded in the expectation that with the freedom to determine the interest rate, banks will be encouraged to actively step into this large volume-low value business segment.

The base rate system is expected to enhance the allocative efficiency of the financial intermediation process, permit an assessment of the relative efficiency and cost structure of banks and improve monetary transmission from the Reserve Bank's policy rate to the bank's lending rates.

It is satisfying to note that banks have made a smooth adjustment to the base rate system. Also, base rates of major banks have converged. The base rate system has improved transparency and transmission of policy rate changes to banks' lending rates.

For instance, between September 2010 and December 2011, the Reserve Bank raised the policy rate by 250 basis points. During the same period, the average base rate and weighted average lending rate of scheduled commercial banks (SCBs) increased by a similar magnitude. After the Reserve Bank reduced policy rate by 50 basis points in May 2012, 26 banks responded with a reduction in their base rates evidencing more efficient monetary policy transmission in both upward and downward directions.

One problem that has persisted even after the introduction of the base rate system relates to the lack of transparency in the customer specific spread charged to a borrower over the base rate. There have been complaints that the spread charged to a customer has been revised upwards without any apparent change in her risk profile. Also, where floating rate loans are concerned, existing customers have been disadvantaged *vis-à-vis* new customers with similar credit ratings, resulting in complaints about discrimination. In order to address this malady, the Reserve Bank constituted a working group under the chairmanship of Deputy Governor Anand Sinha to determine the principles that must govern proper, transparent and non-discriminatory pricing of credit. The working group is expected to submit its report by August 2012.

Savings Deposit Interest Rate

The next on my list of issues is savings deposit interest rate. Up until 1990, India ran a repressed financial system with a complex plethora of administered interest rates on both deposit and lending sides. An important element of the early 1990s financial sector reforms was to deregulate the interest rate structure to spur competitive impulses, improve allocative efficiency and strengthen monetary transmission. The savings deposit rate, however, continued to be regulated; it remained unchanged at 3.5 per cent since March 1, 2003 (revised to 4% in May 2011) even as other deposit rates moved in either direction in response to the Reserve Bank's policy rate calibration.

The advisability of deregulating this last vestige of administered interest rate structure continued to be debated. Several benefits were argued in favour of freeing up the savings deposit rate—competitive pricing, product innovation, more efficient price discovery and improved monetary transmission. The arguments against deregulation were that it would hurt the asset-liability management (ALM) of banks which had built up a dependence on the low cost, large volume and fairly stable savings deposits and that the adjustment to a deregulated regime would set off an unhealthy competition among banks, potentially impairing their balance sheets. There was also an apprehension that deregulation would militate against financial inclusion as, in the business of servicing small customers, banks might see the costs exceeding the benefits.

On two separate occasions - first in 2002-03 and again 2006-07—the Reserve Bank considered deregulation, and on both occasions deferred the issue perceiving the time to be as yet inopportune.

The Reserve Bank revived the issue in 2011 by placing a Discussion Paper on the pros and cons of deregulating the savings bank deposit interest rate on its website, and following that up by generating an active debate. After careful consideration of the feedback, effective October 25, 2011, the savings bank deposit interest rate was deregulated.[1] To protect small customers whose knowledge levels and bargaining power are low, banks were mandated to provide a uniform rate for accounts upto ₹ 100,000 while enjoying flexibility in the rates and charges for accounts over ₹ 100,000.

Belying earlier apprehensions, the adjustment to the deregulation has been fairly smooth. Following the deregulation, seven relatively small private banks raised their saving bank deposit rates and expectedly improved their share of this market segment. The big banks have yet to respond to this but it is expected that whenever that happens, the adjustment will be smooth.

1. With this, the task of interest rate deregulation has been brought to a logical closure. Interest rate on FCNR accounts of NRIs continues to be regulated for purposes of external sector management. Also, the lending rate by NBFC-MFIs has since been regulated as per the rationale explained earlier.

In conclusion of this section, let me also add that the Reserve Bank looks forward to more active play in the saving bank segment with banks coming out with some customer friendly innovations especially aimed at attracting low income households, presently outside the banking sector.

Liberalisation of the Branch Authorisation Policy

The fifth and last issue is liberalisation of the branch authorisation policy. The thrust of the Reserve Bank's branch expansion policy since 1962, when banks were first mandated to open branches in unbanked/banked centres in the ratio of 2:1, has been to ensure banking penetration into the underbanked areas of the country. The precise formula has been continuously tweaked to reflect the changing scenario, but the underlying objective has all along been to link branch licences in urban/metropolitan areas to branches set up in disadvantaged semi urban/rural areas.

Till 2005, the practice was for RBI to issue licences for individual branches. In September 2005 the policy was liberalised, importantly shifting from branch licensing to branch authorisation. The new policy replaced the practice of licences for individual branches from time to time by an aggregate annual approval through a consultative and interactive process. Banks' branch expansion strategies and plans over the medium-term would be discussed by the RBI with individual banks. The medium term framework and the specific proposals would cover opening, closing, shifting, merger and conversion of all categories of branches.

By 2009, there was a growing consensus that further liberalisation would be in order especially so as to enhance banking penetration and promote financial inclusion. Accordingly, in May 2009, a working group under the chairmanship of Executive Director, Vijaya Bhaskar, was constituted to review the branch authorisation policy with a view to providing greater flexibility to banks in opening branches.

Based on the recommendation of the working group, in December 2009, the case by case approval process was given up and domestic banks were given general permission to open branches in

Tier 6 to Tier 3 centres (population up to 49,999) and in rural, semi urban and urban centres in the north eastern states and Sikkim. In November 2011, this general permission was further liberalised to opening of branches in Tier 2 centres (population up to 99,999). Thus presently, only opening of branches in Tier 1 centres, largely urban and metropolitan centres with population of 100,000 and above, requires prior RBI approval. In respect of the north-east states and Sikkim, *laissez faire* operates even for Tier 1 centres.

In 2010, a roadmap was drawn up to provide access to formal banking to every village with a population over 2,000. Under the roadmap, about 74,000 villages with population above 2,000 were identified as unbanked. These villages were allocated to various banks, including regional rural banks (RRBs), for providing banking services by March 2012. Further, in July 2011, banks were advised that at least 25 per cent of the total number of branches proposed to be opened during a year should be in unbanked rural centres. In June 2012, the process was refined further by advising all banks to prepare roadmaps covering all unbanked villages with population of less than 2,000 with banking services especially to facilitate transfer of state benefits (EBT).

This is the long established carrot and stick policy. As an incentive for their outreach, the Reserve Bank has indicated that banks will get licences for branches in urban/metropolitan centres (Tier 1) equal in number to the branches opened in underbanked districts of underbanked states. To ensure that financial inclusion is 'meaningful', banks have also been advised that their application for licences will be evaluated on the basis of the quality of their outreach—the extent of their penetration to unbanked areas, flow of credit to priority sectors, customer service to small account holders particularly by rolling out customer friendly products and innovative use of technology.

One of the issues that comes up in financial inclusion is the deployment of business correspondents (BCs). Since the operation of a brick and mortar branch is expensive, banks have found the BC model to be a cost-effective way of expanding access to the formal financial sector. Latest figures indicate that there are over

110,000 BCs deployed across the country as of now. Benefitting from accumulated experience, the Reserve Bank has liberalised the eligibility norms for appointment as BCs by including retired employees, *kirana* shops, NGOs, societies, post offices, and also large corporates who have a marketing penetration. Recently, we have allowed interoperability of BCs to enable remittance and electronic benefit transfers. Even as the BC model has consolidated by now, two caveats are in order. First, banks should not neglect the importance of brick and mortar branches, and in their financial inclusion plans, should maintain a fair ratio between brick and mortar branches and BCs. Indeed, I think there is a strong case for a much larger effort on innovating a cost effective village branch model. Second, it is important that all BCs are trained in the use of technology, knowledge of bank products and processes, and importantly, in customer service.

Even as branch authorisation has been substantially liberalised, several challenges remain. The biggest challenge, as always in India, is in the numbers. In 1969 when banks were nationalised, there were 8,321 branches with an average population per branch office (APPBO) of about 64,000. That has improved to 97180 branches with an APPBO of about 13,000 by March 2012. But in a country with over 600,000 villages, these numbers, while both impressive and commendable, serve to highlight what remains to be done. In the first index of financial inclusion prepared by the Indian Council for Research on International Economic Relations (ICRIER) to determine the extent of reach of banking services in 100 countries of the world, India has been placed at the 50th spot, below China, Kenya and Morocco.

The second big challenge lies in moving beyond numbers and looking at how we actually make a difference. There is a disappointingly large number of cases of bank branches with low customer footfalls; BCs who drift off after a few months and 'no frills accounts' which remain largely inoperative. This is where issues of perception come in. Unless banks are convinced that reaching out to the common man is not just a forced regulatory imperative but a potential business opportunity, the numbers will remain without life. The Reserve Bank looks forward to competition among banks to develop business models for such small, low staff and low cost branches.

Conclusion

I have so far covered five specific areas: (i) microfinance; (ii) priority sector lending; (iii) lending interest rate system; (iv) savings deposit interest rate; and (v) liberalisation of the branch authorisation policy, to illustrate how the Reserve Bank's regulatory and supervisory policies are guided by the belief that financial inclusion is a necessary prerequisite for inclusive growth.

What financial inclusion requires most of all is efficient and sympathetic customer service by banks. No amount of regulation, rules, policies and plans will deliver sustainable results unless banks serve their customers with efficiency, empathy and courtesy.

Many of you are aware of the Reserve Bank's outreach programme which is an effort to connect with people in the villages. I know that many commercial banks, including IOB, have their own versions of the outreach programmes. These programmes give us all a first hand exposure to the needs and aspirations of less privileged people and also an understanding of their problems and concerns.

In addition to the outreach, I have also included a frontline managers conference in my annual schedule. This is a conference where we bring frontline bank branch managers, MFIs, SHGs and some low income households together for a one day intensive, free flowing and informal discussion on the problems in the supply and demand of banking services to the poor. The last such conference was held in Pune in March 2012. Several of the participants narrated their tales of woe to me—bank managers have no time for them; they have to wait long hours at the end of which they are asked to come some other time; the documentation required of them is not indicated to them all at once, but done piecemeal, frustrating them and multiplying the transaction costs; the paper work is exacting; they discover hidden costs only after the transaction is completed; the attitude of the bank staff is unsympathetic if also uncivil. The general impression I got is that frontline branch managers treat 'no frills' accounts as a 'nuisance' and low income households as an intrusion into their time and their business. This is disappointing to say the least.

As I have said on several previous occasions, banks should look upon financial inclusion not as an obligation but as an opportunity to build 'fortune at the bottom of the pyramid'. I am also conscious that the bulk of our effort so far has been from the supply side—opening branches, appointing BCs and opening accounts that remain largely inoperative. If this is all that happens, the entire effort is both futile and wasteful. We need to supplement that supply side effort by a demand side effort—by reaching out to people left behind, inspiring their trust and confidence in the banking system and supporting them in improving the quality of their lives. Such a change in mindset is very important if we are to achieve meaningful financial inclusion. In other words, 'touching hearts and spreading smiles' requires both a smart mind and a kind heart.

Based on the oration by Dr Duvvuri Subbarao, Governor, Reserve Bank of India, as part of the IOB Platinum Jubilee Oration Series at Chennai, July 4, 2012. RBI Bulletin August 2012.

Index

G

H

I

J

R

S

T

U

V

W

Z